Human Operant Conditioning and Behavior Modification

Human Operant Conditioning and Behavior Modification

Edited by

Graham Davey
The City University, London

and

Chris Cullen
University of St Andrews, Scotland

JOHN WILEY & SONS
Chichester · New York · Brisbane · Toronto · Singapore

Library of Congress Cataloging-in-Publication Data
Human operant conditioning and behavior modification.
    1. Behavior modification. 2. Operant conditioning.
I. Davey, Graham.   II. Cullen, Chris.   [DNLM:
1. Behavior Therapy.   2. Conditioning, Operant.
WM 425 H918]
BF637.B4H85   1988   153.1'52   87–13321
ISBN   0 471 91637 4

British Library Cataloguing in Publication Data:
Human operant conditioning and behavior modification
    1. Operant conditioning
    I. Davey, Graham   II. Cullen, Chris
    153.15   BF319.5.06

    ISBN   0 471 91637 4

Typeset by Witwell Ltd, Liverpool
Printed in Great Britain by St Edmundsbury Press, Bury St Edmunds, Suffolk

Contents

v

List of Contributors

ALAN BARON	University of Wisconsin–Milwaukee
C. M. BRADSHAW	University of Manchester
WILLIAM BUSKIST	Auburn University, Alabama
CHRIS CULLEN	University of St Andrews
GRAHAM DAVEY	The City University, London
W. FRANK EPLING	The University of Alberta
MARK GALIZIO	University of North Carolina at Wilmington
SANDRA HALE	University of Wisconsin–Milwaukee
ALAN E. KAZDIN	University of Pittsburg
HUGH LACEY	Swarthmore College, Pennsylvania
DAVID MORGAN	Auburn University, Alabama
JOEL MYERSON	Cardinal Stritch College, Milwaukee
MICHAEL PERONE	West Virginia University, Morgantown
W. DAVID PIERCE	The University of Alberta
BARRY SCHWARTZ	Swarthmore College, Pennsylvania
E. SZABADI	University of Manchester
J. H. WEARDEN	University of Manchester
ROGER Ll. WOOD	St Andrews Hospital, Northampton

Preface

This volume is an attempt to provide the reader with an insight into recent developments in the theory and application of operant conditioning with humans. Traditionally, both the theory of operant conditioning in humans and its application to management and therapy in human affairs have relied very much on the animal literature, but in recent years operant conditioners have turned their attention to a direct study of operant processes in humans. This interest has manifested itself in a number of ways. First, workers have been attempting to identify the operation of operant processes in various human psychological phenomena; secondly, they have been concerned with direct quantitative analyses of human operant performance; and thirdly, they have been busy developing imaginative ways of applying laboratory-based principles to a variety of applied settings. This volume attempts to reflect all three of these recent developments in operant conditioning.

The main aim of the contributions to this book is to convey some of these recent trends, but, more importantly, to suggest new directions for future developments – in both the theoretical and applied aspects of operant analysis with humans. Specifically, the contributions attempt to cover the following ground: (1) a look at future trends in operant theory and applied behavior analysis; (2) a detailed discussion of the role of animal and laboratory-based operant theory in human operant performance, and in particular the potential role of some neglected aspects of the animal literature in applied behavior analysis with humans; (3) the role of operant analyses in understanding human psychological phenomena, in particular, cooperative and competitive behavior, the effects of aging on discriminative performance, and the effectiveness of rewards and reinforcers on human behavior; and (4) direct quantitative analyses of human operant performance.

Contributors were asked to be as theoretically speculative as they wished, but in particular to consider comparisons of the animal and human literature and the potential of laboratory-based findings for applied behavior analysis. The end result is hopefully a book which will not necessarily provide a bland summary of recent developments in human behavior analysis, but which will provide a source of ideas and new techniques for all psychologists using applied behavior analysis methods.

GRAHAM DAVEY
CHRIS CULLEN

January 1987

Human Operant Conditioning and Behavior Modification
Edited by G. Davey and C. Cullen
© 1988 John Wiley & Sons Ltd

Chapter 1

Trends in Human Operant Theory

GRAHAM C.L. DAVEY
The City University, London

Operant conditioning is a term that is synonymous with a number of approaches and analyses within psychology. Most obviously it is the study of the way in which behavior is modified by its consequences, but it also has associations with a philosophy of the study of behavior – such as radical behaviorism; a technology of behavior change – such as behavior modification; and has its roots in one of the most seminal influences on modern-day psychology – B. F. Skinner. In its heyday in the late 1960s the study of operant conditioning was generally guided by the tenets of radical behaviorism as espoused by Skinner (cf. Skinner, 1950, 1953, 1969, 1972). In this respect, learning theorists were primarily interested in operant conditioning in animals in the belief that any principles they discovered with a limited number of laboratory species would be more or less directly relevant to human behavior. The principles of operant conditioning that they were led to look for involved the search for the variables controlling behavior and the construction of a functional analysis of behavior. This required the extensive study of performance on schedules of reinforcement and of the discriminative control of behavior (e.g. Ferster and Skinner, 1957; Schoenfeld, 1970; Honig, 1966; Reynolds, 1968), and led to refinements in principles of reinforcement, punishment, stimulus control (generalization and discrimination), extinction, and conditioned reinforcement, etc. This obsession with an analysis of operant conditioning in terms of controlling variables meant that the study of the mechanisms (cognitive or otherwise) underlying such learning was neglected, and, even in animals, study of the proximal mechanisms involved in operant conditioning has only recently been broached with any conviction (e.g. Adams and Dickinson, 1981; Dickinson, 1985; Mackintosh, 1983).

1

Early analyses of human operant performance were colored by two particular factors: (1) the radical behaviorists' assumption that many of the basic laws of learning were common to a very wide range of species – including humans; and (2) the initial desire to study human operant performance in conditions which were procedurally and formalistically similar to the operant Skinner-box studies using rats.

Extrapolation from animals to humans

It has never been quite clear on what grounds the assumption that many of the laws of learning are common to a wide variety of species was based, although it has been loosely argued in a number of places that learning about the consequences of one's behavior has important adaptive benefits, and therefore such learning will either have been selected for very early on in the evolution of living organisms or will have been separately selected for in a very wide range of species (cf. Davey, 1981a; Carpenter, 1974; Skinner, 1969). On the basis of this assumption, operant conditioners have seen fit to extrapolate readily from animals to humans (especially Skinner, 1953, 1972), and in many cases these extrapolations have proved useful – especially in the applied fields where animal principles have been utilized successfully in a variety of management and therapeutic settings without first establishing that such principles do in fact apply to humans (e.g. Davey, 1981 b,c). Nevertheless, the liberal use of the principle of extrapolation from animals to humans in learning theory has had a number of important implications.

First, and most obviously, it has led to a relatively 'mechanistic' view of conditioning in humans and the view that conditioning is a 'subhuman' or primitive form of learning which is nothing more than a 'crude slot-machine model' of behavior (Koestler, 1967, pp. 3–18). This in turn has tended to tar the application of such principles with the same brush, such that techniques like behavior modification have been labeled as 'manipulatory' or 'control-oriented' (e.g. Chomsky, 1972; cf. Davey, 1981a, Ch. 15). However, characterizing the operant conditioning process as mechanical or reflexive could not be further from the truth. The modern conception of any kind of conditioning – whether it be operant or Pavlovian – is as a complex information gathering process which utilizes a variety of cognitive and information processing capacities in order to equip the organism with knowledge about important relationships in its environment or between its behavior and its environment (e.g. Mackintosh, 1983; Dickinson, 1980). Furthermore, in humans at any rate, these processes appear to be under the conscious control of the individual (cf. Dawson and Schell, 1986).

A second implication of the extrapolation from animals to humans approach has been to gloss over the nature of the mechanisms which mediate conditioning in different species. A whole range of species are sensitive to contingencies of operant reinforcement, from invertebrates such as drosophila, blow-flies and honey bees, through many species of fish, amphibia and reptiles, to birds and nonhuman mammals (cf. Davey, 1987). This does not, of course, mean that all species negotiate these contingencies using a similar learning mechanism. For instance, many species may be able to modify their behavior successfully in operant conditioning procedures by utilizing a mechanism which has evolved to learn primarily about Pavlovian contingencies. Indeed, a number of learning theorists have outlined models of operant conditioning which rely basically on Pavlovian mechanisms (e.g. Moore, 1973; Bindra, 1974). However, other species may be able to cope with operant contingencies by learning directly about the correlation between their behavior and its consequences and adjusting their behavior accordingly (cf. Dickinson, 1985). Clearly, a bona fide operant conditioning mechanism would be one which enables the animal to learn directly about the contingency relationship between its behavior and the consequences of that behavior. There is emerging evidence that humans, nonhuman mammals and birds can do this in a relatively sophisticated way, and in a way which implies that these classes of species possess underlying cognitive mechanisms with very similar dynamic features (e.g. Alloy and Tabachnik, 1984; Dickinson, Shanks, and Evenden, 1983). Nevertheless, it is almost certain that not all animals share such mechanisms, and to extrapolate blindly without knowledge of underlying mechanisms might frequently lead to erroneous conclusions about the factors which determine human operant performance (see below).

Traditional methods of studying human operant behavior

In the early days of studying human operant performance directly, there was a clear tendency to attempt to replicate animal procedures far too faithfully. The experimental environment would usually be a bare, confined room, the operant manipulandum a telegraph key or button designed to resemble the rat's lever, and reinforcers would be simple discrete events such as the delivery of candy or the clocking up of points on a counter (cf. Davey, 1981a; Lowe 1979; Sidman, 1962; Spradlin and Girardeau, 1966). The immediate result of these endeavors was the discovery that human operant performance seemed to deviate in fairly significant ways from that of animals. First, a variety of studies reported great difficulty in extinguishing a simple learned operant under experimental conditions (e.g. Buchwald, 1959; Bijou and Baer, 1966). Secondly, human performance on schedules of reinforcement exhibited a marked rigidity which distinguished it from the adaptive performance of nonhuman animals. For instance, human responding on schedules of reinforcement frequently entailed erratic rates of responding often interspersed with long and unpredictable pauses (Barrett and Lindsley, 1962; Lindsley, 1960; Orlando and Bijou, 1960; Sidman, 1962; Spradlin and Girardeau, 1966; Weiner, 1969, Lowe, 1979). In particular, human performance on fixed-interval schedules was odd. Whereas nonhuman animals exhibit a slowly accelerating response gradient throughout the interval (the fixed-interval 'scallop'), human subjects tend to emit either a very high, constant rate of responding without pauses, or a very low response rate consisting of just one or two responses at the end of the inter-reinforcement interval (cf. Lowe, 1979, 1983; Davey, 1981a). Similarly, human subjects would often show a distinct lack of adaptivity when it came to transferring from one schedule of reinforcement to another. Humans frequently carry over the response patterning acquired on a previous schedule to the performance on a completely different schedule (e.g. Weiner, 1969, 1972).

These apparently maladaptive aspects of human operant conditioning can to a large extent be explained by the difference between what Skinner (1966) called instruction-controlled versus contingency-controlled behavior. When high-rate fixed-interval performance is observed, subjects frequently adopt an inappropriate response strategy based on some rule they have formulated – largely because the sparsity of the experimental environment and the undemanding nature of the response leaves them ample time and opportunity to ponder on the nature and meaning of the task. Furthermore, the kind of rule that subjects formulate to control their responding appears to be crucially affected by the nature of the instructions given to subjects at the outset of the experiment. High-rate fixed-interval performance results when information is given about the response requirement, while low-rate fixed-interval per- formance from information in the instructions concerning the scheduling of reinforcement (Kaufman, Baron, and Kopp, 1966; Lippman and Meyer, 1967).

What evidence such as this suggests is that much of the human operant performance that is observed in experimental set-ups based directly on the procedure used for nonhuman animals produces performances which are rule- governed rather than contingency-governed. These rules are formulated by the subject during the course of performance, may be influenced by the nature of the instructions given prior to the experiment, and often produce behavior which is inappropriate to the scheduled contingencies. This raises two immediate questions about human operant performance. First, if rule-governed performance can be prevented, does human schedule behavior then show any similarity to that of animals? And secondly, why should human operant performance be so susceptible to control by self-generated rules when animal performance is quite clearly contingency-controlled?

A good number of studies have attacked the first question in a variety of ways: (1) by eliminating instructions and shaping up the operant from scratch (Schimoff, Catania, and Matthews, 1981; Matthews *et al.* 1977); (2) by providing subjects with a concurrent distractor task which deters hypothesis forming (Laties and Weiss, 1963); and (3) by attempting to externalize any self-produced rules and bring those under schedule control (Lowe, Harzem and Hughes, 1978; Lowe, Harzem and Bagshaw, 1978). All of these kinds of studies have been fairly unanimous in demonstrating that once self-produced cues are eliminated or controlled, the contingency-controlled performance of human subjects is formalistically very similar to that of nonhuman animals.

But why does so much human operant performance in these circumstances become rule-governed rather than contingency-governed? Lowe (1983) has suggested that the answer to this question may lie in the unique linguistic abilities possessed by humans. He suggests that it is 'the human subjects' capacity to formulate their own descriptions of reinforcement contingencies, to "self-tact" (Skinner, 1957, p. 138), and to use these descriptions to formulate rules to govern their behavior which results in human operant behavior being so different from that of lower animals' (Lowe, 1983, p. 77). In order to test this theory, Lowe suggested that contingency-governed performance should be found readily in the schedule performance of humans who have not developed language sufficiently well to be able to describe their own behavior and its consequences. In support of this theory Lowe and colleagues (Bentall and Lowe, 1982; Lowe, Beasty, and Bentall, 1983) found that the fixed-interval performance of young infants with very little linguistic ability (2½–4 years) resembled that of animals, while the performance of slightly older children (5–6½ and 7½–9 years) resembled that of adults, and frequently exhibited the maladaptive high-rate responding typical of adult human fixed-interval performance.

Contemporary human operant theory

If there has been any enduring problem with human operant research and application it has been that it has lacked theory. In particular, the momentum of human operant research has been generated largely by comparisons with nonhuman animal performance or by operant analyses of human psychological phenomena, and it has not come necessarily from a pervading interest in how human beings themselves learn about and adapt to operant contingencies. This has left us with a plethora of techniques for analyzing human behavior and conducting functional analyses, etc., but without an integrated body of knowledge on human operant learning. Some recent advances have been made in attempts to update our thinking on human operant performance – especially in relation to recent advances in the animal field (cf. Epling and Pierce, 1983; Pierce and Epling, 1983; Bradshaw and Szabadi, this volume) – but we still have only the merest of insights into how human beings learn about, adapt to, and cognitively process operant contingencies. With this in mind, it seems that contemporary human operant theory requires guidance and impetus from two particular directions: the first being the contemporary animal laboratory and the second being a desire to understand how operant learning in humans is mediated.

The role of contemporary animal theory

The preceding section on traditional approaches to human operant learning illustrates how human schedule performance and its comparison with animal performance had tended to dominate human operant research in the 1960s and 1970s. Yet there are many more phenomena in animal operant research which have been relatively ignored in human operant analyses.

Choice behavior

One of these phenomena is the Matching Law or correlation-based Law of Effect. In the 1970s and subsequently the 1980s, operant researchers have discovered that the behavior of animals in a simple choice situation appears to follow a basic empirical law. This law states that the proportion of responses that an animal will make to one of two choice stimuli will be proportional to the relative rate of reinforcement to that stimulus (Herrnstein, 1961; Baum, 1981). This is known as the Matching Law, and in its simplest form can be expressed in the following equation:

$$\frac{R_a}{R_a + R_b} = \frac{r_a}{r_a + r_b}$$

where R_a and R_b are the rates of responding to the two alternatives and r_a and r_b are the rates of reinforcement earned on each alternative.

When human subjects have been used in procedures analogous to those with animals, the results have been favorably comparable: human subjects do appear to obey the strictures of the Matching Law in a similar way to animals (cf. Bradshaw and Szabadi, this volume).

This has rather important implications for the experimental analysis of human behavior. Most of all, it implies that behavior can be analyzed, not just on the basis of an obvious temporal *contiguity* between responses and reinforcement, but also on the basis of a *correlation* between response rate and relative reinforcement frequency. In most environments individuals are faced with alternative sources of reinforcement and they may allocate their behavior in accordance with the relative rate of reinforcement for those alternatives. This has important implications for the behavior analyst who is conducting a functional analysis of behavior: the analyst may be unable to detect any obvious contingency between a prominent behavior and its reinforcing consequences, yet a more molar analysis may reveal important correlations between the frequency of behavior and the frequency of reinforcing environmental events (see Epling and Pierce, this volume, for a fuller account of these implications in applied settings).

Response allocation and behavioral regulation

Recently, another approach to understanding operant reinforcement in animals has emeged, and this is one that has developed the notions of response hierarchies first outlined by Premack (1965, 1971). Premack proposed that responses could be structured into a kind of preference hierarchy which was based on the probability of occurrence of those behaviors. Within this kind of analysis more probable behaviors could be used to reinforce less probable behaviors. The implication here is that reinforcement is a relational term rather than a 'goal' activity: it defines a relationship between a more probable behavior and a less probable behavior. This has led some operant theorists to ask by what processes more probable behaviors can act to reinforce less probable behaviors. Experiments have revealed two important factors. First, there is competition between different activities such that restricting the opportunity to indulge in one behavior normally acts to increase others (e.g. Dunham, 1971; Hinson and Staddon, 1978; Staddon and Ayres, 1975; Staddon, 1977, 1983). Secondly, there appear to be regulatory mechanisms which maintain different activities in a fixed proportion, and description of these mechanisms has been incorporated into what have come to be known as *behavioral regulation* theories of reinforcement (e.g. Allison, 1983; Hanson and Timberlake, 1983; Timberlake, 1984; Staddon, 1983). These theories assume that the animal allocates its time between activities in an optimal way (as measured by a free-response baseline) and the animal attempts to return to this optimal distribution as best it can whenever a particular activity is restricted. According to this kind of analysis, reinforcement occurs when we restrict a particular behavior (e.g. eating) by imposing a contingency relationship between it and some other behavior (e.g. lever pressing). For example, let us assume that a rat has an optimal allocation of 30 seconds running to each 30 seconds drinking. Now we impose a contingency such that the rat has to run twice as much as it drinks (i.e. it has to run for 60 seconds to get 30 seconds access to drinking). In these situations, behavioral regulation theories assume that the animal will attempt to return as closely as possible to its original optimal distribution of activities. Clearly, in the above example it can never return to exactly the optimal distribution but would probably compromise by increasing its preferred rate of running in order to produce something near its preferred rate of drinking. Thus, drinking has reinforced running.

This model of reinforcement has considerable uses in the analysis of human behavior. First, it assumes that reinforcement effects occur when an individual's optimal distribution of activities is disrupted in some way. Deprivation states do not have to be induced to produce reinforcement effects, nor is there a special class of stimuli which can be called reinforcers. Behavioral regulation accounts assume that the factor which motivates instrumental responding is the regulatory process which is continually attempting to return the animal to its optimal allocation of activities when this has been disrupted. This has a number of implications for the analysis of human behavior change in natural settings and in some restricted settings such as the psychiatric ward. In order to understand how behavior is being allocated in these situations we need to have some idea of the individual's optimal allocation of behaviors in unrestricted circumstances and the individual's preferences for different activities. What is perhaps even more important is that reinforcement effects can be induced if the optimal distribution is disrupted in any way at all, and not necessarily by the imposition of a response–consequence contingency. For instance, if on a psychiatric ward the opportunity to watch television is withdrawn, this disruption of the optimal allocation of behaviors will result in dynamic inter-actions between the remaining activities producing changes which look, prima facie, like contingency-generated reinforcement effects. If some of the behaviors that increase in frequency are undesirable ones, behavioral regulation models assume that these can best be controlled by finding some way in which the original optimal allocation of activities can be restored.

Economic theories of behavioral regulation

A number of animal theorists have noted the similarities that exist between describing reinforcement-generated behavior changes and certain ideas concerning labor supply and consumer demand in microeconomics (e.g. Allison, 1983; Lea, 1978; Staddon, 1980, 1983). Ironically, although these ideas were taken from human behavior and applied to animals, their application back again to human behavior has been slow to precipitate. In general, economic models assume that behavior changes occur in order to maintain some kind of optimal balance between activities and needs, and they provide mathematical formulations which allow us to make certain predictions about behavior changes and make some statements about the constraints that restrict operant learning. For instance, in microeconomics a consumer demand curve expresses the relationship between how much of a commodity is purchased and its price. This notion can be applied to operant learning by conceiving of the reinforcer as the commodity and the number of operant responses required to obtain the reinforcer as the price. Thus, price is equivalent to the value of, say, a fixed-ratio schedule. Some commodities are very sensitive to their price and consumption can fluctuate with changes in price. When the price of a commodity does affect its rate of consumption, then demand for the commodity is called *elastic*. However, when consumption of a commodity is relatively unaffected by its price then demand is known as *inelastic*. Whether demand for a commodity (reinforcer) is elastic or inelastic depends on a number of factors, some of which include the actual need for the product, the wealth of the consumer, and the availability of substitutes. Using such notions to describe the interaction between responses and reinforcers has proved useful in a number of animal studies (e.g. Kagel *et al.*, 1975; Lea, 1978; Lea and Roper, 1977). This kind of analysis has clear advantages when it comes to describing and predicting the behavior of human subjects in closed economy learning environments (such as *token economy schemes*) and in natural settings where the behavioral requirements for certain reinforcers are being continually adjusted.

Schedule-induced behavior

It is a curious fact that animal behaviorists have known about and studied schedule-induced behavior for well over 20 years, yet we are still far from understanding either the mechanisms that underlie it or its function. However, what we do know is something about the variables which generate schedule-induced activities. Schedule-induced behavior is the excessive and stereotyped behavior that often occurs in the inter-reinforcement interval on schedules of reinforcement. Examples that have been cataloged include schedule-induced drinking, aggression, wheel running and wood biting (cf. Davey, 1981a, 1987; Falk, 1971). Yet there are clear analogies here with a number of human behavioral phenomena that still require exploring (see Epling and Pierce, this volume). From a formalistic point of view certain kinds of drug dependency, alcohol dependency, aggressive behavior, 'fidgety' response patterns, self-stimulating rituals in psychotic and mentally handicapped individuals and hyperactivity all share the characteristics of excessiveness and stereotypy possessed by schedule-induced behavior in animals (cf. Foster, 1978; Gilbert, 1974; Fredericksen and Peterson, 1974; Epling and Pierce, this volume). It remains to be discovered whether schedules of reinforcement are the important determinants of these behavioral problems. If they are, then they have clear implications for the control and prediction of such social problems as alcoholism, drug addiction and certain kinds of aggressive outbursts (see Epling and Pierce, this volume, for a fuller account of these implications).

Cognitive aspects of operant learning in humans

An important goal of human operant theory is to understand the processes by which humans come to learn about the relationship between their behavior and its consequences, and how they translate this knowledge into behavior. Basically, these two goals represent the learning and performance dichotomy traditionally found in animal learning and they have rarely been broached in human operant research – largely because of the analytical rather than deductive nature of the research generally carried out in this field. Nevertheless, a full understanding of human operant performance still requires that we should know something about the cognitive processes that underlie response-consequence learning, given that we possess the experimental techniques suitable for studying such factors. There are at least two issues we need to approach here. First, what factors determine an individual's perception of an association between his or her behavior and the effects of that behavior? Secondly, what mechanisms act to generate an increase in the occurrence of a particular response once it has been reinforced? Both of these questions are relatively novel ones in human operant research, but some preliminary studies have suggested the kind of direction we should travel in to seek answers.

First, there is a good deal of literature available on the detection of relationships between events by human subjects – both the detection of relationships between covarying stimuli and between behavior and its outcome (e.g. Crocker, 1982; Nisbett and Ross, 1980; Alloy and Tabachnik, 1984). What is perhaps more interesting from the present point of view is that the factors which affect covariation assessment appear to be very similar in both humans and animals, and can be integrated under a single theoretical framework (Alloy and Tabachnik, 1984). In a recent study, Dickinson, Shanks, and Evenden (1983) have looked explicitly at human action-outcome assessments using a simulated video game procedure. In this procedure subjects had to assess to what extent they believed their own actions were important in causing events to occur on the video screen. Dickinson *et al.* found that the patterning and bias in contingency judgments could be explained in terms of contemporary conditioning models of associative learning such as the Rescorla–Wagner (1972) and Pearce–Hall (1980) models. Thus, the extent to which a human subject judged that his or her own actions had a particular outcome appeared to be determined by some of the same factors which determine associative strength in other conditioning procedures. This theoretical development is important because it permits an integration of a number of hitherto different areas of psychology: namely, animal associative learning, human operant performance and human covariation assessment.

The above paragraph alludes to the way in which humans learn about the relationship between their behavior and its outcomes. But what factors lead them to act on this knowledge? In traditional operant terms, this question is asking about the mechanisms that lead to an increase in the frequency of responding following operant reinforcement. At the present time we know very little about the answer to this question – even in animal operant conditioning (cf. Davey, 1987, Ch. 7; Dickinson, 1985). Nevertheless, some inferential techniques are being devised which allow us to infer the kinds of cognitive factors which mediate the operant response in animals (e.g. Adams and Dickinson, 1981; Dickinson, 1985). Such techniques have been successfully utilized in the study of factors mediating conditioned responding in human Pavlovian conditioning (Davey and Arulampalam, 1982; Davey and McKenna, 1983), and there is no reason why in the future such techniques cannot be applied to human operant performance.

References

Adams, C.D., and Dickinson, A. (1981). Actions and habits: Variations in associative representations during instrumental learning. In N.E. Spear and R.R. Miller (eds), *Information Processing in Animals: Memory Mechanisms*, Hillsdale, NJ: Erlbaum, pp. 143–165.

Allison, J. (1983). *Behavioral Economics*, New York: Praeger.

Alloy, L.B., and Tabachnik, N. (1984). Assessment of covariation by humans and animals: The joint influence of prior expectations and current situational information, *Psychological Review*, **91**, 112–149.

Barrett, B.H. and Lindsley, O.R. (1962). Deficits in acquisition of operant discrimination and differentiation shown by institutionalized retarded children, *American Journal of Mental Deficiency*, **67**, 424–436.

Baum, W.M. (1981). Optimization and the matching law as accounts of instrumental behavior, *Journal of the Experimental Analysis of Behavior*, **36**, 387–403.

Bentall, R.P., and Lowe, C.F. (1982). Developmental aspects of human operant behavior: The role of instructions and self-instructions, *Behavior Analysis Letters*, **2**, 186.

Bindra, D. (1974). A motivational view of learning, performance and behavior modification, *Psychological Review*, **81**, 199–213.

Bijou, S.W., and Baer, D.M. (1966). Operant methods in child behavior and development. In W.K. Honig (ed.), *Operant Behavior: Areas of Research and Application*, New York: Appleton-Century-Crofts.

Buchwald, A.M. (1959). Extinction after acquisition under different verbal reinforcement combinations, *Journal of Experimental Psychology*, **57**, 43–48.

Carpenter, F. (1974). *The Skinner Primer*, London: The Free Press.

Chomsky, N. (1972). Psychology and ideology, *Cognition*, **1**, 11–46.

Crocker, J. (1982). Biased questions in judgment of covariation states, *Personality and Social Psychology Bulletin*, **8**, 214–220.

Davey, G.C.L. (1981a). *Animal Learning and Conditioning*, London: Macmillan.

Davey, G.C.L. (1981b). Conditioning principles, behaviourism and behaviour therapy. In G.C.L. Davey (ed), *Applications of Conditioning Theory*, London: Methuen.

Davey, G.C.L. (1981c). How Skinner's theories work: Behaviour analysis and environmental problems, *Bulletin of the British Psychological Society*, **36**, 75–91.

Davey, G.C.L. (1987). *Ecological Learning Theory*, London: Methuen.

Davey, G.C.L. and Arulampalam, T. (1982). Second-order 'fear' conditioning in humans: Persistence of CR2 following extinction of CR1, *Behaviour Research and Therapy*, **20**, 391–396.

Davey, G.C.L. and McKenna, I. (1983). The effects of postconditioning revaluation of CS1 and UCS following Pavlovian second-order electrodermal conditioning in humans, *Quarterly Journal of Experimental Psychology*, **358**, 125–133.

Dawson, M.E., and Schell, A. (1986). The role of 'controlled' and 'automatic' cognitive processes in human autonomic classical conditioning. In G.C.L. Davey (ed.), *Cognitive Processes and Pavlovian Conditioning in Humans*, Chichester: John Wiley.

Dickinson, A. (1980). *Contemporary Animal Learning Theory*, Cambridge: Cambridge University Press.

Dickinson, A. (1985). Actions and habits: The development of behavioural autonomy, *Philosophical Transactions of the Royal Society of London*, **308**, 67–78.

Dickinson, A., Shanks, D., and Evenden, J. (1983). Judgement of act–outcome contingency: The role of selective attribution, *Quarterly Journal of Experimental Psychology*, **36A**, 29–50.

Dunham, P.J. (1971). Punishment: Method and theory, *Psychological Review*, **78**, 58–70.

Epling, W.F., and Pierce (1983). Applied behavior analysis: New directions from the laboratory, *Behavior Analyst*, **6**, 27–37.

Falk, J.L. (1971). The nature and determinants of adjunctive behavior, *Physiology and Behavior*, **6**, 577–588.

Ferster, C.B., and Skinner, B.F. (1957). *Schedules of Reinforcement*, New York: Appleton-Century-Crofts.

Foster, W.S. (1978). Adjunctive behavior: an underreported phenomenon in applied behavior analysis, *Journal of Applied Behavior Analysis*, **11**, 545–546.

Fredericksen, L.W., and Peterson, G.L. (1977). Schedule-induced aggression in humans and animals: A comparative parametric review, *Aggressive Behavior*, **3**, 57–75.

Gilbert, R.M. (1974). Schedule-induced ethanol polydipsia in rats with restricted fluid availability, *Psychopharmacologia*, **38**, 151–157.

Hanson, S.J., and Timberlake, W. (1983). Regulation during challenge: A general model of learned performance under schedule constraint, *Psychological Review*, **90**, 261–282.

Herrnstein, R.J. (1961). Relative and absolute strength of response as a function of frequency of reinforcement, *Journal of the Experimental Analysis of Behavior*, **4**, 267–272.

Hinson, J.M., and Staddon, J.E.R. (1978). Behavioral competition: A mechanism for schedule interactions, *Science*, **202**, 432–434.

Honig, W.K. (1966). *Operant Behavior: Areas of Research and Application*, New York: Appleton-Century-Crofts.

Kagel, J.H., Rachlin, H., Green, L., Battalio, R.C., Basmann, R., and Klemm, W.R. (1975). Experimental studies of consumer demand behavior using laboratory animals, *Economic Inquiry*, **13**, 22–38.

Kaufman, A., Baron, A., and Kopp, R.M. (1966). Some effects of instructions on human operant behavior, *Psychonomic Monograph Supplements*, **1**, 243–250.

Koestler, A. (1967). *The Ghost in the Machine*, London: Hutchinson.

Laties, V.G., and Weiss, B. (1963). Effects of a concurrent task on fixed-interval responding in humans, *Journal of the Experimental Analysis of Behavior*, **3**, 431–436.

Lea, S.E.G., (1978). The psychology and economics of demand, *Psychological Bulletin*, **85**, 441–466.

Lea, S.E.G. and Roper, T.J. (1977). Demand for food on fixed-ratio schedules as a function of the quality of concurrently available reinforcement, *Journal of the Experimental Analysis of Behavior*, **27**, 371–380.

Lindsley, O.R. (1960). Characteristics of the behavior of chronic psychotics as revealed by free-operant conditioning methods, *Diseases of the Nervous System (Monograph Supplements)*, **21**, 66–78.

Lippman, L.G., and Meyer, M.E. (1967). Fixed-interval performance as related to instructions and to subjects' verbalizations of the contingency, *Psychonomic Science*, **8**, 135–136.

Lowe, C.F. (1979). Determinants of human operant behavior. In M.D. Zeiler and P. Harzem (eds), *Advances in Analysis of Behavior* (**Vol. 1**), Chichester: John Wiley.

Lowe, C.F. (1983). Radical behaviorism and human psychology. In G.C.L. Davey (ed.), *Animal Models of Human Behavior*, Chichester: John Wiley, pp. 71–93.

Lowe, C.F., Beasty, A., and Bentall, R.P. (1983). The role of verbal behavior in human learning: Infant performance on fixed-interval schedules, *Journal of the Experimental Analysis of Behavior*, **39**, 157–164.

Lowe, C.F., Harzem, P., and Bagshaw, M. (1978). Species differences in temporal control of behavior II: Human performance, *Journal of the Experimental Analysis of Behavior*, **29**, 351–361.

Lowe, C.F., Harzem, P., and Hughes, S. (1978). Determinants of operant behavior in humans: Some differences from animals, *Quarterly Journal of Experimental Psychology*, **30**, 373–386.

Mackintosh, N.J. (1983). *Conditioning and Associative Learning*, Oxford: Oxford University Press.

Matthews, C.B.A., Shimoff, E., Catania, C., and Sagvolden, T. (1977). Uninstructed responding to ratio and interval contigencies, *Journal of the Experimental Analysis of Behavior*, **27**, 453–467.

Moore, B.R. (1973). The role of directed Pavlovian reactions in simple instrumental learning in the pigeon. In R.A. Hinde and J. Stevenson-Hinde (eds), *Constraints on Learning*, New York: Academic Press.

Nisbett, R.E., and Ross, L. (1980). *Human Inference: Strategies and Shortcomings of Social Judgment*, Englewood Cliffs, NJ: Prentice-Hall.

Orlando, R., and Bijou, S.W. (1960). Single and multiple schedules of reinforcement in developmentally retarded children, *Journal of the Experimental Analysis of Behavior*, **3**, 339–348.

Pearce, J.M., and Hall, G. (1980). A model for Pavlovian learning: Variations in the effectiveness of conditioned but not of unconditioned stimuli, *Psychological Review*, **87**, 532–552.

Pierce, W.D., and Epling, W.F. (1983). Choice, matching and human behavior: A review of the literature, *Behavior Analyst*, **6**.

Premack, D. (1965). Reinforcement theory. In D. Levine (ed.), *Nebraska Symposium on Motivation* (Vol. 13), Lincoln: Univ. Nebraska Press.

Premack, D. (1971). Catching up with common sense, or two sides of a generalization: Reinforcement and punishment. In R. Glaser (ed.), *The Nature of Reinforcement*, New York: Academic Press.

Rescorla, R.A., and Wagner, A.R. (1972). A theory of Pavlovian conditioning: Variations in the effectiveness of reinforcement and nonreinforcement. In A.H. Black and W.F. Prokasy (eds), *Classical Conditioning II: Current Research and Theory*, New York: Appleton-Century-Crofts.

Reynolds (1968). *A Primer of Operant Conditioning*, Glenville, Illinois: Scott Foresman & Co.

Schoenfeld, W.N. (1970). *The Theory of Reinforcement Schedules*, New York: Appleton-Century-Crofts.

Shimoff, E., Catania, A.C., and Mathews, B.A. (1981). Uninstructed human responding: Sensitivity of low-rate performance to schedule contingencies, *Journal of the Experimental Analysis of Behavior*, **36**, 207–220.

Sidman, M. (1962). Operant techniques. In A.J. Bachrach (ed.), *Experimental Foundations of Clinical Psychology*, New York: Basic Books, pp. 170–210.

Skinner, B.F. (1950). Are theories of learning necessary? *Psychological Review*, **57**, 193–216.

Skinner, B.F. (1953). *Science and Human Behavior*, New York: Macmillan.

Skinner, B.F. (1957). *Verbal Behavior*, New York: Appleton-Century-Crofts.

Skinner, B.F. (1969). *Cumulative Record*, New York: Appleton-Century-Crofts.

Skinner, B.F. (1972). *Beyond Freedom and Dignity*, New York: Alfred A. Knopf.

Spradlin, J., and Girardeau, F. (1966). The behavior of moderately and severely retarded persons. In N. Ellis (ed.), *International Review of Research in Mental Retardation*, New York: Academic Press, pp. 132–168.

Staddon, J.E.R. (1977). Schedule-induced behavior. In W.K. Honig and J.E.R.

Staddon (eds), *Handbook of Operant Behavior*, Englewood Cliffs, NJ: Prentice-Hall.

Staddon, J.E.R. (1980). Optimality analyses of operant behavior and their relation to optimal foraging. In J.E.R. Staddon (ed.), *Limits to Action*, New York: Academic Press.

Staddon, J.E.R. (1983). *Adaptive Behaviour and Learning*, Cambridge: Cambridge University Press.

Staddon, J.E.R., and Ayres, S.L. (1975). Sequential and temporal properties of behavior induced by a schedule of periodic food delivery, *Behaviour*, **54**, 26–49.

Timberlake, W. (1984). Behavior regulation and learned performance: Some misapprehensions and disagreements, *Journal of the Experimental Analysis of Behavior*, **41**, 355–375.

Weiner, H. (1969). Controlling human fixed-interval performance, *Journal of the Experimental Analysis of Behavior*, **12**, 349–373.

Weiner, H. (1972). Controlling human fixed-interval performance with fixed-ratio responding or differential reinforcement of low-rate responding in mixed schedules, *Psychonomic Science*, **26**, 191–192.

Human Operant Conditioning and Behavior Modification
Edited by G. Davey and C. Cullen
© 1988 John Wiley & Sons Ltd

Chapter 2

Applied Behavior Analysis: Contemporary and Prospective Agenda

CHRIS CULLEN
University of St Andrews

Behavior analysis is the term adopted by those working with an operant conditioning perspective. Depending on the procedures and target groups, the behavior analyst might be either *applied* or *experimental* (but cf. Baer, 1978). There is little doubt that procedures which have evolved from a conditioning perspective have become dominant in the various fields of applied psychology. This is especially so with regard to clinical areas, and is becoming more so in the educational, criminological and occupational fields. In his Presidential Address to the Association for Behavior Analysis, Jack Michael referred to this as 'the good news' (Michael, 1980). He described the development of the behavioral approach from its true beginning in the 1940s — Watson's pioneering work had little practical impact — by charting key publications and university courses taught by influential figures such as B. F. Skinner, W. N. Schoenfeld, and F. S. Keller.

Today the good news is as good as ever. The premier journal in the field —*Journal of Applied Behavior Analysis* — continues to publish research reports of increasingly important social validity. It is instructive to review briefly here some of the developments since Michael's address.

Client groups

It has always been true that behaviorists have tackled the problems of mentally handicapped people, chronically mentally ill people, children and delinquents. It was with these populations that they were initially allowed and encouraged to work, and it was in these areas that some powerful procedures (such as the token economy) were developed.

However, behavior analysts have been helping new and different client groups. Many are recipients of health care, such as cancer patients (Friman *et al.*, 1986), dental patients (Iwata and Becksfort, 1981; Reiss and Bailey, 1982), head injured youths (Gajar *et al.*, 1984), burn patients (Kelly *et al.*, 1984; Mahon, Neufeld, and Christopherson, 1984), drug addicts (McCaul *et al.*, 1984), comatose patients (Boyle and Greer, 1983), and people suffering from Raynaud's disease (Keefe, Surwit, and Pilon, 1980). Some are the providers of health care, such as counselors (Whang, Fletcher and Fawcett, 1982), medical technicians (Seaman, Greene, and Watson–Perczel, 1986), and dentists (Greene and Neistat, 1983).

Members of the general public have been the subject of a number of studies. For example, drivers and pedestrians (cf. Geller, Bruff, and Nimmer, 1985; Jason and Liotta, 1982), smokers (Stitzer and Bigelow, 1984; Stitzer *et al.*, 1986), consumers (Greene *et al.*, 1984), TV viewers (Jason, 1985; Winett *et al.*, 1985), diners in a cafeteria (Dubbert *et al.*, 1984), and snorers (Josephson and Rosen, 1980).

Employees in industry, such as plastics and industrial workers (Hopkins *et al.*, 1986; Sulzer-Azaroff and de Santamaria, 1980), have received the attentions of behavior analysts, as have sports people (Allison and Ayllon, 1980) and the police (Kirchner *et al.*, 1980; Larson *et al.*, 1980).

New responses

With an increasing emphasis on working with a wide range of people has come the need to analyze a wide range of responses. No longer are behaviorists simply interested in self-care skills and problem behaviors. They are dealing with responses which are important to society at large. Some of the emphasis is on improving health by dealing with dental care (cf. Dalquist and Gil, 1986), smoking (Stitzer *et al.*, 1986), testicular self-examination (Friman *et al.*, 1986), immunization (Yokley and Glenwick, 1984), sensible eating (Dubbert *et al.*, 1984), and insulin use (Epstein *et al.*, 1981). Conservation has become the watchword in present-day society, and behavior analysts have devised procedures to improve energy conservation (cf. Luyben, 1980; Winett *et al.*, 1985), resource recycling (Jacobs, Bailey, and Crews, 1984), littering and litter control (Bacon-Prue *et al.*, 1980; O'Neill, Blanck, and Johner 1980). Safety has been addressed with research on driving behavior (cf. Van Houten, Malenfant, and Rolider 1985), home safety (Peterson, 1984), resuscitation skills (Seaman *et al.*, 1986), self-defence (Poche, Bouwer, and Swearingen, 1981), and policing practices (Larson *et al.*, 1980). Personal well-being has been addressed by programs for sharing (Bryant and Budd, 1984), sports skills (Allison and Ayllon, 1980; Koop and Martin, 1983), drug abuse (Caudill and Lipscomb, 1980; Stitzer *et al.*, 1982), job independence (Sowers *et al.*, 1985), and community participation (Sanford and Fawcett, 1980).

If I had allowed myself to include articles from the other major journals publishing behavioral work, the lists of new client groups and new response classes would be longer, and would include some very important areas such as organizational behavior management (cf. *Journal of Organizational Behavior Management*, 1977 onwards; *Analysis and Intervention in Developmental Disabilities*, 1983, 3 (2/3)). But enough is enough, and the point is probably well made. This is the 'good news'.

Michael (1980) went on, though, to describe the 'bad news'. He argued that the considerable success in applying behaviorism was resulting in a problem. The 'circle', which used to be the province of a select few who had attended particular universities and who had sat at the feet of the originators of the field, is now widened so far that it is getting hard to tell who are the real behaviorists. There has been a shift in emphasis, away from the scientific to the technical. It isn't necessary any more to understand basic behavioral principles in order to apply them. The 'demands of the marketplace' have made it necessary to undertake projects which result only in measurably successful outcomes. There is little interest in investigating basic behavioral processes while there are so many problems awaiting an application of the solutions we have available now. Michael's fear is that this will result in stagnation and a drift back to the old mentalistic psychologies which behaviorism has replaced. His warning is justified by an analysis of the change in types of articles published since Baer, Wolf, and Risley's germinal paper of 1968. They identified a number of characteristics of applied behavior analysis as a discipline, four of which Hayes, Rincover, and Sotnick (1980) examined in papers published in the *Journal of Applied Behavior Analysis*. These dimensions were as follows:

- *Applied* — the extent to which a response is socially important.
- *Analytic* — the demonstration of experimental control by manipulation of putative causes.
- *Generality* — concerned with the longevity of behavior change, and the extent to which it is restricted only to the intervention setting.
- *Conceptual* — a measure of how the research is related to, illuminates or throws up basic principles of behavior.

Their analysis revealed that behaviorists are becoming less concerned with basic principles of behavior and more concerned with techniques for behavior change.

But, perhaps the bad news isn't so bad? After all, if there are a number of procedures which are effective in achieving behavior change, and they are being used, then we may be some way on toward Skinner's (1972) hope of a technology of behavior which can help solve some of 'the terrifying problems that face us in the world today' (p. 1). Perhaps it doesn't really matter if academic psychology drifts back towards cognitivism (cf. Skinner, 1985) or if clinicians describe their procedures in terms such as 'cognitive behavior modification' (cf. Cullen, 1982). We may have lost the battle of words yet still have won the war. On succeeding Jack Michael as President of the Association for Behavior Analysis, Don Baer argued that it is a good thing that there are people around whose job it is to apply well-tried and tested behavioral solutions, especially if they can do it efficiently. It is also a good thing that there are behavior analysts who are not particularly interested in applying their work but who are interested in identifying new principles of behavior. The two will work alongside each other and only time will tell how the relationship will go.

The debate will no doubt continue, but there are still problems to be addressed by behavior analysts, and the solutions will have both practical and theoretical significance. I will consider briefly just four.

The place of research with nonhuman animals

Behavior analysis is rightly considered a branch of biology, along with physiology, anatomy, evolutionary theory, and so on. It would be inappropriate to assert the existence of a qualitative discontinuity between humans and other animals (cf. Poling, 1984) yet there is still a question mark over the value of further work with nonhuman animals for our continued progress in understanding the behavior of humans. The initial insights gained by Skinner and his co-workers have undoubtedly been of great benefit, although very few behaviorists have advocated a *simple* extrapolation across species. Certainly Skinner himself has always recognized that some behavior is influenced by phylogenic contingencies and hence might be peculiar to one particular species (cf. Skinner, 1975a) and he concluded his first major report of findings from studies of the behavior of rats with the words '[this is] nothing more than an experimental analysis of a representative sample of behavior. Let him extrapolate who will' (Skinner, 1938, p. 442). However, the myth has built up over the years that behavior analysis depends for its success and conceptual basis on the investigation of nonhuman behavior. This is far from the truth. There are still interesting and relevant findings from laboratory work with rats and pigeons — for example the recent contributions by Epstein (1981, 1985) which simulate behavior in pigeons which is generally considered to involve 'higher cognitive process' — and some authors contend that there are behavioral processes currently being investigated with nonhuman animals which might have relevance for human affairs (cf. Epling and Pierce, 1983), but the evidence is that such work is declining in influence within applied behavior analysis. Poling *et al.* (1981) conducted a systematic citation analysis and showed that sources which traditionally report work with nonhuman subjects have been referenced increasingly infrequently since 1965 by authors who are presenting findings of relevance to practitioners. Notwithstanding even arguments that applied behavior analysis findings could be influencing basic research (Epling and Pierce, 1986) perhaps we have heeded the word of Baer (1978, p. 14):

Quite a lot of bar presses, key pecks, switch closings, alley runs, and barrier leaps have already been analysed and found amenable to reinforcement variables. A good deal of red and green, squares and triangles and other odd shapes, and myriad tones and buzzes have been discriminated under the press of a reinforcement contingency. Hardly anything else seems worth trying reinforcement on but language and social problems.

Verbal behavior

1957 saw the publication of one of the most controversial books in the history of psychology: *Verbal Behavior* (Skinner, 1957). It was greeted with a furore of protest by psychologists and linguists, and it has continued to generate controversy since that time. McPherson *et al.* (1984) show that there is an increasing trend in the number of citations per year for the book, and the number of fields in which the book is cited gives some indication of the widespread influence of the work. For Skinner, verbal behavior involves talking, thinking, imagining, and writing. It is social behavior, i.e. behavior whose reinforcement is mediated by another organism. His analysis pointed to several different response classes, each with their own characteristics. McLeish and Martin (1975) showed that there was strong experimental justification for the operant classes which Skinner had suggested in his book. (It is important to note that Skinner's 1957 analysis was *not* itself an experimental analysis, but was a plausible interpretation based upon his experimental work.)

However, even though behaviorists have some confidence in the conceptual analysis offered by Skinner (1957), the hallmark of a radical behaviorists' approach — the gaining of experimental control over the subject matter, thereby demonstrating the utility of the approach — is largely absent. There have been relatively few empirical studies using *Verbal Behavior* as their starting point (McPherson *et al.*, 1984).

This has practical as well as theoretical importance, since there are many areas (such as speech therapy and in the field of mental handicap) where an empirical analysis leading to teaching and corrective procedures would be of great value. Education, in general, would benefit from a functional analysis of areas such as creativity (cf. Vargas, 1978; Zoellner, 1969), and special educators need improved procedures for dealing with delayed language (cf. Reynolds and Risley, 1968) and reading difficulties (cf. Lee and Pegler, 1982). Clinicians who have clients with self-control problems need to know more about the relation between rule-governed and contingency-shaped verbal behavior (cf. Hayes *et al.*, 1986) so that they can give more effective advice on, for example, temper and anger control (Cullen, Black, and Dickens, 1986).

So far, the surface of the field of verbal behavior has hardly been scratched, and is an important challenge for the future.

The generalization problem

It is (relatively) easy to change behavior under conditions of strict experimental control, but far more difficult to ensure that newly acquired repertoires are displayed in non-experimental or clinical situations. This is referred to as the generalization problem (cf. Stokes and Baer, 1977). However, it is not a problem inherent in behavior analysis but is really a shorthand way of saying that behavior is complexly and multiply determined, and that the failure so far by behavior analysts has been to devise ways of identifying conditions in a person's normal environment which will maintain changed behavior. The problem is more acurately described as one of a failure to identify appropriate forms of stimulus control.

There appear to be two main options. One is to establish a new environment to replace the one which was maintaining behaviors which originally caused the person to seek help. This is the option realized when token economies are used as permanent (habilitative) rather than therapeutic (rehabilitative) settings in which people live (Cullen, Hattersley, and Tennant, 1977; Kazdin, this volume). It is also the option adopted within the field of organizational behavior management when management practises are changed to support new behavior on the part of staff (cf. Frederiksen, 1982). Unfortunately, though, behavior analysts rarely have the luxury of designing new and permanent large-scale environments, although they do have their fantasies (Skinner, 1948).

The second option is to identify natural contingencies which will 'trap' the new repertoire. Baer and Wolf (1970) articulated this possibility, but Kohler and Greenwood (1986) point out that there is still a long way to go before an effective technology of trapping is available. They present five types of evidence which should be produced in the search for traps. These are: Demonstrations that behavior occurs in settings different from the training setting, or the emergence of related behaviors which have not specifically been trained; the maintenance of behavior long after the intervention has ceased; demonstrations that social stimuli regularly follow or precede behavior outside the clinical setting; an experimental analysis of these social stimuli to demonstrate their functions as reinforcers or discriminative/setting events; the application of these stimuli to other behaviors within the setting to demonstrate their generality.

The immediate task for behavior analysts is to incorporate these five paradigms into their experimental and applied work. By so doing, important parameters will be uncovered which will help in addressing the generalization question, and will increase confidence that behavior analysis has something useful to contribute.

Dissemination

It is a constant source of wonder to behavior analysts that procedures they know to be effective are not adopted wholesale by the wider community. In fact, not only are the procedures not adopted, but behavior analysts even have considerable difficulty in gaining a hearing (cf. Morse and Bruns, 1983) and their endeavors are misrepresented to other psychologists (Todd and Morris, 1983) and to the public at large (Morris, 1985). Stolz (1981) was moved to ask 'does anybody care?' Disseminating research findings in a way which will lead to their adoption is another challenge for the future.

Because a functional analysis — in the sense of an analysis where putative causes are experimentally manipulated — would be near impossible in the public policy-making arena, Stolz (1981) examined four examples of the adoption by governmental agencies of behavioral procedures. Her purpose in doing this was to elucidate possibly crucial variables which were common to each situation. She identified ten, amongst which were included the existence of a pressing management problem, data showing the procedure to be effective, and the availability of funds for implementation. The strongest single variable, though, she surmised to be 'personal interaction, or the influence of the colleagues of the policymaker' (p. 501). This is not particularily good news for behavior analysts who wish to see their important research findings adopted by policymakers. Stolz's suggestion that we devote considerable energy to investigating ways in which public policies may be influenced is a sound one.

Paine and Bellamy (1982) propose a three-stage continuum for considering the development and dissemination of behavioral procedures. Initially, when a *technique* is developed, dissemination is to fellow professionals and service providers and is for information only. It will be achieved by conference presentations and journal articles, the intention being to have the procedures adopted by others for their own use. The next stage is when the techniques are collected together with an administrative structure, to form a *demonstration*. Dissemination of demonstrations is most appropriate to the general public by way of program visits and media coverage. A desired outcome for this type of dissemination is to achieve support for the program.

The third stage only occurs when the demonstrations have been field-tested and the resultant *models* are shown to be viable in non-experimental settings. The target audience for dissemination are planners, decisionmakers and service providers, and they must be offered manuals, training, technical assistance, and so forth. The aim is to get them to adopt the program.

Clearly, behavior analysts are concerned that their research helps people, and becomes widely accepted, but there is still some way to go before an adequate technology of dissemination is developed.

Conclusion

We have come a long way in a relatively short period of time, and many other approaches within psychology have fallen by the wayside. However, the dominant mode of thinking about human behavior in Western society is still mentalistic, influenced more by Plato than by any scientific approach to the subject. There is a strong urge to want to look for the causes of behavior inside the organism rather than in the environment. It is even the case that the subject matter itself is thought by many to be what is going on 'inside' (e.g. associations, cognitions) rather than what people *do*. There is still a 'steep and thorny way to a science of behavior' (Skinner, 1975b).

References

Allison, M. G., and Ayllon, T. (1980). Behavioral coaching in the development of skills in football, gymnastics, and tennis, *Journal of Applied Behavior Analysis*, **13**, 297–314.

Bacon-Prue, A., Blount, R., Pickering, D., and Drabman, R. (1980). An evaluation of three litter-control procedures: trash receptors, paid workers, and the marked item technique. *Journal of Applied Behavior Analysis*, **13**, 165–170.

Baer, D. M. (1978). On the relation between basic and applied research. In A. C. Catania and T. A. Brigham (eds), *Handbook of Applied Behavior Analysis: Social and Instructional Processes*, New York: Irvington.

Baer, D. M., and Wolf, M. M. (1970). The entry into natural communities of reinforcement. In R. Ulrich, T. Stachnik and J. Mabry (eds), *Control of Human Behavior*. Glenview, Ill: Scott Foresman.

Baer, D. M., Wolf, M., and Risley, T. R. (1968). Some current dimensions of applied behavior analysis. *Journal of Applied Behavior Analysis*, **1**, 91–97.

Boyle, M. E., and Greer, R. D. (1983). Operant procedures and the comatose patients. *Journal of Applied Behavior Analysis*, **16**, 3–12.

Bryant, L. E., and Budd, K. S. (1984). Teaching behaviourally handicapped pre-school children to share. *Journal of Applied Behavior Analysis*, **17**, 45–56.

Caudill, B., and Lipscomb, T. R. (1980). Modeling influences on alcoholics' rates of alcohol consumption, *Journal of Applied Behavior Analysis*, **13**, 355–365.

Cullen, C. (1982). Questioning the foundations of cognitive behavior modification. In C. J. Main (ed.), *Clinical Psychology and Medicine: A Behavioral Perspective*, New York: Methuen.

Cullen, C., Black, L., and Dickens, P. (1986). Anger control with mentallly handicapped adults. Unpublished manuscript.

Cullen, C., Hattersley, J., and Tennant, L. (1977). Behaviour modification — some implications of a radical behaviorist's view, *Bulletin of the British Psychological Society*, **30**, 65–69.

Dalquist, L. M., and Gil, K. M. (1986). Using parents to maintain improved dental flossing skills in children, *Journal of Applied Behavior Analysis*, **19**, 255–260.

Dubbert, P. M., Johnson, W. G., Schlundt, D. G., and Montague, N. W. (1984). The influence of caloric information on cafeteria food choices, *Journal of Applied Behavior Analysis*, **17**, 85–92.

Epling, W. F., and Pierce, W. D. (1983). Applied behavior analysis: New directions from the laboratory, *The Behavior Analyst*, **6**, 27–37.

Epling, W. F., and Pierce, W. D. (1986). The basic importance of applied behavior analysis, *The Behavior Analyst*, **9**, 89–99.

Epstein, L. H., Beck, S., Figueroa, J., Farkas, G., Kazdin, A. E., Daneman, D., and Becker, D. (1981). The effects of targeting improvements in urine glucose of metabolic control in children with insulin dependent diabetes, *Journal of Applied Behavior Analysis*, **14**, 365–376.

Epstein, R. (1981). On pigeons and people: a preliminary look at the Columbian Simulation Project, *The Behavior Analyst*, 4 (1), 43–55.

Epstein, R. (1985). The spontaneous interconnection of three repertoires, *The Psychological Record*, 35, 131–141.

Frederiksen, L. M. (ed.) (1982). *Handbook of Organizational Behavior Management*, New York: Wiley.

Friman, P. C., Finney, J. W., Glassock, S. G., Weigel, J. W., and Christopherson, E. R. (1986). Testicular self-examination: Validation of a training strategy for early cancer detection, *Journal of Applied Behavior Analysis*, 19, 87–92.

Gajar, A., Schloss, P. J., Schloss, C. N., and Thompson, C. K. (1984). Effects of feedback and self-monitoring on head trauma youths' conversation skills, *Journal of Applied Behavior Analysis*, 17, 353–358.

Geller, E. S., Bruff, C. D., and Nimmer, J. G. (1985). 'Flash for life': Community-based prompting for safety belt promotion, *Journal of Applied Behavior Analysis*, 18, 309–314.

Greene, B. F., and Neistat, M. D. (1983). Behavior analysis in consumer affairs: Encouraging dental professionals to provide consumers with shielding from unnecessary X-ray exposure, *Journal of Applied Behavior Analysis*, 16, 13–27.

Greene, B. F., Rouse, M., Green, R. B., and Clay, C. (1984). Behavior analysis in consumer affairs: Retail and consumer response to publishing food price information, *Journal of Applied Behavior Analysis*, 17, 3–21.

Hayes, S. C., Brownstein, A. J., Haas, J. R., and Greenway, D. E. (1986). Instructions, multiple schedules, and extinction: Distinguishing rule-governed from schedule-controlled behavior, *Journal of the Experimental Analysis of Behavior*, 46, 137–147.

Hayes, S. C., Rincover, A., and Solnick, J. V. (1980). The technical drift of applied behavior analysis, *Journal of Applied Behavior Analysis*, 13, 275–285.

Hopkins, B. L., Conrad, R. J., Dangel, R. H., Fitch, H. G., Smith, M. J., and Anger, W. K. (1986). Behavioral technology for reducing occupational exposures to styrene, *Journal of Applied Behavior Analysis*, 19, 3–11.

Iwata, B. A., and Becksfort, C. M. (1981). Behavioral research in preventive dentistry: Educational and contingency management approaches to the problems of patient compliance, *Journal of Applied Behavior Analysis*, 14, 111–120.

Jacobs, H. E., Bailey, J. S., and Crews, J. I. (1984). Development and analysis of a community-based resource recovery program, *Journal of Applied Behavior Analysis*, 17, 127–145.

Jason, L. A. (1985). Using a token-actuated timer to reduce television viewing, *Journal of Applied Behavior Analysis*, 18, 269–272.

Jason, L. A., and Liotta, R. F. (1982). Pedestrian jaywalking under facilitating and nonfacilitating conditions, *Journal of Applied Behavior Analysis*, 15, 469–473.

Josephson, S. C., and Rosen, R. C. (1980). The experimental modification of sonorous breathing, *Journal of Applied Behavior Analysis*, 13, 373–378.

Keefe, F. J., Surwit, R. S., and Pilon, R. N. (1980). Biofeedback, autogenic training, and progressive relaxation in the treatment of Raynaud's Disease: A comparative study, *Journal of Applied Behavior Analysis*, 13, 3–11.

Kelley, M. L., Jarvie, G. J., Middlebrook, J. L., McNeer, M. F., and Drabman, R. S. (1984). Decreasing burned children's pain behavior: Impacting the trauma of hydrotherapy, *Journal of Applied Behavior Analysis*, 17, 147–158.

Kirchner, R. E., Schnelle, J. F., Domash, M., Larson, L., Carr, A., and McNees, M. P. (1980). The applicability of a helicopter patrol procedure to diverse areas: A cost-benefit evaluation, *Journal of Applied Behavior Analysis*, 13, 143–148.

Kohler, F. W., and Greenwood, C. R. (1986). Toward a technology of generalization: the identification of natural contingencies of reinforcement, *The Behavior Analyst*, 19–26.

Koop, S., and Martin, G. L. (1983). Evaluation of a coaching strategy to reduce swimming stroke errors with beginning age-group swimmers, *Journal of Applied Behavior Analysis*, **16**, 447–460.

Larson, L. D., Schnelle, J. F., Kirchner, R. Jr., Carr, A. F., Domash, M., and Risley, T. R. (1980). Reduction of police vehicle accidents through mechanically aided supervision, *Journal of Applied Behavior Analysis*, **13**, 571–581.

Lee, V. L., and Pegler, A. M. (1982). Effects on spelling of training children to read, *Journal of the Experimental Analysis of Behavior*, **37**, 311–322.

Luyben, P. D. (1980). Effects of informational prompts on energy conservation in college classrooms, *Journal of Applied Behavior Analysis*, **13**, 611–617.

Mahon, L. M., Neufeld, M. M. M., and Christopherson, E. R. (1984). The effect of informational feedback on food intake of adult burn patients, *Journal of Applied Behavior Analysis*, **17**, 391–396.

McCaul, M. E., Stitzer, M. L., Bigelow, G. E., and Liebeson, I. A. (1984). Contingency management interventions: Effects on treatment outcome during methadone detoxification, *Journal of Applied Behavior Analysis*, **17**, 35–43.

McLeish, J., and Martin J. (1975). Verbal behavior: A review and experimental analysis, *Journal of General Psychology*, **93**, 3–66.

McPherson, A., Bonem, M., Green, G., and Osborne, J. G. (1984). A citation analysis of the influence on research of Skinner's *Verbal Behavior*, *The Behavior Analyst*, **7**, 157–167.

Michael, J. L. (1980). Flight from behavior analysis, *The Behavior Analyst*, **3**(2), 1–22.

Morris, E. K. (1985). Public information, dissemination and behavior analysis, *The Behavior Analyst*, **8**, 95–110.

Morse, L. A., and Bruns, B. J. (1983). Nurturing behavioral repertoires within a non-supportive environment, *The Behavior Analyst*, **6**, 19–25.

O'Neill, G. W., Blanck, L. S., and Johner, M. A. (1980). The use of stimulus control over littering in a natural setting, *Journal of Applied Behavior Analysis*, **13**, 379–381.

Paine, S. C., and Bellamy, G. (1982). From innovation to standard practice: Developing and disseminating behavioral procedures, *The Behavior Analyst*, **5**, 29–43.

Peterson, L. (1984). Teaching home-safety and survival skills to latch-key children: A comparison of two manuals and methods, *Journal of Applied Behavior Analysis*, **17**, 279–293.

Poche, C., Bower, R., and Swearingen, M. (1981). Teaching self-protection to young children, *Journal of Applied Behavior Analysis*, **14**, 169–176.

Poling, A. (1984). Comparing humans to other species: We're animals and they're not infra-humans, *The Behavior Analyst*, **7**, 211–212.

Poling, A., Picker, M., Grossett, D., Hall-Johnson, E., and Holbrook, M. (1981). The schism between experimental and applied behavior analysis: Is it real and who cares? *The Behavior Analyst*, **4**, 93–102.

Reiss, M. L., and Bailey, J. S. (1982). Visiting the dentist: A behavioral community analysis of participation in a dental health screening and referral program, *Journal of Applied Behavior Analysis*, **15**, 353–362.

Reynolds, N. J., and Risley, T. R. (1968). The role of social and material reinforcers in increasing talking of a disadvantaged preschool child, *Journal of Applied Behavior Analysis*, **1**, 253–262.

Sanford, F. L., and Fawcett, S. B. (1980). Consequence analysis: Its effects on verbal statements about an environmental project. *Journal of Applied Behavior Analysis*, **13**, 57–64.

Seaman, J.E., Greene, B.F., and Watson-Perczel, M. (1986). A behavioral system for assessing and training cardiopulmonary resuscitation skills among emergency medical technicians, *Journal of Applied Behavior Analysis*, **19**, 125–135.

Skinner, B.F. (1938). *The Behavior of Organisms*, New York: Appleton-Century-Crofts.

Skinner, B.F. (1948), *Walden Two*. New York: Macmillan.

Skinner, B.F. (1957), *Verbal Behavior*. New York: Appleton-Century-Crofts.

Skinner, B.F. (1972). *Beyond Freedom and Dignity*, London: Jonathan Cape.

Skinner, B.F. (1975a). The shaping of phylogenic behavior, *Acta Neurobiologiae Experimentalis*, **35**, 409–415.

Skinner, B.F. (1975b). The steep and thorny way to a science of behavior, *American Psychologist*, **30**, 43–49.

Skinner, B.F. (1985). Cognitive science and behaviorism, *British Journal of Psychology*, **76**, 291–301.

Sowers, J.A., Verdi, M., Bourbeau, P., and Sheehan, M. (1985). Teaching job independence and flexibility to mentally retarded students through the use of a self-control package, *Journal of Applied Behavior Analysis*, **18**, 81–85.

Stitzer, M.L., and Bigelow, G.E. (1984). Contingent reinforcement for carbon monoxide reduction: Within-subjects effects of pay amount, *Journal of Applied Behavior Analysis*, **17**, 477–483.

Stitzer, M.L., Bigelow, G.E., Liebson, I.A., and Hawthorne, J.W. (1982). Contingent reinforcement for benzodiazepine-free urines: Evaluation of a drug abuse treatment intervention, *Journal of Applied Behavior Analysis*, **15**, 493–503.

Stitzer, M.L., Rand, C.S., Bigelow, G.E., and Mead A.M. (1986). Contingent payment procedures for smoking reduction and cessation, *Journal of Applied Behavior Analysis*, **19**, 197–202.

Stokes, T.F., and Baer, D.M. (1977). An implicit technology of generalization, *Journal of Applied Behavior Analysis*, **10**, 349–367.

Stolz, S.B. (1981). Adoption of innovations from applied behavior analysis: 'Does anybody care?' *Journal of Applied Behavior Analysis*, **14**, 491–505.

Sulzer-Azaroff, B., and de Santamaria, M.C. (1980). Industrial safety hazard reduction through performance feedback, *Journal of Applied Behavior Analysis*, **13**, 287–295.

Todd, J.T., and Morris, E.K. (1983). Misconception and miseducation: Presentations of radical behaviorism in psychology textbooks, *The Behavior Analyst*, **6**, 153–160.

Van Houten, R., Malenfant, L., and Rolider, A. (1985). Increasing driver yielding and pedestrian signaling with prompting, feedback, and enforcement, *Journal of Applied Behavior Analysis*, **18**, 103–110.

Vargas, J.S. (1978). A behavioral approach to the teaching of composition, *The Behavior Analyst*, **1**, 16–24.

Whang, R.L., Fletcher, R.K., and Fawcett, S.B. (1982). Training counselling skills: An experimental analysis and social validation, *Journal of Applied Behavior Analysis*, **15**, 325–334.

Winnett, R.A., Leckliter, I.N., Chinn, D.E., Stahl, B., and Love, S.Q. (1985). Effects of television modeling on residential energy conservation, *Journal of Applied Behavior Analysis*, **18**, 33–44.

Yokley, J.M., and Glenwick, D.S. (1984). Increasing the immunization of pre-school children: An evaluation of applied community interventions, *Journal of Applied Behavior Analysis*, **17**, 313–325.

Zoellner, R. (1969). Talk-write: A behavioral pedagogy for composition, *College English*, **30**, 263–319.

Human Operant Conditioning and Behavior Modification
Edited by G. Davey and C. Cullen
© 1988 John Wiley & Sons Ltd.

Chapter 3

What Applied Studies of Human Operant Conditioning Tell Us About Humans and About Operant Conditioning*

BARRY SCHWARTZ and HUGH LACEY
Swarthmore College

During the 'Golden Age of Learning Theory' that dominated experimental psychology from about 1940 to 1960, investigators studied the behavior of rats or pigeons, in streamlined experimental situations, with full confidence that the principles revealed by these simple creatures in simple experiments could eventually be built into a comprehensive theory of behavior. Though the origins of such a theory might be humble, its ultimate scope and explanatory power would be grand. What was true of rats and pigeons in mazes and boxes would also be true, with suitable parameter adjustments, of people in their everyday environments. While there was great debate about exactly which general theory (Hull's, Skinner's, Tolman's, Guthrie's) would win the day, it was generally accepted that there would be a winner.

Much has happened in the last 25 years to dampen this enthusiasm. First, it has turned out that even the principles that govern the behavior of rats and pigeons, in simple situations, are more complex, and more elusive, than anyone would have guessed. And second, it appears that even when such principles are discovered, they may be specific to both the situation and the species under investigation. The early promise of a general behavior equation that could be applied, willy nilly, to one situation after another, has dissolved into a wide array of different research programs, each focused on understanding some

* This chapter was prepared with the help of National Science Foundation grants SES-83604 (to H. L.) and BNS 82-06670 (to B. S.). Portions of it appear, in slightly altered form, in Lacey and Schwartz (1987).

particular phenomenon, without much concern for its generality. The past presumption that what was true of pigeons would be true of people is gone. It has been replaced by attempts to study people directly, as the contents of this book can attest. Also gone, with one exception, are the grand theorists and their global theories.

But that one exception is notable. Among the contestants of the 1940s, B. F. Skinner has survived. He continues to hold the view that a general account of behavior can be derived from principles uncovered in the animal laboratory. He and his followers continue to construct explanations of everyday, human phenomena based on speculative extrapolations from the animal laboratory. If the growing body of literature on conditioning in humans, in both laboratory and applied settings, has relevance to any general theory of behavior, it is to his. For at the moment, Skinner's is the only game in town.

The purpose of this chapter is to examine the relevance of studies of conditioning in humans to a general theory of behavior. Our arguments are intended to apply to any theory, though, since Skinner's is the only current candidate, they will be applied directly to his. Our focus will be logical, not empirical. We will not be concerned with assessing how closely principles uncovered in studies of humans parallel principles uncovered in studies of rats or pigeons. For the purpose of this discussion, we can assume that the parallels are close, or if not, that some cogent account can be given of where and why the parallels break down. Our question, therefore, is this: Under the best of circumstances, in which studies of operant conditioning in humans systematically confirm and extend what is already known about animals, what does research on human conditioning tell us about human behavior in general? The answer that we will suggest is that such studies tell us less than is typically assumed.

Assessing theoretical comprehensives

The researcher who is deeply involved in determining why and when 'blocking' occurs in Pavlovian conditioning (Kamin, 1968; Mackintosh, 1975), or whether pigeons 'match' or 'maximize' in choosing among different schedules of reinforcement (e.g. Prelec, 1982), rarely pauses to consider how general his solution to the problem will turn out to be. The sensible view seems to be to put first things first: solve the problem in the limited domain in which it has been formulated, and then let future empirical investigation determine the scope of the solution. It seems premature at best, and pointless at worst to attempt to assess how comprehensive a theory will be in what are relatively early stages in its development.

In contrast to this view, we suggest that assessments of comprehensiveness are important at all stages of theoretical development — even the early ones. There are three reasons for this view:

1. Theories develop and experimental research is conducted within the framework of a research program (Lakatos, 1978). A research program provides positive guidelines for research, in large part by constraining what constitutes proper research — what are proper methods, research strategies and hypotheses. It is defined by some object of inquiry (e.g. learning, memory, behavior), and by a broadly sketched class of parameters whose effects it systematically and progressively investigates so as to include more and more signficiant features of its object of inquiry within its explanatory scope. It provisionally assumes that the class of parameters it investigates is broad enough to encompass its object of inquiry. Without some claims about the general characteristics of the object of inquiry, together with plausibility arguments defending those claims, there are no grounds for holding that the significant variables which control the object are in fact under investigation, and so for restricting inquiry in the manner required by the research program. Thus, for example, the behavior theorist can study an animal's allocation of its scarce behavioral resources without investigating the animal's 'rationality' (Rachlin, 1980). From within the research program of behavior theory, it can be defended that such an approach does not exclude significant variables, though it is doubtful that a similar defense could be made from within the research program of microeconomics.

2. Often, research programs rest on foundational assumptions that are in conflict with the assumptions that guide the practices of everyday life. This is obviously clear in the case of Skinnerian behavior theory. Its commitment to the views that behavior is lawful, that it can be fully explained by appeal to relations between it and a small set of environmental factors, both past and present, and that it is typically controlled by these environmental factors, so that by manipulating the environment one can manipulate behavior in lawful, predictable ways is radically incompatible with our everyday inclination to assign a fair measure of autonomy and responsibility to human agents. This incompatibility is, of course, the point. Skinner has written often to defend these commitments against the explanatory language of everyday life (e.g. Skinner, 1971). In his words: 'A person is not an originating agent; he is a locus, a point at which many genetic and environmental variables come together in a joint effort' (Skinner, 1974, p. 168).

If our everyday conception, the one that informs most of our social practices, is correct, the research program of behavior theory cannot produce a comprehensive account of behavior. In contrast, if behavior theory is correct, and if it becomes widely accepted, social practices justified by our everyday conception will be undermined, and eventually displaced. There can be no compromise here; either behavior theory is importantly incomplete, or important social practices are ill-conceived. The determination of which of these possibilities is correct is essentially a determination of the comprehensiveness of behavior theory.

3. Most good scientific theories yield practical, technological applications. Indeed, it is often the applications that people point to as evidence for the power of the theory. In the case of behavior theory, Skinner has often argued that the impressive, burgeoning technology of behavior control, as much as anything else, is what demands our allegiance to the behavior theorist's research program. Now, for an application to be justified, two conditions must be met. First, it must succeed in bringing about its intended effect. Second, it must not produce any undesirable side-effects. The first condition is straightforward; either the application does what it is supposed to or it doesn't. However, assessing side-effects is less straightforward. To evaluate side-effects, one needs to explore the range of variables upon which the application could have an impact. But how does one know what these variables are? One is guided by the research program itself.

Suppose, for example, it is true that behavior is almost exclusively controlled by prevailing contingencies of reinforcement coupled with the organism's past history of reinforcement. If so, one need not look beyond the scope of behavior theory itself to check for side-effects, and one could reasonably expect that an application that merely recasts environmental variables that are already controlling behavior anyway would have no adverse side-effects. But suppose instead that human beings are characterized by a measure of autonomy and responsibility, and that applications of behavior theory undermine these human characteristics. This is indeed a side-effect of the application (whether it is adverse or not could be argued, but for present purposes this is beside the point). However, it is a side-effect that cannot even be recognized or acknowledged from within the research program of behavior theory. The behavior theorist rarely looks for side-effects that are presumed to operate on variables that are significant to rival research programs, but not to his own. Whether or not this myopia is reasonable depends upon whether behavior theory is comprehensive. Is it myopic not to look for unicorns? Is it myopic not to look for charmed quarks? Our answers to these questions are parasitic on the explanatory framework we adopt in answering them. In any case it is clear that one cannot generally justify the applications of behavior theory without an assessment of its comprehensiveness.

For these three reasons, it is important to assess the comprehensiveness of a theory. In the case of behavior theory, one of the most important guides to that assessment comes from the extension of conditioning principles derived from the study of animals to human beings, both in the laboratory and in application. Behavior theorists have always asserted that their theory was comprehensive, and now empirical research is substantiating the assertion. This, at any rate, is the commonplace view; successful applications confirm the general theories that give rise to them. Let us then turn to an examination of this view.

The relation between theory and application

A theory predicts that a given application will work. The application is attempted. It works. The theory is confirmed. It is by this standard logic of confirmation that we regard such applications as automobiles, satellites, bridges, computers and the like as evidence for the various physical theories that give rise to them. And the logic seems straightforward enough. A theory says that such and such variables, in combination, will give rise to such and such an effect. We find that effect desirable, so we combine the variables as the theory says. The effect occurs. This gives us simultaneously a desired application and support for the theory. In terms of theory confirmation, there is really nothing to distinguish successful applications from successful experiments. We perform experiments in the light of theory-based predictions that these values of these variables combined in this way will yield a particular outome. The outcome is 'desired' in the case of experiments only because it will support the theory, and it is support for the theory that we are after. So applications really are experiments of a particular sort; they are experiments whose results are of some use to us at the same time that they confirm the theory from which they were derived. Thus Skinner could argue that attempted applications of behavior theory principles are simply real-world tests of the theory. Indeed, they are the most impressive tests, just because they are 'real-world' and because they produce good results.

This view of the relation between sucessful application and theory has a significant implication. It makes applications, in an important sense, value-free. To the question 'should there be atomic energy?', the physicist can reply 'there is atomic energy. Perhaps we can debate whether or how it should be used, but its presence is a fact of nature.' To the question 'should there be genetic control of human beings?', the molecular biologist can reply 'there is genetic control of human beings. Perhaps we can debate whether or when it is appropriate to manipulate genes surgically or to abort fetuses, but genetic control is a fact of nature.' And to the question 'should human behavior be manipulated and controlled?', the behavior theorist can reply 'it is already controlled. Perhaps we can debate which contingencies can be manipulated to produce which behaviors, but the control of behavior is a fact of nature.' In each of these cases, an important piece of the justification of application comes by appeal to some natural process or law from which the application derives. What the justification says is that, in a real sense, the application isn't actually changing anything; it is simply harnessing and directing a universal, natural process. Part of what underlies justifications like these is an (often implicit) assumption that the relevant theory is comprehensive. What gives the claim that such and such is a fact of nature its justificatory force is the presumption that it is a fact of *all* of nature, or at least of all the relevant domain.

There are a number of assumptions that underly this presumed relation between theory and practice. First, it is assumed that the phenomena of nature are lawful, that nature can be 'carved at the joints', and the business of science is to discover where the joints are. Second, it is assumed that the joints can be studied, in the laboratory, or manipulated, in application, in isolation from each other, and in this way, deep truths about them can be revealed. Third, it is assumed that nature's joints work the same way in isolation as they do in combination. This last step is crucial to the view that successful experimentation or application tells us not just about experiments and applications, but about the world in general.

We want to suggest that this pattern of assumptions that underlies the presumed relation between theory and practice is unwarranted or, at least, problematic. Consider these two claims:

- *Claim 1* : Behavior is controlled by contingencies of reinforcement.
- *Claim 1A*: Behavior can be controlled by contingencies of reinforcement.

The first of these claims is a statement of a universal, natural law. It says that we can understand all behavior, in all circumstances, as the product of past and present environmental reinforcement contingencies. (Of course, it isn't really this general, since certain classes of behavior, like reflexes, are excluded, but to keep the exposition simple, we will ignore this qualification.) The second claim is much more restricted. It says that there are certain (unspecified) circumstances in which reinforcement controls behavior. Just how general this claim is depends on just how general these circumstances are.

The second of these claims is completely uncontroversial. What makes behavior theory interesting and challenging is its view that the first claim is approximately true, or at least that behavior under the control of contingencies of reinforcement represents the paradigm case, defining a norm from which departures may be explained by appeal to subsidiary principles. The debates that occur between behavior theorists and their critics are not debates about the truth of falsity of the principle of reinforcement (for surely it is true), they are debates about whether the circumstances of its applicability are properly viewed as paradigmatic.

Distinguishing between these two claims may seem like nit-picking, but if it were to turn out that Claim 1A rather than Claim 1 were true, some important implications would follow. If behavior can be, but need not be, controlled by reinforcement, it seems natural to ask whether it should be. Should social institutions be structured so that Claim 1A holds or not? Will such institutions make for a good society and good people? Is this the best way for people to live their lives? All of these questions require moral judgments. They require a conception of what the good life is, so that we can determine whether the conditions in which the truth of Claim 1A is manifested support for that good life. But as we saw before, behavior theorists tend to deny the need for moral judgments of this sort by suggesting that the control of behavior by reinforcement is just a fact of nature.

Now consider these two claims:

* *Claim 2* : Falling objects have the same constant acceleration.
* *Claim 2A*: Falling objects can have the same constant acceleration.

These two claims parallel Claims 1 and 1A, but this time the domain is physics. In this case we know that Claim 2A and not Claim 2 is true. Usually, the falling bodies in our experience satisfy not Claim 2, but Claim 2':

* *Claim 2'*: The acceleration of falling bodies varies with their densities.

Concerning the falling bodies of our experience, Claim 2 is rarely true and Claim 2' is almost always true, and where we experience Claim 2 to be true, it is almost always in circumstances that we have created experimentally. Nevertheless, for the purposes of post-Galilean scientific practice, Claim 2 is taken as more important, more fundamental, than Claim 2'. Falling bodies of which it is true are taken as paradigms, departures from which are to be explained by subsidiary principles. Thus, the motions of the far more common falling bodies of which Claim 2' is true are explained as departures from the norm because air resistance has quantitatively different effects on objects depending, among other things, on their density. Claim 2, a fundamental principle of Galilean physics, holds *ceteris paribus* (other things being equal), that is, if there are no causes for the motions of falling bodies to depart from the norm which it represents. It is taken to represent a norm, not because of its direct and immediate applicability to the falling bodies of our common experience, but because it is readily embedded in Newtonian mechanics, a general framework that is applicable to much more than falling bodies, and that enables the exact definition of the conditions under which it is exemplified and the systematic articulation of subsidiary principles that can explain the quantitative details of departures from the norm. Claim 2', a fundamental principle of pre-Galilean physics, though it applies more widely than Claim 2 to the falling bodies of our common experience, is not now held to be a norm since it cannot be readily embedded in a much more general framework. Rather, it is now treated as a special case. The principle represented by Claim 2 enters into its explanation in conjunction with subsidiary principles. Indeed, this principle figures as a central part of the explanation of all falling bodies, under any conditions whatsoever (for example, objects falling on the moon), whereas the principle of Claim 2' applies only to objects falling in a medium. Claim 2', therefore, is just an empirical generalization that applies under special (albeit widespread in our experience) conditions, and which offers no explanatory insight outside those conditions. In contrast, Claim 2 is not only a generalization that applies under certain conditions, it also represents a norm against which *ceteris paribus* clauses can be given exact meaning, and it enters as a key component into the explanation of falling bodies under all conditions.

Interpreted simply as generalizations, both Claims 2 and 2′ are true of falling bodies only under certain conditions. Cartwright (1983) has presented a compelling argument that no scientific principle, even of the greatest generality, applies generally without recourse to *ceteris paribus* clauses. Like Claim 1A, only Claim 2A is literally true. This is what led us to ask whether or not behavior should be controlled by contingencies of reinforcement. Does this mean that we should now ask whether objects should fall with the same constant acceleration or should fall with accelerations that vary with density? Obviously not, for such questions are intelligible only of moral agents. The question would remain pointless even if we recast it to ask whether conditions should be brought about such that all objects fall with the same constant acceleration. The question would be pointless because people are powerless to bring about the relevant conditions that would make this generalization uniformly true.

Is the same true of the control of behavior by reinforcement? Are the circumstances under which people are reinforcement-governed circumstances over which we are powerless, or are they circumstances we can do something about, circumstances subject to human discretion, intervention, and alteration? We believe that circumstances can be manipulated so that reinforcement exerts more or less control over behavior, and that both successful experiments and successful applications are examples of that manipulation. If this is true, the successes of behavior theory in human applications are support for Claim 1A, not Claim 1. Even so, we must ask whether Claim 1 is closer to Claim 2 or to Claim 2′? If the former, then while reinforcement principles would not provide the whole story, they would still be an essential part of the explanation of any instance of behavior. If the latter, then Claim 1 would be simply an empirical generalization that applies under special conditions. We will argue that Claim 1 is indeed parallel to Claim 2′, and that from the perspective of a broader explanatory framework (provided by the categories of ordinary purposive explanation) the conditions under which it is approximately true can be defined. This will strengthen our contention that the successful applications of behavior theory do not obviate the need for discussion about whether such applications should occur. Let us turn to the argument.

Applications as human creations

As we indicated at the outset of this paper, we concede, for purposes of the present discussion, that both laboratory and applied conditioning research with people confirms and extends the general principles initially discovered with animals. We concede, in short, that a contingency between a conditioned and an unconditioned stimulus is sufficient to produce Pavlovian conditioning in people, and that contingencies of reinforcement can be manipulated to control human behavior. The question is what these extensions of conditioning principles tell us about the comprehensiveness of behavior theory. And the answer, we propose, is not much.

Think about the various applications of the basic sciences of physiology and pharmacology that appear as modern medical treatment. First, consider the case of two widely used and effective drugs, insulin and aspirin. Insulin is used to treat diabetes. It is supplied to the body exogenously to make up for inadequate endogenous supply. The physiologist would say that insulin supplied from outside performs just the same functions, in just the same way, as endogenous insulin. Thus external insulin mimics the effects of internal insulin, and its success in controlling the symptoms of diabetes constitutes confirmation of the physiologist's understanding of the role played by insulin in normal body function.

Now consider aspirin. Aspirin has multiple effects. It alleviates pain, it reduces fever, it thins blood, it reduces inflammation, and so on. Does aspirin work like insulin, mimicking endogenous bodily processes, or does it work by dwarfing or overriding those processes? If there are endogenous processes that work like aspirin, it is not presently known what they are. That is, no single endogenous process that has all aspirin's effects, that aspirin can be said to mimic, has as yet been identified. Thus aspirin's effectiveness in application confirms no particular theory of normal body function. Eventually it may, that is, eventually an endogenous process that aspirin mimics may be identified. But at the moment, aspirin is a technological achievement with no clear implications for the understanding of physiology. What this shows is that an application may be successful without confirming any particular theory of natural functioning.

Now consider another example, artificial hearts. One doesn't need to know how the heart works to build an effective artificial heart. One needs to know the functions it performs, but not *how* it performs them. There is no reason to suppose that the most effective artificial heart will be one that mimics the natural heart in every detail. Evolution is not, after all, a mechanical engineer. And the same story can be told of the dialysis machine. These examples also show that successful applications need not confirm basic physiological theories.

As a final example, closer to psychology, consider the digital computer. Computers perform feats of artificial intelligence. They store and retrieve data from memory, they perform various calculations, they draw pictures and transform them in various ways. Does the existence of the digital computer and its ability to perform various intelligent activities provide confirmation of a theory of human intelligence, or of human brain function? Obviously no. Computer circuitry is not like the human brain, and computers typically perform their functions in ways that are radically different from the ways that people perform similar functions. Computers work in ways that capitalize on features of their design (large memory, high processing speed, and so on) that are importantly different (so far as is known) from features of the design of human cognitive capacity. Of course, one could use the computer as a tool in the study of human cognition by building into its operation constraints and functions that are thought to mimic the way humans operate. But the mere fact of computer intelligence need have no bearing whatsoever on theories of human intelligence.

And so it is with applications of conditioning. One can use principles of stimulus control, together with shaping by successive approximation, to teach children to cross the street only when the light is green. One can also explain what traffic lights are for, and what the consequences of crossing on red might be. The fact that both of these techniques might work is no reason to infer that one is reducible to the other, that instruction is just shaping and stimulus control by another name. Of course it might be, but the mere fact that two superficially quite different operations yield the same result does not imply that it must be.

Though the point is often overlooked, there is nothing startling, or even controversial about the claim that successful applications are not necessarily confirmations of the theory that spawned them. Nor is this peculiar to psychology. Precisely the same reasoning applies to physics. Showing that the laws of motion hold in a vacuum, or on a frictionless surface, is no guarantee that they have much to do with the motions of objects in the real world. Neither would some invention constructed in accord with the laws of motion. Both the experiment and the invention are human creations. What really convinces us that the laws of motion capture an important piece of reality is that we see them exemplified in the behavior of natural objects, with no intervention from physicists. They are exemplified in the motions of the planets, and neither Newton nor his successors had much to do with that. So what we need to find are some naturally occurring phenomena that exemplify the behavior theorist's principles without his intervention. If we found such phenomena, and if they were widespread, it would inspire confidence that Claim 1, and not Claim 1A, is true, or at least that it might represent a behavioral paradigm.

And there are such phenomena to be found. All one has to do is look at the modern, industrial workplace. There it is common for people to engage in essentially arbitrary, repetitive tasks, in which their behavior is virtually completely controlled by the operative contingencies of reinforcement. There is little to distinguish the factory worker sewing hems on a piece rate schedule of pay from the pigeon pecking keys on a ratio schedule of reinforcement. The workplace seems like the behavior theorist's equivalent of the planets.

However, as we have argued elsewhere (Schwartz, Schuldenfrei, and Lacey, 1978), this equivalence is more apparent than real. An examination of the evolution of the modern workplace leads us to the following conclusions:

1. Medieval work, the precursor to modern work, cannot be analyzed as exemplifying reinforcement contingencies in operation, at least not straightforwardly. This is in part because medieval work was variegated, flexible, and socially integrated.
2. Important features of the modern workplace developed slowly in the nineteenth century. As they emerged, certain customary and traditional work practices were suppressed, and gradually replaced by wages as the worker's predominant concern in the workplace.
3. Only with the suppression of these traditional practices did behavior in the workplace become describable and explicable in informative detail in terms of principles of reinforcement.
4. The structuring of the modern workplace was completed under the heavy influence of the Scientific Management Movement (Taylor, 1911/1967) at the turn of this century, in the light of principles virtually identical to those of behavior theory.
5. Therefore, the settings in which reinforcement principles are clearly exemplified are not generally characteristic of human societies. Instead, they have been constructed, much like other applications of behavior theory, in the course of recent history. Rather than being a natural exemplification of principles of reinforcement in operation, the modern workplace is just another human creation.

Note that this account does not deny the efficacy of conditioning principles in controlling behavior. On the contrary, the modern workplace is testimony that under the right conditions, conditioning principles can be extraordinarily effective. What it does do is question the workplace as an exemplification of a universal, natural law. In consequence, it leaves open the question of whether the 'right' conditions for the operation of reinforcement principles should be established.

How does one go about answering this question? In part, as suggested above, it depends upon some theory of how people should live. But even in the absence of a well-articulated theory of this sort, one can approach the question of whether conditions under which conditioning principles operate should be established by looking for side-effects in circumstances where they are established. One study of this sort was reported by Schwartz (1982). In that study, college students were required to push two buttons. If they pushed the buttons in an appropriate sequence, of which there were many, they earned points that were ultimately convertible into cash. All students quickly came to produce only appropriate sequences. Of special interest was the fact that although many such sequences were possible, each student fixated on one particular sequence, to the virtual exclusion of all others. That is, contingent reinforcement succeeded in producing highly stereotyped and efficient operant behavior.

The 'side-effect' came later, when these subjects were instructed to discover the rule that governed whether or not their response would earn points. In comparison to a group of subjects that had been exposed to the rule-discovery task with no pretraining, pretrained subjects were less likely to discover the rules, and took longer to do so. The pretraining that made them extremely efficient at producing particular sequences that worked had the side-effect of making them inefficient at discovering general principles or rules. Pretraining had turned amateur scientists into factory workers, at least temporarily.

This is not an isolated example. Other demonstrations of side-effects, of the 'hidden costs of reward', have been collected by Lepper and Greene (1978). What they indicate collectively is that control of behavior by reinforcement can be achieved by creating situations from which other potential sources of influence have been eliminated. Just as the vacuum eliminates air resistance, and the factory eliminates tradition, reinforcement contingencies can eliminate an orientation to effective hypothesis testing and problem solving.

What is the justification for calling this a 'side-effect'? Perhaps it is a main effect that merely reflects poorly designed contingencies. Perhaps different contingences could improve hypothesis-testing and problem-solving behavior rather than undermining it. When we discussed earlier the importance of assessing a theory's comprehensiveness, one of the issues that arose was the issue of side-effects. If a theory is comprehensive, there can be no side-effects. Comprehensiveness implies that all effects are main effects, all effects are the result of the operation of known variables on a known domain. Not all effects will necessarily be anticipated, so that what we are calling side-effects might properly be reinterpreted as surprising main effects, but if a theory is comprehensive, these effects, whatever they are called, will lie within its explanatory compass. So having raised the question of comprehensiveness before, it is now time to sketch an answer to it. Is behavior theory, buttressed by the growing literature on conditioning in humans, comprehensive?

We believe that the answer to this question is no. Behavior theory is not comprehensive; it is importantly incomplete. Seeing this is difficult in the absence of an alternative explanatory framework that is more comprehensive. Fortunately, there is such an explanatory framework, the one that guides the explanation of action in everyday life, that treats behavior as purposive, goal-directed, and teleological. This framework has the virtue of accounting both for situations in which principles of behavior theory are powerful and situations in which they are not. In addition, it accounts for what must be done to situations of the latter type to turn them into situations of the former type.

A teleological alternative to behavior theory

We have sketched the general features of such a teleological explanatory framework elsewhere (Lacey and Schwartz, 1987; Schwartz and Lacey, 1982,

Ch. 9). This framework does not constitute a theory in the way that theory is usually understood in scientific practice. Briefly, a theory is a set of interconnected generalizations which explains particular phenomena by deducing (or probabilistically inferring) them from the theory together with relevant *ceteris paribus* clauses and initial conditions. At the same time, in order that such deductions are possible, a theory also provides a set of categories for the description of phenomena. A theory explains by revealing concretely the lawfulness of phenomena, and so a phenomenon has been explained when it has been described in such a way that its being an instance of certain theoretical generalizations is apparent. The teleological framework offers explanations in another mode. Where the background metaphysical assumption of theoretical explanation is that events are lawful, that of the teleological framework is that action is explicable in terms of an agent's goals and beliefs. More explicitly, theoretical explanation proceeds by filling in the schema:

'b' occurred because 'b' is a 'B' and it was preceded by 'a' which is an 'A', and *ceteris paribus*, whenever an 'A' occurs a 'B' follows.

Here 'b' and 'a' represent particular events, 'B' and 'A' kinds of events which are identified by categories provided by the theory, and the stated generalization (which usually will be more complex) is deducible from the fundamental hypotheses of the theory.

In contrast, teleological explanation proceeds by filling in the schema:

'X' did 'b' because 'X' had the goal 'g' and 'X' believed that doing 'b' would further 'g'.

Here 'X' represents an agent and 'b' an action. The framework provides a rich variety of concepts to capture goals and beliefs—intentions, motives, emotions, character, virtues, and so on, which we all deploy with ease in daily life, and without which we would be utterly unable to interact humanly with our fellows, even partially anticipate the future course of social events, or make sense of our own lives and projects.

We are not aware of any compelling arguments that the teleological schema can be reduced to or ought to be replaced by the theoretical. The teleological framework often provides illuminating explanations that are not implicated in generalizations, although it is a framework in which there can be formulated powerful generalizations (for example, 'power corrupts'). Because of the vast gulf which separates the fundamental presuppositions of the two frameworks, it is difficult to make an item by item comparison with behavior theory. (But see Davidson, 1980; and Taylor, 1964. See also Schwartz and Lacey, 1982, Ch. 8; and Lacey, 1985 in which we suggest that the categories of teleological explanation better explain important instances of successful applied procedures than do general behavioral principles, contrary to the concession we made at the outset of this chapter.) Nevertheless, the network of goal-directed, purposive concepts that people appeal to in explaining action in everyday life can illuminate both the successes of behavior theory and its inadequacies.

The application of behavior theory principles is conspicuously successful in situations that have the following characteristics: Only a few reinforcers are available, and usually, only one has special salience; the experimenter (behavior modifier) has control over conditions of deprivation and access to reinforcers; there is only one, or at most a few, available means to the reinforcers; the performance of clearly defined, specific tasks is reinforced; different tasks are effectively interchangeable for the one that is reinforced; the contingencies of reinforcement are imposed and varied by agents not themselves being subjected to the contingencies; and there are no effective alternatives to being in the situation. Let us call situations that have these properties closed settings. Clearly, all experimental situations, and most applied situations, have these properties. The evolution of work that we sketched above can be understood as the transformation of the workplace from a largely open to a largely closed setting. Demonstrating that behavior theory has explanatory success in closed settings does not suffice to show that it is comprehensive, if not all settings are closed. And the everyday framework of teleology suggests that many settings are not closed (for details, see Lacey and Schwartz, 1987).

The teleological framework presupposes that human behavior is goal-directed. Goal-directedness can, in a few steps, be translated into the conceptual scheme of behavior theory. To be goal directed is to be controlled by anticipated consequences. To be controlled by anticipated consequences is to be controlled by actual past consequences. To be controlled by past consequences is to be controlled by past contingencies of reinforcement. Thus, any consequence that controls behavior necessarily becomes a reinforcer, from which it is often inferred that any goal is a reinforcer. But this translation and inference are only licit in a closed setting. Strictly, 'behavior is under the control of reinforcement' has the very precise meaning that 'behavior occurs because of the contingencies of reinforcement that have affected earlier instances of the behavior.' But in open settings, behavior may occur to bring about a certain consequence without previous instances of the behavior ever having been reinforced, or even ever having occurred. Examples of such behavior include the invention of the Skinner box, of concurrent reinforcement schedules, and of 'mands' and 'tacts'. Further, again strictly, something is a reinforcer only if it increases the probability of behaviors on which it is contingent. But in open settings, there are many goals for which a person may act that do not have this property, goals that, once achieved, render irrelevant or unnecessary the further repetition of the behaviors that eventuated in the goals. Conducting a successful experiment does not induce one to repeat it. Rather, it obviates the need for repetition. So does the receipt of a salt shaker in response to the behavior 'please pass the salt.'

One cannot treat goals like these as reinforcers without radically changing the precise meaning of the term reinforcement.

The teleological framework has no trouble distinguishing goals from reinforcers. It offers explicit and detailed explanations of a broad class of phenomena—goal-directed behaviors—in open settings. These explanations employ parameters (goal, expectancy, plan, reason, intention, purpose, and so on) that have no place within the framework of behavior theory. These explanations have broad empirical support; we use them effectively to predict the behavior of others. Principles of behavior theory, or of conditioning theories generally, currently offer no explanation of this class of phenomena. And this is especially important since these phenomena are not peripheral to human life. Instead, they are characteristic of it. The teleological framework treats current principles of behavior theory as special cases, that obtain only when the conditions that define closed settings obtain. In these closed settings, behavior is still purposive. That it exhibits the law-like regularities characteristic of conditioned behavior is a consequence of the limited options and means to bring them about that characterize closed settings. Goals become reinforcers only in closed settings, and principles of behavior theory are clearly exemplified only when the key conditions that prevail in open settings are suppressed. Stated more generally, the teleological framework implies that we will find law-like regularities relating behavior to environmental factors, past and present, only when environmental conditions are held sufficiently constant that intelligent variation of goals and of beliefs concerning how they may be reached is not likely to occur.

It should be noted that the teleological framework views the role of the environment in influencing behavior as no less significant than does the behavior theory framework. The environment is both a constraint on behavior and an object of behavior. It limits what it is possible to do, and what is done is always a modification of the environment. Modification of the environment is, indeed, the explicit object of intentions. It is just that the relation between environment and action is not one that can be captured by a behavioral law.

With the teleological explanatory framework in mind, we can illuminate some of the 'side-effects' mentioned above. It seems to be (or it can be) a side-effect of the reinforcement-induced repetition of what works, that the flexibility characteristic of purposive behavior in open settings in the setting of goals and the finding of means to achieve them is impaired. Such flexibility is not required of the factory worker, so his behavior can be captured by the framework of behavior theory. It is required of the factory manager, however, just as it is required of the scientist. The transformation of open into closed settings, while creating the context for the apparent confirmation of behavior theory principles, can also turn goals into reinforcers, scientists into factory workers.

What, then, do experiments and applications of operant conditioning with humans tell us about conditioning and about humans? About conditioning, we believe they tell us that under a certain set of highly restricted conditions, human behavior obeys the principles of behavior theory; behavior is controlled by contingencies of reinforcement. Furthermore, these conditions are not difficult to establish. They are not at present especially general in the everyday environment, but they could become more general with the widespread application of behavior theory in existing social institutions. About human beings, we believe these studies tell us that people are the sort of creatures whose purposive, flexible, goal-directed activities can degenerate into law-governed, operant behavior in environments that have the characteristics of closed settings. Such law-governed behavior is not yet characteristic of people because their environments are not yet characteristically closed. But this too could change. Should it change? It is hard to imagine many chapters like this one, in collections like this one, emerging from environments whose settings are predominantly closed.

References

Cartwright N. (1983). *How the Laws of Physics Lie*, Oxford: Clarendon Press.

Davidson, D. (1980). *Essays on Actions and Events*, Oxford: Clarendon Press.

Kamin, L. (1968). Predictability, surprise, attention and conditioning. In B. A. Campbell and R. M. Church (eds), *Punishment and Aversive Behavior*, New York: Appleton-Century-Crofts.

Lacey, H. (1985). Pain behavior: How to define the operant, *The Behavioral and Brain Sciences*, **8**, 64–65.

Lacey, H., and Schwartz, B. (1987). The explanatory power of radical behaviorism. In S. Modgil and C. Modgil (eds), *B. F. Skinner: Consensus and Controversy*. London: Falmer Press.

Lakatos, I. (1978). *The Methodology of Scientific Research Programmes*, Cambridge: Cambridge University Press.

Lepper, M. R., and Greene, D. (eds) (1978). *The Hidden Costs of Reward*, Hillsdale, NJ: Erlbaum.

Mackintosh, N. J. (1975). A theory of attention, *Psychological Review*, **82**, 276–298.

Prelec, D. (1982). Matching, maximizing, and the hyperbolic reinforcement feedback function, *Psychological Review*, **89**, 189–230.

Rachlin, H. (1980). Economics and behavioral psychology. In J. E. R. Staddon (ed.), *Limits to Action*, New York: Academic Press.

Schwartz, B. (1982). Reinforcement induced behavioral stereotypy: How not to teach people to discover rules, *Journal of Experimental Psychology: General*, **111**, 23–59.

Schwartz, B., and Lacey, H. (1982). *Behaviorism, Science, and Human Nature*, New York: W. W. Norton.

Schwartz, B., Schuldenfrei, R., and Lacey, H. (1978). Operant psychology as factory psychology, *Behaviorism*, **6**, 229–254.

Skinner, B. F. (1971). *Beyond Freedom and Dignity*, New York: Knopf.

Skinner, B. F. (1974). *About Behaviorism*, New York: Knopf.

Taylor, C. (1964). *The Explanation of Behaviour*, London: Routledge and Kegan Paul.

Taylor, F. W. (1911/1967). *Principles of Scientific Management*, New York: W. W. Norton.

Human Operant Conditioning and Behavior Modification
Edited by G. Davey and C. Cullen
Published by John Wiley & Sons Ltd

Chapter 4

Applied Behavior Analysis: New Directions from the Laboratory*

W. FRANK EPLING and W. DAVID PIERCE
University of Alberta

Applied behavior analysis as a scientific enterprise began with the extension of laboratory-based principles to the understanding and control of socially significant human behavior (Baer, Wolf, and Risley, 1968). Such an extension was predicted by Skinner (1953) and evidenced by the subsequent application of basic principles to a variety of human problems (e.g. Risley, 1968; Hart *et al.*, 1968; Keller, 1968; Barrish, Saunders, and Wolf, 1969; Lovaas and Simmons, 1969). This extension also included theoretically important advances in the analysis of contingencies of reinforcement operating at the human level (e.g. Baer, Peterson, and Sherman, 1967; Gerwritz, 1969). Historically, the link between applied behavior analysis and operant principles has been a successful strategy. Thus, it is important to detail some of the recent developments in basic research which may suggest new applications and tactics for behavior change.

A current issue of concern for behavior analysts is the apparent separation of applied and basic research. Several papers have documented this separation and have suggested the continuing relevance of laboratory research for applied behavior analysis (Dietz, 1978; Hayes, Rincover and Solnick, 1980; Pierce and Epling, 1980; Michael, 1981; Poling *et al.*, 1982). Other investigators have also recognized this divergence but have argued that it is inevitable and may have positive implications (Baer, 1982). In this debate, a major problem may be that basic researchers have not communicated how continued attention to

---

* This chapter first appeared in *The Behavior Analyst*, 1983, **6**, 27–37. Copyright 1983 by the Society for the Advancement of Behavior Analysis (SABA). Reprinted by permission.

laboratory data and principles could or would be important for applied behavior analysis.

An acquaintance with basic research could have two major effects. First, applied behavior analysts, who are in the best position to identify socially relevant problems, would be able to work out new applications. Second, basic research may suggest new ways of analyzing socially important behavior. A number of currently available behavior principles have implications for applied behavior analysis. In addition, there are analyses and paradigms in existence which challenge some currently held tenets. The remainder of this chapter will be devoted to illustrating some of these principles, analyses, and paradigms.

Schedule-induced behavior

Researchers have described classes of behavior which occur as side-effects of schedules of reinforcement (e.g. Staddon and Simmelhag, 1971; Falk, 1966). This behavior is not specified by the contingencies and is therefore called schedule-induced (Staddon, 1977; Falk, 1971). Schedules of reinforcement may induce a variety of behavior patterns, including exaggerated water drinking (Falk, 1966), attack (Flory, 1969), wheel running (Levitsky and Collier, 1968), licking at an air stream (Mendelson and Chillag, 1970), and smoking in humans (Wallace and Singer, 1976). These behavior patterns are typically excessive and resistant to change by manipulation of operant contingencies. Thus, when an analysis of response–consequence relationships does not indicate clear controlling variables, behavior could be schedule-induced. Foster (1978) has pointed to the absence of clinical investigations of induced or adjunctive behavior with humans and has suggested that:

> Potential candidates for human adjunctive behaviors range from (a) 'normal' time-filling or 'fidgety' patterns such as playing, idle conversing, finger tapping and beard stroking, through (b) 'neurotic' obsessive–compulsive or 'nervous-habit' patterns such as nail biting, snacking, and hand washing, to (c) 'psychotic' patters such as self-stimulating rituals, manic episodes, and rage outbursts. Potential candidates for human 'inducing' schedules include home, office, classroom and ward routines, whose time, effort, and consequence properties have long been suspected of side-effects by lay and professional people. (p. 545)

Side-effects of schedules of reinforcement may have implications for other problem behaviors. There is suggestive evidence from animal studies that some problems of drug addiction, including alcohol (Freed and Lester, 1970; Samson and Falk, 1975; Gilbert, 1974), narcotics (Leander, McMillan and Harris, 1975), barbiturates (Kodluboy and Thompson, 1971; Meisch, 1969), and nicotine (Lang *et al.*, 1977) may be induced by the operating contingencies of reinforcement. The applied analyst who deals with drug dependency might gain new insight by a consideration of this literature. Of equal importance, basic researchers in these areas should attempt to communicate the applied relevance of their findings.

In addition to drug dependencies and psychiatric disturbances, there may be other socially important human activities which arises as a by-product of schedules of reinforcement. In particular, there is growing evidence that some classes of aggressive behavior are induced. At the animal level, several studies have demonstrated that birds responding on food reinforcement schedules will attack another bird or a visual representation of another pigeon (Azrin, Hutchingson, and Hake, 1966; Cohen and Looney, 1973; Flory and Ellis, 1973; Flory and Everist, 1977). A similar effect is produced with rats maintained by schedules of food or water reinforcement (Gentry and Schaeffer, 1969; Thompson and Bloom, 1966). Also, primates have shown induced biting of a rubber hose with positive or negative reinforcement schedules in effect (Hutchinon, Azrin, and Hunt, 1968; De Weese, 1977). Importantly, these findings have been extended to humans. Fredericksen and Peterson (1974) report that 16 five-year-old nursery school children increased their hitting of a Bobo doll when extinction for monetary reinforcers was scheduled. In a later review of induced aggression in humans and animals, Fredericksen and Peterson (1977) examined the variables controlling schedule-induced attack across species; in most instances animal and human data were remarkably similar.

Some problems of classroom management may have to do with the generation of induced aggression by contingencies operating in the school. Temporal properties of work assignments, classroom routines, the allocation of recess periods, and schedules of teacher attention are likely facilitators of such side-effects. For example, increased physical and verbal aggression would be expected when reinforcement is temporarily delayed. This might occur in line-ups when coming into the school, assembly, washroom, or other activities. Educators who recognize how these behaviors are produced may be able to design school programs which reduce the likelihood of aggressive behavior.

Another behavior of clinical interest that may be induced by reinforcement schedules is excessive locomotor activity. Epling, Pierce, and Stefan (1981, in press) have argued for an activity model of anorexia nervosa. These researchers have suggested that the hyperactivity observed in some anorectic patients (Kron et al., 1978; Crisp et al. 1980) is central to an understanding of what they call 'activity-based anorexia'. They have further argued that this hyperactivity is induced by food schedules. In support of this model, Epling et al. have demonstrated that rats and mice will excessively increase wheel-running behavior (up to 20000 revolutions per day), decrease food ingestions, and die of starvation when they are placed on a restricted meal schedule and allowed access to an activity wheel on a non-contingent basis. Control animals placed on the same food schedule but not provided with the opportunity to run increase food intake and survive. In this model of activity anorexia, the authors suggest that excessive wheel running is induced by properties of the meal schedule (see also, Wallace, Samson, and Singer, 1978). Further, this high rate activity functions to suppress and eventually reduce food intake. This is a paradoxical effect, since it would be expected that organisms who are expending large amounts of energy and declining in body weight would increase (rather than decrease) food ingestion.

The determinants of induced behavior were described by Falk (1977). Two critical factors are the length of the inter-reinforcement interval and the deprivation status of the organism with respect to the scheduled reinforcer. Schedule-induced behavior is an increasing monotonic function of deprivation. However, the relationship of schedule-induced activity to the inter-reinforcement interval (IRI) is more complex. Research (Falk, 1966; Flory, 1971) indicates that as the length of the IRI increases from small values (approximately 2 seconds) to medium values (between 120 and 180 seconds), there is a direct increase in schedule-induced responses. As the length of the interval is increased beyond these medium values, induced behavior declines and reaches a low level at approximately 300 seconds.

Of course, the IRI values explored in this literature are of such short duration that the effects reported are not directly applicable to most human situations. One way the interval values may be extended is to consider that a small amount of food is delivered to an animal after a brief temporal interval. Schedule-induced behavior in humans might be generated over longer time intervals with relatively large reinforcers. In order to draw more convincing parallels from animals studies, it is necessary to generate research focused directly on human subjects in both laboratory and natural settings. An understanding of the parameters that control schedule-induced behavior in humans might lead to new types of treatment and improved long-term follow-up results.

The schedule-induced literature demonstrates that high-strength behavior can occur as a by-product of programmed contingencies. Thus, contingency control of behavior may not always be a productive way of viewing environmental control in applied settings. Another branch of research suggests that close temporal proximity between behavior and consequence is not a necessary requirement for the control of behavior. This literature on the correlation-based law of effect may explain some problems of treatment and suggest new intervention strategies.

The correlation-based law of effect

Many applied researchers pursue modification programs based on principles that stipulate a relationship between behavior and its immediate consequences (e.g. Skinner, 1953). There are good reasons for an analysis of response–

consequence relationships; contingencies of reinforcement have proven to be an effective behavior change strategy. However, there is increasing evidence that behavior is not always maintained in a direct linear manner. In environments where many sources of reinforcement are available, operants may be acquired and maintained on the basis of correlations between rate of response and rate of reinforcement (Herrnstein, 1961; Baum, 1973). Such correlations may occasionally be critical to an analysis and modification of behavior, especially when behavior is maintained in human environments which contain multiple sources of reinforcement.

The analysis of behavior can be problematic when only contingency–contiguity principles are assumed to operate. These analytical difficulties were addressed by Rachlin (1974) when he recounted the research by Herrnstein and Hineline (1966) on aversive control of bar pressing in the rat. In this research, there was no direct connection between responses and their consequences but only a correlation between bar pressing and rate of shock. Results indicated that rats acquired bar pressing when followed by a reduced frequency of shocks over time, although no particular bar press terminated the shocks. An observer faced with this behavior would have difficulty accounting for it on the basis of contingency–contiguity principles. At any point in time, the analyst could infer: (1) that there was no relationship between bar presses and shocks; (2) that shocks were causing bar presses; and (3) that bar presses were causing shocks. In fact, Rachlin (1974) states 'the cause of bar presses is the relationship between pressing and shocks as it is experienced by the rat'.

This implies that observers trained primarily to identify response–consequence relationships may occasionally arrive at incorrect conclusions about behavior and its controlling variables. Additionally, introducing manipulations of consequences may have correlational effects that are unexpected. To illustrate, 'pestering behavior' emitted by a child in a classroom could be maintained by a correlation between that behavior and teacher attention. This might occur if rate of attention increased with the child's rate of pestering. The increase of attention could occur as a result of reinforcing a different target behavior. An overall increase in reinforcement accidentally correlated with pestering would be expected to increase the frequency of the behavior. Thus, it is possible that behavior in applied settings can be controlled without direct response–consequence relationships.

The value of the correlation-based law of effect in applied settings is the emphasis it places on environment–behavior relations over extended periods of time. Professionals have suspected and occasionally made use of this relationship. The clinical interview where a history is taken may be seen as an attempt to take the correlation between behavior and consequence into account. Thus, the therapist may obtain a family history which correlates with problematic behavior. This is seen in cases of child abuse where a parent's behavior is related to punitive socialization practices (Conger, Burgess, and

Barrett, 1979). However, the therapist is often faced with the problem of identifying immediately present events that can be altered to change the behavior of the client. There are many instances in which particular environmental events that directly follow behavior cannot be isolated. In such instances, applied analysts with a contingency–contiguity viewpoint are often forced to seek explanation for behavior through hypothetical cognitive constructs.

When a client is behaving 'neurotically' but there are not conspicuous controlling variables, behavior is sometimes explained in terms of hopes, expectations, or feelings (Bandura, 1977). At this point, applied behavior analysts may abandon their concern with specification of environment–behavior relations. However, the correlation-based law of effect suggests that the environment interacts with behavior over long periods of time. Rachlin (1970) has made the point that we cannot understand why a man continues to shovel coal into a fire since the immediate effect is to dampen the flames. But with a long-range view we see that the reason the man shovels is the positive correlation between amount of heat and rate of shoveling. The behavior can now be understood, and it is clear that we must modify the correlation between amount of heat and rate of shoveling in order to modify the man's activity. The variables for behavior change remain in the environment from the correlation point of view.

As a specific instance of the applied importance of the correlation-based law of effect, Rachlin (1970) pointed to the learned helplessness phenomenon (Seligman, Maier, and Soloman, 1969). The research on helplessness concerns first exposing a person or an animal to an environment where there is a zero correlation between rate of response and rate of punishment. There are no behaviors which allow escape from the aversive stimuli. The environment is subsequently rearranged so that a positive correlation exists between behavior and reduction of aversive stimuli. But the previous exposure to a zero correlation interferes with the acquisition of escape responses. The animals of the Seligman group's research give up and accept their fate. Such effects in humans might be ascribed to 'endogenous depression', but an environmental analysis suggests that the observable zero correlation between responding and reduction of aversive stimuli is the cause of giving up. With attention focused on the environment, it is clear that one treatment strategy would involve training escape behavior in an environment which arranges for a positive correlation between escape responding and rate of (negative) reinforcement. This is, in fact, what animal analogues of learned helplessness have done.

The correlation-based law of effect proposes that only regular covariation, planned or adventitious, over time is necessary to produce behavior change. The researchers dealing with concurrent operants have recognized this principle and have shown how it governs behavioral choice.

Behavioral choice and the matching law

Human environments typically contain many possible sources of reinforcement. These reinforcers compete for behavior and provide for a number of response alternatives. Goldiamond (1975) has discussed the linear model based on a response followed by a consequence and an alternative view in which an individual behaves in accord with several reinforcement contingencies. The applied importance of alternatives and choice is stressed in Goldiamond's account of an interview with a 'mental' patient:

> A patient I interviewed at a state mental hospital clearly indicated the existence of such alternatives. To attain sustenance and shelter when he had outworn his stays at all homes of his friends and relatives, he could either engage in criminal behavior and be sent to prison, or engage in crazy behavior and be sent to the mental hospital, or engage in neither behavior and die of exposure. Viewed unilinearly, engaging in behaviors whose consequence is confinement in a ward in a state hospital does not make 'sense', hence is 'crazy'... (However), his 'crazy' behavior did not represent 'psychosis', nor would criminal behavior have represented 'criminality'. Both were (alternative behaviors) maintained by the same consequences, namely, sustenance and shelter. (pp. 60–61)

Operant researchers have often accounted for choice in terms of the matching law (Baum, 1974). This principle states that relative behavior (or time) matches relative rate of reinforcement delivered on two or more concurrent alternatives. The person distributes behavior in accord with the relative, rather than absolute, payoffs received over a period of time. A formal statement of this relationship (Herrnstein, 1961) is presented in equation 4.1.

$$B_1/(B_1 + B_2) = R_1/(R_1 + R_2) \qquad [4.1]$$

The values B_1 represent the amount of behavior (or time) given to the respective alternatives and the R_1 values represent the amount of reinforcement obtained from these alternatives. This proportional equation makes it clear that a given target behavior must always by analyzed with respect to all simultaneously available sources of reinforcement.

At the present time there are a number of studies which have investigated the matching law with humans in laboratory settings (see Pierce and Epling, 1983). Humans are found to match visual responding to concurrently scheduled targets (Baum, 1975; Schroeder and Holland, 1969). Also, Bradshaw and his associates (e.g. Bradshaw, Szabadi, and Bevan, 1976, 1979) report that relative rate of key pressing in humans matches relative rate of monetary reinforcement. Finally, Conger and Killeen (1974) found that human conversation was distributed in accord with the relative rate of agreement provided by concurrently available listeners.

At the applied level, the proportion equation suggests that in order to modify the rate of occurrence of behavior, the analyst may alter the rate of reinforcement on a target alternative, or alter the rate of reinforcement from other sources. Thus, in order to change the rate of child compliance (see Patterson, 1976) toward the mother, the applied analyst must consider the father or others as additional sources of reinforcement. Rate of compliance may be low toward one parent because this behavior is concurrently reinforced by the other. To illustrate, if maternal reinforcement is at a relatively lower rate than father's reinforcement schedule, modification of the rate of maternal attention for compliance will increase the rate of the behavior only if father's rate of reinforcement remains at former levels. Often, however, modifications in maternal attention to the child produce a shift in reinforcement rate for the father. An increase in father's rate of attention would further lower the rate of child compliance to mother, while a decrease would enhance the modification procedure. With consideration and measurement of such changes in alternative sources of reinforcement, predictions of treatment outcomes may be enhanced.

While a proportion equation has predictive and control power when alternatives differ only in rate of reinforcement, other variables such as effort, quality of reinforcement, punishment and stimulus control, may affect the distribution of behavior in applied settings. These conditions can, however, be represented in a more general form of the Matching Equation when only two alternatives are considered (Baum, 1974). Equation 4.2 presents the Matching Law in terms of the ratio of behavior relative to the ratio of reinforcement.

$$B_1/B_2 = K(R_1/R_2)^a \qquad\qquad [4.2]$$

As in equation 4.1, B_1 values represent the amount of behavior distributed to respective alternative and R_1 values represent the amount of reinforcement from these alternatives. When the coefficient k and the exponent a are equal to 1, equation 4.2 is an alternative form of equation 4.1. However, when a is not equal to 1 this is called under- (or over-) matching and a unit increase in relative reinforcement systematically produces less than (or greater than) a unit increase in relative behavior. For example, if a discrimination is poorly established between concurrently available schedules of reinforcement, this will typically be reflected by the exponent assuming a value less than 1 (i.e. undermatching).

When the coefficient k departs from 1 this is called bias (Baum, 1974) and a systematic preference for one alternative is indicated. Bradshaw, Ruddle, and Szabadi (1981) have shown with humans that if alternatives differ with respect to effort there is a preference, over and above the relative reinforcement, for the lower effort alternative. Thus, changing the rate of reinforcement on a target alternative without considering these conditions may produce behavior change that is unexpected in direction or frequency. At the present time, the variables which control these values (i.e. a and k) are being researched at the basic level.[1] This research may suggest strategies of behavior management that will be of practical importance to the applied analyst.

Animal research on concurrent schedules often employs a two-key procedure (Ferster and Skinner, 1957). The animal changes back and forth between two separate keys with different reinforcement schedules on each key. This experimental paradigm has external validity and practical importance to the extent that human behavior in everyday settings is described as responding or time spent on simultaneously arranged reinforcement schedules. Recently, for instance, Sunahara and Pierce (1982) have argued for the external validity of this model in representing human social interaction. Thus, an individual is viewed as distributing time and behavior among social others who reinforce responding on concurrently available schedules. This experimental model can be presented as a social interaction involving a central individual, A, who has two (or more) alternatives, X and Y, as partners. In this setting, it is assumed that A exchanges reinforcers with X and Y over time. This kind of situation is researched more effectively if the number of alternatives is limited to two, but evidence suggest that the analysis can be extended to situations which provide multiple alternatives (Herrnstein, 1974; Miller and Loveland, 1974; Pliskoff and Brown, 1976). Also, while X and Y do not interact in this model, this restriction can be relaxed in applied research. The effects of X and Y's interaction would be to alter the rate of reinforcement to A, therefore altering the distribution of A's behavior to these social alternatives.

Another way of programming concurrent schedules has been described by Findley (1958). According to this procedure, reinforcement is delivered for responding on a single key with alternative schedules signaled by different discriminative stimuli. A changeover key is also provided, and a response on this key changes the schedule of reinforcement and the associated discriminative stimulus on the response key. Basic researchers have not made a distinction between the two procedures. However, Sunahara (1980) has suggested that a single-key model might represent another socially important phenomenon. He notes that the individual can be viewed as 'playing different roles' depending on the stimulus conditions. The person is an employee, and work behavior is reinforced by the employer on a given schedule; the same individual is also a spouse, with marital behavior reinforced by the partner on a different schedule. The person changes between these respective schedules, sometimes behaving as an employee and sometimes as a spouse. The distribution of behavior (or time) between work and the marital relation can become quite disproportional on the basis of the respective reinforcement schedules. Concurrent schedules can give rise to the common complaints that 'he or she is never home' or 'he or she never pays attention to me'. The behavior which these reports describe is often a prime target for change by the applied analyst.

The Matching Law suggests multiple sources of environmental control are operating in most human settings. Even when the applied analyst focuses on a single target behavior, the control exerted by alternative sources of reinforcement can be important. Herrnstein's (1970) statement of the quantitative Law of Effect demonstrated that principles governing the single operant could be derived from the Matching Law. In recent papers, McDowell (1981, 1982) has shown that clinically relevant behavior conforms to Herrnstein's equation for single operants. He reports that the self-injurious scratching of an eleven-year-old boy was described by considering rate of scratches to be a function of rate of verbal reprimands (McDowell, 1981). When McDowell fitted the boy's data to Herrnstein's hyperbolic equation, he explained 99.67 per cent of the variance in this self-mutilating behavior. Another applied example is provided by the research of Szabadi, Bradshaw, and Ruddle (1981). In this study, parameters of the single operant equation varied systematically and in the expected direction for two manic-depressive patients depending on mood state. The implications were that monetary reinforcers, which maintained button pressing on several variable interval schedules, were less valued in depressive periods and of greater value during manic episodes. Thus, the degree of control by (at least some) reinforcers may vary with affective disturbance. Also, this research suggests that parameters of Herrnstein's equation may be useful in diagnosis of some behavior disorders. These applied implications were addressed by McDowell (1982) and he concluded that:

> Herrnstein's equation is considerably more descriptive of natural human environments than Skinner's earlier view of reinforcement. It is not always easy to isolate Skinnerian response–reinforcement units in the natural environment. Herrnstein's equation makes efforts to do so unnecessary and, moreover, obsolete. The equation can help clinicians conceptualize cases more effectively and design treatment regimens more efficiently. It also suggests new intervention strategies that may be especially useful in difficult cases. (p. 778)

The literature dealing with behavioral choice and the quantitative law of effect has been extensive enough to be considered a major paradigm within the experimental analysis of behavior. There are other paradigms suggested by basic research that require a reconsideration of the assumptions held by behavior analysts. These models are generally not as well developed as those presented previously. However, they may ultimately provide new information important to the understanding and control of behavior in applied settings.

Recent paradigms

A recent paradigm that relates behavior to environmental determinants has been suggested by Collier, Hirsch, and Kanarek (1977). When an organism receives an entire meal contingent on responses, behavior differs from that maintained by typical operant strategies. The paradigm employs long food intervals and analyzes behavior between entire meals while the more usual operant analysis employs short food intervals and analyzes behavior within a single meal. Collier *et al.* have provided data which demonstrate that even a non-deprived rat will emit up to 5000 bar presses with the consequence being a single meal. Additionally, these researchers have shown that behavior can change in unexpected ways when it is maintained in accord with this paradigm. For example, increasing the size of a reinforcer for a food-deprived animal typically results in an increase in rate of response. Thus, the clinician may increase the size of reinforcement in order to increase the rate of pro-social behavior. However, the between-meal paradigm shows that behavior slows in rate when size of meal is increased. It follows then, that depending on the maintenance conditions, behavior may or may not change in predicted directions as a function of increasing the size of the reinforcer.

While this paradigm has been explored only with nonhuman subjects and has focused on feeding behavior, it may have further implications for applied behavior analysts. For example, the intiation and maintenance of behavior chains that take a person to a concert, a visit at a friend's house, or to a university class, etc., might be best understood by a consideration of the between-meal paradigm. Once an individual has arrived at the concert, visit or class, behavior would likely operate according to the more traditional operant paradigm. Of course the Collier *et al.* model may not explain human behavior, particularly when it is maintained by conditioned reinforcers. What is needed is an analysis of human behavior in accord with this approach. The analysis might also increase the predictive utility and precision of some behavioral treatment programs.

There are other major conceptual shifts in the literature. Morse and Kelleher (1977) have questioned the continued use of the terms reinforcer and punisher:

> The modification of behavior by a reinforcer or by a punisher depends not only upon the occurrence of a certain kind of consequent environmental event but also upon the qualitative and quantitative properties of the ongoing behavior preceding the event and upon the schedule under which the event is presented. (p. 176)

Thus, the transitional properties of reinforcers and punishers are questioned. In addition, Morse and Kelleher present data which demonstrate consequent events change in function as a result of scheduling. Applied behavior analysts have recognized for some time that a change in environment (discriminative stimulus properties) may change the function of a reinforcer or punisher. For example, the child whose behavior is reinforced by teacher attention in the classroom may show the effects of punishment with the same attention on the playground. However, Morse and Kelleher's data suggest that the reinforcing effects of teacher attention could change to punishing in the same environment as a result of an increase or decrease in frequency of delivery. This has been recognized by lay persons and in a non-systematic way by professionals. The person who occasionally tells another 'well done' probably reinforces that other person. The effect on behavior is, however, very different when 'well done', 'great', 'good job', etc. are delivered on a continuous reinforcement schedule.

Summary

This chapter has presented examples of basic research that may have implications for applied behavior analysis. The research presented is not exhaustive, nor are the implications. The intention of this manuscript was to suggest some of the behavior principles which are currently available to applied behavior analysts.

Much of the basic work points to multiple sources of behavior control. A possible reaction to this complexity would be to give up any attempt to analyze or modify human behavior. This reaction is not necessary. Applied behavior analysis has produced a powerful technology of behavior that, as it stands, seems superior to any other approach. However, case failures, problems of follow-up, and excessive variance in data may be functions of principles presented here or other processes which are undiscovered or unknown. In short, current laboratory evidence continues to suggest new directions for applied behavior analysis.

References

Azrin, N. H., Hutchinson, R. R., and Hake, D. F. (1966). Extinction-induced aggression. *Journal of the Experimental Analysis of Behavior*, **9**, 191–204.

Baer, D. M. (1981). A flight of behavior analysis, *The Behavior Analyst*, **4**, 85–91.

Baer, D. M., Peterson, R., and Sherman, J. (1967). The development of imitation by reinforcing behavioral similarity to a model, *Journal of the Experimental Analysis of Behavior*, **10**, 405–416.

Baer, D. M., Wolf, M. M., and Risley, T. R. (1968). Some current dimensions of applied behavior analysis, *Journal of Applied Behavior Analysis*, **1**, 91–97.

Bandura, A. (1977). *Social Learning Theory*, New Jersey: Prentice-Hall.

Barrish, H. H., Saunders, M., and Wolf, M. M. (1969). Good behavior game: Effects of individual contingencies for group consequences on disruptive behavior in a classroom, *Journal of Applied Behavior Analysis*, **2**, 119–124.

Baum, W. M. (1973). The correlation-based law of effect, *Journal of the Experimental Analysis of Behavior*, **20**, 137–153.

Baum, W. M. (1974). On two types of deviation from the matching law: Bias and undermatching, *Journal of the Experimental Analysis of Behavior*, **22**, 321–342.

Baum, W. M. (1975). Time allocation in human vigilance, *Journal of the Experimental Analysis of Behavior*, **23**, 45–53.

Bradshaw, C. M., Ruddle, H. V., and Szabadi, E. (1981). Studies of concurrent performances in humans. In C.M. Bradshaw, E. Szabadi, and C.F. Lowe (eds), *Quantification of Steady-State Operant Behavior*, Amsterdam: Elsevier/North-Holland Biomedical Press.

Bradshaw, C.M., Szabadi, E., and Bevan, P. (1976). Behavior of humans on variable-interval schedules of reinforcement, *Journal of the Experimental Analysis of Behavior*, **26**, 135–141.

Bradshaw, C.M., Szabadi, E., and Bevan, P. (1979). The effect of punishment on free-operant choice behavior in humans, *Journal of the Experimental Analysis of Behavior*, **32**, 65–74.

Cohen, P.S., and Looney, T.A. (1973). Schedule-induced mirror responding in the pigeon, *Journal of the Experimental Analysis of Behavior*, **19**, 395–408.

Collier, G., Hirsch, E., and Kanarek, R. (1977). The operant revisited. In Honig, K. Werner, and J.E.R. Staddon (eds), *Handbook of Operant Behavior*, Englewood Cliffs, NJ: Prentice-Hall.

Conger, R.D., Burgess, R.L., and Barrett, C. (1979). Child abuse related to life change and perceptions of illness: Some preliminary findings, *Family Coordinator*, Jan., 73–78.

Conger, R., and Killeen, P. (1974). Use of concurrent operants in small group research, *Pacific Sociological Review*, **17**, 399–416.

Crisp, A.H., Hsu, L.K.G., Harding, B., and Hartshorn, J. (1980). Clinical features of anorexia nervosa: A study of a consecutive series of 102 female patients, *Journal of Psychosomatic Research*, **24**, 179–191.

de Villiers, P.A. (1977). Choice and concurrent schedules and a quantitative formulation of the Law of Effect. In W.K. Honig and J.E.R. Staddon (eds), *Handbook of Operant Behavior*, New York: Prentice-Hall.

De Weese, J. (1977). Schedule-induced biting under fixed-interval schedules of food or electric shock presentation, *Journal of the Experimental Analysis of Behavior*, **27**, 419–431.

Dietz, S.M. (1978). Current status of applied behavior analysis: Sciences versus technology, *American Psychologist*, **33**, 805–814.

Epling, W.F., Pierce, W.D. and Stefan, L. (1981). Schedule-induced self-starvation. In C.M. Bradshaw, E. Szabadi, and C.F. Lowe (eds), *Quantification of Steady-State Operant Behavior*, Amsterdam: Elsevier/North-Holland Biomedical Press.

Epling, W.F., Pierce, W.D., and Stefan, L. (in press). A theory of activity-based anorexia, *International Journal of Eating Disorders*.

Falk, J.L. (1966). Schedule-induced polydipsia as a function of fixed interval length, *Journal of the Experimental Analysis of Behavior*, **9**, 37–39.

Falk, J.L. (1971). The nature and determinants of adjunctive behavior, *Physiology and Behavior*, **6**, 577–588.

Falk, J.L. (1977). The origin and functions of adjunctive behavior, *Animal Learning and Behavior*, **5**, 325–335.

Ferster, C.B., and Skinner, B.F. (1957). *Schedules of Reinforcement*, Englewood Cliffs, NJ: Prentice-Hall.

Findley, J.D. (1958). Preference and switching under concurrent scheduling, *Journal of the Experimental Analysis of Behavior*, **1**, 123–144.

Flory, R.K. (1969). Attack behavior as a function of minimum interfood interval, *Journal of the Experimental Analysis of Behavior*, **11**, 545–546.

Flory, R.K. (1971). The control of schedule-induced polydipsia: Frequency and magnitude of reinforcement, *Learning and Motivation*, **12**, 825–828.

Flory, R.K., and Ellis, B.B. (1973). Schedule-induced aggression against a slide-image target, *Bulletin of the Psychonomic Society*, **2**, 287–290.

Flory, R. K., and Everist, H. D. (1977). The effect of a response requirement on schedule-induced aggression, *Bulletin of the Psychonomic Society*, **9**, 383–386.

Foster, W. S. (1978). Adjunctive behavior: An under-reported phenomenon in applied behavior analysis, *Journal of Applied Behavior Analysis*, **11**, 545–546.

Frederiksen, L. W., and Petersen, G. L. (1974). Schedule-induced aggression in nursery school children, *Psychological Record*, **24**, 343–351.

Frederiksen, L. W., and Peterson, G. L. (1977). Schedule-induced aggression in humans and animals: A comparative parametric review, *Aggressive Behavior*, **3**, 57–75.

Freed, E., and Lester, D. (1970). Schedule-induced consumption of ethanol: Calories or chemotherapy? *Physiology and Behavior*, **5**, 555–560.

Gentry, W. D., and Schaeffer, R. W. (1969). The effect of FR response requirement on aggressive behavior in rats, *Psychonomic Science*, **14**, 236–238.

Gerwitz, J. L. (1969). Mechanisms of social learning: Some roles of stimulation and behavior in early human development. In D. A. Goslin (ed.), *Handbook of Socialization Theory and Research*, Chicago: Rand McNally, pp. 57–212.

Gilbert, R. M. (1974). Schedule-induced ethanol polydipsia in rats with restricted fluid availability, *Psychopharmacologia*, **38**, 151–157.

Goldiamond, I. (1975). Alternative sets as a framework for behavioral formulations and research, *Behaviorism*, **3**, 49–86.

Hart, B. M., Reynolds, N. J., Baer, D. M., Brawley, E. R., and Harris, F. R. (1968). Effect of contingent and non-contingent social reinforcement on the cooperative play of a preschool child, *Journal of Applied Behavior Analysis*, **1**, 73–76.

Hayes, S. C., Rincover, A., and Solnick, J. V. (1980). The technical drift of applied behavior analysis, *Journal of Applied Behavior Analysis*, **13**, 275–285.

Herrnstein, R. J. (1961). Relative and absolute strength of response as a function of frequency of reinforcement, *Journal of the Experimental Analysis of Behavior*, **4**, 267–272.

Herrnstein, R. J. (1970). On the law of effect, *Journal of the Experimental Analysis of Behavior*, **13**, 243–266.

Herrnstein, R. J. (1974). Formal properties of the matching law, *Journal of the Experimental Analysis of Behavior*, **21**, 159–164.

Herrnstein, R. J., and Hineline, P. N. (1966). Negative reinforcement as shock-frequency reduction, *Journal of the Experimental Analysis of Behavior*, **9**, 421–430.

Hutchinson, R. R., Azrin, N. H., and Hunt, G. M. (1968). Attack produced by intermittent reinforcement of a concurrent operant response, *Journal of the Experimental Analysis of Behavior*, **11**, 489–495.

Keller, F. S. (1968). Good-bye teacher ... *Journal of Applied Behavior Analysis*, **1**, 79–89.

Kodluboy, D. W., and Thompson, T. (1971). Adjunctive self-administration of barbiturate solutions, *Proceedings of the Annual Convention of the American Psychological Association*, **6**, 749–750.

Kron, L., Katz, J. L., Gorzynski, G., and Weiner, H. (1978). Hyperactivity in anorexia nervosa: A fundamental clinical feature, *Comprehensive Psychiatry*, **19**, 433–440.

Lang, W. J., Latiff, A. A., McQueen, A., and Singer G. (1977). Self-administration of nicotine with and without a food delivery schedule, *Pharmacology, Biochemistry and Behavior*, **7**, 65–70.

Leander, J., McMillan, D. E., and Harris, L. S. (1975). Schedule-induced oral narcotic self-administration: Acute and chronic effects, *Journal of Pharmacology and Experimental Therapeutics*, **195**, 279–287.

Levitsky, D., and Collier, G. (1968). Schedule-induced wheel running. *Physiology and Behavior*, **3**, 571–573.

Lovaas, I. W., and Simmons, J. Q. (1969). Manipulation of self-destruction in three retarded children, *Journal of Applied Behavior Analysis*, **2**, 143–157.

McDowell, J. J. (1981). On the validity and utility of Herrnstein's hyperbola in applied behavior analysis. In C. M. Bradshaw, E. Szabadi, and C. F. Lowe (eds), *Quantification of Steady-State Operant Behavior*, Amsterdam: Elsevier/North-Holland Biomedical Press.

McDowell, J. J. (1982). The importance of Herrnstein's mathematical statement of the law of effect for behavior therapy. *American Psychologist*, **37**, 771–779.

Meich, R. A. (1969). Self-administration of pentobarbital by means of schedule-induced polydipsia. *Psychonomic Science*, **16**, 16–17.

Mendelson, J., and Chillag, D. (1970). Schedule-induced air licking in rats, *Physiology and Behavior*, **5**, 535–537.

Michael, J. L. (1980). Flight from behavior analysis, *The Behavior Analyst*, **3**, 1–21.

Miller, H. L. and Loveland, D. H. (1974). Matching when the number of response alternatives is large, *Animal Learning and Behavior*, **2**, 106–110.

Morse, W. H., and Kelleher, R. T. (1977). Determinants of reinforcement and punishment. In W. K. Honig and J. E. R. Staddon (eds), *Handbook of Operant Behavior*, Englewood Cliffs, NJ: Prentice-Hall.

Patterson, G. R. (1976). The aggressive child: victim and architect of a coercive system. In E. J. Mash and L. A. Hammerlynk (eds), *Behavior Modification and Families*, New York: Brunner/Mazel.

Pierce, W. D., and Epling, W. F. (1980). What happened to analysis in applied behavior analysis? *Behavior Analyst*, **3**, 1–9.

Pierce, W. D., and Epling, W. F. (1983). Choice, matching and human behavior: A review of the literature, *The Behavior Analyst*, **6**.

Pierce, W. D., and Epling, W. F., and Greer, S. M. (1981). Human communication and the Matching Law. In C. M. Bradshaw, E. Szabadi, and C. F. Lowe (eds), *Quantification of Steady-State Operant Behavior*. Amsterdam: Elsevier/North-Holland Biomedical Press.

Pliskoff, S. S., and Brown, T. G. (1971). Matching with a trio of concurrent variable-interval schedules of reinforcement, *Journal of the Experimental Analysis of Behavior*, **25**, 69–73.

Poling, A., Picker, M., Grossett, D., Hall-Johnson, E., and Holbrook, M. (1981). The schism between experimental and applied behavior analysis: Is it real and who cares? *The Behavior Analyst*, **4**, 93–102.

Rachlin, H. (1970). *Introduction to Modern Behaviorism*, San Francisco: W. H. Freeman.

Rachlin, H. (1974). Self control, *Behaviorism*, **2**, 94–107.

Risley, T. R. (1968). The effects and side-effects of punishing the autistic behaviors of a deviant child, *Journal of Applied Behavior Analysis*, **1**, 21–34.

Samson, H. H., and Falk, J. L. (1975). Pattern of daily blood ethanol elevation and the development of physical dependence, *Pharmacology, Biochemistry and Behavior*, **3**, 1119–1123.

Schroeder, S. R., and Holland, J. G. (1969). Operant control of eye movements, *Journal of Applied Behavior Analysis*, **1**, 161–168.

Seligman, M. E. P., Maier, S. F., and Solomon, R. L. (1969). Pavlovian fear conditioning and learned helplessness. In R. Church and B. Campbell (eds), *Aversive Conditioning and Learning*, New York: Appleton-Century-Crofts.

Skinner, B. F. (1953). *Science and Human Behavior*, New York: Macmillan.

Staddon, J. E. R. (1977). Schedule-induced behavior. In W. K. Honig and J. E. R. Staddon (eds), *Handbook of Operant Behavior*, Englewood Cliffs, NJ: Prentice-Hall.

Staddon, J.E.R., and Simmelhag, V.L. (1971). The 'superstition' experiment: A reexamination of its implications for the principles of adaptive behavior, *Psychological Review*, **78**, 3–43.

Sunahara, D.F. (1980). *Social Exchange Theory and the Matching Law*, Ph.D. dissertation, Department of Sociology, The University of Alberta.

Sunahara, D.F. and Pierce, W.D. (1982). The matching law and bias in a social exchange involving choice between alternatives, *Canadian Journal of Sociology*, **7**, 145–165.

Szabadi, E., Bradshaw, C.M., and Ruddle, H.V. (1981). Reinforcement processes in affective illness: Towards a quantitative analysis. In C. M. Bradshaw, E. Szabadi, and C.F. Lowe (eds), *Quantification of Steady-State Operant Behavior*, Amsterdam: Elsevier/North-Holland Biomedical Press.

Thompson, T., and Bloom, W. (1966). Aggressive behavior and extinction-induced response rate increase, *Psychonomic Science*, **5**, 335–336.

Wallace, M., Sanson, A., and Singer, G. (1976). Adjunctive behavior and smoking induced by a maze solving schedule in humans. *Physiology and Behavior*, **17**, 849–852.

Human Operant Conditioning and Behavior Modification
Edited by G. Davey and C. Cullen
© 1988 John Wiley & Sons Ltd

Chapter 5

The Relevance of Animal-Based Principles in the Laboratory Study of Human Operant Conditioning*

MICHAEL PERONE
West Virginia University

MARK GALIZIO
University of North Carolina at Wilmington

ALAN BARON
University of Wisconsin-Milwaukee

Introduction

Operant behavior is defined in terms of its environmental consequences, and central to the analysis is the experimental manipulation of contingencies between responding and consequences, particularly reinforcing ones (Ferster and Skinner, 1957). Indeed, for many researchers systematic study of schedules of reinforcement has been the major distinguishing feature of operant psychology (e.g. Zeiler, 1977, 1984). Those convinced of the fundamental nature of schedule effects have suggested that they must be taken into account whenever behavior is studied. As Dews (1963, p. 148) wrote, 'schedule influences operate generally in psychology; ... when these influences can operate, they will; and ... a student of any problem in psychology—in motivation, generalization, discrimination, or the functions of the frontal lobes—ignores the consequences of the precise scheduling arrangements of his experiments at his peril'.

* Supported by a Senate Grant for Research and Scholarship from West Virginia University to the first author and by Grant AG02513 from the National Institute on Aging to the third author.

The experimental analysis of schedule effects began with the study of nonhuman organisms (hereafter called 'animals'). Laboratory procedures for use with pigeons and rats were standardized, and the vast majority of operant studies have involved, and continue to involve, these species (Buskist and Miller, 1982; Grossett *et al.*, 1982). But psychology ultimately must be concerned with the behavior of humans, and a longstanding issue has been the applicability of the principles discovered in the animal laboratory to human performances. The prevailing strategy to understand human behavior has been one of extrapolation (Baron and Perone, 1982). Operant principles have suggested procedures for modifying human behavior in the clinic, classroom, and other applied settings. Operant principles also have served as the basis for interpretation and clarification of such topics as creativity, social conflict, and political and economic behavior. The paucity of laboratory experiments that directly address schedule effects in humans is a curious incongruity within the study of operant conditioning—the rigor of the animal laboratory is accompanied by loose extrapolations to complex, less controlled settings.

Although uncommon, laboratory experiments on human responses to schedules of reinforcement have been conducted over the past three decades (early efforts include Ader and Tatum, 1961; Azrin, 1958; Baer, 1960; Holland, 1958; Lindsley, 1956; Weiner, 1962), and there appears to be a growing interest in the use of human subjects in operant conditioning research. The effort has produced a diverse and somewhat contradictory literature, one that has been interpreted in diametrically opposed ways. At one extreme, the findings are viewed as confirming principles discovered in the animal laboratory, and thus as supporting their applicability to the broad domain of human affairs (e.g. Rachlin, 1980; Skinner, 1969a). At the other extreme is the view that there are discontinuities between human and animal performances and thus a need for major revisions in conceptions of human operant behavior (e.g. Brewer, 1974; Lowe, 1979).

The latter objections to the possibility of a unified conceptual framework rest on the claim that human behavior is qualitatively different because it is relatively free of control by environmental contingencies. Cognitively oriented critics have argued that human responses to schedules are mediated by thoughts, beliefs, and hypotheses (Bandura, 1969; Brewer, 1974; Schwartz, Schuldenfrei, and Lacey, 1978; Spielberger and DeNike, 1966; Thoresen and Mahoney, 1974). These internal happenings, rather than the schedule or other aspects of the environment, are said to be the controlling variables. A more behavioral account, but one which nonetheless relies on mediating processes, postulates that human subjects verbally describe experimental contingencies to themselves and that these covert 'self-instructions' play a more important role than the contingencies themselves (Lowe, 1979). Whether formulated in cognitive or behavioral terms, these objections express doubt about the environment as the locus of control over human behavior, that is, about the relevance of schedules of reinforcement.

The purpose of this chapter is to evaluate critically the evidence favoring the view that 'the effects of reinforcement are altered qualitatively when subjects acquire the skill of generating verbal descriptions ... of their own behavior and its consequences' (Lowe, 1984, p. 563). After summarizing current concerns about discrepancies, we address some empirical and methodological shortcomings in the comparative analysis of human and animal behavior. We then consider the evidence that verbal capability is the factor that makes the human performances different, and go on to argue that investigators of human behavior should be more circumspect in their reliance on language as an explanatory variable. Finally, we reach a position similar to one expressed by Skinner (1953) when he discussed the relevance of animal experiments to the world of human affairs. As the evidence now stands, it appears premature (as it did to Skinner some years ago) to conclude that there are fundamental differences in the principles underlying the operant behavior of humans and animals.

Human–animal differences

Operant conditioning experiments with human subjects provide important tests of the interspecies generality of behavioral principles. Confidence in these principles is inductively supported when laboratory performances of humans and animals are similar. Because the strategy has been to study animals first, the behavior of rats and pigeons provides the standard of comparison, and the concern is whether principles derived from such subjects can be extrapolated to humans. The fundamental question, as Lowe and Horne (1985, p. 111) put it, is: 'To what extent and under what conditions is human behavior under direct contingency control and governed by reinforcement principles as we know them in animals?'

Apparent discrepancies in the laboratory performances of humans and animals have raised doubts about the generality of reinforcement principles. We will not attempt a comprehensive survey of the literature on this topic. Detailed consideration of the various problems and theoretical issues has been provided in recent reviews and commentaries (Baron and Galizio, 1983; Baron and Perone, 1982; Bradshaw and Szabadi, 1988; Dinsmoor, 1983; Hake, 1982; Higgins and Morris, 1984; Lowe, 1979, 1983, 1984; Lowe and Horne, 1985; Perone, 1985; Perone and Baron, 1983; Poppen, 1982; Weiner, 1983). It will be sufficient to summarize some of the human–animal discrepancies that have attracted attention. Three matters are of significance.

1. *Different procedures are required to establish responding at the outset of an experiment.* With animals, a successful conditioning procedure is first to

train the subjects to eat from the food magazine and then to leave them to encounter the contingency between responding and the food reinforcers (sometimes, to speed the process, successive approximations of the lever-press or key-peck response may be reinforced—'shaping'). In studies of shock avoidance (negative reinforcement) magazine training is unnecessary and subjects may simply be exposed to the schedule (e.g. Bolles and Popp, 1964; Sidman, 1953). When similar procedures have been tried with humans, however, an assortment of problems ensue. For example, when Ader and Tatum (1961) exposed students to shock avoidance schedules without telling them 'anything about the nature of the experiment' (p. 275), many failed to acquire the target response (pressing a conspicuous red button) and received repeated shocks as a consequence. Later work showed that one way to facilitate acquisition is to tell subjects that there is something they can do to prevent the aversive event (e.g. Baron and Kaufman, 1966). A similar approach has been effective with positive reinforcement. Ayllon and Azrin (1964) arranged for psychiatric patients to receive treats contingent upon appropriate behavior at mealtime. After 20 meals with no improvement, the problem was solved by instructing the patients about the contingency. These and other studies have led to the suggestion that conventional operant procedures may be insufficient to engender appropriate behavior in humans.

2. *Response patterns differ on simple schedules of reinforcement.* The most intensively studied schedule with humans has been the fixed interval: The reinforcer is presented contingent upon the first response after a specified period of time. Descriptions of animal performances on this schedule have emphasized control by its temporal features (e.g. Dews, 1970; Mackintosh, 1974). Responding has been described as occurring in a distinctive pattern beginning with a pause in responding at the outset of the interval followed by positively accelerating response rates until presentation of the reinforcer (a 'scallop' in the cumulative record). By comparison, scalloped patterns are not the rule when humans respond on fixed-interval schedules (Weiner, 1969). Some subjects respond at high rates throughout the interval, without any evidence of pausing. Others assume low rates, pausing for most of the interval and responding just once or twice at the end. An increasingly popular account of these different patterns points to the influence of the different ways in which individual subjects verbally formulate the contingencies (e.g. rapid responders describe the schedule as one requiring many responses, whereas slow responders describe the schedule's temporal features; see Lowe's, 1979, review).

3. *Humans are less sensitive to changing schedule conditions.* Performances of rats and pigeons have been found to vary in orderly ways as a function of schedule parameters. This has been shown on single interval and ratio schedules when the duration of the interval or the size of the ratio is varied,

as well as on procedures with different concurrent variable-interval schedules (deVilliers, 1977; Zeiler, 1977). By comparison, human responding is inconsistently affected by parametric variations (e.g. Takahashi and Iwamoto, 1986; Weiner, 1969). Moreover, human behavior may be insenstive to gross qualitative changes in the reinforcement schedule. For example, responding may not differ when ratio schedules normally supporting high rates alternate with time-based schedules normally supporting low to moderate rates (Hayes *et al.*, 1986; Matthews *et al.*, 1977), or even when reinforcement has been suspended altogether (Kaufman, Baron, and Kopp, 1966).

If comparable laboratory procedures produced similar performances in human and animal subjects, a straightforward interpretation would be in terms of a unified set of behavioral principles. By comparison, discrepant performances of the sort outlined above make the proper interpretation considerably less clear.

A conservative approach is to view the discrepancies in the same way one might view discrepant findings within any body of research literature. Thus, differences may be viewed as a consequence of defective techniques of experimental control, perhaps accompanied by incomplete, imprecise, or erroneous specification of the relevant variables. From this standpoint, human-animal discrepancies are reflections of ignorance—the experimenter's ignorance of either the critical variables or the means of controlling them. Resolution of the discrepancies is thus an important research objective as well as a criterion by which to judge current understanding of human and animal behavior.

Quite different is the interpretation described earlier, that discrepancies reflect fundamental incompatibilities between the principles governing human and animal behavior. Despite the example set by research and theory within the biological sciences, the conclusion has been reached that few if any behavioral principles are characterized by interspecies generality (Brewer, 1974). A less extreme position may admit a role for the animal-based principles, but only in the exceptional case where more important principles—uniquely human—are prevented from operating (Lowe, 1979). Either way, serious questions are raised about the relevance of animal research to the analysis of human behavior. The goal of developing a truly general set of behavioral principles is seen as unrealistic and outdated.

Animal performance as a 'benchmark'

In conjunction with the discrepancies mentioned above, recent discussions offer the view that animal performances are more consistent and predictable. Throughout this literature are references to the 'characteristic', 'typical', and even 'classic' performances of rats and pigeons on schedules of reinforcement. By comparison, human performances are viewed as erratic and unpredictable. But close scrutiny suggests caution in using the animal literature as a benchmark for evaluating human performances.

We will discuss two reasons why strong conclusions may be premature. First, the regularity observed in animal experiments has emerged from a set of standard laboratory procedures. Appropriate counterparts are not in common use in operant research with humans, with the consequence that one cannot be certain whether discrepant human performances reflect idiosyncratic features of the laboratory procedures or fundamental differences in the nature of the relevant behavioral principles. Second, unexplained variability is by no means unique to studies with human subjects. Characterizations of animal performances that overlook such variation may paint an exalted and unrealistic picture of what is known about operant conditioning.

Standard procedures

By comparison with the relatively uniform apparatuses and procedures of the animal laboratory, the methods of human operant conditioning experiments are diverse. In research with rats and pigeons, well-known procedures are available for such matters as setting the deprivation level, habituating the subject to the apparatus, and selecting the events to serve as discriminative stimuli, reinforcers, and punishers. These and many other procedures are documented in the literature, and also may be learned routinely from teachers and colleagues. By comparison, the investigator of human operant conditioning does not have the advantage of clear precedents for many of the decisions that must be made in designing and executing an experiment. Consequently, different workers arrive at idiosyncratic solutions to methodological problems, and the variation in methods may lead to variation in experimental results as well.

To illustrate this point, we focus on the aforementioned finding that human subjects often fail to acquire the target response. To meet this problem, researchers have employed, with varying degrees of success, a range of procedures including instructions, demonstration, and shaping. Beyond the observation that human performances appear more variable than those of animals, it is difficult to specify the exact influence of these different procedures. But if findings from animal research are any guide, one might expect that histories engendered by the different procedures interact in complex ways with subsequent control by the reinforcement schedule. Thus, avoidance procedures which are inefficient in promoting response acquisition also may lead to anomalous performances by those subjects who do manage to acquire the response. In the case of positive reinforcement, the shaping of unusual topographies or excessive initial training with continuous reinforcement schedules may inhibit adjustment to more complex schedules.

Also to be emphasized is that failures of response acquisition when subjects are simply exposed to contingencies are by no means unique to research with humans. Instructive in this regard is the literature on free-operant avoidance with rats. Researchers who simply have placed animals within a test chamber and started the shock schedule have found that many of the rats do not acquire the lever-press response. According to one author, 'there are investigators who have never been able to get it in any subjects' (Bolles, 1971, p. 201). Although different theoretical interpretations may be placed on these failures, the important point is that standard procedures are available which markedly increase the likelihood that the response will be rapidly acquired. In our own studies of avoidance in rats, the standard procedure is to shape the response, with the consequence that most animals begin lever pressing during the initial session and with minimal exposure to the shock, and are proficient avoiders during subsequent phases of the experiments (e.g. DeWaard, Galizio, and Baron, 1979; Perone and Galizio, 1987; see also Ferrari, Todorov, and Graeff, 1973).

Within the animal laboratory, longstanding influences of initial training procedures may be reduced in research designs that emphasize stability of performance from session to session within a given experimental condition. In his classic treatise on research methods, Sidman (1960) described stable behavior as representing a 'steady state', a point of equilibrium in the reciprocal interaction between behavior and the variables that influence it. Extended exposure to contingencies is needed to establish steady-state performances, and such exposure may eventually counteract complications caused by the initial procedures. Unfortunately, this antidote usually is not available in human research, where exposure to contingencies can be quite brief, often lasting no more than a few hours. This limitation, in conjunction with the diverse procedures used in different experiments, would seem to make variations in outcomes all but inevitable.

Irregularities in animal performance

The second reason why strong conclusions about human–animal discrepancies are premature pertains to the unsettled state of the literature on animal performances. It is a serious error, or at least a gross oversimplification, to regard the animal literature as a monolithic structure of regular findings and well agreed-upon principles. On the contrary, animal experimentation on the conditioning process characteristically has been in a state of ferment, and controversy reigns with regard to matters that outsiders—including many investigators of human behavior—may view as settled. The list of controversies is a long one. In this section we survey some illustrative cases, paying special attention to work on fixed-interval and avoidance schedules, as these have received extensive review in discussions of human operant conditioning (Higgins and Morris, 1984; Lowe, 1979).

Discrepancies between rats and pigeons

First, consider some persistent species differences. By comparison with pigeons, rats have been found to be more susceptible to control by temporal contingencies, including fixed-interval and differential-reinforcement-of-low-rate schedules. When fixed-interval schedules are replaced with fixed-time schedules that deliver response-independent food at regular intervals, pigeons continue responding across a range of schedule parameters, whereas rats' responding is markedly reduced (Lowe and Harzem, 1977). On multiple schedules in which a reinforcement schedule alternates with extinction, pigeons show increased rates in the reinforcement component (by comparison with rates on a baseline schedule with two reinforcement components). This effect, called 'behavioral contrast', has been an elusive phenomenon when rats are the subjects (e.g. Pear and Wilkie, 1971).

In accounting for these discrepancies, some authors have pointed to Pavlovian influences that operate on the pigeon's key-peck but not the rat's lever-press (Schwartz and Gamzu, 1977). But further research, particularly on behavioral contrast, has shown this account to be unsatisfactory. Convincing demonstrations of contrast have been obtained with responses that presumably are not susceptible to Pavlovian influences: Lever pressing by rats (Gutman, 1977) and treadle pressing by pigeons (McSweeney, 1983). Additional complications are that contrast effects depend on subtle variations in the way multiple-schedule stimuli are introduced (Kodera and Rilling, 1976; Terrace, 1963), and that some studies have found that contrast dissipates after extended training (Terrace, 1966) but others have not (Hearst, 1971).

Generality of functional relations

Even when species differences are not of concern, there continue to be discrepancies in the description of basic functional relationships. Three illustrations should make the point. The first concerns the relationship between the size of a fixed-ratio schedule and running response rates (rates exclusive of any post-reinforcement pause). One conclusion is that rates are more or less invariant (Felton and Lyon, 1966; Powell, 1968), but another is that rate and ratio size are inversely related (Mazur, 1983). A second issue concerns reinforcer magnitude. Although this basic variable has been studied intensively in the animal laboratory, Kling and Schrier (1971, p. 630) wrote that it 'comes as something of a shock' to discover that such a seemingly important and robust variable often is 'an ineffective variable when manipulated in laboratory studies, and that there is considerable discrepancy between the results of studies which appear to be equally well designed and executed' (the state of knowledge does not appear to have changed since then; cf. Harzem and Harzem, 1981). Third is a recent controversy about whether variability is a dimension of operant behavior, and thus subject to control by reinforcement along with other behavioral dimensions such as response topography and rate. One series of experiments reached the conclusion that reinforcement induces stereotypy in behavior and thus cannot engender variability (Schwartz, 1982), but another, using similar procedures and subjects, reached the opposite conclusion (Page and Neuringer, 1985).

Fixed-interval schedules

Given the attention that has been paid to human performances on fixed-interval schedules, it is important to consider rather carefully whether animal responses to this type of schedule provide a suitable standard of comparison. Our reading of the literature is that there continues to be difficulty in reaching firm conclusions about findings from the animal laboratory.

Cumulative response records from Ferster and Skinner's (1957) seminal research with pigeons often serve as examples of the smooth acceleration in response rates known as the fixed-interval scallop. But close examination indicates considerable variation from interval to interval. A convenient example is found in a summary of this research by Skinner (1957/1969b, Figure 2, p. 129). One of the cumulative records, illustrating what Skinner described as 'characteristic performance', shows scallops in some intervals, but three additional patterns also are present: Abrupt transitions from zero to high rates ('break-and-run' pattern; cf. Schneider, 1969); low rates with just one or perhaps two responses late in the interval; and the interruption of response runs midway in the interval. One might infer that Skinner's records may not be 'characteristic' after all, but similar variability is not difficult to find in other reports. For example, all of the patterns described above can be seen from interval to interval in the records from pigeons and rats presented by Lowe and Harzem (1977, Figure 3, p. 193). Their records also show decelerating response rates in some intervals—negative or inverted scallops—as well as substantial variation in overall response rates, with nearly zero rates in some intervals but rates over 70 responses per minute in other intervals within the same session. In his comprehensive review of animal schedule performance, Zeiler (1977) acknowledged the existence of irregularities such as these and discussed some of the variables deserving further research.

In the face of this variation, one might wonder about the origin of the consensus that has developed about the 'fixed-interval scallop' in rats and pigeons. Perhaps this has come about because some experimenters have dealt with irregularities by averaging over several intervals. Thus, the classic scallop may be a construction rather than an accurate depiction of the organism's actual performance (see Shull, 1979). Interestingly, the scallops presented by some authors are idealized representations rather than actual records (e.g. Reynolds, 1975, Figure 6.4, p. 81). These portrayals may fit certain theoretical expectations more closely than actual empirical outcomes.

An aspect of fixed-interval performance needing fuller recognition is that response patterns may depend on the extent of exposure to the schedule. This may help account for disagreements about whether temporal control by the schedule is manifested in a break-and-run pattern rather than smooth scallops. Mackintosh (1974) presented the plausible view that these different patterns represent different stages in the evolution of temporal control. Early in training, when control is lacking, responding occurs throughout the interval. As control develops, the scalloped pattern emerges. Finally, with extended exposure precise control develops; the pause is lengthened and terminal responding is at high, steady rates. We noted earlier that all three of these patterns have been observed in studies of fixed-interval performances. One can only speculate on whether the variations in human performances reflect different histories with fixed-interval schedules—prior to, as well as during, the experiment.

Free-operant avoidance

Research and theory on avoidance also have been the focus of controversy. We already have noted the difficulties encountered by some experimenters in establishing the avoidance response in their animal subjects. With regard to response maintenance, Higgins and Morris (1984) concluded that rates of rats tend to be somewhat irregular, low, and close to the minimal rates required by the schedule. By comparison, human rates sometimes are steady, high, and thus insulated from frequent contact with the schedule (e.g. Baron and Kaufman, 1966; Galizio, 1979).

But as with fixed-interval schedules, results from the animal laboratory make it hazardous to characterize 'typical' performance on avoidance schedules. Contrary to the view that rats make close contact with the schedule, Anger (1963) commented that after extensive training with Sidman's (1953) free-operant schedule, rats' responding is proficient enough to reduce substantially contact with shock—and thus the schedule itself. (In more technical terms, Anger noted that proficient avoiders virtually never encounter the 'shock–shock' interval of the schedule, and only occasionally encounter the 'response–shock' interval.) This has been the result in our own work as well. Following appropriate training, rats may receive as few as three or four shocks per hour, and in fact may respond for several hours without receiving shocks at all (DeWaard *et al.*, 1979; Perone and Galizio, 1987), results not too different from those in some studies with humans (e.g. Baron and Kaufman, 1966). A reasonable account, similar to the one reached about fixed-interval schedules, is that the efficiency of shock avoidance depends on the extent of exposure to the schedule as well as the procedures followed when the response was initially acquired. Proper conclusions about the literature require that each experiment be examined carefully in light of these considerations.

With regard to avoidance learning in general, we can only note in passing the considerable disagreement about theoretical mechanisms such as the roles of shock-frequency reduction, conditioned fear, species-specific defense reactions, and the safety period that follows the response (for different views see Bolles, 1971; Dinsmoor, 1977; Herrnstein, 1969; Hineline, 1981). These controversies, well known in the area of animal conditioning, underline the theme of this section. It seems premature to conclude that human avoidance performances differ from those of animals when the animal literature is in such an unsettled state.

Comparing human and animal performances

To some, our discussion of research from the animal laboratory may provide additional ammunition for attacks against a unified conceptual framework. We have added to the original objection—that human performances are discrepant from those observed in the animal laboratory—the further objection that disagreements about the conditioning process on the animal level do not provide a very good basis for comparisons. Taken together, these objections might suggest the need for a fresh start in the study of human operant conditioning. But we do not see things that way.

The methods and theories developed in the animal laboratory provide a framework for the study of operant conditioning that has barely been tapped by behavioral researchers. But in turning to the animal laboratory as a source for the study of human conditioning, it is easy to forget that the study of conditioning in animals as well as in humans is a dynamic and changing endeavor. On the one hand, the controversy we have described is indicative of the vitality of the effort (if all the empirical and theoretical problems of operant conditioning already were solved, there would be little point in conducting research in the area). On the other hand, the controversy suggests prudence in reaching conclusions about the implications of the findings for human behavior.

The role of verbal behavior

The most obvious difference between humans and animals is that of verbal capability. Consequently, it is not surprising that discrepant human performances in operant experiments have been attributed to the interaction of verbal and nonverbal behavior. The view that verbal behavior dominates nonverbal behavior is a common one in psychology. The individual is conceived as telling himself what to do, listening to the commands, and then proceeding to obey them.

In discussing control of human schedule performances by verbal stimuli, it is useful to classify studies in terms of the source of the stimuli. One type of study examines the effects of experimenter-provided instructions. Such procedures arrange verbal episodes (Skinner, 1957) in which the experimenter functions as speaker and the subject as listener. In the other type of study, the experimenter is eliminated from the verbal episodes and the subject functions not only as listener but also as speaker, first by generating the stimuli through 'self-instructions' (or 'self-rules') and then by responding to them.

Despite these procedural differences, both approaches focus on the competition between verbal stimuli and reinforcement contingencies for control of nonverbal behavior. The outcome of this competition reveals whether responding on the schedule of reinforcement is 'rule-governed' or 'contingency-shaped' (Skinner, 1969a). At issue, then, is whether explanation of schedule performances by verbal humans requires principles beyond those traditionally associated with performances of nonverbal animals.

Instructions: Effects of the experimenter's verbal behavior

Interest in instructional control of human operant behavior extends well beyond the study of schedule effects (Baron and Galizio, 1983). From a practical standpoint, instructions constitute the primary means of effecting behavioral change in social and educational settings. From an experimental standpoint, some sort of verbal exchange must occur in research with humans, raising basic procedural questions about the degree to which instructional effects may obscure those of the independent variable. From a theoretical standpoint, Skinner (1963) argued that control by instructions in the form of descriptions of contingencies should be different from control by the contingencies themselves.

An often-stated conclusion about experimenter-provided instructions is that they have the special property of reducing sensitivity to reinforcement contingencies (Higgins and Morris, 1984; Lowe, 1979). Data bearing on this issue have come from procedures in which instructions do not correspond to the actual contingencies, thereby revealing the relative contribution of each to performances (see Baron and Galizio's 1983 review). For example, Kaufman, Baron, and Kopp (1966) gave college students various instructions in conjunction with training on a variable-interval schedule. Instructions describing the schedule as a fixed interval led to low rates and occasional scalloped patterns, whereas instructions describing a variable-ratio schedule led to high steady rates. Because performances were characteristic of the contingencies described in the instructions rather than the actual contingency, this study illustrates how instructions can override schedule control.

There is no doubt that strong instructional control over behavior can make the effects of contingencies difficult to discern. But it seems erroneous, or at least an oversimplification, to conclude that a *necessary* property of instructions is to reduce sensitivity to contingencies. Other considerations indicate that instructions may enhance as well as reduce schedule control. Such a conclusion emerges readily from a view of instruction effects as the outcome of a competition between responses to the instructions and responses to the actual schedule. The interactions may be complex, but the analysis follows that for more familiar interacting variables.

Consider, for example, the effects of an organism's history with a schedule on performances when the schedule is abruptly altered. A history with schedules that generate high steady rates shields the organism from the temporal contingencies of a subsequent fixed-interval schedule, whereas a history with schedules that differentially reinforce low rates has the opposite consequence of producing a greater degree of contact with the fixed interval (Weiner, 1969). In a parallel way, instructions about a schedule also can generate either high or low response rates, and, depending on the actual schedule, contact with the contingencies may either be facilitate or impeded (Galizio, 1979; Hayes *et al.*, 1986). An essential feature of the interaction is the strength of the stimulus control exerted by the instructions. Research from the animal laboratory shows that responding under strong stimulus control can dominate control by subsequent contingencies. In the case of instructions, one might suppose that the subject's natural history gives this source of control considerable strength by comparison with the reinforcers available within the confines of the laboratory.

Whether instructions sensitize or desensitize subjects to contingencies depends heavily on the extent to which instruction-generated behaviors are reinforced by the prevailing schedule. In Kaufman *et al.*'s (1966) study, subjects given variable-ratio instructions responded at excessive rates, given the actual variable-interval schedule, but such responding had the consequence of maximizing the reinforcement available from the schedule. Under such circumstances, it is not surprising that a response pattern at odds with the schedule was maintained. By comparison, when responding controlled by instructions—or for that matter by prior histories or discriminative stimuli—leads to loss of reinforcement, the advantage in the competition shifts, and control is transferred to the contingencies (e.g. Galizio, 1979; Hayes *et al.*, 1986; Weiner, 1969).

Self-instructions: Effects of the subject's verbal behavior

We now turn to the case where the same individual functions as speaker as well as listener. To study the influences of self-generated instructions or rules on responding to reinforcement schedules, investigators somehow must gain access to the subject's 'self-instructions'. A common approach is that of exposing subjects to schedules, asking them questions about the schedules during post-session interviews, and then determining the correlations between schedule performances and the answers to the questions. This research strategy has been used in connection with a variety of topics, often as a source of subsidiary data, and our impression is that both its popularity and its contribution to the analysis of results are increasing (e.g. Ader and Tatum, 1961; Buskist, Bennett, and Miller 1981; Case, Fantino, and Wixted, 1985; Duvinsky and Poppen, 1982; Lippman and Meyer, 1967; Rosenfeld and Baer, 1970; Sidman and Tailby, 1982; Vaughan, 1985; Wasserman and Neunaber, 1986; Wearden and Shimp, 1985).

Despite the correlational nature of studies relating verbal reports and schedule performances, the verbal reports sometimes have been used as explanatory variables, that is, as evidence for control of performances by rules. Given the increasing reliance on this approach, it deserves careful scrutiny. Many of the pitfalls may be found in the developmental studies reported by Lowe and his colleagues (Bentall, Lowe, and Beasty, 1985; Lowe, Beatsy, and Bentall, 1983). Their results indicated that the responses to fixed-interval schedules of infant subjects (less than a year old) resembled those of pigeons and rats, whereas the patterns of older children (three–nine years) did not. In accounting for this outcome, the authors observed that the infants could not describe the contingencies, whereas the older children could, a finding documented by quoting some answers to open-ended questions (along the lines of 'What makes the apparatus work?'). The investigators concluded that the infants' lack of verbal behavior allowed control by the fixed-interval schedule, whereas the verbal descriptions produced by the older subjects served as rules that interfered with schedule control (Bentall *et al.*, 1985).

This sort of reliance on post-session interviews, particularly when the subjects are children, is easy to criticize. As Shimoff (1984) noted, a subject's verbal behavior during an interview may be unrelated to whatever verbal behavior occurred during the session. Answers to questions can be controlled by a host of variables, including the subject's pre-experimental and experimental histories before the interview as well as the discriminative stimuli and reinforcers at work during the interview. Although post-session descriptions of experimental contingencies could be veridical with verbalizations that occurred during the session, it is also possible that the subject had never described the contingency until prompted to do so. Compounding the problem is the casual manner in which verbal reports sometimes are evoked, recorded, and summarized. In Bentall *et al.*'s (1985) paper, information about the interview procedures and results is incomplete, and the verbal reports themselves are presented by way of anecdotes and the authors' general impressions.

If a major role is to be ascribed to verbal processes in theoretical interpretations of human schedule performance, much closer attention must be paid to the development of precise, reliable, and valid instruments to collect verbal data. The need for caution in the collection and interpretation of verbal reports is intensified when the subjects are children whose verbal proficiency is naturally lower than that of adults. [This is demonstrated memorably by Brown and Bellugi's classic studies of language acquisition in children. These investigators frequently asked a two-year-old boy to report on his verbal and nonverbal behavior. At one point they asked a straightforward question about pluralization: 'Adam, which is right—"two shoes" or "two shoe"?' Adam's answer, emitted with explosive enthusiasm, was 'Pop goes the weasel!' (Brown and Bellugi, 1964/1968, p. 413)].

The studies by Lowe's group illustrate the major obstacles standing in the way of the conclusion that one behavioral repertoire, the responding reinforced by the schedule, is controlled by a second repertoire, the verbal description of the schedule. A correlation between these two behavioral systems—in so far as a relationship has been established—does not provide acceptable evidence that one system actually controls the other. Several variables besides the verbal ones were correlated with the different schedule performances, and any of these may have contributed to the performances. The infants and older children were tested in different laboratories with different manipulanda. The reinforcers for the infants were customized and likely more potent than the reinforcers presented to the older children. Sessions were terminated when natural contingencies competed with the fixed-interval schedule for control of the infants' behavior—influences described as 'nappy wetting and various minor ailments that are inevitable features of infant research' (Lowe *et al.*, 1983, p. 159). By comparison, sessions for the older children were continued despite evidence of a variety of competing behaviors including withdrawal from the apparatus and wandering about the laboratory (Bentall *et al.*, 1985). In addition to these important procedural factors, the subjects differed in terms of numerous behavioral characteristics, including motor coordination, attention, and general intellectual development. Of special importance may be that older children have been exposed to a much wider range of reinforcement contingencies, including temporal ones. Thus, to isolate verbal capability as the explanatory variable is tempting, and possibly correct, but at present this theoretical formulation awaits improved methods for its verification.

Promise of such an advance may be seen in a recent study by Matthews, Catania, and Shimoff (1985) in which verbal reports were objectively observed under well-specified conditions, recorded on a more or less continuous basis, and brought under some degree of experimental control. In this experiment college students earned money by button pressing on multiple random-interval random-ratio schedules and, after every exposure to the pair of schedules, by writing statements about either the contingencies or the appropriate way to press the buttons. Correct statements were shaped by reinforcing successive approximations with money. When subjects were trained to describe performances, their button pressing fit the descriptions, even if the descriptions were inappropriate to the actual contingencies. By comparison, when subjects were trained to describe contingencies, button pressing sometimes was and sometimes was not in accord with the descriptions. Thus, the findings point to the limits of interactions between verbal and nonverbal behavior: The pattern of button pressing paralleled verbal descriptions of performance but not descriptions of contingencies.

This line of research is original and the procedures and analyses are, understandably, in need of refinement. Although central to the aims of the research, the shaping procedure and resulting verbal responses were not described as precisely as one would like. The experiments lasted just a few hours, and it is important to determine how verbal and nonverbal behavior might interact in the long term, after performances are allowed to stabilize. The inconsistent relationship between contingency descriptions and schedule performances suggests that identification of the controlling variables is incomplete. Unfortunately, the procedures cannot isolate the contributions of several possible sources of control over the verbal descriptions, for example, the shaping procedure, the multiple schedule, the operant performances maintained by the schedule, or the interaction among these variables. Until such matters can be sorted out, the relationship between the verbal descriptions and the schedule performances must be viewed essentially as correlational, not causal. Despite these problems, Matthews *et al.*'s study represents an important step in the development of procedures in which verbal behavior can be studied as operant behavior, directly and objectively measured and, most importantly, brought under explicit control of environmental contingencies of reinforcement.

Conceptual issues regarding the effects of verbal stimuli

In addressing the role of verbal capability in human operant behavior, we considered the effects of two forms of verbal stimuli on schedule performances— stimuli generated by the experimenter (instructions) and those generated by the subjects themselves (self-instructions). Close analysis of these effects is important for understanding the control that rules can exert over behavior.

A starting point is the recognition that the study of experimenter-provided instructions can be conducted within the traditional framework of the experimental analysis of behavior. It bears repetition that instructional stimuli represent a source of external control whose influences, although complex, are amenable to objective investigation. Put simply, instructions can be manipulated in the same way as nonverbal sources of behavioral control.

Hayes and Brownstein (1984) noted that research on instructions provides a vehicle for the experimental analysis of rule-governed behavior in 'subjects as listeners'. The concept of 'rule-governance', although increasingly regarded as a major characteristic of human behavior, seems to us to be ill-defined. But if the effects of rules are to be studied experimentally, we agree that the direct manipulation of verbal stimuli, along the lines of research on instructional control, appears necessary. Regardless of how rules are to be studied, there is the further question of whether their understanding is to be pursued in terms of the familiar and fundamental processes that underlie other forms of operant behavior, that is, in terms of environmental contingencies involving discriminative stimuli and reinforcers. Brownstein and Shull (1985) expressed concern about movement by behavior analysts away from this goal, noting that injudicious distinction between rule-governed versus contingency-shaped behavior 'encourages the view that control by rule-like instructions operates according to *principles* that are unique to human language' (p. 266). The view of rule-governed behavior needing emphasis, then, is not its basis in verbal capability, but rather 'the possibility of a systematic interpretation that is continuous with interpretations of simpler cases with nonhuman animals' (p. 266). A unified conceptual framework calls for a view of rule-governed behavior as a form of discriminated operant created by contingencies, not as an exception to operant principles. Skinner, the originator of the distinction between rule-governed and contingency-shaped behavior (as well as distinctions among other discriminated operants such as 'tacts', 'mands', 'echoics', and 'textuals'), has long argued along similar lines: 'All behavior is. . . contingency shaped. We . . . follow rules because of reinforcing consequences' (Skinner, 1984, p. 577).

This brings us to the case of the subject as speaker as well as listener. Questions about discriminative control of nonverbal behavior by verbal stimuli do not appear well served by procedures in which the researcher relinquishes control of the stimuli, as in most studies relying on subjects' verbal reports about schedule performances. Nevertheless, interest in verbal reports has been defended on philosophical grounds. The argument is that radical behaviorism recognizes the importance of covert verbal events such as self-instructions and self-rules in human behavior, by comparison with methodological behaviorism which restricts study to publicly observable events. Lowe (1983, p. 83) put it this way:

Skinner's radical behaviorism, in contra-distinction to the methodological variety, has established its theoretical identity largely on the basis of its recognition of the importance of covert events in human behavior and Skinner, moreover, has argued that being able, through language, to describe our own behavior to ourselves has resulted in a form of 'consciousness' which is unique in the animal world. It is remarkable, therefore, that the role of covert events and the transformation in human behavior brought about by language, have been almost completely ignored in radical behaviorist research.

Verbal reports are, of course, behavior and thus a legitimate object of behavior analysis. But like other forms of verbal behavior, they are multiply determined and cannot be taken as a direct measure of private events or as an accurate indicator of stimuli (private or public) controlling nonverbal behavior (Branch and Malagodi, 1980). Zuriff (1985), in his explication of Skinner's radical behaviorism, provides the reasons why radical behavioral researchers (including Skinner himself) are reluctant to invoke covert verbal events as explanatory mechanisms. Zuriff (p. 234) summarized the matter as follows:

> Skinner ... can be interpreted as maintaining that covert events, or 'private events', are observed stimuli rather than inferred hypothetical constructs. Nevertheless, he, in fact, does not make use of first-person reports as observational reports for a science of behavior because he considers them to be unreliable discriminations of private events. ... Skinner hypothesizes that the verbal community establishes first-person reports by contingencies of reinforcement that rely on public correlates of private stimuli. However, in the absence of the public correlates, the verbal community cannot be certain that the private discriminative stimulus for the first-person report is consistent. With no public stimuli to serve as guides, the verbal community cannot maintain precise contingencies to ensure a rigid discriminative relationship between the verbal response and the private stimuli. Therefore, the association between the verbal response and the private stimulus cannot be considered a reliable one, and first-person reports are not to be used as observational reports of private stimuli.

Introspection as a technique for data gathering has had a checkered career within psychology. It seems ironic to us that this questionable method is defended in the name of Skinnerian behaviorism.

But what about approaches in which verbal behavior is treated as no more than behavior? Methodological obstacles in the way of appropriate procedures for evoking, recording, and summarizing verbal reports are formidable, although Catania and his colleagues have taken initial steps to remove these obstacles (Catania, Matthews, and Shimoff, 1982; Matthews *et al.*, 1985). But even if these concerns are laid to rest, the fact remains that data on verbal–nonverbal interactions are, in essence, correlational in nature, and thus insufficient to the task of developing causal explanations. This limitation in the interpretation of verbal behavior as a cause of nonverbal behavior needs fuller recognition and discussion. The issue has been laid out by Hayes (1986, p. 361):

> In a behavior–analytic approach, all 'causes' are ultimately restricted to environmental events. Behavioral causes are not ultimately acceptable because no one can change behavior without changing its context (e.g. through instructions, drugs, consequences, settings). Behavioral influences are often thought to be important aspects of an overall causal chain, but for philosophical reasons the search is never ended until sources of environmental control are established.

All this is not to say that behavior–behavior correlations have no place in the study of human operant conditioning. Such information can contribute to a better understanding of the structure of behavioral systems. Questions of structure have not been given their due by behavior analysts who traditionally have focused on questions of function (Catania, 1973; see also Baron, Myerson, and Hale, 1988). But from the standpoint of the variables controlling the operant conditioning process, correlational studies cannot bear the explanatory burden that some authors have placed on them, nor can they provide a substitute for an experimental analysis of behavior that seeks environmental causes (cf. Skinner, 1963).

We can best conclude this section by pointing to the need for careful and systematic research on experimenter-provided and subject-generated instructions. Information about the role that verbal stimuli play in human operant conditioning will broaden our understanding of the conditioning process as it operates on the human level. But we also emphasize that we can find nothing in the literature thus far that undermines application of an 'animal model' to such understanding.

Summary and conclusions

Current understanding of operant conditioning principles derives from decades of research in the animal laboratory. Much evidence for the generality of these principles at the human level has been indirect, having been provided by their successful use in interpreting human society and in modifying human behavior in applied settings. Paradoxically, when more direct evidence has been sought in laboratory studies of human operant conditioning, the animal-based principles do not appear to fit nearly as well, particularly with regard to control by schedules of reinforcement. Our purpose in this chapter has been to consider the bearing of such discrepancies on the adequacy of operant principles in the analysis of human behavior.

One view points to the unique verbal capability of humans and argues that the principles must undergo major revision to account for the behavior of organisms who can describe contingencies between responding and its consequences. On this view, the key to human operant conditioning lies in the verbal descriptions of the contingencies rather than the contingencies themselves. Covert events, conceptualized as implicit verbal behaviors, are assigned a central explanatory role.

An alternative view, the one advocated here, is that strong conclusions about human–animal discrepancies are premature, given the limited effort thus far to study human operant conditioning within the laboratory. Discrepancies are not to be regarded as limits on the development of a unitary set of operant conditioning principles, but rather as evidence that our current understanding of these principles is incomplete. On this view, the ability to resolve discrepancies serves as the criterion for judging the status of the principles developed to date.

Controversy about the relevance of animal-based principles to the understanding of human behavior is by no means a new development on the operant scene. Skinner (1953) anticipated current expressions of dissatisfaction in his seminal work on human operant conditioning. He also provided a rejoinder.

> [Animal research] often meets with the objection that there is an essential gap between man and the other animals, and that the results of one cannot be extrapolated to the other. To insist upon this discontinuity at the beginning of a scientific investigation is to beg the question. Human behavior is distinguished by its complexity, its variety, and its greater accomplishments, but the basic processes are not therefore necessarily different . . . It would be rash to assert at this point that there is no essential difference between human behavior and the behavior of the lower species; but until an attempt has been made to deal with both in the same terms, it would be equally rash to assert that there is (p. 38).

At issue, then, is whether over the ensuing years a proper attempt has been made to deal with animal and human behavior 'in the same terms'. The paucity of investigations of human performances under controlled conditions suggests otherwise to us.

Our assessment of the literature on human–animal discrepancies leads to the conclusion that the available data on human schedule performances do not support the need for qualitatively different principles. This conclusion is supported by three sets of observations and arguments.

First, direct comparisons of human and animal research are complicated by uneven development of appropriate techniques of experimental control. Animal research is characterized by standard laboratory procedures and observations of steady-state performances after long-term exposure to the experimental variables. In contrast, human research is characterized by procedures which differ from one laboratory to the next, and observation of stable performances often is not possible because of abbreviated exposure to the variables.

Second, despite the rigorous experimental control that is possible in the animal laboratory, unexplained variation persists and questions about fundamental variables and processes still await firm answers. Given this unsettled state of affairs, normative statements about 'typical' or 'characteristic' schedules performances are oversimplifications, and do not provide a sound basis for assessing the degree to which human performances reflect sources of control other than the schedule.

Third, experimental support is lacking for the hypothesis that control by verbal stimuli such as rules and instructions can supplant control by contingencies and thus account for differences in human and animal performances. What is at issue is not whether verbal stimuli can exert major influences on behavior (indeed, we ourselves have contributed to the evidence on this point; e.g. Baron and Galizio, 1983; Baron, Kaufman, and Stauber, 1969; Galizio, 1979). Rather, the essential questions pertain to the research methods and the theoretical interpretations best suited to the analysis of such control. On the level of methodology, it is essential that experiments be designed in ways that bring verbal influences under direct control. Procedures in which verbal stimuli are presented through experimenter-provided instructions have considerable merit in this regard, in so far as the characteristics of instructions can be manipulated in much the same way as other environmental variables. Considerably less adequate are procedures in which the subjects themselves are the source of stimuli, so-called 'self-instructions'. Regardless of whether such behavior is inferred from interviews at the end of the experiment or from verbalizations during the course of the experiment, the critical stimuli are not under experimental control within this procedure. Consequently, results fall short of a true experimental analysis and cannot bear an explanatory burden. Concerning theory, the issue is whether understanding the interactions between the influences of verbal stimuli and schedules of reinforcement requires a new set of principles. To the contrary, similarities with the effects of more familiar variables, such as schedule history and stimulus control, suggest the possibility of a common analysis in terms of competition between the variables for control of behavior.

In summary, the broad issue raised by current discussions of human operant conditioning is whether psychological theory should continue to incorporate data from both humans and animals into a unified account comprised of interchangeable methods and explanatory variables. The view that the study of human operant conditioning is logically continuous with animal research and, indeed, that it is critical to the elaboration of a truly general theory of operant behavior, has been an essential feature of the historical development of operant psychology. It also has long been under attack by advocates of frankly cognitive points of view. But, we fear, the unified view also may be falling out of favor among behaviorally oriented psychologists as fascination with the verbal capability of humans increases. This would be unfortunate because advocacy of a unified account does not discourage the study of verbal behavior. Instead, extending operant methods to the experimental analysis of human behavior demands that due attention be paid to control by verbal stimuli. But when human and animal subjects respond differently under putatively similar conditions, it is inconsistent with the operant tradition to resort to an account in terms of special abilities possessed by the human organism.

Much more constructive at this stage of knowledge is to approach such discrepancies in the same way as when the subjects providing the conflicting data are of the same species, that is, simply as instances in which the environmental influences over behavior remain to be identified or controlled. For example, one of the more exciting developments in the analysis of complex behavior has been the demonstration that classes of equivalent stimuli with properties of identity, symmetry, and transitivity may emerge following conditional discrimination training in humans but not animals (Sidman and Tailby, 1982; Sidman *et al.*, 1982). The possible relevance of equivalence class formation to an operant account of language is suggested by an intriguing study which found that equivalence classes were formed readily by normal and retarded children who used language, but not by language-disabled children (Devany, Hayes, and Nelson, 1986). The investigators noted, however, that the data permit differing interpretations. It is unclear whether ability to form equivalence classes is necessary for language and other kinds of symbol use, whether the ability to use symbols is necessary to form equivalence classes, or whether these two abilities are manifestations of a common process. A further possibility is that, if as yet undetermined conditions are met, stimulus equivalence may be observed in animals and nonverbal humans. Thus, in our view, it still is premature to abandon the search for continuity in the principles underlying human and animal behavior.

Our position that assumptions of discontinuities are premature has a counterpart in Sidman's (1960) own discussion of comparative psychology and its role in explicating questions of interspecies similarities and differences:

> Comparative psychology has become a discipline largely devoted to discovering *differences* in the behavior of various species of organism. When similarities, the stuff of which most sciences are made, are found, they are dismissed as unimportant phenomena. ... [Yet] a comparative psychology that seeks to determine differences rather than similarities among species really has an easy time of it. Differences are not difficult to find (p. 55).

When comparisons are made between the performances of humans and animals, discrepancies also are not difficult to find and, in themselves, provide little basis for satisfaction. The challenge for the student of human operant conditioning is to identify the similarities in the variables underlying the discrepant performances and ultimately to bring them under experimental control.

References

Ader, R., and Tatum, R. (1961). Free-operant avoidance conditioning in human subjects, *Journal of the Experimental Analysis of Behavior*, **4**, 275–276.
Anger, D. (1963). The role of temporal discriminations in the reinforcement of Sidman avoidance behavior, *Journal of the Experimental Analysis of Behavior*, **6**, 477–506.
Ayllon, T., and Azrin, N. H. (1964). Reinforcement and instructions with mental patients, *Journal of the Experimental Analysis of Behavior*, **7**, 327–331.
Azrin, N. H. (1958). Some effects of noise on human behavior, *Journal of the Experimental Analysis of Behavior*, **1**, 183–200.
Baer, D. M. (1960). Escape and avoidance response of pre-school children to two

schedules of reinforcement withdrawal, *Journal of the Experimental Analysis of Behavior*, **3**, 155–159.

Bandura, A. (1969). *Principles of Behavior Modification*, New York: Holt, Rinehart, & Winston.

Baron, A., and Galizio, M. (1983). Instructional control of human operant behavior, *The Psychological Record*, **33**, 495–520.

Baron, A., and Kaufman, A. (1966). Human, free-operant avoidance of 'time-out' from monetary reinforcement, *Journal of the Experimental Analysis of Behavior*, **9**, 557–565.

Baron, A., Kaufman, A., and Stauber, K.A. (1969). Effects of instructions and reinforcement feedback on human operant behavior maintained by fixed-interval reinforcement. *Journal of the Experimental Analysis of Behavior*, **12**, 701–712.

Baron, A., Myerson, J., and Hale, S. (1988). An integrated analysis of the structure and function of behavior: Aging and the cost of dividing attention. In G.C.L. Davey and C. Cullen (eds), *Human Operant Conditioning and Behavior Modification*, Chichester: John Wiley, pp. 139–166.

Baron, A., and Perone, M. (1982). The place of the human subject in the operant laboratory, *The Behavior Analyst*, **5**, 143–158.

Bentall, R.P., Lowe, C.F., and Beasty, A. (1985). The role of verbal behavior in human learning: II. Developmental differences, *Journal of the Experimental Analysis of Behavior*, **43**, 165–181.

Bolles, R.C. (1971). Species-specific defense reactions. In F.R. Brush (ed.), *Aversive Conditioning and Learning*, New York: Academic Press, pp. 183–233.

Bolles, R.C., and Popp, R.J., Jr. (1964). Parameters affecting the acquisition of Sidman avoidance, *Journal of the Experimental Analysis of Behavior*, **7**, 315–321.

Bradshaw, C.M., and Szabadi, E. (1988). Quantitative analysis of human operant behaviour. In G.C.L. Davey and C. Cullen (eds), *Human Operant Conditioning and Behavior Modification*, Chichester: John Wiley, pp. 225–259.

Branch, M.N., and Malagodi, E.F. (1980). Where have all the behaviorists gone? *The Behavior Analyst*, **3**, 31–38.

Brewer, W.F. (1974). There is no convincing evidence for operant or classical conditioning in adult humans. In W.B. Weimer and D.S. Palermo (eds), *Cognition and the Symbolic Processes*, Hillsdale, NJ: Erlbaum, pp. 1–33.

Brown, R., and Bellugi, U. (1968). Three processes in the child's acquisition of syntax. In N.S. Endler, L.R. Boulter, and H. Osser (eds), *Contemporary Issues in Developmental Psychology*, New York: Holt, Rinehart & Winston. (Original work published 1964), pp. 411–424.

Brownstein, A.J., and Shull, R.L. (1985). A rule for the use of the term, 'rule-governed behavior', *The Behavior Analyst*, **8**, 265–267.

Buskist, W.F., Bennett, R.H., and Miller, H.L., Jr. (1981). Effects of instructional constraints on human fixed-interval performance, *Journal of the Experimental Analysis of Behavior*, **35**, 217–225.

Buskist, W.F., and Miller, H.L., Jr. (1982). The analysis of human operant behavior: A brief census of the literature: 1958–1981, *The Behavior Analyst*, **5**, 137–141.

Case, D.A., Fantino, E., and Wixted, J. (1985). Human observing: Maintained by negative informative stimuli only if correlated with improvement in response efficiency, *Journal of the Experimental Analysis of Behavior*, **43**, 289–300.

Catania, A.C. (1973). The psychologies of structure, function, and development. *American Psychologist*, **28**, 434–443.

Catania, A.C., Matthews, B.A., and Shimoff, E. (1982). Instructed versus shaped human verbal behavior: Interactions with nonverbal responding, *Journal of the Experimental Analysis of Behavior*, **38**, 233–248.

Devany, J. M., Hayes, S. C., and Nelson, R. O. (1986). Equivalence class formation in language-able and language-disabled children, *Journal of the Experimental Analysis of Behavior*, **46**, 243–257.

deVilliers, P. (1977). Choice in concurrent schedules and a quantitative formulation of the law of effect. In W. K. Honig and J. E. R. Staddon (eds), *Handbook of Operant Behavior*, Englewood Cliffs, NJ: Prentice-Hall, pp. 233–287.

DeWaard, R. J., Galizio, M., and Baron, A. (1979). Chained schedules of avoidance: Reinforcement within and by avoidance situations, *Journal of the Experimental Analysis of Behavior*, **32**, 399–407.

Dews, P. B. (1963). Behavioral effects of drugs. In S. M. Farber and R. H. L. Wilson (eds), *Conflict and Creativity*, New York: McGraw-Hill, pp. 138–153.

Dews, P. B. (1970). The theory of fixed-interval responding. In W. N. Schoenfeld (ed.), *The Theory of Reinforcement Schedules*, New York: Appleton-Century-Crofts, pp. 43–61.

Dinsmoor, J. A. (1977). Escape, avoidance, and punishment: Where do we stand? *Journal of the Experimental Analysis of Behavior*, **28**, 83–95.

Dinsmoor, J. A. (1983). Observing and conditioned reinforcement, *Behavioral and Brain Sciences*, **6**, 693–728.

Duvinsky, J. D., and Poppen, R. (1982). Human performance on conjunctive fixed-interval fixed-ratio schedules, *Journal of the Experimental Analysis of Behavior*, **37**, 243–250.

Felton, M., and Lyon, D. O. (1966). The post-reinforcement pause, *Journal of the Experimental Analysis of Behavior*, **9**, 131–134.

Ferrari, E. A., Todorov, J. C., and Graeff, F. G. (1973). Nondiscriminated avoidance of shock by pigeons pecking a key, *Journal of the Experimental Analysis of Behavior*, **19**, 211–218.

Ferster, C. B., and Skinner, B. F. (1957). *Schedules of Reinforcement*, Englewood Cliffs, NJ: Prentice-Hall.

Galizio, M. (1979). Contingency-shaped and rule-governed behavior: Instructional control of human loss avoidance, *Journal of the Experimental Analysis of Behavior*, **31**, 53–70.

Grossett, D., Roy, S., Sharenow, E., and Poling, A. (1982). Subjects used in JEAB articles: Is the snark a pigeon? *The Behavior Analyst*, **5**, 189–190.

Guttman, A. (1977). Positive contrast, negative induction, and inhibitory stimulus control in the rat, *Journal of the Experimental Analysis of Behavior*, **27**, 219–233.

Hake, D. F. (1982). The basic-applied continuum and the possible evolution of human operant social and verbal research, *The Behavior Analyst*, **5**, 21–28.

Harzem, P., and Harzem, A. L. (1981). Discrimination, inhibition, and simultaneous association of stimulus properties: A theoretical analysis of reinforcement. In P. Harzem and M. D. Zeiler (eds), *Advances in Analysis of Behaviour: Vol. 2. Predictability, Correlation, and Contiguity*, New York: Wiley, pp. 81–124.

Hayes, S. C. (1986). The case of the silent dog–verbal reports and the analysis of rules: A review of Ericsson and Simon's *Protocol Analysis: Verbal Reports as Data*, *Journal of the Experimental Analysis of Behavior*, **45**, 351–363.

Hayes, S. C., and Brownstein, A. J. (1984). Verbal behavior: Is the human operant lab an ideal place to begin? *Experimental Analysis of Human Behavior Bulletin*, **2**, 11–13.

Hayes, S. C., Brownstein, A. J., Zettle, R. D., Rosenfarb, I., and Korn, Z. (1986). Rule-governed behavior and sensitivity to changing consequences of responding, *Journal of the Experimental Analysis of Behavior*, **45**, 237–256.

Hearst, E. (1971). Contrast and stimulus generalization following prolonged discrimination training, *Journal of the Experimental Analysis of Behavior*, **15**, 355–363.

Herrnstein, R.J. (1969). Method and theory in the study of avoidance, *Psychological Review*, 76, 49–69.

Higgins, S.T., and Morris, E.K. (1984). Generality of free-operant avoidance conditioning to human behavior, *Psychological Bulletin*, 96, 247–272.

Hineline, P.N. (1981). The several roles of stimuli in negative reinforcement. In P. Harzem and M.D. Zeiler (eds), *Advances in Analysis of Behaviour: Vol. 2. Predictability, Correlation, and Contiguity*, New York: Wiley, pp. 203–246.

Holland, J.G. (1958). Human vigilance, *Science*, 128, 61–67.

Kaufman, A., Baron, A., and Kopp, R.E. (1966). Some effects of instructions on human operant behavior, *Psychonomic Monograph Supplements*, 1, 243–250.

Kling, J.W., and Schrier, A.M. (1971). Positive reinforcement. In J.W. Kling and A.L. Riggs (eds), *Experimental Psychology* (3rd edn), New York: Holt, Rinehart, & Winston, pp. 615–702.

Kodera, T.L., and Rilling, M. (1976). Procedural antecedents of behavioral contrast: A re-examination of errorless learning, *Journal of the Experimental Analysis of Behavior*, 25, 27–42.

Lindsley, O.R. (1956). Operant conditioning methods applied to research in chronic schizophrenia, *Psychiatric Research Reports*, 5, 118–139.

Lippman, L.G., and Meyer, M.E. (1967). Fixed-interval performance as related to instructions and to subjects' verbalizations of the contingency, *Psychonomic Science*, 8, 135–136.

Lowe, C.F. (1979). Determinants of human operant behavior. In M.D. Zeiler and P. Harzem (eds), *Advances in Analysis of Behaviour: Vol. 1. Reinforcement and the Organization of Behaviour*, New York: Wiley, pp. 159–192.

Lowe, C.F. (1983). Radical behaviorism and human psychology. In G.C.L. Davey (ed), *Animal Models of Human Behavior*, Chichester, England: Wiley, pp. 71–93.

Lowe, C.F. (1984). The flight from human behavior, *Behavioral and Brain Sciences*, 7, 562–563.

Lowe, C.F., Beasty, A., and Bentall, R.P. (1983). The role of verbal behavior in human learning: Infant performance on fixed-interval schedules, *Journal of the Experimental Analysis of Behavior*, 39, 157–164.

Lowe, C.F., and Harzem, P. (1977). Species differences in temporal control of behavior, *Journal of the Experimental Analysis of Behavior*, 28, 189–201.

Lowe, C.F., and Horne, P.J. (1985). On the generality of behavioral principles: Human choice and the matching law. In C.F. Lowe, M. Richelle, D.E. Blackman, and C.M. Bradshaw (eds), *Behaviour Analysis and Contemporary Psychology*, London: Erlbaum, pp. 97–115.

Mackintosh, N.J. (1974). *The Psychology of Animal Learning*, London: Academic Press.

Matthews, B.A., Catania, A.C., and Shimoff, E. (1985). Effects of uninstructed verbal behavior on nonverbal responding: Contingency descriptions versus performance descriptions, *Journal of the Experimental Analysis of Behavior*, 43, 155–164.

Matthews, B.A., Shimoff, E., Catania, A.C., and Sagvolden, T. (1977). Uninstructed human responding: Sensitivity to ratio and interval schedules, *Journal of the Experimental Analysis of Behavior*, 27, 453–467.

Mazur, J.E. (1983). Steady-state performance on fixed-, mixed-, and random-ratio schedules, *Journal of the Experimental Analysis of Behavior*, 39, 293–307.

McSweeney, F.K. (1983). Positive behavioral contrast when pigeons press treadles during multiple schedules, *Journal of the Experimental Analysis of Behavior*, 39, 149–156.

Page, S., and Neuringer, A. (1985). Variability is an operant, *Journal of Experimental Psychology: Animal Behavior Processes*, 11, 429–452.

Pear, J.J., and Wilkie, D.M. (1981). Contrast and induction in rats on multiple schedules, *Journal of the Experimental Analysis of Behavior*, **15**, 289–296.

Perone, M. (1985). On the impact of human operant research: Asymmetrical patterns of cross-citation between human and nonhuman research, *The Behavior Analyst*, **8**, 185–189.

Perone, M., and Baron, A. (1983). Can reinforcement by information be reconciled with a Pavlovian account of conditioned reinforcement? *Behavioral and Brain Sciences*, **6**, 713–714.

Perone, M., and Galizio, M. (1987). Variable-interval schedules of timeout from avoidance, *Journal of the Experimental Analysis of Behavior*, **47**, 97–113.

Poppen, R. (1982). The fixed-interval scallop in human affairs, *The Behavior Analyst*, **5**, 127–136.

Powell, R. W. (1968). The effect of small sequential changes in fixed-ratio size upon the post-reinforcement pause, *Journal of the Experimental Analysis of Behavior*, **11**, 589–593.

Rachlin, H. (1980). *Behaviorism in Everyday Life*, Englewood Cliffs, NJ: Prentice-Hall.

Reynolds, G. S. (1975). *A Primer of Operant Conditioning* (rev. edn), Glenview, Ill: Scott, Foresman, & Company.

Rosenfeld, H. M., and Baer, D. M. (1970). Unbiased and unnoticed verbal conditioning: The double-agent robot procedure, *Journal of the Experimental Analysis of Behavior*, **14**, 99–105.

Schneider, B. A. (1969). A two-state analysis of fixed-interval responding in the pigeon, *Journal of the Experimental Analysis of Behavior*, **12**, 677–687.

Schwartz, B. (1982). Failure to produce response variability with reinforcement, *Journal of the Experimental Analysis of Behavior*, **37**, 171–181.

Schwartz, B., and Gamzu, E. (1977). Pavlovian control of operant behavior. In W. K. Honig and J. E. R. Staddon (eds), *Handbook of Operant Behavior*, Englewood Cliffs, NJ: Prentice-Hall, pp. 53–97.

Schwartz, B., Schuldenfrei, R., and Lacey, H. (1978). Operant psychology as factory psychology, *Behaviorism*, **6**, 229–254.

Shimoff, E. (1984). Post-session questionnaires, *Experimental Analysis of Human Behavior Bulletin*, **2**, 1.

Shull, R. L. (1979). The postreinforcement pause: Some implications for the correlational law of effect. In M. D. Zeiler and P. Harzem (eds), *Advances in Analysis of Behavior: Vol. 1. Reinforcement and the Organization of Behavior*, New York: Wiley, pp. 193–221.

Sidman, M. (1953). Avoidance conditioning with brief shock and no exteroceptive warning signal, *Science*, **118**, 157–158.

Sidman, M. (1960). *Tactics of Scientific Research*, New York: Basic Books.

Sidman, M., and Tailby, W. (1982). Conditional discrimination vs. matching to sample: An expansion of the testing paradigm, *Journal of the Experimental Analysis of Behavior*, **37**, 5–22.

Sidman, M., Rauzin, R., Lazar, R., Cunningham, S., Tailby, W., and Carrigan, P. (1982). A search for symmetry in the conditional discriminations of rhesus monkeys, baboons, and children, *Journal of the Experimental Analysis of Behavior*, **37**, 23–44.

Skinner, B. F. (1953). *Science and Human Behavior*, New York: Macmillan.

Skinner, B. F. (1957). *Verbal Behavior*, Englewood Cliffs, NJ: Prentice-Hall.

Skinner, B. F. (1963). Operant behavior, *American Psychologist*, **18**, 503–515.

Skinner, B. F. (1969a). *Contingencies of Reinforcement*, New York: Appleton-Century-Crofts.

Skinner, B. F. (1969b). The experimental analysis of behavior. In B. F. Skinner (ed),

Cumulative Record, (3rd edn), pp. 125–157. (Original work published 1957.) New York: Appleton-Century-Crofts.

Skinner, B. F. (1984). Coming to terms with private events, *Behavioral and Brain Sciences*, 7, 572–581.

Spielberger, C. D., and DeNike, L. D. (1966). Descriptive behaviorism versus cognitive theory in verbal conditioning experiments, *Psychological Review*, 73, 306–326.

Takahashi, M., and Iwamoto, T. (1986). Human concurrent performances: The effects of experience, instructions, and schedule-correlated stimuli, *Journal of the Experimental Analysis of Behavior*, 45, 257–267.

Terrace, H. S. (1963). Discrimination learning with and without 'errors', *Journal of the Experimental Analysis of Behavior*, 6, 1–27.

Terrace, H. S. (1966). Behavioral contrast and the peak shift: Effects of extended discrimination training, *Journal of the Experimental Analysis of Behavior*, 9, 613–617.

Thoresen, C. E., and Mahoney, M. J. (1974). *Behavioral Self-Control*, New York: Holt, Rinehart, & Winston.

Vaughan, M. E. (1985). Repeated acquisition in the analysis of rule-governed behavior, *Journal of the Experimental Analysis of Behavior*, 44, 175–184.

Wasserman, E. A., and Neunaber, D. J. (1986). College students' responding to and rating of contingency relations: The role of temporal contiguity, *Journal of the Experimental Analysis of Behavior*, 46, 15–35.

Wearden, J. H., and Shimp, C. P. (1985). Local temporal patterning of operant behavior in humans, *Journal of the Experimental Analysis of Behavior*, 44, 315–324.

Weiner, H. (1962). Some effects of response cost upon human operant behavior, *Journal of the Experimental Analysis of Behavior*, 5, 201–208.

Weiner, H. (1969). Controlling human fixed-interval performance, *Journal of the Experimental Analysis of Behavior*, 12, 349–373.

Weiner, H. (1983). Some thoughts on discrepant human–animal performances under schedules of reinforcement, *The Psychological Record*, 33, 521–532.

Zeiler, M. D. (1977). Schedules of reinforcement: The controlling variables. In W. K. Honig and J. E. R. Staddon (eds), *Handbook of Operant Behavior*, Englewood Cliffs, NJ: Prentice-Hall, pp. 201–232.

Zeiler, M. D. (1984). The sleeping giant: Reinforcement schedules, *Journal of the Experimental Analysis of Behavior*, 42, 485–493.

Zuriff, G. E. (1985). *Behaviorism: A Conceptual Reconstruction*, New York: Columbia University Press.

Human Operant Conditioning and Behavior Modification
Edited by G. Davey and C. Cullen
© 1988 John Wiley & Sons Ltd

Chapter 6

Clinical Constraints Affecting Human Conditioning

RODGER Ll. WOOD
St Andrews Hospital, Northampton

Introduction

For some time there has been an acknowledged discrepancy between conditioning *theory* and those conditioning *techniques* which are used to produce changes in human behavior (London, 1972). Davey (1981) suggests this is the reason why, when specific procedures do not work, it is more often the technique that is questioned rather than the 'theoretical underpinnings'. By the same token, one may accept that behavior modification techniques are successful at improving behavior in a number of settings while at the same time acknowledging a problem when trying to link this success (unequivocally) to the conditioning techniques explicit in such procedures.

Traditionally, the approach adopted by practitioners of behavior modification is based on the 'radical' view that all behavior can be reduced to a series of S–R associations. While it is accepted that behavior may be intelligent or adaptive it is still regarded as reflecting a process of *association*, independent of whether the method of conditioning is Pavlovian or operant. Cognitive or neuro-psychological interpretations have largely been avoided to the point where the part played by memory would be explained by persistent associations (frequent pairings of stimulus and response) while the attention process can be attributed to more or less *salient stimuli*. In this model, the individual does not execute choice, there is just a system whereby responses become more strongly associated with one stimulus configuration than another. The critical element in this conceptualization is that behavior, no matter how intelligent it may appear to be, develops according to some learned S–R association, which is dependent upon, or controlled by, stimuli that are present at the time the behavior occurs (Bolles, 1979).

Clinical observation of patients involved in behavior modification often produces an irresistible urge to interpret behavioral change in humans as something which is largely cognitive in nature. This is because in operant systems of learning, stimuli which are present at the time behavior occurs do not seem to have any direct control over the response (unlike many experimental animal studies) and simply act as signs or signals for the outcome of behavior. At most, the stimuli tell individuals what they should do, so that over time the individual comes to expect or anticipate some behavioral outcome in terms of the reward or punishment contingency that has prevailed in the past. However, this interpretation still depends on the *process of association*, so it becomes possible to consider the likely outcome of behavioral techniques, not only in terms of cognitive learning versus conditioning, but also in terms of what factors may prevent effective associations being formed and thereby interfere with the efficiency of response acquisition.

Certain clinical conditions place constraints on associative learning and human behavior. These include:

1. *Neuropsychologically mediated disorders of behavior*:
   (a) Disorders of attention which can interfere with the maintenance of an attentional set.
   (b) The focusing of attention in order to select environmental cues which act as antecedents in associative learning.
2. *Organically mediated disorders of behavior*:
   (a) Impulsive behaviors which occur in association with 'limbic' epilepsy.
   (b) Loss of emotional control, usually seen in association with frontal-lobe disorders.
   (c) Disorders of insight and the awareness of environmental cues.
   (d) Disorders of drive which can occur as a consequence of diffuse cortical injury or certain psychotic disorders.
3. *Disorders of personality and motivation*:
   (a) Anhedonia and problems of reinforcement incentive.
   (b) Hysteria and avoidance reactions.

These constraints are determined by the condition of the organism (Wood and Eames, 1981) and the integrity of the reward mechanism of the brain (Olds and Milner, 1954; Eames and Wood, 1984). In some cases these constraints act as major obstacles to human conditioning procedures. They exert an effect in two main ways. On one hand, the constraints on associative learning have a direct influence on the conditioning process, because the neuropsychological systems which mediate such learning are damaged. This may mean that the antecedents or environmental cues which initiate and direct behavior are not perceived.

Alternatively (or even concurrently) the reinforcement incentive of the individual may be diminished, thus reducing habit strength and the desirability of some goal.

Constraints on behavior, on the other hand, can mean that factors which usually initiate, regulate or inhibit behavior are not instrumental in controlling the expression of the specific behavior under observation. The implication is that in certain clinical conditions specific behaviors occur, not in response to environmental contingencies, but according to factors 'internal' to the organism, e.g. paroxysmal electrical discharges, as in temporal-lobe disorders, or bizarre and sometimes aggressive behavior which is in response to some hallucinatory or delusional command.

The fact that some disorders may be 'organically mediated' does not mean that they are immune to those environmental contingencies that can be used in the process of behavioral change. However, it does mean that the conditionability of such behaviors cannot be taken for granted and that psychological techniques of behavior change may need to run parallel with pharmacological methods to obtain a successful clinical outcome.

The experience which has led to these observations has mainly been collected on a unit which specializes in the rehabilitation of adults who have suffered a severe brain injury. Many of these individuals present major management problems because of: (1) inappropriate social behavior; (2) difficulty in controlling response to frustration; and (3) physical aggression. The illustrations given to explain the effects of different constraints on associative learning will be based mainly on such patients. However, it must be emphasized that clinical experience with other types of patients has demonstrated the generality of these constraints.

The influence of these constraints will be discussed in the context of operant conditioning procedures. Human conditioning in clinical settings uses operant learning far more than Pavlovian procedures because operant procedures are more suitable to the management of groups of patients and also because it is easier to conceptualize and manipulate a wide range of responses in natural settings, where the identification of specific eliciting stimuli is not easily achieved.

The effect of an attentional impairment on behavioral learning

One important characteristic shared by brain injured, psychotic, and mentally handicapped patients, which is capable of affecting psychological aspects of treatment, is a slow rate of learning. Wood and Eames (1981) described this as a prominent feature affecting rehabilitation in severely brain injured patients. Zeaman and House (1963) also point to the slow rate of learning in mentally handicapped patients. They suggest that the reasons for this learning difficulty cannot be attributed to a failure of instrumental learning (operant conditioning) but can be explained on the basis of attentional capabilities. They found that in a group of mentally handicapped patients the difference between fast and slow learning was not determined by the rate of improvement from trial to trial *once* learning had started, but rather in the number of trials needed *before* learning started.

In their experiments they presented subjects with two stimuli, differing on a number of dimensions (color, size, and form). The subjects were rewarded if they pointed to the stimulus defined by the experimenter as correct (e.g. blue, on one of the dimensions). They found that the normal and mentally handicapped groups did not differ in the *rate* of moving from the level of chance performance to 100 per cent correct performance. Where they differed was in the number of chance responses which occurred prior to learning. Whereas normal subjects needed few trials to start moving from chance to 100 per cent correct responses, the mentally defective subjects remained at the chance level of performance for an inordinate length of time. Once learning commenced, however, progress from the chance level of performance to criterion was at a similar rate to that made by the normals. From these results, Zeaman and House concluded that an inability to attend selectively to relevant stimulus cues was the main reason why mentally handicapped subjects show a poor overall performance on discrimination learning. The defect of learning can be regarded as secondary to a defect of attention.

Fisher and Zeaman (1973) reviewed the importance of attentional components in learning and suggest that in the Zeaman and House paradigm, learning to respond to the correct stimulus can be broken down into two processes: (1) learning to attend to the correction dimension; and (2) learning to associate the correct value of that dimension with a reward. If the subject fails to attend to the correct dimension, performance over a series of trials would be expected to remain at chance levels. However, once a degree of selective attention had been established, learning could occur, determined by the subject's ability to associate a particular response with a specific stimulus cue.

The type of learning that is required during the process of rehabilitation includes the acquisition of appropriate social behavior for independent daily living. Bandura (1969) and Kanfer and Phillips (1970) have emphasized that a major factor in social learning is the ability to *discriminate* relevant cues within the environment. This means that stimulus–response contiguity must be accompanied by discriminative observations to produce learning. For this to occur, it is necessary that the stimulus variables required for learning are identifiable to the learners. There have, of course, been studies on normal individuals indicating learning without 'awareness' of a stimulus cue (Hefferline Keenan, and Harford, 1959; Keehn, 1967). Bandura, on the other hand, argues that 'simply exposing an individual to repeated stimuli does not guarantee that he will select from the total stimulus complex those cues necessary for learning to occur'. This also appears to be true for subjects with congenital brain damage, as Cullen (1978) has shown.

The poor discrimination learning shown by the mentally handicapped, and its apparent relationship to attention, may have major implications for understanding the influence of attentional deficits on social learning and human conditioning. This may be of particular importance for behavior change and social learning following brain injury, especially if we consider the ample clinical and experimental evidence for defects of attention occurring after head injury (Meyer, 1904; Conkey, 1938; Goldstein, 1939; Dencker and Lofving, 1958; Miller, 1970; Gronwall and Sampson, 1974; Miller and Cruzat, 1981).

To determine the influence of attention on conditioning in the severely brain injured, Wood (1985) conducted a study which compared the discrimination learning ability of three groups of subjects: (1) severely brain injured, N = 38; (2) high grade mental handicap, N = 20; and (3) normal controls, N = 20. Comparisons of discrimination learning ability as well as differences in the speed of learning were obtained. The relationship of intelligence and attentional performance to discrimination learning ability was also examined.

All subjects were initially tested on a simple discrimination learning task. This required them to select one of two stimuli, differing both in color (yellow and blue) and shape (square, triangle, and circle). Each stimulus shape was approximately one and a half inches in diameter. They were placed three inches apart in front of the subject. The correct stimulus was a square, meaning that the subject had to ignore color (the irrelevant dimension) and the position of the square in relation to shape.

Color and position were randomized over 100 trials. The 100 presentations took approximately 30 minutes, which was considered (from pilot studies) to be the limit of endurance for the two patient groups. Subjects were told whether their response was correct or not, the two patient groups receiving praise (social reinforcement) for accuracy. Learning was regarded as reaching criterion when 20 successive discriminations were made (see Oakley, 1983, for a similar procedure).

Following discrimination learning, all subjects were given two tests which measured the ability to focus and sustain attention and to select relevant information from a stimulus set. The first test involved auditory attention. The subject was presented with a series of random digits at a rate of one per second while, at random intervals, a target (a series of three odd digits) was presented. The subject had to identify the presence of each target by simultaneously tapping the table. The task lasted 30 minutes and 50 target sets were included. The score was the total number of misses and false-positive responses. The second task employed a six-choice visual reaction time, with the stimulus lights being randomized over the array. One hundred reaction times were recorded and the inter-stimulus interval was 4 seconds.

In addition to the attention measures, a measure of intelligence was obtained by pro-rating a 'short version' of the Wechsler Adult Intelligence Scale. This was composed of verbal measures of vocabulary and similarity, and performance measures of block design and picture arrangement.

The performance of the three groups showed an inevitable difference in learning ability—principally between the normal control group and the two patient groups. The control group reached criterion within 30 trials (allowing for the 20 consecutive correct responses needed to reach criterion), whereas neither patient group reached criterion in the 100 trials allowed.

An analysis of variance was used to calculate the difference between the three groups. This showed that although the three groups made a significant improvement (responses above chance level) over the 100 trials ($F = 23.024$; df = $9/675$; $p < 0.01$), the learning ability of the three groups was significantly different ($F = 6.707$; df = $2/75$; $p < 0.01$). A *post hoc* analysis of the difference between means, using the Tukey test, showed that the difference between groups 1 and 2 is not significant (mean diff. = 0.35; critical difference [C.diff] = 0.389, whereas both groups 1 and 2 are significantly different from group 3 (mean diff. = 1.02 and 1.37; p. < 0.05 respectively).

This latter result was predicted, but the lack of a between-groups effect for the two patient groups suggests that if intelligence was an important factor in discrimination learning then the brain injured group (mean IQ = 87) should perform at an intermediate level in terms of learning ability—better than the mental handicap group (mean IQ = 62) and worse than the normal controls (mean IQ = 99). These data, however, show that although there is a 25 IQ point difference betwen the two patient groups ($F = 106.273$; df = $2/73$; $p < 0.0001$), the brain injury group are statistically no different to the mentally handicapped on simple discrimination learning. Even when a within-group analysis was made, comparing the IQ levels of the learners with the nonlearners of the brain injury group, there was no evidence of a significant difference ($t = 1.655$, df = 32).

Ability on the two attention measures seems to have been a much more important factor determining discrimination learning. Both measures showed a significant between-group difference (CRT: $F = 6.059$, df=$2/65$, $p<0.05$; aud. attention: $F= 32.968$, df = $2/66$, $p<0.001$). *Post hoc* comparisons show the main difference to be in the performance of the brain injury group. Comparisons between the other groups failed to produce any significant differences, with group 2 continuing to be intermediate in terms of attentional ability. A within-group analysis of the brain injury group indicates that performance on the attention tasks was related to discrimination learning ability. Both tasks record a significant difference (CRT: $t= 3.257$, df= 25, $p<0.01$; aud. attention: $t = 3.652$, df=34, $p<0.01$) between learners and nonlearners on the discrimination task in the direction of good attentional performance being compatible with good discrimination learning.

If we exclude from the analysis the data of those subjects in groups 1 and 2 who failed to reach criterion (N = 12 and 6 respectively), we find that only five subjects in group 1 and one in group 2 failed to learn by the 50th trial. A second repeated measures ANOVA on these 50 trials showed that the between-group difference is eliminated ($F = 2.628$; df = $2/55$). However, when the number of correct responses made by each group before reaching criterion was analyzed, a significant between-groups difference was revealed (F = 4.972; df = 2/56; p < 0.01). This suggests that although all the remaining subjects are capable of learning, their *speed* of learning remains quite different. A *post hoc* comparison of means showed the significant difference to be between the brain injured and normal controls (mean diff. = 9.21; C diff. = 7.89; p < 0.05). No difference was found between the patient groups (mean diff. = 5.07; C diff. = 7.89). On this occasion, however, the mentally handicapped group (intermediate in terms of ability) did not significantly differ from the normal controls (mean diff. = 4.14, C diff. = 7.89). This suggests that slow response acquisition is more characteristic of the brain injured than mildly retarded individuals.

Differences in the speed of learning can be illustrated by converting the data into backward learning curves (Hayes, 1953). This technique has been used by Zeaman and House (1963), and more recently Oakley (1983), to demonstrate group curves in the vicinity of criterion.

Figure 6.1 shows the data for all subjects (learners and nonlearners). The number of responses at chance level for the two patient groups can be contrasted against the rapid progress towards criterion made by the controls. This can be seen more clearly in Figure 6.2, which presents the data of the learners from the three groups as separate graphs (group 1, N = 24; group 2, N = 14; group 3, N = 20).

The learning curves for each of the three groups show the difference in the number of trials at chance level. They also show the number of subjects responding at chance level before the sudden and rapid increase in accurate discriminations from chance level to the 100 per cent correct. It is interesting to note that, proportionally, there are more brain injured patients making up the tail of their learning curve than is the case with the mental handicap group.

The results of this study suggest that problems of attention may interfere with associative learning and, subsequently, affect aspects of social learning and brain injury rehabilitation. The data would appear to support the Zeaman and House (1963) hypothesis that discrimination learning, of the kind measured here, relies more on attentional factors than on intellectual ones. The measures of intelligence suggest that if IQ were a relevant factor, the discrimination learning of the mentally handicapped group would be far inferior to the other two groups, in particular the normal controls. The fact that they fall intermediate between the normal and brain injured groups, and not significantly different in their rate of learning from either, suggests that some other variable, such as attention, has a far greater influence in associative learning than might previously have been expected.

The importance of attention in behavioral (as opposed to cognitive) learning has been commented on in the recent animal literature (Oakley, 1979, 1981). However, this is not a recent observation. As early as 1935, Lashley described neocortically damaged animals as deficient in attention but recognized that, at

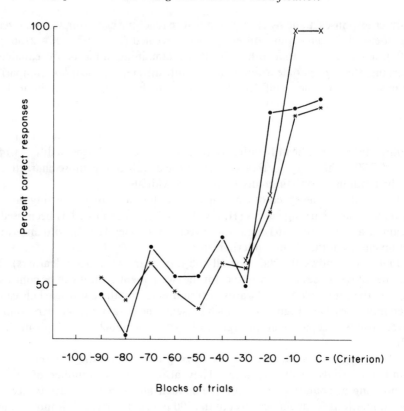

Figure 6.1   Backward learning curve showing the performance of *all*
subjects on a color/form discrimination learning task

the time, this was an unpopular and unacceptable explanation for observed
responses. Oakley (1983) argued that the associative mechanisms underlying
operant learning operate independently of cognitive processes following severe
brain injury. He bases this statement on the results of clinical studies which
show success in behavior modification programs, irrespective of the level of
residual cognitive ability in the patients involved and also on his own experience
of operant conditioning with decorticate rats. Oakley found that such animals
were still able to learn, in some cases as well as normal animals, but that
attention was an important factor in such learning. The speed at which
decorticate animals learned was improved if, first of all, they were trained in
procedures which helped them focus attention on relevant cues. This is an
important consideration when preparing many brain injured adults for behavior
modification.

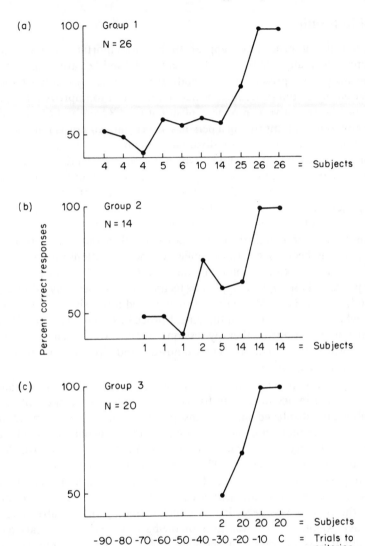

Figure 6.2   Discrimination learning in brain injured retarded and normal subjects. (a) Group 1. Backward learning curve showing percent correct responses in a group of 26 severely brain injured patients on a color/form discrimination task. (b) Group 2. Backward learning curve for fourteen mentally handicapped. (c) Group 3. Backward learning curve for 20 normal adult humans

Attention training

Attention training procedures appear to be an important prerequisite for conditioning in many brain injured patients. Methods of training and their rationale have been presented by Wood (1984b). These are often based on computer administered procedures which are assumed to improve information processing (the cognitive component of attention). Recently, however, it has become apparent that improving a person's 'processing ability' is not enough. It may be more important for an individual to maintain an attentional set (the behavioral component of attention which requires a degree of effort and motivation) in order to make use of any improvement in information processing capability. One of the most simple yet efficient ways of helping a patient maintain a level of concentration is to apply an operant conditioning procedure using a schedule of fixed-interval reinforcement.

Increasing attention span through contingent token reinforcement is not a new idea. It has been successfully applied to increase attention and decrease overactivity in hyperkinetic children (Staats, 1968). Until recently there have been no published attempts to apply this technique to the severely brain injured (see Wood, 1984a). The effectiveness of such procedures is shown in Figures 6.3 and 6.4, which use a positive reinforcement procedure to increase the duration of directed attention during therapy sessions. Tokens were given to the patient for directing attention (maintaining head posture and directing gaze toward the therapist during therapy sessions.

The two patients studied were similar in many respects. Both had sustained a very severe brain injury in road traffic accidents four years earlier. Both were distractable and displayed short spans of attention. Their cooperation in therapy was minimal, not because they were beligerent or deliberately uncooperative but because they were continually attending to things which were not part of the therapy activity. This made any kind of treatment program difficult to pursue and was a source of continuous irritation to the therapy staff.

A time-sampling procedure was used to record behavior. At two-minute intervals the patient was recorded as either attending or not attending to a therapy task. Reinforcement was given on the basis of this simple binary record. If the patient was attending at the end of the two-minute interval, token reinforcement was delivered. Non-attending resulted in no token payment. A maximum of 15 tokens could be earned during a 30-minute session. The patient had to earn more than a designated number of tokens in order to exchange them for a reward (sweets, cigarette, etc.) immediately after the therapy session. The number was fixed by the staff (without the patient's knowledge) and organized according to a sliding scale, which increased as the patient's behavior improved.

Figure 6.3 shows the response of patient 1. Two therapy activities (speech and occupational therapy) were incorporated into this training procedure. An improvement in behavior was observed which was somewhat variable. The

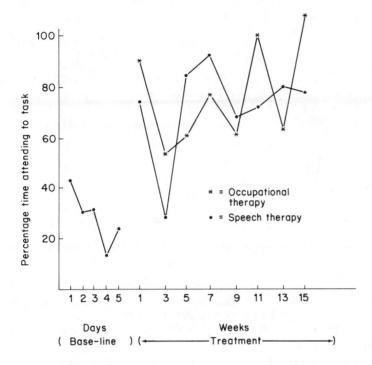

Figure 6.3 Improvement in attending to therapy activities in speech and occupational therapy during a program of contingent positive reinforcement delivered on the basis of two-minute time-samples of behavior

trends toward improvement were not significant, either for the speech (F = 1.096; df = 1/6) or occupational therapy activities (F = 1.434; df = 1/6). However, there was a significant improvement when the treatment phases were compared to baseline using a Student's t analysis: Occupational therapy (t = 6.54; df = 7; p < 0.001); speech therapy (t = 6.12; df = 7; p < 0.001).

Figure 6.4 (patient 2) attempts to record a treatment effect (applying the same procedure as above) by using an A–B–A–B design. The baseline (A) phases were recorded for one hour each day over two five-day intervals. The recordings took place in different therapy activities during that time. It was not possible to restrict these measures to one particular therapy activity because the treatment timetable varied from day to day and week to week. Length of treatment in each phase was determined by other rehabilitation needs and, in particular, the need to avoid carrying out such training procedures at times when medication, which might alter arousal (and probably attention), was being used.

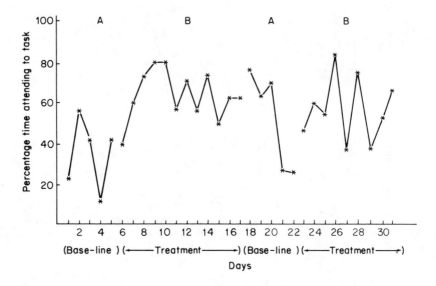

Figure 6.4   An–B–A–B design confirming a treatment effect using the same reinforcement procedure as Figure 6.3

A non-significant trend was recorded for the first treatment phase (F = 1.98; df = 1/7) although there was a significant improvement compared to baseline (t = 8.11; df = 7; p < 0.001). On completion of the first treatment phase the behavior recording shows a rapid return to pre-treatment levels (the second A phase). The reintroduction of the reinforcement procedure produced another nonsignificant trend towards improvement (F = 1.22; df = 1/7) but again the treatment phase was significantly better than the first baseline (t = 3.57; df = 7; p < 0.01), suggesting that the changes in attention are due to a treatment effect, rather than some artifact of the general rehabilitation program.

Organically determined disorders of behavior

There are two broad categories of behavior which can be considered to be organically mediated. One category contains behaviors which are produced or elicited as a direct result of some neurological event. These can be designated *positive behavior disorders*. The other category consists of behavior which is characterized by a general lack of responsiveness on the part of an individual, referred to as *negative behavior disorders* (Wood, 1984a). These are not mutually exclusive categories of behavior; a patient may present any combination of behaviors from either category, whether at the same or different times. Their significance as separate categories lies in the fact that the behaviors result from essentially different types of neurological (or neuropsychological) processes and produce quite different patterns of behavior.

Positive behavior disorders

Positive disorders include behaviors which actively interfere with the social acceptability of the patient. They are largely antisocial behaviors and can, in turn, be divided into at least two major subcategories, aggression and disinhibition.

Aggression

Systematic observations of aggressive behavior in a clinical setting (Wood and Eames 1981; Wood 1984a) suggest that aggressive responses can occur independently of the environmental contingencies that commonly act as antecedents of such behavior. This type of aggression also seems isolated from any form of positive reinforcement, however vicarious. Some support for this is derived from the fact that many individual show genuine remorse for their actions, over which they feel they have little or no control. These observations would predict that some kinds of aggression will respond less well to operant methods of control. It does not mean that reinforcement contingencies will have no controlling influence over such behavior.

The implication is that some aggressive behavior is mediated by internal mechanisms which are wholly or partly independent of those environmental stimuli normally assumed to elicit behavior. If this is the case it may be necessary to make inferences about the neurological (or, more strictly, neuropsychological) systems that mediate or promote aggressive acts when planning conditioning programs to eliminate such behavior. It would also be wise to take the opportunity to observe the effects of medication as an alternative or complementary form of clinical management. A behavior modification system allows us to hold the environment relatively constant, therefore we should be able to determine the effectiveness of drugs used either independently or in association with behavior modification techniques.

'Limbic epilepsy' and aggression One particular form of aggressive behavior occurs as a result of damage to the medial structures of the temporal lobes. The behavior pattern involves a fairly sudden, often unprovoked, outburst of aggressive behavior, quite primitive in nature and poorly organized. It is usually directed at the nearest object or person and has a very destructive quality, smashing furniture, spitting, scratching or other frenzied activity. It is usually short-lived and often followed by a feeling of remorse. Awareness of such behavior varies. Some patients have total amnesia for this aggressive period while others have a vague idea of what they are doing while they are doing it.

The remainder have full awareness of their behavior, yet little or no control over their actions. This form of aggression is often due to an epileptic abnormality, referred to either as temporal-lobe epilepsy or limbic epilepsy. In epileptic conditions behavior is particularly purposeless and unmotivated, in contrast to learned or gratuitous forms of aggressive behavior, usually characterized by its purposeful and directed quality.

Epileptic aggression does not necessarily occur in isolation. It can be precipitated by specific stresses which overwhelm the individual's tolerance or capacity for self-control. From clinical observation, Eames (personal communication) reports that many cases of aggression are restricted to the family environment or close friends, implying that the constraint affects modulatory mechanisms or the inhibitory control of behavior. If this is the case we can assume that environmental factors still influence this type of behavior but are blunted by some form of neuropathology. This would explain the more frequent expression of the behavior in conditions which do not demand the same social awareness and control as would be the case at work or in less familiar social surroundings.

Evidence to support the claim that organically mediated behavior is difficult to condition can be seen by referring to Figures 6.5 and 6.6. These show the lack of a conditioned response when epileptic aggression results in a negative punishment contingency. This involved placing the patient in a locked time-out room for five minutes (or multiples of five minutes if the behavior continues to be disturbed), plus a loss of tokens which results in a temporary withdrawal of privileges. The graphs compare the procedure under two conditions: (1) when conditioning was used in isolation; and (2) when an appropriate anticonvulsant (carbamazepine) was added to control the focal epileptic disturbance presumed to underlie this type of aggressive disorder. It is clear that behavior change occurred only when medication, which controlled the neurological antecedent of the behavior, was introduced. Another example of neurologically mediated behavior is given in Figure 6.7. In this case, the aggression was originally presumed to be a form of temporal-lobe epilepsy and treatment was given which incorporated the time-out room procedure described above, plus carbamazepine. This only achieved a temporary reduction in aggression, and it was ten weeks before staff realized that the patient suffered from intermittent hydrocephalus as well. This meant that intracranial pressure increased to the point where it precipitated an aggressive outburst. At the ten-week stage of management a ventriculo-peritoneal shunt was inserted to control intracranial pressure and this led to an immediate and permanent reduction in the aggressive behavior.

Frontal-lobe injury and reduced emotional control The difficulty that many patients have inhibiting an emotional response is frequently seen after head injury and often enough in relative isolation from other problems to suggest it may be founded in some focal cerebral pathology (Lishman, 1978). Individuals

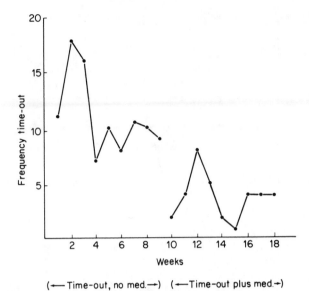

Figure 6.5   Neurologically mediated aggression. Comparison of nine weeks of time-out for aggressive behavior to nine weeks using time-out + carbamazepine

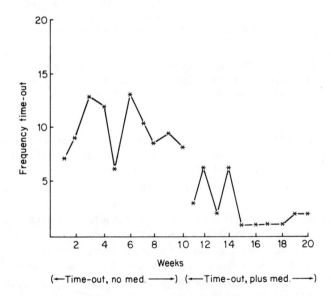

Figure 6.6   Neurologically mediated behavior. Comparison of ten weeks of time-out for aggressive behavior to ten weeks using time-out + carbamazepine

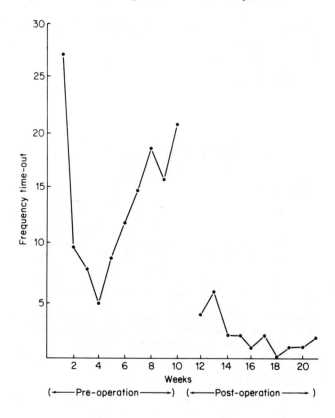

Figure 6.7   Neurologically mediated behavior. The effect of
post-traumatic hydrocephalus on the incidence of aggressive
outbursts during a time-out program for aggression

with this difficulty typically over-react to minor provocation or frustration. The
characteristic pattern is for an emotional response to escalate, quite out of
proportion to the eliciting event. Once this emotional outburst starts, the person
seems to have little or no control over its course.

The escalation of behavior probably occurs because the inhibitory or
modulatory function of the frontal lobes has been affected by the injury. Some
support for this idea is derived from the fact that aggression, in association with
frontal injury, often occurs as part of a more global 'frontal-lobe syndrome'
which includes a blunting of social skills and a tendency toward coarse behavior.
Evidence from experimental psychology has been provided by Teuber (1964)
and Luria (1966), showing that frontal injuries disturb the 'modulating' function
which the frontal lobes exert on complex sets of signals that regulate our
interaction with the environment. Luria extrapolates from his neuro-

psychological studies to suggest that, in everyday life, such deficits could have a profound effect on many aspects of behavior.

Teuber's studies suggest that patients with frontal-lobe injury are able to anticipate the future course of events but lack the ability to picture themselves as a potential agent in relation to those events. Luria's studies suggest that frontal-lobe damage has a disruptive effect on the programming of complicated activities, with the result that many aspects of behavior are not properly regulated. His experiments revealed not only a disturbed regulation of activity but disordered feedback and the failure to correct errors. He extrapolates from such neuropsychological studies to state that, in everyday life, such deficits could impair many aspects of behavior. The disordered regulation of activity may underlie the apathy and aspontaneity of many patients with frontal-lobe lesions, while impaired feedback may account for their lack of critical attitude toward the results of their own behavior and their failure to modify it.

It is at the clinical level of observation that the neurological basis of such behavior is made clear. Clinicians who have been able to study focal damage to the frontal areas, for example after missile wounds (Jarvie, 1954; Lishman, 1968), agree that the behavior occurs either independently of, or in disproportion to, any eliciting environmental event. Bond (1984) summarized this point of view well: 'The problem for the patient is that he has minimum or no control over sudden shifts of mood, basic drives and behavior, and such control as he has, if any, is usually short lived.' The lack of control associated with this type of behavior probably accounts for the difficulty experienced when operant techniques are used to modify the response.

Figures 6.8 and 6.9 illustrate this by giving examples of fairly typical extinction curves seen during negative punishment procedures for the treatment of frontal-lobe-mediated behavior. These programs employed the time-out room procedure described above (patients being placed in a time-out room for intervals of five minutes following disruptive, abusive, sexual or aggressive behavior). The main points to be noted are: (1) the loss of (learned) control after the first drop in aggression; (2) the variable response rate until the behavior finally comes under control; and (3) the length of time taken to achieve control. These features can be compared with similar programs for aggressive behavior in other patients who had sustained very severe brain injury but without primary frontal-lobe damage (Figures 6.10 and 6.11).

Disinhibited behaviors

The one characteristic common to all 'frontal' brain damage is the presence of a certain degree of disinhibition. Bond (1984) considered that disinhibition presents a variety of behavior patterns, with varying disturbance of intellect. Behavior is characterized by coarse social comments and over-familiarity. Disinhibited patients often make gross errors of judgment, are tactless, over-

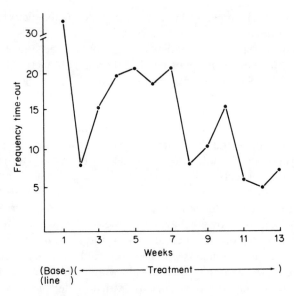

Figure 6.8 Neurologically mediated behavior. Response to a time-out program for verbal abuse by a patient with severe frontal-lobe damage

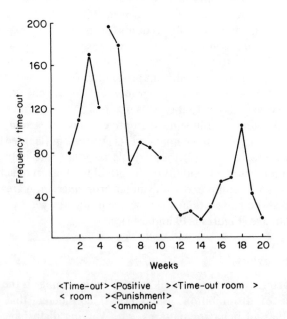

Figure 6.9 The response of negative and positive punishment programs used to control verbal outbursts in a patient with frontal-lobe injury

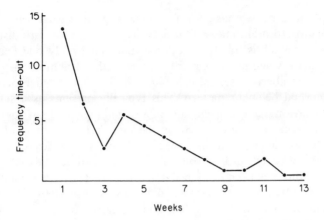

Figure 6.10 Time-out room program to control an
aggressive response to frustration

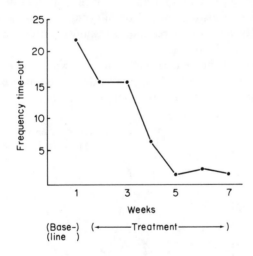

Figure 6.11 A time-out room program to
control learned aggressive behavior

talkative, and show a marked indifference to the effect their behavior has on
others. One of the more common and socially important aspects of disinhibition
is inappropriate sexual behavior. This varies considerably in its nature and
intensity, from tactless attempts at intimacy, conversation loaded with sexual
innuendo, inappropriate touching, lewd remarks and, in more severe cases,
indecent exposure and public masturbation.

There appear to be two basic forms of inappropriate sexual behavior which occur in relation to brain injury. One is typically associated with disinhibition because the behavior is not specifically sexual, but simply one feature of a behavior pattern which includes many aspects of the 'disinhibition syndrome'. Another kind of aberrant sexual behavior can be isolated which occurs in an otherwise normal behavior pattern. This typically presents as a sudden and impulsive behavior change, specifically of a sexual type, and has some form of epileptic involvement, characterized by the fact that the inter-ictal (between seizure) behavior appears normal in every way. This tends to distinguish 'temporal lobe' sexual disorders from a frontal lobe disorder. Sexuality which is epileptic in nature has been described as producing: (1) hypersexual episodes (Blumer, 1970); (2) transvestism (Davis and Morganstern, 1960); (3) exhibition-ism (Hooshmand and Brawley, 1970); and (4) fetishism (Mitchell, Falconer, and Hill, 1954). Powell (1981) discusses these conditions, concluding that they are probably due to the influence of an epileptic discharge upon the limbic structures linked to the temporal lobe, such as the amygdala and hypothalamus.

The response of such behavior to various types of negative punishment contingency varies, depending upon the extent of neurological involvement. If the sexual behavior forms part of a 'frontal syndrome' and a general state of disinhibition which includes aggression, a response pattern may be obtained similar to that seen in Figure 6.12.

Here, a time-out room procedure has been used which tries to improve the process of association between an unpleasant consequence (the imposed isolation of a time-out room) and the inappropriate behavior. In this respect,

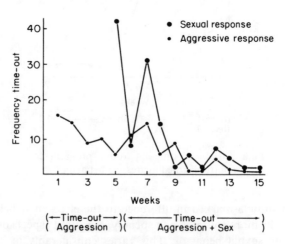

Figure 6.12 Control of inappropriate sexual behavior. The significant trend for aggression is reversed when, at week 6, the program is expanded to include time-out for sexual behavior

reinforcement can act as an aid to discrimination learning which, because of reduced insight, is often seriously impaired in such individuals. This particular time-out room procedure requires a member of staff to present a 'cue word' or a 'signal phrase' to the patient immediately before he or she enters the time-out room. This word/phrase is directly related to the inappropriate behavior, for example in the case of a patient making an embarrassing sexual comment the phrase may be 'sexual talk'.

The graph in Figure 6.12 shows the response of a 20-year-old male who was placed under a compulsory treatment order of the Mental Health Act because of sexually unacceptable behavior. This developed after he sustained a head injury, with subsequent intracranial hemorrhage into the frontal lobes. He lacked insight into his behavior and usually failed to realize why he was being placed in the time-out room following inappropriate 'touching' of female patients. This led to the development of a 'cue-word' technique to help the patient focus attention on the unacceptable behavior, thereby facilitating the process of association.

Initially, the program was directed at his aggressive behavior, using the time-out procedure described above. The frequency of this behavior progressively diminished over the first five weeks of treatment. Sexual behavior was then included as part of the time-out room program. This appeared to precipitate a 'relapse' in his aggressive behavior and reduced the extent to which this former behavior had been brought under control, reflecting the poor control and length of time needed to consolidate behavioral change in this type of behavior problem. The increased pressure and frustration caused by bringing both aggression and sexual behavior under the same reinforcement contingency resulted in a very unsettled period where neither behavior showed a trend toward extinction. This pattern continued for four weeks and it was not until the ninth week that behavior control began to be consolidated.

Insight Disorders of insight almost inevitably involve some disorder of attention, awareness or consciousness (Eames and Wood, 1985). Its inclusion in this section on organically mediated disorders of behavior rather than the section on attention, is merited by the fact that some lack of insight is an almost inevitable consequence of severe frontal-lobe injury and usually accompanies disinhibited behavior. Bond (1984) goes as far as stating that the degree of a behavior disorder and cognitive impairment are closely related to the extent to which insight has been lost. This phenomenon appears to underlie, and in part explain, the curious anomalies of reasoning and judgment which become particularly marked when matters bearing on the patient's own conception of his circumstances are discussed. In such cases the patient may utterly reject evidence which is at variance with his own beliefs and will attempt to reconcile any inconsistencies stemming from this in the most facile and implausible manner (Whitty and Zangwill, 1977).

The brain damage which produces loss of insight must also affect our sense of 'other-awareness' because individuals appear impervious to both the response of other people to their behavior as well as the nature of their behavior. An example to illustrate this is given in Figure 6.13 showing the lack of success of a selective reinforcement program modeled on the one described by Ayllon and Michael (1959) to reinforce appropriate (nonpsychotic) speech in a schizophrenic girl. When used for exactly the same purpose (except the speech was repetitive conversational themes—see Wood and Eames, 1981) with a woman suffering from frontal damage and some loss of insight, the reinforcement contingency had no effect. This is presumably because the reinforcement procedure—positive social reinforcement for appropriate speech and negative punishment (ignoring her) when she produced inappropriate speech—was not *perceived* by the patient as a reinforcement contingency. Unless the information processing system of the brain can respond to changes in environmental cues, reinforcement cannot be effective.

Negative behavior disorders

Blunted affect, psychomotor retardation, and loss of initiative are commonly observed behavioral characteristics of many psychiatric conditions and frequently follow brain injury. The patient is often unwilling (or unable) to initiate behavior and can display great difficulty trying to perform the most routine activity of ordinary life. Behaviors that were once automatic can now

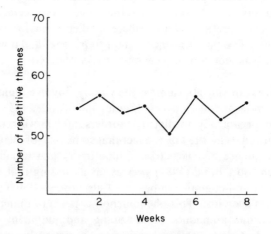

Figure 6.13   The influence of severe frontal-lobe injury on a TOOTS program for inappropriate conversation. The patient was unable to recognize the cues used in this type of reinforcement contingency

only be carried out with a great deal of effort. The main feature of such behavior is a loss of drive. This manifests itself as a state of apathy and lethargy. It is what the patient *won't* do that becomes the problem, rather than the inappropriate or threatening behaviors which characterize the positive disorders referred to above. It should be emphasized that the clinical condition *imposes* this behavioral state, over which the patient has little or no control. This can pose very difficult problems for rehabilitation and independent living.

The extent to which purposeful or goal-directed behavior is disrupted usually depends upon the extent to which the mechanisms of arousal are involved in the drive disorder. Arousal is generally used to describe a state of an organism on some continuum, such as sleep–wakefulness. Frequently, this continuum is referred to as *consciousness*. Basically, there are two major aspects of conscious behavior: *content of awareness* and *arousal*. Content represents the sum of cognitive and affective mental functions. Obviously we can never gain direct access to this area but it is reasonable to infer that brain injury or some psychotic process can interfere with cognition and, therefore, the interpretive functions of the brain. This must also reduce, to some extent, the person's awareness of himself and his environment. Arousal on the other hand is a physiological construct, more closely related, behaviorally at least, to alertness. While it is evident that cognition cannot occur without some degree of arousal, evidence presented by Plum and Posner (1980) shows that arousal in itself does not guarantee cognition.

Behavior disorders which occur in the context of drive or arousal problems vary. Patients may show a reduction in their level of activity, described by Lishman (1978) as aspontaneity, slowing, and inertia. Speech may be slow and . labored and there occur periods during which mental and physical activity virtually come to a halt. Luria (1973) remarks that the problems arising from small lesions become particularly manifest when patients are expected to complete relatively difficult behavioral tasks that require the formation of a plan. When large lesions of the frontal lobes are involved, anergy is usually the main behavioral characteristic. This results in a major breakdown of purposeful and directed behavior. Luria describes an extreme form of arousal disorder which he attributes to 'massive damage of the frontal lobes', called the apathico-akinetic-abulic syndrome. In this state, patients lie completely passive, express no wishes or desires and make no requests, to the point that not even a state of hunger may rouse them to take necessary action—'even if hungry and thirsty they make no active attempt to take food or drink placed on their table'.

Luria emphasized that although there is a breakdown of organized behavior in such cases, patients are visibily aware of any change taking place in their environment, such as 'someone coming in, a squeaking of a door, or coughing by a patient in the next bed'. These events often arouse 'a strong orientation reflex, most frequently manifested as movement of the eyes or sometimes turning the head toward the stimulus'. Such patients still find it almost impossible to perform a definite action in response to a command. However, they will perform various automatic actions, such as pulling at a sheet, picking up and dropping, in a repetitive manner, articles with their fingers, or repeatedly scraping the wall near their bed. Often they appear involuntarily attracted by a small spot on the wall and will make attempts to clean it, not stopping even when asked. In contrast, they rarely take an examiner's hand when instructed, but if the examiner puts his own hand into theirs they are likely to grasp it, often without being able to terminate this grasping reflex.

Another well-known arousal disorder, linked to brain stem damage, is akinetic mutism. This was described by Cairns (1952) and Plum and Posner (1980) as a state in which the patient lies immobile and mute, but appears fully alert, although he or she exhibits virtually no spontaneous movement or speech. However, such patients do follow moving objects and keep their eyes vigilant. Lishman draws attention to the fact that although such patients are apparently in an akinetic state of muteness and immobility, they can, if forcibly roused, prove to be normally orientated. Luria describes patients lying passively, frequently in a drowsy or an 'oneroid' state, making no effort to follow instructions which involve displaying a motor or verbal response, but still showing a tendency to respond spontaneously to 'irrelevant stimuli'. Cairns, in his original description of akinetic mutism (Cairns *et al.*, 1941), also supports the apparent existence of an orientating response by stating that 'when following the movement of objects, they may be diverted by sound'.

Sokolov (1963) regarded arousal as being important for maintaining in the individual the readiness to respond. It is linked by Posner (1975) to a state of 'consciousness' which 'affects general receptivity to input of information'. This makes arousal an important factor determining drive, even suggesting that an individual's given level of drive is dependent upon the variable state of arousal. This relationship would appear to re-state the 'Yerkes–Dodson' law which postulates an inverted U-shaped function of efficiency depending on the degree of arousal of the organism. Thus, not only alertness but also the appropriateness of behavior will depend upon the individual being optimally aroused.

Arousal disorders can interfere with both the reception of information and the capacity of the system to generate effort or drive. In conditions we describe as *amotivational*, the information appears to be processed and analyzed correctly but without the 'evaluation criteria' which determine the pleasurability of that information and, therefore, the purposeful effort or drive necessary for a response to occur. In the normal individual, drive strength has been related to a state of *need* on the one hand and the attractiveness of the stimulus (reward) on the other (Hull, 1943). The behavioral distinction between motivation and drive is that drive does not contribute to the *direction* of behavior. If we interpret drive as a physiological component (arousal), any increase in this state will lead to agitated and non-directed behavior. This is because the individual feels more alert and energetic yet may not have any idea how to direct such energy or have the ability to put together a sequence of behaviors to achieve some goal. This has been observed in many of our patients who have received stimulant medication in an attempt to increase their level of activity. From a clinical point of view the procedure can be counter-therapeutic because it *creates* treatment problems instead of alleviating them.

If however, the individual is able to attribute an increase in drive to a state of need, the behavior can become goal directed. In negative behavior disorders, this appears to be precisely where the breakdown between drive and motivation occurs. A frontal-lobe patient, for example is often incapable of consistently directing behavior toward a goal. This was first alluded to by Lashley (1938). He separated motivation from drive by stating that motivation could not involve 'general drive'. He also appears to emphasize the cognitive aspect of motivation by linking it to emotion, which 'evaluates' the content of information being processed by the brain before behavior is emitted. Gray (1972) also appears to make this distinction. He distinguishes drive from emotion and motivation. Drive is described as an 'internal process, affected by changes internal to the organism'. Emotions were also regarded as internal states but these are mainly related to changes taking place external to the organism.

Disorders of personality and motivation

Motivation is a concept which has largely been regarded as irrelevant in the process of conditioning. This may be true for animal studies but Wood and Eames (1981) and Eames and Wood (1985) have taken quite a different view where human conditioning is concerned. The essence of their argument is that, in humans, motivation may not promote learning as such but a lack of motivation can profoundly interfere with learning, especially in the case of brain damaged individuals. Belmont (1969) also described how brain injured patients are particularly vulnerable to motivational deficits, in ways which impede the progress of rehabilitation.

Some individuals appear to have an anhedonic personality (Meehl, 1962) and lack the ability to experience pleasure. Hedonic responsiveness may, therefore, be an important characteristic determining motivation. Unless an individual is able to identify a particular experience as pleasant and therefore desirable, or, at the very least, has the ability to acknowledge other experiences as unpleasant or painful and seeks to avoid or escape them, any kind of associational learning, relying as it does on positive or negative reinforcement contingencies, will be compromised. Anhedonia may limit an individual's potential for treatment because the presence of a 'neutral' attitude reduces motivation and the effort needed to overcome obstacles which stand in the way of recovery. Attempts to change behavior by the application of selective rewards are undermined because such patients fail to perceive any value or sense of pleasure in the reward.

Kraepelin (1913), Bleuler (1911), and later Bleuler (1950) viewed the loss of the experience of pleasure as one aspect leading to deterioration during a schizophrenic illness. Rado (1956, 1962) gave anhedonia a more central role in the development of schizophrenia, suggesting that it was genetically transmitted and may be present both in 'overt schizophrenics' and also in 'schizo-types' who do not actually undergo a psychotic breakdown. Anhedonia is presumed to prevent the development of a normal and healthy sexual interest, reduces zest for life, impairs the ability to relate with other people, and weakens the feelings for joy, affection, love, pride, and self-respect. In addition to its role in schizophrenia Klein (1974) and Klein, Gittleman, and Quitkin (1980) considered anhedonia to have a central role in endogenous depression. Klein hypothesized that anhedonic depression was associated with a more favorable response to tricyclic antidepressant medication than was likely from other depressions.

A neurological and biological basis for anhedonia has been postulated more recently. Meehl (1962, 1973) integrated anhedonia into a theory of neurological dysfunction and schizophrenia. He proposed that a defect in the organizing action of pleasure or reward means that the integrating mechanisms of behavior, and hence the organization and control of goal directed thinking and behavior, become impaired. Wise and Stein (1973) take up this argument, suggesting that anhedonia is the result of a genetic defect, produced by excessive 6-hydroxydopamine, which damages the brain's reward mechanism. Wise (1980), in a review of the evidence, concludes that there is a motivational role for dopamine in behavior. This involves the signaling of *reward*, 'which is translated into the *hedonic* messages we receive as pleasure or euphoria'. He described the dopamine synapse as the site in the brain where 'the hedonic impact of the sensory message is first associated with the sense impressions of the external events which constitute *natural rewards*'.

Wood and Eames (1981) discuss hedonic responsiveness in the context of motivational problems following severe brain injury. Clinically, they associate this concept with hysterical or dissociative states which radically interfere with motivation. Because of the nature of traumatic brain damage, anhedonia may result from damage to the frontal regions or their connections with limbic structures. This receives some support from Wise (1980) who thought that the anatomically critical 'dopamine synapse' was in the frontal cortex. He felt that damage to this area can 'leave patients in contact with the sensory dimensions but not the hedonic impact of their environment'. Further reference was made to this problem in Wood (1984a). Here it is associated with an intrinsic lack of drive which limits the incentive value of many reinforcers used to increase effort and motivation in a behavior management approach to head injury rehabilitation. The existence of anhedonia means that a person's thoughts, feelings, and actions are not directed by a unifying concept, purpose or goal. This in turn affects motivation and progress toward recovery through rehabilitation.

The association of anhedonia with a dissociative disorder of behavior depends to what extent the person is aware of the behavior he or she presents. This involves concepts such as 'alteration of consciousness'. In the case of dissociation, there appears to be a blocking of awareness preventing an individual from understanding the intentionality of behavior. Dissociative mechanisms are able, quite selectively, to block awareness of restricted sets of information. At one level, for example the instance of paralysis and loss of sensation from an entire limb makes it possible to interpret the clinical state in terms of a disturbance of selective attention, an interpretation based on the concept of central sensory gating mechanisms (Ludwig, 1972).

Silverman (1968) offered an alternative paradigm for the study of 'altered states' based on observations of different attentional styles in normal and psychiatric populations. Silverman identifies three major attentional styles described as intensive, extensive, and selectiveness. *Intensive* refers primarily to responses which individuals make on a stimulus continuum ranging from very weak to very strong. *Extensivity* refers to the degree to which elements in a stimulus field are sampled. *Selectivity* of attention or 'field articulation' refers to responses which determine which elements in a stimulus field exert a dominant influence on the perceiver.

Silverman describes a paradox in sensory functioning, most evident in individuals with altered states of consciousness, which may explain certain dissociative characteristics. On the one hand, they have lowered sensory thresholds and over-react to subliminal or marginal stimulation; on the other hand, they are under-responsive to high intensity stimulation and therefore have higher pain tolerance. Pavlov (1957) explained such a paradox using the concept of 'protective inhibition'. This means that individuals who are hypersensitive to low intensity sensory stimulation, respond more strongly to it and require a compensatory adjustment (under-responsiveness) to protect themselves from strong stimulation.

Scanning of information may be different in ordinary states from altered states of consciousness. Individuals with altered consciousness *appear* preoccupied with a very narrow circle of ideas and are limited in the range of environmental stimuli to which they respond. Evidence from studies on normals and schizophrenics using measures of size constancy (Gardner and Long, 1962; Silverman, 1968) showed the latter to underestimate consistently. The differences in size or other 'constancies' (when they occurred) depended on the number of cues available when making the judgment. It might be reasonable to expect the same underestimation from the brain injured because of the evidence suggesting their poor use of environmental cues. This may reduce motivation because of the patient's inability to perceive the true value of the reward.

Silverman stated that conditions of extensiveness and selectiveness result in people thinking in very subjective and egocentric ways. The conditions are concerned with ways in which the individual is prepared to *see* the world. This suggests that there may be certain parallels between the perceptions and behavior of hysterics following a major emotional crisis (such as would be experienced in severe head injury) and the theory of learned helplessness which results in depression and passivity (Seligman, 1975).

Operant conditioning often confronts the individual with the consequences of behavior. This could possibly precipitate an avoidance reaction, even a conscious decision not to cooperate, producing behavior similar to that traditionally described as 'hysterical' but which, in a conditioning paradigm, could be described as 'learned helplessness' (Seligman, 1975). Seligman presents a theory of helplessness which claims that exposure to uncontrollable events leads to a state of passive acceptance or withdrawal. In such conditions, animals learn that making a response to change their circumstances is ineffective. He used laboratory data from animal studies to show that *uncontrollability reduces motivation*, decreasing responses during instrumental learning, undermining the ability to perceive success, which finally heightens emotionality.

The effect of non-contingent electric shock or unavoidable aversive conditioning and its relationship to what was described as 'experimental neurosis' has been known for some time (see Stroebel, 1969, for a review). This model does not offer a complete explanation of dissociative behavior because it does not account for the fact that many of the 'hysterics' observed in our rehabilitation program, were not in any way passive in their response. Rather, they appear to make considerable effort to retain the *status quo*, thereby working in direct opposition to the rehabilitation team who are trying to facilitate recovery. In this respect their behavior is characterized by active game playing, approximate answers (Ganser Syndrome), and definite conversion symptoms, all preventing the achievement of greater independence. Other patients react in a way which is far more characteristic of the Seligman model. When faced with a distressing situation over which they perceive they have no control, many develop a resigned, passive acceptance of their situation. This 'blocks' their ability to recognize response alternatives, focusing their efforts on maintaining their current state, probably as a compensation strategy because they perceive more reward in being a total invalid than in being a functioning 'cripple'!

The incentive to initiate voluntary responses (make an effort!) could, on the one hand, be impaired by alterations in hedonic responsiveness and, on the other, by the experience during early recovery, that effort of any kind is not going to result in significant or rapid progress towards a 'cure'. This results in a feeling of loss of control over the situation. The patient feels that outcome is independent of effort, diminishing the probability for any kind of constructive response. Maier and Testa (1975) showed that loss of control, in itself, was not sufficient to produce a state of helplessness in rats. More important was whether a rat could see the relationship between response and outcome. If such perceptions were possible then animals learned the response without difficulty. If, however, they were unable to see response–outcome contingencies, learning ability was reduced, making any response less likely. Their conclusion was that a *cognitive deficit* of some kind increases the potential for learned helplessness in the rat (and probably for other organisms). Experiencing a lack of control results in increased emotionality. Experimental studies show that there is a time factor involved in producing helplessness after uncontrollable shock. If animals are returned to the shuttle box more than 72 hours after first experiencing uncontrollable shock and are then given a normal shock-avoidance test, they will learn normally; before 72 hours they are still likely to show helplessness. If, however, the animals are subjected to many uncontrollable experiences over time, the duration of helplessness is significantly increased and interference with response initiation may become permanent (Seligman, Klein, and Miller 1974).

Summary

Many behavioral problems presented by psychiatric patients or the brain injured can be controlled or eliminated and need not prevent them from being accepted back into society. Behavior modification techniques offer an important service as part of a complete program of mental health care. This is because they help patients to learn more constructive and adaptive forms of social behavior, whereas drug treatment alone is often restricted to controlling the illness process. There are several ways in which brain injury or psychiatric illness can affect neurological modulatory mechanisms, cognition or 'personality', interfering with associative learning. To obtain a successful outcome from behavioral methods, these 'constraints' must be considered. In human conditioning it is important to establish not just that behavioral methods work, but circumstances where they are likely to fail or, at least, require either a longer time-frame to achieve success or assistance from drugs. By examining the problem of clinical constraints on human conditioning we are reminded that cognitive and other factors 'internal' to the organism can affect the process of conditioning and that these must be considered if successful behavioral change is to be obtained.

References

Ayllon, T., and Michael, J. (1959). The psychiatric nurse as behavioral engineer, *Journal of the Experimental Analysis of Behavior*, **2**, 323–334.
Bandura, A. (1969). *Principles of Behavior Modification*, New York: Holt, Rinehart and Winston.
Belmont, I. (1969). Effects of cerebral damage on motivation in rehabilitation, *Archives of Physical and Medical Rehabilitation*, **50**, 507–511.
Bleuler, F. (1911). *Dementia Praecox or the Group of Schizophrenias*, New York: University Press.
Bleuler, F. (1950). Psychiatry of cerebral diseases, *British Medical Journal*, **2**, 1233.
Blumer, D. (1970). Hypersexual episodes in temporal lobe epilepsy, *American Journal of Psychiatry*, **126**, 1099–1106.

Bolles, R. C. (1979). *Learning Theory* (2nd edn), New York: Holt, Rinehart and Winston.
Bond, M. R. (1984). The psychiatry of closed head injury. In D. N. Brooks (ed), *Closed Head Injury: Psychological, Social and Family Consequences*, Oxford University Press.
Cairns, H. (1952). Disturbances of consciousness with lesions of the brain and diencephalon, *Brain*, **75**, 109-146.
Cairns, H., Oldfield, R. C., Pennybacker, J. B., and Whitteridge, D. (1941). Akinetic mutism with an epidermoid cyst of the third ventricle, *Brain*, **64**, 273-290.
Conkey, R. C. (1938). Psychological changes associated with head injuries, *Archives of Psychology*, **33**, 1-62.
Cullen, C. N. (1978). Errorless learning with the retarded, *Journal of the Practical Approach to Developmental Handicap*, **2**, 21-24.
Davey, G. (1981). *Animal Learning and Conditioning*, London: Macmillan.
Davis, B. M., and Morgenstern, F. S. (1960). A case of cysticercosis, temporal lobe epilepsy, and transvestism, *Journal of Neurology, Neurosurgery, and Psychiatry*, **23**, 247-250.
Dencker, S. J., and Lofving, B. (1958). A psychometric study of identical twins discordant for closed head injury, *Acta Psychiatrica Neurologica Scandinavica*, **33**, Suppl. 122.
Eames, P. G., and Wood, R. Ll. (1984). Consciousness in the brain damaged adult. In M. Stevens (ed), *Clinical Aspects of Consciousness*, Oxford: Oxford University Press.
Fisher, M. A., and Zeaman, D. (1973). An attention–retention theory of retardate discrimination learning. In N. R. Ellis (ed), *International Review of Research in Mental Retardation*, New York: Academic Press.
Gardner, G. E., and Long, P. (1962). Control, defence and centration effect: A study of scanning behavior, *British Journal of Psychiatry*, **53**, 129-140.
Goldstein, K. (1939). *The Organism*, New York: American Book Co.
Gray, J. A. (1972). The psychophysiological nature of introversion–extraversion: A modification of Eysenck's theory. In V. D. Nebylitsyn and J. A. Gray (eds), *Biological Bases of Individual Behaviour*, London: Academic Press.
Gronwall, D. M. A., and Sampson, H. (1974). *The Psychological Effects of Concussion*, Auckland University Press.
Hayes, K. J. (1953). The backward curve: A method for the study of learning, *Psychological Review*, **60**, 269-75.
Hefferline, R. F., Keenan, B., and Harford, R. A. (1959). Escape and avoidance conditioning in human subjects without their observation of the response, *Science*, **130**, 1338-1339.
Hooshmand, H., and Brawley, B. W. (1970). Temporal lobe seizures and exhibitionism, *Neurology*, **9**, 1119-1124.
Hull, C. L. (1943). *Principles of Behavior*, New York: Appleton.
Jarvie, N. F. (1954). Frontal lobe wounds causing disinhibition: A study of six cases, *Journal of Neurology, Neurosurgery, and Psychiatry*, **17**, 14-32.
Kanfer, F. H., and Phillips, J. S. (1970). *Learning Foundations of Behavior Therapy*, New York: Wiley.
Keehn, J. D. (1967). Experimental studies of 'the unconsciousness': Operant conditioning of unconscious eye-blinking, *Behavior Therapy*, **5**, 95-102.
Klein, D. (1974). Endomorphic depression, *Archives of General Psychiatry*, **31**, 447-454.
Klein, D., Gittelman, R., and Quitkin, F. (1980). *Diagnosis and Drug Treatment of Psychiatric Disorders*, Baltimore: Williams and Wilkins.
Kraepelin, E. (1913). *Dementia Praecox and Paraphrenia*, Edinburgh: E. and S. Livingstone.

Lashley, K. S. (1935). Studies of cerebral function in learning. The behavior of the rat in latch-box situations, *Comparative Psychological Monographs*, **11**, 5–40.

Lashley, K. S. (1938). Factors limiting recovery after central nervous system lesions, *Journal of Neurology and Mental Disorders*, **88**, 733–755.

Lishman, W. A. (1968). Brain damage in relation to psychiatric disability after head injury, *British Journal of Psychiatry*, **116**, 373–410.

Lishman, W. A. (1978). *Organic Psychiatry*, Oxford: Blackwell.

London, P. (1972). The end of ideology in behavior modification, *Annals of Psychology*, **27**, 913–920.

Ludwig, A. M. (1972). Hysteria: A neurobiological theory, *Archives of General Psychiatry*, **27**, 771–777.

Luria, A. R. (1966). *Higher Cortical Functions in Man*, London: Tavistock.

Luria, A. R. (1973). *The Working Brain*, London: Allen Lane, The Penguin Press.

Maier, S. F., and Testa, T. (1974). Failure to learn to escape by rats previously exposed to inescapable shock is partly produced by associative interference, *Journal of Comparative and Physiological Psychology*, 88, 554–564.

Meehl, P. (1962). Schizotaxia, schizotopy, schizophrenia, *American Psychologist*, **17**, 827–838.

Meehl, P. (1973). *Psychodiagnosis: Selected Papers*, Minneapolis: University of Minnesota Press.

Meyer, A. (1904). The anatomical facts and clinical varieties of traumatic insanity, *American Journal of Insanity*, **60**, 373–441.

Miller, E. (1970). Simple and choice reaction time following severe head injury, *Cortex*, **6**, 121–127.

Miller, E., and Cruzat, A. (1981). A note on the effects of irrelevant information on task performance after mild and severe head injury, *British Journal of Social and Clinical Psychology*, **20**, 69–70.

Mitchell, W., Falconer, M. A., and Hill, D. (1954). Epilepsy with fetishism relieved by temporal lobectomy, *Lancet*, **2**, 626–636.

Oakley, D. A. (1979). Learning with food reward and shock avoidance in neodecorticate rats, *Experimental Neurology*, **63**, 627–642.

Oakley, D. A. (1981). Performance of de-corticated rats in a two-choice visual discrimination apparatus, *Behavior and Brain Research*, **3**, 55–69.

Oakley, D. A. (1983). Learning capacity outside neocortex in animals and man. In G. Davey (ed), *Animal Models of Human Behavior*, London: Wiley.

Olds, J., and Milner, P. (1954). Positive reinforcement produced by electrical stimulation of septal area and other regions of rat brain, *Journal of Comparative and Physiological Psychology*, **47**, 419–427.

Pavlov, I. (1957). General types of animal and human higher nervous activity. In *Experimental Psychology and Other Essays*, New York: Philosophical Libraries.

Plum, F., and Posner, J. B. (1980). *The Diagnosis of Stupor and Coma*, Philadelphia: F. A. Davis.

Posner, M. I. (1975). The psychobiology of attention. In M. S. Gazzaniga and C. Blakemore (eds), *Handbook of Psychobiology*, New York: Academic Press, pp. 441–480.

Powell, G. E. (1981). *Brain Function Therapy*, London: Gower.

Rado, S. (1956). *Psychoanalysis of Behavior: Collected Papers*, New York: Grune and Stratton.

Rado, S. (1962). *Psychoanalysis of Behavior*: Vol. 2, New York: Grune and Stratton.

Seligman, M. E. P. (1975). *Helplessness: On Depression, Development and Death*, San Francisco: W. H. Freeman.

Seligman, M. E. P., Klein, D. C., and Miller, W. (1974). Depression. In H. Leitenberg (ed), *Handbook of Behavior Therapy*, Englewood Cliffs, NJ: Prentice-Hall.

Silverman, J. (1968). The problem of attention in research and theory in schizophrenia, *Psychological Review,* 71, 352–379.

Sokolov, Y. N. (1963). *Perception and the Conditioned Reflex*, New York: Macmillan.

Staats, A. W. (1968). *Learning, Language and Cognition*, New York: Holt, Rinehart and Winston.

Stroebel, C. F. (1969). Biological rhythm correlates of disturbed behaviour in the rhesus monkey, *Bibliotheca Primatologica*, 9, 91–105.

Teuber, H. L. (1964). The riddle of frontal lobe function in man. In J. M. Warren and U. Akert (eds), *The Frontal Granular Cortex and Behavior*, New York: McGraw-Hill, pp. 410–444.

Whitty, C. W. M., and Zangwill, O. L. (1977). *Amnesia: Clinical, Psychological and Medicolegal Aspects*, London: Butterworths.

Wise, R. A. (1980). The dopamine synapse and the notion of 'pleasure centres'. In *Trends in Neurosciences*, 22, 91–95.

Wise, R. A., and Stein, L. (1973). Dopamine b-hydroxylase deficits in the brains of schizophrenic patients, *Science*, 181, 344–347.

Wood, R. Ll. (1984a). Behavior disorders following severe brain injury: Their presentation and management. In D. N. Brooks (ed.), *Closed Head Injury: Psychological, Social, and Family Consequences*, Oxford: Oxford University Press, pp. 195–219.

Wood, R. Ll. (1984b). The management of attention disorders following severe brain injury. In B. A. Wilson and N. Moffat (eds), *Clinical Management of Memory Problems*, London: Croom Helm, pp. 148–170.

Wood, R. Ll. (1985). *A Behavioral Approach to the Rehabilitation of Severe Brain Injury*, Unpublished Ph. D. thesis. Leicester University.

Wood, R. Ll. and Eames, P. G. (1981). Behaviour modification in the rehabilitation of brain injury. In G. Davey (ed), *Applications of Conditioning Theory*, New York: Methuen, pp. 81–101.

Zeaman, D., and House, B. J. (1963). The role of attention in retardate discrimination learning. In N. R. Ellis (ed), *Handbook of Mental Deficiency*, New York: McGraw-Hill.

Human Operant Conditioning and Behavior Modification
Edited by G. Davey and C. Cullen
Published by John Wiley & Sons Ltd

Chapter 7

The Token Economy: A Decade Later*

ALAN E. KAZDIN
Western Psychiatric Institute and Clinic, University of Pittsburgh School of
Medicine

In the middle and late 1960s, the token economy emerged as a promising intervention in treatment, rehabilitation, and educational settings. Major impetus for the development of the token economy was the pioneering work of Ayllon and Azrin (1965, 1968b) who developed and evaluated a program for chronic psychiatric patients. Several other programs emerged for psychiatric patients, delinquents, the mentally retarded, children in classroom settings, and other populations (see Kazdin and Bootzin, 1972; O'Leary and Drabman, 1971). Since the late 1960s and early 1970s, the breadth of applications has increased greatly. Within areas that already received attention, programs extended to diverse subpopulations. For example, within psychiatric populations, the token economy has been extended beyond chronic psychiatric patients to patients with acute disorders (Gershone *et al.*, 1977), organic brain syndromes (Murphy, 1976), psychosomatic disorders (Wooley, Blackwell, and Winget, 1978), and autistic children (Hung, 1977), to mention a few. The token economy has also been extended to new areas of research such as behavioral medicine (Ferguson and Taylor, 1980), behavioral ecology (Lloyd, 1980), community psychology (Glenwick and Jason, 1980), and geriatric psychology (Hussain, 1981).

Within the last decade, extension of the token economy has also been evident in the number of studies comparing the token economy with other interventions (e.g. Bushell, 1978; Paul and Lentz, 1977; Stoffelmayr, Faulkner, and Mitchell,

---

1979) and examining the potential benefits of combining a token economy with other procedures (e.g. Greenberg *et al.*, 1975; McCreadie, Main, and Dunlop, 1978). The most dramatic extension has been the application of token economies on a much larger scale than had been the case previously. Perhaps the largest extension has been the Behavior Analysis Follow Through project for disadvantaged elementary school children (Bushell, 1978). The Follow Through program was developed to follow up the gains provided by an earlier intervention program, Head Start. However, the Follow Through project was designed specifically to test different models of intervention including behavior analysis. The program has been implemented in kindergarten through third grades and has included over 7000 children in approximately 300 classrooms and 15 separate cities throughout the United States. Other programs, even though smaller in scale, still represent major extensions of the token economy in educational settings by encompassing entire schools (e.g. Boegli and Wasik, 1978) and classes from several different schools (Rollins *et al.*, 1974; Thompson *et al.*, 1974).

A decade ago, Bootzin and I evaluated the token economy research and identified several issues and obstacles (Kazdin and Bootzin, 1972). These included (1) maintaining behavior and ensuring generalization; (2) training staff to implement the token economy; (3) increasing client responsiveness to the contingencies; and (4) overcoming client resistance to the program. Since the earlier review, the literature has proliferated and considerable progress has been made. An evaluative review of research is now well beyond the confines of a chapter or journal article (see Kazdin, 1977; O'Leary, 1978). This chapter discusses issues raised by token economies in light of applications over the last decade. The purpose is to examine progress on salient issues identified previously as in need of research and significant issues that have recently emerged.

Progress on salient issues

Enhancing effects of token economies

From the inception of the token economy, reports indicated that some number of participants may not respond to the contingencies. For example, Ayllon and Azrin (1965), reported that 18 per cent ($n = 8$) of chronic psychiatric patients were generally unaffected by the procedures. Since this report, other programs with psychiatric patients, the mentally retarded, delinquents, and children in school settings have continued to report a small but consistent percentage of participants who fail to respond (see Hemsley, 1978; Kazdin, in press).

Research has examined whether particular client variables contribute to responsiveness to the token economy, but the evidence has been inconsistent.

For example, in token economies for psychiatric patients, degree of patient withdrawal, social isolation, and length of hospitalization are negatively correlated with improvement in some studies (Ayllon and Azrin, 1968b; Fullerton, Cayner, and McLaughlin-Reidel, 1978) but unrelated or even positively correlated with reponsiveness in other studies (Allen and Magaro, 1971; Mishara, 1978). Similarly, conflicting evidence within and across target populations has been provided for the relations between age, IQ, and gender and responsiveness to the contingenices (e.g. Fullerton *et al.*, 1978; Mishara, 1978; Moran, Kass, and Munz, 1977).

A significant development over the last decade is recognition that lack of responsiveness to the token economy may reflect more on the program than on clients who fail to respond. Lack of responsiveness usually refers to the failure of some clients to respond to a set of contingencies that is standardized across all clients. The model on which the token economy is based does not propose that identical contingencies will be universally effective. Considerable evidence exists that persons who do not respond initially to a program may readily respond when some alterations are made in the contingencies.

Several procedures can be used to improve responsiveness. Perhaps the most obvious one is to vary the magnitude of reinforcement. Increases in the number of tokens or the value of back-up events enhance clinet responsiveness (e.g. Ayllon *et al.*, 1979; Bassett, Blanchard, and Koshland, 1975; Rickard *et al.*, 1973). Another procedure for improving responsiveness is reinforcer sampling (Ayllon and Azrin, 1968b) which consists of exposing the client to a portion of the back-up reinforcer such as a part of a meal or a few minutes of special social activity. By sampling a portion of the reinforcers on a noncontingent basis, the client is more likely to purchase the event with tokens and consequently to engage in token-earning behaviors (e.g. Ayllon and Azrin, 1968a, 1968b; Curran, Lentz, and Paul, 1973). Allowing clients to preselect the back-up reinforcers for which they will be working (Kazdin and Geesey, 1980) or to earn their way off the token system for meeting high criterion levels of performance (Kazdin and Mascitelli, 1980) can also enhance responsiveness.

Viewing a token program from the standpoint of an economic system has also identified variables that can be manipulated to enhance performance (see Fisher *et al.*, 1978). Essentially, token-earning behaviors represent work output; the token represents income or wages; back-up events represent expenditures; and accumulated tokens can be viewed as savings. Altering the amount of savings clients are permitted to accrue, increasing the costs of back-up events (inflation), increasing the consumption of back-up events by expanding the range of attractiveness of these events, stimulating spending through occasional sales, or placing expiration dates on the tokens to promote spending, have increased responsiveness (e.g. Hung, 1977; Milby *et al.*, 1977; Winkler, 1973).

Responsiveness to token reinforcement can also be enhanced by involving peers in the program. For example, permitting peers to share the consequences earned by a particular individual has increased responsiveness of that individual to the contingencies (Feingold and Migler, 1972; Kazdin and Geesey, 1977). Using a peer–manager system of reinforcement in which a member of the peer group administers and withdraws tokens can enhance performance as well (Phillips *et al.*, 1973). Finally, the addition of response cost or fines can improve client performance in a token economy (e.g. McLaughlin and Malaby, 1977; Walker, Hops, and Fiegenbaum, 1976).

When persons initially fail to respond, performance can be improved by different program variations. The fact that many variables may overcome initial unresponsiveness to the program does not mean that token economies do not 'fail' to produce the desired changes or ultimate treatment goals. However, the lack of responsiveness often can be readily controverted with changes in the contingencies.

Staff training

Training the staff who administer a token economy has been recognized as an important issue throughout the history of reinforcement programs. In recent years, the importance has been substantiated by demonstrations showing that the extent to which staff administer the contingencies as intended (e.g. Jackson, 1976; McLaughlin *et al.*, in press) is directly related to client behavior change. In the last decade a great deal has been learned about alternative training procedures and their effects.

Several methods have been evaluated and include variations of instructions, modeling and role playing, informative feedback, and direct reinforcement using approval and attention, special privileges or 'tokens' (e.g. money, trading stamps). Procedures that combine several techniques and include direct reinforcement of staff performance have been especially effective, as demonstrated in school, hospital, and community settings (see Bernstein, 1982; Kazdin, 1980b).

An important issue is integrating staff training within the constraints of existing settings. For example, many potent reinforcers that might be used to develop staff performance are usually unavailable for contingent application. The problem has been circumvented in many programs by creative use of such reinforcers as certificates of recognition and approval from supervisors (Burg, Reid, and Lattimore, 1979; Busheil, 1978; Montegar *et al.*, 1977). A remaining issue is determining whether training can be effectively carried out on a large scale. Promising results along these lines have already emerged in the context of training teachers to administer the Behavior Analysis Follow Through project (see Bushell, 1978; Jackson, 1976).

Over the last decade, additional information has emerged related to staff training and administration of token economies. Several studies have shown that staff behaviors often change as a function of administering a program. Across different populations and settings, the administration of a token economy has been associated with staff increases in nonverbal and verbal approval for appropriate client behavior and decreases in disapproval and withdrawal of privileges for inappropriate behavior (Boegli and Wasik, 1978; Breyer and Allen, 1975; Trudel *et al.*, 1974). Also, staff working on a token economy ward show more positive attitudes toward patients and toward treatment than staff working on wards with conventional treatments (McReynolds and Coleman, 1982; Milby, Pendergrass, Clarke, 1975). The social climate or ward atmosphere of token economy wards has also been found to be more positive on several dimensions (e.g. spontaneity, affiliation) than on conventional wards (Wilkinson and Repucci, 1973). Thus, the token economy appears to produce changes in several facets of the social climate in which staff and clients function.

Client resistance to the program

Client resistance refers to expressions of anger, complaints, and rule breaking in response to the token economy. Although only a few reports indicate client resistance, adverse client reactions are important to discuss for different reasons. First, a token economy restructures much of the reward system in most settings. Consequently, the potential for coercion is great. Conceivably, basic amenities previously provided noncontingently might be withheld until they are earned. Second, legal issues raised by token economies in institutional settings have received increased attention in the United States (Martin, 1975). In specifying patient rights and basic conditions of institutional care, the courts have influenced the types of events that can be used as reinforcers (see Kazdin, 1977).

Within legal guidelines, it is still possible to design programs that clients find aversive. For example, Biklen (1976) reported a token economy in a psychiatric hospital that led to patient anger at the system and rejection of the tokens. Objections were based in part on the contingent delivery of many rewards that were given freely before the program. Also, many of the reinforced activities seem puerile (e.g. games, crafts, childlike parties). Similarly, Zeldow (1976) noted adverse reactions of psychiatric patients to a system that seemed to consist of inflexible rules that staff rigidly imposed and the lack of patient recourse for complaints about the system.

Consideration of client reactions to token economies is critical because, in institutional settings, residents usually have the legal right to withdraw from the program. Because the courts have been involved increasingly in the rights of involuntarily confined persons, programs have changed. The onus has fallen on investigators to identify and to provide reinforcers that are ordinarily unavailable in the setting rather than to use basic amenities to which persons are entitled by right (Wexler, 1973). With creative selection of incentives, client resistance is less likely to result because existing reinforcers from the setting are not lost. Indeed, because of the diverse rewards that are added to the program, there is an incentive for participants to remain willingly in the program. Also, in some programs, clients are explicitly given the option of leaving the program without penalty (e.g. Ayllon *et al.*, 1979). Other procedures can be used to overcome client resistance and to help protect client rights. For example, providing opportunities for clients to have input into the system such as selecting rewards or negotiating the contingencies may increase reactions to the program (see Karraker, 1977; Kazdin, 1980a). In short, several options are available to overcome client resistance.

To operationalize client resistance, an important point of departure would be to assess client reactions to the program (see Wolf, 1978). The relationship between client reactions and responsiveness to the contingencies could then be more systematically evaluated than has been the case in current research. Moreover, interventions could be designed to have impact on client evaluations of, and participation in, the program.

Long-term effects: Response maintenance and transfer to training

An issue of obvious importance in any intervention program is whether the effects are maintained after the program is terminated and continue outside of the treatment setting. These issues, referred to as response maintenance and transfer, respectively, or as generalization collectively, have been of special concern in token economy research for different reasons. First, token economies and other contingency-based programs are often evaluated in experimental designs (e.g. ABAB) where the intervention is temporarily suspended and behavior returns to or near baseline levels. Thus, even during evaluation of the program, therapeutic gains may be lost or partially lost. Second, token economies often represent environmental arrangements that depart dramatically from the usual environments to which individuals will return. Thus, little transfer of training might be expected from treatment to extratreatment settings.

In the last decade, several developments can be identified regarding maintenance and transfer of intervention effects. To begin with, many more programs are available that report follow-up data than in previous years. Also, for many programs, the follow-up date are reported after the program has been in effect for protracted periods (e.g. several months or a few years). Thus, the long-term effects of treatment have been given a better test than in demonstration projects with short intervention phases.

The results from different studies show that gains produced by token economies are not inevitably lost. For example, Paul and Lentz (1977) compared social learning, milieu therapy, and routine hospital care for the treatment of chronic psychiatric patients. The social learning program was based primarily on a token economy where patients received incentives for a variety of adaptive behaviors on the ward such as attending activities and engaging in self-care activities or social interaction. Although patients in both social learning and milieu programs improved, the social learning program was consistently more effective on measures in the hospital, discharge of patients, and status in the community from 1.5 up to 5 years after termination of the program.

In school settings, follow-up data have also indicated that intervention effects are at least partially maintained. For example, the changes in academic achievement obtained from the Behavior Analysis Follow Through program had been terminated and the children had entered classrooms in which token programs were not in effect (Bushell, 1978). Similarly, in a junior high school program for serious behavior problem adolescents, token economies led to reductions in expulsions, suspensions, and grade failure. At follow-up three to four years later, gains were still evident (Heaton, and Safer, 1982; Safer, Heaton and Parker, 1981). Adolescents who participated in the program showed higher rates of entrance into high school and school attendance, better classroom conduct, and lower rates of withdrawal from school relative to control subjects. However, by the end of senior high school, token economy and control groups showed comparable rates of school enrolment and high school graduation.

With delinquent youths, follow-up results have been obtained for the teaching-family model (based on Achievement Place) (Wolf *et al.*, 1976). The model has been extended to approximateley 150 different group homes throughout the United States and a few foreign countries (Jones, Winrott, and Howard, Note 1). (Actually, the token economy is only part of a much larger program in the teaching-family model and relies on self-government, a skills training curriculum, a relationship with the teaching parents, and procedures to reintegrate youths into the community [Kirigin *et al.*, 1982].) Evaluations of large-scale extensions of the model have shown that measures of offences and reinstitutionalization from one to three years after the program are no different for youths who complete the program and those who participate in more traditional programs (Kirigin *et al.*, 1982; Jones *et al.*, Note 1). In contrast, an extensive evaluation of the Achievement Place home where the procedures have been especially well developed and monitored has shown that youths who participate in the program have much lower rates (approximately one-half) of reinstitutionalization, and a much higher rate of school attendance in the community than youths in a more traditional detention setting (Kirigin *et al.*, 1979). However, in the follow-up period, contact with the police and the courts was not different between groups. The absence of differences on police and court contacts is difficult to interpret. Non-Achievement Place youths were more likely to be reinstitutionalized at follow-up and hence were no longer candidates for police and court contacts.

In general, the above programs show that the effects of participation in a token economy may still be evident up to a few years after the program has been terminated. However, important qualifiers need to be highlighted to place the follow-up data in perspective. First, in many instances a token economy is only one component of the program. For example, in school programs the token economy has been associated with smaller classroom size, individualized instruction, parent involvement in classroom procedures, home-based reinforcement, and other procedures that may contribute to maintenance and transfer in their own right (e.g. Bushell, 1978; Safer *et al.*, 1981). Similarly, in the Achievement Place program, the token economy is only part of a much more comprehensive program including multiple procedures noted earlier. Thus follow-up results cannot be attributed specifically to the token reinforcement contingencies. However, the primary applied concern is whether, after participation in a token economy, the gains in behavior are necessarily lost; several programs indicated that they are not.

Second, in many cases, follow-up data show that gains are sustained in some areas of performance but lost in others. Thus, the long-term effects of a program are not simply evaluated by whether the gains are retained or not. For example, in the junior high school program of Safer *et al.* (1981), some measures reflected maintenance of intervention effects (school attendance) and others did not (graduation from high school). The same was true for the comparison of Achievement Place and other facilities where follow-up gains for delinquents were different on some measures but not on others (Kirigin *et al.*, 1979, 1982; Jones *et al.*, Note 1).

Third, with long-term follow-up, intervening experiences (e.g. hospital aftercare) can obfuscate the effects of the original program. Intervening and current environmental contingencies may exert more immediate impact on performance than a program a few years earlier. Thus, it is no surprise that several investigators have cautioned that token programs may have immediate impact but perhaps should not be expected to alter future performance unless the environments to which persons return promote continuation of the gains (Bushell, 1978; Kirigin *et al.*, 1982; Paul and Lentz, 1977).

Although many programs have shown that the effects of token economies are partially maintained, maintenance and transfer continue to be salient issues. Whether intervention effects will be maintained is still not entirely predictable. Several programs have shown that behavioral gains are lost when the program is terminated. Why behaviors are maintained after some programs but not others is not obvious. Simple hypotheses such as those stating that particular target behaviors are likely to be maintained are not easily supported. Reponses that might be expected to be maintained by the natural environment (e.g. social interaction) are lost in some studies and maintained in others (see Kazdin, 1980b). Programs that have shown long-term changes often have been in effect for relatively long periods. Protracted participation in a program may develop greater stability in the target behaviors so that they are less likely to be lost or to depend on immediate changes in the environment once the client leaves the program.

As a general rule, it is still prudent to assume that behavioral gains are likely to be lost in varying degrees once the client leaves the program. Thus, special efforts are required to ensure that the gains are maintained, a point cogently made by Baer, Wolf, and Risley in 1968 and frequently (and deservedly) cited ever since. In the last decade, considerable progress has been made in identifying strategies that increase the likelihood that behaviors are maintained and extend to new settings (see Kazdin, 1980b; Stokes and Baer, 1977). The proposed strategies include: Removing the token economy gradually so that behaviors are maintained with less direct reinforcement; reinforcing behaviors under a variety of situations so that the behaviors are not restricted to a limited range of cues; substituting naturally occurring reinforcers such as praise and activities in place of tokens; altering the schedule and delay of reinforcement to prolong extinction; and using peers and clients themselves as reinforcing agents to sustain long-term performance across a variety of situations.

Emergent issues

Advances over the last decade have not entirely resolved the questions about the token economy and variables that contribute to behavior change. However, over the years other issues have emerged that directly pertain to the limitations of token economies. The issues pertain to the feasibility of implementing effective token economies outside the domain of research and demonstration projects.

Integrity of treatment

The essential ingredients for beginning a token economy typically include identifying the target behaviors, the medium of exchange (tokens) and back-up reinforcers and specifying the relations among performance, token earnings, and expenditures. The success of token economies is largely attributed to what the program is, i.e. the specific contingencies, rather than how the program is conducted. Too little attention has been accorded the manner in which the program is monitored and implemented. Several procedures are often included in the program to help monitor the treatment to ensure that the program is carried out correctly. These procedures may be critical to the successful implementation of token economies.

To appreciate the point, reconsider the program of Paul and Lentz (1977) which produced marked changes in chronic psychiatric patients. Several features of the Paul and Lentz study probably contributed to the success of the token program. First, training of staff to implement the treatments was extensive. Clinical staff received academic training that consisted of carefully planned instruction in the different procedures, using a detailed treatment manual as a guide. Training included opportunities for role playing, modeling, rehearsal, and feedback. The academic training was followed with on-the-job training and supervised practice.

Second, monitoring of treatment was extensive to ensure that the programs were administered as planned. (The assessment procedures used to monitor treatment are detailed in a series of papers published in a special issue of the *Journal of Behavioral Assessment*, 1979, 1(3).) Supervisory staff monitored data on staff–patient interaction daily and provided positive feedback to staff for flawless performance or corrective feedback for departures from the desired procedures. Professional observers monitored staff and patients over the entire course of the program which provided a further check on execution of the program.

Third, the program included several personnel in roles that depart from the usual staffing of impatient programs. Among the positions were several interns who helped implement and evaluate the program, persons to monitor staff–patient interaction, professional observers, already mentioned, Ph.D. level staff to supervise the research, and so on. The mere presence of separate research and clinical staff and Ph.D. level research supervisors to monitor the day-to-day program, added a special feature to ensure proper implementation of the treatments.

Finally, the treatment procedures were relatively complex, as would be expected with techniques that focus on difficult clinical problems. The treatment was described in manual form. Constant updating of procedures was handled through memoranda to clarify implementation of practices, to answer questions, and so on. Both the subtle day-to-day details and the resources to have knowledgeable personnel to address such questions are very special program features that may have helped ensure that treatment was conducted as intended.

Characteristics such as those mentioned above may have had major bearing on the clinical impact of treatment and the generality of result to other clinical settings. The results, viewed superficially, suggest that a token economy can produce dramatic in-hospital and extra-hospital changes and return chronic patients to the community. However, the Paul and Lentz program was implemented with multiple procedures to evaluate and monitor the execution of treatment. Programs without these latter procedures may fall quite short of the mark in producing similar changes.

One of the major problems of treatment and program evaluation is ensuring the integrity of treatment, i.e. that treatment is carried out as intended (Rossi, 1978; Scheirer, 1981; Sechrest *et al.*, 1979). Monitoring the integrity of treatment is essential to ensure that the program is being conducted correctly. Different reports have indicated that token economies deteriorate when supervision over execution of the program is withdrawn or is not in place from the beginning. For example, Bassett and Blanchard (1977) reported a token economy in a prison setting for male adult offenders. When the director took a leave of absence and provided supervision only on a consulting basis, the program deteriorated rapidly. Specifically, staff withheld tokens for appropriate behaviors, increased the use of fines, and became inconsistent in the magnitude of fines that were invoked. The eventual return of the program's director and careful monitoring of the contingencies returned the program to its original state.

Similarly, Scheirer (1981) described a token economy for female chronic psychiatric patients that failed from the beginning, in part because of the absence of personnel within the program to supervise staff directly and to ensure their proper execution of the contingencies. No single person was in a position of authority to coordinate and supervise the day-to-day details of running the program as part of the ward routine.

Finally, Rollins, Thompson, and their colleagues developed token economies in several elementary school classrooms (Rollins *et al.*, 1974; Thompson *et al.*, 1974). The programs were quite effective in altering student deportment and academic achievement. When the investigators left the setting the resources for supervision and data collection were also withdrawn. When they returned one year later for follow-up assessment, the programs had been discontinued and teacher and student behavior had returned to preprogram rates.

In general, the potent effects of token economies may result in part from procedures included to ensure treatment integrity. Perhaps, a minimal condition to monitor treatment execution is the continuous data collection on client or staff behavior. Assessment procedures have been carefully developed and tested by Paul and his colleagues to monitor patient and staff behavior and program execution in institutional settings (see Engel and Paul, 1979; Licht, 1979; Mariotto, 1979; Power, 1979; Redfield, 1979). Of course, in many institutional settings, continuous data collection is often difficult to implement unless special consultants with outside resources are available (see Scheirer, 1981). With little or no feedback about direct execution of the program or its effects on client behavior, the integrity of treatment and the efficacy of the program are likely to be sacrificed.

Administrative and organizational issues

Token economies are frequenty implemented in institutional settings such as schools, psychiatric facilites, and institutions for the mentally retarded. Programs must work within the confines of organizational structures, administrative hierarchies, and external regulatory procedures. Organizational and administrative issues frequently dictate the extent to which implementing an effective token economy is feasible (see Scheirer, 1981). Constraints in permissible practices within the institution, lack of authority or power to follow through on program decisions, limited resources, and a variety of other sociopolitical issues may interfere with beginning the program and maintaining the integrity of treatment once the program is initiated. Although organizational obstacles have long been recognized in applied research (e.g. Tharp and Wetzel, 1969), their significance in delimiting the effects of token economies has only been fully appreciated relatively recently (Ayllon *et al.*, 1979; Bushell, 1978; Liberman, 1979; Reppucci and Saunders, 1974; Scheirer, 1981).

Professionals who are responsible for designing, implementing, and evaluating token economies may not initially recognize organizational and administrative issues as central to the program. However, the issues come into sharp focus as they affect more familiar variables that are known to influence program effectiveness. For example, limited resources within an institution may be translated into a small budget for back-up reinforcers, insufficient staff to reward clients as frequently as might be required, and absence of personnel to assess behavior of clients or staff. In one instance, a limited budget resulted in the absence of back-up reinforcers in the store when psychiatric patients were to spend their tokens (Scheirer, 1981).

Administrative and institutional obstacles often become obvious when beginning staff training. As noted earlier, the administration of direct reinforcement to staff has been an important ingredient in many staff training programs. Yet, potent reinforcers (e.g. money, vacations, shift preferences, work breaks) usually are unavailable for contingent application. Thus, staff training programs often rely on in-service training, workshops, and feedback which by themselves may be less effective training procedures than when used in conjunction with potent reinforcers. Even if incentives (e.g. certificates, recognition in an institutional newsletter) are provided, staff behavior is not always easily assessed to ensure that incentives are applied contingently.

Whether the program variations known to be effective can be implemented, or implemented routinely, in applied settings is a major question facing the field at the present time. Questions about the feasibility of extending the token economy have become more prominent over the last decade because they have direct implications for the dissemination of the token economy, as discussed below.

Dissemination of the token economy

Merely demonstrating that the token economy is effective is not enough for it to be widely adopted. A dramatic illustration of the processes and obstacles associated with program adoption was provided by Fairweather and his colleagues who developed an effective aftercare program (community lodge) for psychiatric patients. A research project was designed to disseminate the program to hospitals throughout the United States and to evaluate alternative methods of promoting program adoption. The results revealed a very small proportion (approximately 10 per cent) of the settings adopted the program (Fairweather, Sanders, and Tornatzky, 1974) but provided important information about the progression from research and development to dissemination and social policy change (Fairweather and Tornatzky, 1977).

The characteristics of programs that may contribute to their widespread adoption have been elaborated by Fawcett, Mathews, and Fletcher (1980) in the context of behavioral community psychology. Drawing from work on dissemination in other fields (e.g. extension of technology to underdeveloped countries), Fawcett *et al.* (1980) discussed the notion of an 'appropriate technology' which refers to procedures that are compatible with the context, resources, philosophy, and values of the settings in which they will be used. Interventions that are contextually appropriate and likely to be adopted should be (1) effective, (2) relatively inexpenisive, (3) decentralized and controlled by local participants, (4) flexible enough to permit local input, (5) sustainable with local rather than outside resources, (6) relatively simple and comprehensible, and (7) compatible with existing values, goals, and perceived needs of the setting.

A few of the conditions of an appropriate technology have begun to be addressed in relation to token economics. For example, the expense (cost) of token economies has been examined in different ways. Operating costs, cost-effectiveness, and cost-benefit analyses have shown that major benefits accrue from adopting token economies in relation to existing alternatives such as routine psychiatric care or detention centers for juvenile offenders (e.g. Foreyt *et al.*, 1975; Kirigin *et al.*, 1979; Paul and Lentz, 1977).

A major issue that has not been addressed is the extent to which successful programs can be sustained by local resources. Token economies reported in the research literature often have federal, state, or local funding to provide many of the resources that promote effective program implementation (e.g. money for staff who collect data, special reinforcers). Also, consultants with interests in research and affiliations with academic departments often play an important role in program development and implementation. Resources not otherwise available in the institution (e.g. undergraduates) are often drawn upon to serve critical functions to maintain and evaluate the program.

For example, the Behavior Analysis Follow Through project was part of a specially funded demonstration project (Bushell, 1978). Execution of the program was monitored centrally and locally and teacher and student performance were regularly evaluated. The favorable results suggest that the token economy could be extended on a large scale provided the mechanisms for monitoring and supervision are in place as well. Whether the program could obtain the effects without outside resources included as part of a special research project remains to be seen. Even with the program closely monitored and supervised, treatment integrity and program effectiveness varied across different sites.

If effective token economies are to be disseminated, they may need to be designed to depend less on extraneous resources. Some attempts have been reported to reduce outside monitoring and input. For example, token programs in the schools developed by Rollins *et al.* (1974) depended on extensive training and supervision by outside consultants. To make the program less dependent on outside resources, principals were trained in behavioral techniques so they could return to their schools, train teachers, and monitor the programs (Rollins and Thompson, 1978). Extra-institutional resources continued to be used to monitor program effectiveness. Yet, the attempt to develop programs that can function autonomously with minimal outside resources is an important step.

Flexibility of the token economy warrants special comment in so far as it may relate to treatment integrity. The willingness of administrators, staff, and others to adopt a particular program may be a function of the perceived or actual flexibility of the procedures. Yet, there may be clear limitations in allowable flexibility to ensure that changes in behavior are achieved. Procedural flexibility to promote local adoption and treatment integrity to ensure effective applications may need to be balanced. It may be critical to delineate program characteristics that are known or are likely to be essential for behavior change and those that are not. For example, in a token economy, reinforcers generally need to be delivered contingently and behaviors that compete with the target behavior should not be inadvertently or directly reinforced. On the other hand, many of the details of the program such as the selection of target behaviors, tokens, or back-up reinforcers, and the use of staff or patients to administer consequences, individual or group contingencies, and other features can vary widely (Kazdin, 1977). Dissemination of the token economy may be facilitated by delineating the principles that need to be followed and the alternative ways in which they can be translated into effective procedures. In this way, flexibility can be delineated even for essential ingredients of the program.

The attention that token economies have received in research, claims made about their effects, and their seeming ease of implementation may already have fostered their dissemination. The extent to which token economies are in use is not known; published reports of individual programs, of course, greatly underestimate their actual prevalence. Programs conducted in most applied settings may not be evaluated or, if evaluated, their effects may not be reported. Whether such programs conducted routinely in applied settings vary procedurally from those reported in research and whether the outcomes approach those reported in well-monitored programs remain to be determined.

General comments

Substantive questions about the token economy and variables that contribute to its efficacy are by no means resolved. The array of program variations and their relative effectiveness warrant continued research. However, within the last decade other issues that have become salient pertaining to the requirements of implementing token economies effectively in applied settings as part of routine care. The demands for maintaining the integrity of treatment, the ability to integrate token economies with administrative and organizational constraints, and the ease of disseminating the token economy effectively on a large scale appear to be especially relevant issues at this time in dictating the future of the token economy.

Summary

The token economy has been extended greatly in recent years in terms of the range of populations, settings, and target problems to which it has been applied.

A decade ago, salient issues pertained to how to improve client responsiveness to the program and how to promote maintenance and transfer. Since then, several advances have been made in these areas. The paucity of follow-up data, a perennial issue in outcome research, still characterizes the token economy. However in the last decade, several studies have indicated that the effects of token economies are at least partially maintained and extended to extra-treatment settings.

Salient issues have emerged related to the extension of the techique as part of routine practice in treatment, rehabilitation, and educational settings. Many issues for effectively implementing the token economy have been identified related to the requirements for maintaining the integrity of treatment and integrating the program within administrative constraints of institutional settings in which such programs are likely to be useful. The primary question is whether the token economy can be implemented effectively outside the context of demonstration or research projects which include special features to sustain the integrity of treatment and to overcome institutional obstacles. Apart from continuing to refine the technique and understanding the variables that may contribute to its efficacy, the next step for research is to explore and evaluate procedures to integrate token economies routinely into settings where programs are likely to be of use.

References

Allen, D. J., and Magaro, P. A. (1979). Measures of change in token-economy programs, *Behaviour Research and Therapy*, **9**, 311–318.

Ayllon, T., and Azrin, N. H. (1965). The measurement and reinforcement of behavior of psychotics, *Journal of the Experimental Analysis of Behavior*, **8**, 356–383.

Ayllon, T., and Azrin, N. H. (1968a). Reinforcer sampling: A technique for increasing the behavior of mental patients, *Journal of Applied Behavior Analysis*, **1**, 13–20.

Ayllon, T., and Azrin, N. H. (1968b). *The token economy: A Motivational System for Therapy and Rehabilitation*, New York: Appleton-Century-Crofts.

Ayllon, T., Milan, M. A., Robert, M. D., and McKee, J. M. (1979). *Correctional Rehabilitation and Management: A Psychological Approach*, New York: Wiley.

Baer, D. M., Wolf, M. M., and Risley, T. R. (1968). Some current dimensions of applied behavior analysis, *Journal of Applied Behavior Analysis*, **1**, 91–97.

Bassett, J. E., and Blanchard, E. B. (1977). The effect of the absence of close supervision on the use of response cost in a prison token economy, *Journal of Applied Behavior Analysis*, **10**, 375–379.

Bassett, J. E., Blanchard, E. B., and Koshland, E. (1975). Applied behavior analysis in a penal setting: Targeting 'free world' behaviors, *Behavior Therapy*, **6**, 639–648.

Bernstein, G. S. (1982). Training behavior change agents: A conceptual review, *Behavior Therapy*, **13**, 1–23.

Biklen, D. P. (1976). Behavior modification in a state mental hospital: A participant-observer's critique, *American Journal of Orthopsychiatry*, **46**, 53–61.

Boegli, R. G., and Wasik, B. H. (1978). Use of the token economy system to intervene on a school-wide level, *Psychology in the Schools*, **15**, 72–78.

Breyer, N. L., and Allen, G. J. (1975). Effects of implementing a token economy on teacher attending behavior, *Journal of Applied Behavior Analysis*, **8**, 373-380.

Burg, M. M., Reid, D. H., and Lattimore, J. (1979). Use of a self-recording and supervision program to change institutional staff behavior, *Journal of Applied Behavior Analysis*, **12**, 363-375.

Bushell, D., Jr. (1978). An engineering approach to the elementary classroom: The Behavior Analysis Follow Through project. In A. C. Catania and T. A. Brigham (eds), *Handbook of Applied Behaviour Analysis: Social and Instructional Processes*, New York: Irvington.

Curran, J. P., Lentz, R. J., and Paul, G. L. (1973). Effectiveness of sampling-exposure procedures on facilities utilization by psychiatric hard-core chronic patients, *Journal of Behavior Therapy and Experimental Psychiatry*, **4**, 201-207.

Engle, K. L., and Paul, G. L. (1979). Systems use to objectivify program evaluation, clinical and management decisions, *Journal of Behavioral Assessment*, **1**, 221-238.

Fairweather, G. W., Sanders, D. H., and Tornatsky, L. G. (1974). *Creating Change in Mental Health Organizations*, New York: Pergamon.

Fairweather, G. W., and Tornatsky, L. G. (1977). *Experimental Methods for Social Policy Research*, Oxford: Pergamon.

Fawcett, S. B., Mathews, R. M., and Fletcher, R. K. (1980). Some promising dimensions for behavioral community technology, *Journal of Applied Behavior Analysis*, **13**, 505-518.

Feingold, L., and Migler, B. (1972). The use of experimental dependency relationships as a motivating procedure on a token economy ward. In R. B. Rubin, H. Fenstrheim, J. D. Henderson, and L. P. Ullman (eds), *Advances in Behavior Therapy*, New York: Academic Press.

Ferguson, J. M., and Taylor, C. G. (eds) (1980). *The Comprehensive Handbook of Behavior Medicine, Vol. 3: Extended Applications and Issues*, New York: Spectrum.

Fisher, E. F., Jr., Winkler, R. C., Krasner, L., Kagel, J., Battalio, R. C., and Basmann, R. L. (1978). Economic perspectives in behavior therapy: Complex interdependencies in token economies, *Behavior Therapy*, **9**, 391-403.

Foreyt, J. P., Rockwood, C. E., Davis, J. C., Desvousges, W. H., and Hollingsworth, R. (1975). Benefit-cost analysis of a token economy program, *Professional Psychology*, **6**, 26-33.

Fullerton, D. T., Cayner, J. J., and McLaughlin-Reidel, T. (1978). Results of a token economy, *Archives of General Psychiatry*, **35**, 1451-1453.

Gershone, J. R., Errickson, E. A., Mitchell, J. E., and Paulson, D. A. (1977). Behavioral comparison of a token economy and a standard psychiatric treatment ward, *Journal of Behavior Therapy and Experimental Psychiatry*, **8**, 381-285.

Glenwick, D., and Jason, L. (eds) (1980). *Behavioral Community Psychology: Progress and Prospects*, New York: Praeger.

Greenberg, D. J., Scott, S. B., Pisa, A., and Friersen, D. D. (1975). Beyond the token economy: A comparison of two contingency programs, *Journal of Consulting and Clinical Psychology*, **43**, 498-503.

Heaton, R. C., and Safer, D. J. (1982). Secondary school outcome following a junior high school behavioral program, *Behavior Therapy*, **13**, 226-231.

Hemsley, D. R. (1978). Limitations of operant procedures in the modification of schizophrenic functioning: The possible relevance of studies of cognitive disturbance, *Behavioral Analysis and Modification*, **2**, 165-173.

Hung, D. W. (1977). Generalization of 'curiosity' questioning behavior in autistic children, *Journal of Behavior Therapy and Experimental Psychiatry*, **8**, 237-245.

Hussain, R. A. (1981). *Geriatric Psychology: A Behavioral Perspective*, New York: Van Nostrand Reinhold.

Jackson, D. A. (1976). Behavior analysis certification: A plan for quality control. In T. A. Brigham, R. Hawkins, J. Scott, and T. F. McLaughlin (eds), *Behavior Analysis in Education: Self-Control and Reading*, Dubuque, Iowa: Kendall/Hunt.

Karraker, R. J. (1977). Self versus teacher selected reinforcers in a token economy, *Exceptional Children*, **43**, 454–455.

Kazdin, A. E. (1977). *The Token Economy: A Review and Evaluation*, New York: Plenum.

Kazdin, A. E. (1980a) Acceptability of time out from reinforcement procedures for disruptive child behavior, *Behavior Therapy*, **11**, 329–344.

Kazdin, A. E. (1980b). *Behavior Modification in Applied Settings* (2nd edn), Homewood, Ill: Dorsey.

Kazdin, A. E. (in press). Failure of persons to respond to the token economy. In E. B. Foa and M. G. Emmelkamp (eds), *Failures in Behavior Therapy*, New York: Wiley.

Kazdin, A. E., and Bootzin, R. R. (1972). The token economy: An evaluative review, *Journal of Applied Behavior Analysis*, **5**, 343–372.

Kazdin, A. E., and Geesey, S. (1977). Simultaneous-treatment design comparisons of the effects of earning reinforcers for one's peers versus for oneself, *Behavior Therapy*, **8**, 682–693.

Kazdin, A. E., and Geesey, S. (1980). Enhancing classroom attentiveness by preselection of back-up reinforcers in a token economy, *Behavior Modification*, **4**, 98–114.

Kazdin, A. E., and Mascitelli, S. (1980). The opportunity to earn oneself off a token system as a reinforcer for attentive behavior, *Behavior Therapy*, **11**, 68–78.

Kirigin, K. A., Wolf, M. M., Braukmann, C. J., Fixsen, D. L., and Phillips, E. L. (1979). Achievement Place: A preliminary outcome evaluation. In J. S. Stumphauzer (ed), *Progress in Behavior Therapy with Delinquents*, Springfield, Ill.: Charles C. Thomas.

Kirigin, K. A., Braukmann, C. J., Atwater, J. D., and Wolf, M. M. (1982). An evaluation of teaching-family (Achievement Place) group homes for juvenile offenders, *Journal of Applied Behavior Analysis*, **15**, 1–16.

Liberman, R. P. (1979). Social and political challenges to the development of behavioral programs in organizations. In P. Sjoden, S. Bates, and W. S. Dockens, III (eds), *Trends in Behavior Therapy*, New York: Academic Press.

Licht, M. H. (1979). The Staff–Resident Interaction Chronograph: Observational assessment of staff performance, *Journal of Behavior Assessment*, **1**, 185–197.

Lloyd, K. E. (1980). Reactions to a forthcoming energy shortage: A topic in behavioral ecology. In G. L. Martin and J. G. Osborne (eds), *Helping in the Community: Behavioral Applications*, New York: Plenum.

Mariotto, M. J. (1979). Observational assessment systems use for basic and applied research, *Journal of Behavioral Assessment*, **1**, 239–250.

Martin, R. (1975). *Legal Challenges to Behavior Modification: Trends in Schools, Corrections and Mental Health*, Champaign, Ill.: Research Press.

McCreadie, R. G., Main, C. J., and Dunlop, R. A. (1978). Token economy, primozide and chronic schizophrenia, *British Journal of Psychiatry*, **133**, 179–181.

McLaughlin, T. F., and Malaby, J. E. (1977). The comparative effects of token-reinforcement with and without a response cost contingency with special education children, *Educational Research Quarterly*, **2**, 34–41.

McLaughlin, T. F., Williams, R. L., Truhlicka, M., Cady, M., Ripple, B. J., and Eakins, D. (in press). Model implementation and classroom achievement in the Northern Cheyenne Behavior Analysis Follow Through project, *Child and Family Behavior Therapy*.

McReynolds, W. T., and Coleman, J. (1972). Token economy: Patient and staff changes, *Behaviour Research and Therapy*, **10**, 29–34.

Milby, J. B., Pendergrass, P. E., and Clarke, C. J. (1975). Token economy versus control ward: A comparison of staff and patient attitudes toward ward environment, *Behavior Therapy*, **6**, 22–29.

Milby, J. B., Clarke, C., Charles, E., and Willcutt, H. C. (1977). Token economy process variables: Effects of increasing and decreasing the critical range of savings, *Behavior Therapy*, **8**, 137–145.

Mishara, B. L. (1978), Geriatric patients who improve in token economy and general milieu treatment programs: A multivariate analysis, *Journal of Consulting and Clinical Psychology*, **46**, 1340–1348.

Montegar, C. A., Reid, D. H., Madsen, C. H., and Ewell, M. D. (1977). Increasing institutional staff to resident interactions through in-service training and supervisor approval, *Behavior Therapy*, **8**, 533–540.

Moran, E. L., Kass, W. A., and Munz, D. C. (1977). In-program evaluation of a community correctional agency of high-risk offenders, *Corrective and Social Psychology*, **23**, 48–52.

Murphy, S. T. (1976). The effects of a token economy program on self-care behaviors of neurologically impaired inpatients, *Journal of Behavior Therapy and Experimental Psychiatry*, **7**, 145–147.

O'Leary, K. D. (1978). The operant and social psychology of token systems. In A. C. Catania and T. A. Brigham (eds), *Handbook of Applied Behavior Analysis: Social and Instructional Processes*, New York: Irvington.

O'Leary, K. D., and Drabman, R. (1971). Token reinforcement programs in the classroom: A review, *Psychological Bulletin*, **75**, 379–398.

Paul, G. L., and Lentz, R. J. (1977). *Psychosocial Treatment of Chronic Mental Patients: Milieu Versus Social-Learning Programs*, Cambridge, Mass.: Harvard University Press.

Phillips, E. L., Phillips, E. A., Wolf, M. M., and Fixsen, D. L. (1973). Achievement Place: Development of the elected manager system, *Journal of Applied Behavior Analysis*, **6**, 541–561.

Power, C. T. (1979). The Time-Sample Behavioral Checklist: Observational assessment of patient functioning, *Journal of Behavioral Assessment*, **1**, 199–210.

Redfield, J. (1979) Clinical Frequencies Recording System: Standardizing staff observations by event recording, *Journal of Behavioral Assessment*, **1**, 211–219.

Reppucci, N. D., and Saunders, J. T. (1974). Social psychology of behavior modification: Problems of implementation in natural settings, *American Psychologist*, **29**, 649–660.

Richard, H. C., Melvin, K. B., Creel, J., and Creel, L. (1973). The effects of bonus tokens upon productivity in a remedial classroom for behaviorally disturbed children, *Behavior Therapy*, **4**, 378–385.

Rollins, H. A., and Thompson, M. (1978). Implementation and operation of a contingency management program by the elementary school principal, *American Educational Research Journal*, **15**, 325–330.

Rollins, H. A., McCandless, B. R., Thompson, M., and Brassell, W. R. (1974). Project Success Environment: An extended application of contingency management in inner-city schools, *Journal of Educational Psychology*, **66**, 167–178.

Rossi, P. H. (1978). Issues in the evaluation of human services delivery, *Evaluation Quarterly*, **2**, 573–599.

Safer, D. J., Heaton, R. C., and Parker, F. C. (1981). A behavioral program for disruptive junior high school students: Results and follow-up, *Journal of Abnormal Child Psychology*, **9**, 483–494.

Scheirer, M. A. (1981). *Program Implementation: The Organizational Context*, Beverly Hills, Calif.: Sage.

Sechrest, L., West, S. G., Phillips, M. A., Redner, R., and Yeaton, W. (1979). Some neglected problems in evaluation research: Strength and integrity of treatments. In L.

Sechrest, S. G. West, M. A. Phillips, R. Redner, and W. Yeaton (eds), *Evaluation Studies: Review Annual* (Vol. 4), Beverly Hills, Calif.: Sage.

Stoffelmayr, B. E., Faulkner, G. E., and Mitchell, W. S. (1979). The comparison of token economy and social therapy in the treatment of hard-core schizophrenic patients, *Behavioral Analysis and Modification*, 3, 3–17.

Stokes, T. F., and Baer, D. M. (1977). An implicit technology of generalization, *Journal of Applied Behavior Analysis*, 10, 349–367.

Tharp, R. G. and Wetzel, R. J. (1969). *Behavior Modification in the Natural Enviroment*, New York: Academic Press.

Thompson, M., Brassell, W. R., Persons, S., Tucker, R., and Rollins, H. (1974). Contingency management in the schools: How often and how well does it work? *American Educational Research Journal*, 11, 19–28.

Trudel, G., Boisvert, J., Maruca, F., and Leroux, P. (1974). Unprogrammed reinforcement of patients' behaviors in wards with and without token economy. *Journal of Behavior Therapy and Experimental Psychiatry*, 5, 147–149.

Walker, H. M., Hops, H., and Fiegenbaum, E. (1976). Deviant classroom behavior as a function of combinations of social and token renforcement and cost contingency, *Behavior Therapy*, 7, 76–88.

Wexler, D. B. (1973), Token and taboo: Behavior modification, token economies, and the law, *California Law Review*, 61, 81–109.

Wilkinson, L., and Reppucci, N. D. (1973). Perceptions of social climate among participants in token economy and non-token economy cottages in a juvenile correctional institution, *American Journal of Community Psychology*, 1, 36–43.

Winkler, R. C. (1973). An experiment analysis of economic balance, savings and wages in a token economy, *Behavior Therapy*, 4, 22–40.

Wolf, M. M. (1978). Social validity: The case of subjective measurement or how applied behavior analysis is finding its heart, *Journal of Applied Behavior Analysis*, 11, 203–214.

Wolf, M. M., Phillips, E. L., Fixsen, D. G., Braukmann, C. J., Kirigin, K. A., Willner, A. G., and Schumaker, J. B. (1976). Achievement Place: The teaching-family model, *Child Care Quarterly*, 5, 92–103.

Wooley, S. C., Blackwell, G., and Winget, C. (1978) A learning theory model of chronic illness behavior: Theory treatment and research, *Psychosomatic Medicine*, 40, 379–401.

Zeldow, P. B. (1976). Some antitherapeutic effects of the token economy: A case point, *Psychiatry*, 39, 318–324.

Human Operant Conditioning and Behavior Modification
Edited by G. Davey and C. Cullen
© 1988 John Wiley & Sons Ltd

Chapter 8

An Integrated Analysis of the Structure and Function of Behavior: Aging and the cost of dividing attention*

ALAN BARON, JOEL MYERSON, AND SANDRA HALE
Departments of Psychology, University of Wisconsin-Milwaukee and Cardinal Stritch College

Introduction

Basic processes of operant conditioning are studied most often in the animal laboratory, and the results have had important implications for the world of human affairs as well as for theories of behavior (Myerson and Hale, 1984). However, direct investigations with human subjects are not only desirable but also quite possible (Baron and Perone, 1982). The purpose of this chapter is to examine some complex instances of stimulus control as they have been revealed by the laboratory study of human behavior. Our discussion of stimulus control uses the language and concepts of behavioral (operant) psychology. But our analysis also draws heavily from two areas of inquiry more traditionally allied with cognitive theory. The first is that of divided attention. Although processes of attention have not been ignored completely in the study of operant conditioning, the concept of attention plays a less vital role than in the study of information processing. The second area pertains to the psychological changes that accompany advancing age. With rare exception, investigations of the performance capabilites of older adults have been conducted within cognitive

*Supported by Grant AGO2513 from the National Institute on Aging to the first author and by Grant BNS–8403607 from the National Science Foundation to the second. We thank Len Green for his comments and suggestions on an earlier version of this manuscript.

rather than behavioral frameworks (for exceptions see Baron, Menich, and Perone, 1983; Baron and Menich, 1985). Our consideration of these and related issues is directed towards several goals: To illustrate some unrecognized inter-relationships between the concepts of cognitive and behavioral psychology; to develop an integrated analytic approach based on these interrelationships; and to apply this approach to the question of whether there are age differences in divided attention.

Stimulus control and attention

As the term suggests, stimulus control refers to the extent to which antecedent stimuli determine the strength of a response. The important features of this phenomenon have been identified in numerous experiments conducted in the animal laboratory. A primary role is played by differential reinforcement, that is, a higher probability of reinforcement in the presence of one stimulus relative to another (discrimination training). Stimulus control is manifested by higher response rates in the presence of the stimulus associated with the higher probability. Control also depends in important ways upon features of the discriminative events. Not surprisingly, control develops more readily when stimuli have markedly different characteristics (as when a rat is reinforced for pressing a lever when the chamber is illuminated but not when it is darkened), than when the two are more similar (different levels of illumination). Although stimulus control is most readily accomplished by explicit discrimination training, the procedure of simply reinforcing responding in the presence of a single stimulus may suffice. This outcome is seen when single stimulus training is followed by extinction tests with other stimuli; responding characteristically declines as the test stimuli are made more disparate from the training stimulus (stimulus generalization).

Stimulus control is a reliable aspect of operant conditioning. For this reason, instances when control appears to fail are of special interest, as when a stimulus unmistakably present during the reinforcement of a response fails to control responding. It is here that the concept of attention often is invoked. The issues are illustrated by Jenkins and Harrison's (1960) often-cited study of auditory generalization in the pigeon. In their procedure, key pecking was reinforced in the presence of a particular tone (single stimulus training), and then the birds were tested with a range of tones (generalization tests). Similar procedures with visual stimuli (colored lights projected on the response key) are well known to produce decremental generalization gradients. When tones were the stimuli, the surprising finding was that gradients were essentially flat, indicating that the training stimulus had not assumed differential control. Moreover, there could be no question about the ability of the birds to discriminate the tones because decremental gradients were found after discrimination training (responding was reinforced when the training tone was on but not when it was off).

An account of these and similar findings in terms of the concept of attention rests on the assumption that not all aspects of the stimuli associated with reinforced responding necessarily are attended to. In the case of pigeons, for example, it may be the case that auditory events do not ordinarily serve as effective stimuli. Differential reinforcement compels attention to auditory characteristics of the environment, and thus allows stimulus control to develop. However, various writers have urged caution in the use of attention to explain instances of deficient stimulus control (e.g. Rodewald, 1979; Terrace, 1966). Under some circumstances, attention can be regarded as an actual response that can be directly measured, as when the organism orients itself toward some stimulus other than the one associated with reinforcement. But usually, the only basis for determining whether or not the organism has paid attention is whether stimulus control has been accomplished. Without independent evidence, the concept of attention is better regarded as descriptive than explanatory. This is the way we will use the term in our consideration of divided attention: To describe (rather than explain) instances when the control exerted by concurrent stimuli is less than the sum of the control exerted by these stimuli presented individually.

Age differences in attention

A widely accepted conclusion is that attentional processes decline with advancing age. Such changes have been viewed within cognitive theories of aging as important contributors to a range of other deficits, including those in the areas of memory, psychomotor performances, and perceptual functioning in general (Burke and Light, 1981; Craik, 1977). Regardless of theoretical framework, one can see the value of including age as a variable in the study of attention. In addition to gaining interesting information about adult development, the analysis of stimulus control is expanded when the procedures include individuals with different discriminative capabilities.

There is an extensive literature on cognitive aspects of age–attention relationships (see Kausler, 1982, for a review). In the present discussion we focus on studies concerned with the phenomenon of divided attention, that is, performances in situations in which the individual must deal simultaneously with two or more stimuli. Operant psychologists have not shown much interest in divided attention (and especially not in whether there are age differences in this regard). Divided attention, however, implies a process of competition, and response competition has been a matter of considerable theoretical interest within operant psychology, particularly in connection with responding under concurrent schedules of reinforcement (de Villiers, 1977). Thus, analyses of divided attention in terms of a competition between responses may serve as a bridge between cognitive and behavioral conceptions of stimulus control.

The procedures used by cognitive psychologists to study divided attention are diverse, and there is controversy about the proper interpretation to be placed on the results (see Somberg and Salthouse, 1982). However, a characteristic outcome may be seen in research on dichotic listening. Subjects wear stereo headphones, through which pairs of auditory stimuli (e.g. digits) are presented simultaneously to the two ears (the two channels). Following the last pair, tests of memory are conducted, first for one channel and then for the other. Research comparing adults of different ages has indicated that older adults are not as accurate as younger ones on this task, but the extent of the deficit depends on details of the procedure. For example, if the subject is free to determine which channel will be reported first, the age-related deficit primarily involves the second channel. When the order of testing is placed outside the subject's control (and not announced until after the sequence is completed), deficits are found in both channels.

These sorts of findings have been used to support the contention that older individuals are particularly deficient in situations requiring the simultaneous processing of stimuli from different sources. When the tasks are simple, available resources may be sufficient to allow efficient performances of the simultaneous activities. But when increasing demands are placed on the capabilities of the individual, attention paid to one task must be at the expense of the other. In dichotic listening, for example, the attention paid to one channel leaves insufficient residual capacity for effective processing of the other channel. Thus, from a cognitive standpoint, deficient performances by older individuals are seen as the consequence of either reduced processing resources or a difficulty in allocating these resources.

Competition and divided attention

A behavioral description

From a behavioral standpoint, divided attention can be viewed as the competition between different stimuli for control. Consider the simple case in which two aspects of the environment (either two stimuli or a single stimulus with two dimensions) compete for control of behavior. Within this framework, the term *divided attention* describes those situations in which strong control by one stimulus reduces control by the other. This relationship is exemplified by Reynolds' (1961) study of attention in the pigeon. Following discrimination training with a red triangle and a green circle, responding came under the control of the form of the stimulus or its color, but not both. For example, during generalization tests, one pigeon responded exclusively to an achromatic triangular form and another to the color red.

It may be seen that an account of divided attention in terms of relative degrees of stimulus control requires the assumption of a tradeoff. Increased control by one stimulus produces weakening of control by a concurrent stimulus. If, in addition, the total amount of stimulus control possible in a given situation is assumed to be finite, the relationship may be stated in the following mathematical form:

$$S_1 + S_2 \leq A \tag{8.1}$$

where S_1 and S_2 are the amounts of control exerted by the first and second stimulus, respectively, and A is the maximum amount of control possible in a given situation. An important feature of equation 8.1 is that the values of S_1 and S_2 may increase independently until their sum equals the limit set by the value of A. Beginning at this point, there must be a linear tradeoff in stimulus control, that is, a further gain in control by one stimulus must be accompanied by a loss of equal size by the other stimulus.

The assumptions of a finite attentional capacity and a linear tradeoff have been described in the behavioral literature as 'the inverse hypothesis' (Thomas, 1970), and may be found in Mackintosh's (1977) effort to deal with divided attention in behavioral terms. But it also is the case that these assumptions are prominent features of cognitive models where they define 'the principle of complementarity' (Eysenck, 1984; Norman and Bobrow, 1975). Almost all recent cognitive models of attention, either explicity proposed or incorporated into information processing systems, appear to contain the assumption that attention is either a resource shared among different activities or the mechanism for allocating available resources (e.g. Kahneman, 1973; Norman and Bobrow, 1975; Schneider and Schiffrin, 1977). Thus, despite major differences in language, research strategies, and avowed goals, both behavioral and cognitive views of divided attention rely heavily on the notion of competition. Depending on theoretical predilection, stimuli may be said to compete with one another for the control of behavior or for the allocation of processing resources.

We noted above the common assumption that tradeoffs in stimulus control are linear. Such an assumption, however, is by no means a necessary feature of models of divided attention, and other relationships can be envisioned (Navon and Gopher, 1979). In later sections, we present evidence showing that when simultaneously presented stimuli compete for control, outcomes can be characterized by a range of possible tradeoffs, including nonlinear as well as linear ones.

The attention operating characteristic

The recently proposed concept of the attention operating characteristic (AOC) represents an important advance in determining the nature of the competition when attention is divided. Working in the information processing tradition, Sperling and Melchner (1978) developed this method as a quantitative description of the competition between stimuli for processing. But the AOC also has relevance for behavior analysis when the issues are recast in terms of competing sources of stimulus control.

The concept of the AOC and the procedures for determining it can be described using the data reported by Sperling and Melchner (1978, Exp. I). The subjects observed a compound stimulus consisting of an inner and an outer array of letters, each of which included a numeral (target) that the subjects tried to identify. Division of attention between the arrays was manipulated through instructions. Under different conditions the subjects were told to vary the distribution of their attention: Under one condition to attend to one array to the exclusion of the other (undivided attention); under another to attend mainly to one ('give it 90 per cent of your attention'); and finally, to attend equally to both. To determine the AOC, control by one stimulus is expressed as a function of control by the other. Figure 8.1 shows the outcome of such an analysis for the two subjects in Sperling and Melchner's study (to simplify the present discussion, we averaged multiple replications, and normalized values by representing them as proportions of detections in the undivided condition). The resulting functions reveal a reciprocal relationship in the control exerted by the two stimuli, in that decreased control by one stimulus was accompanied by increased control by the other.

The dashed horizontal and vertical lines in Figure 8.1 correspond to performances under conditions of undivided attention for each of the stimuli. Thus, the lines demark the maximal control that can be achieved, and the enclosed space the range of possible performances. Of special *significance* is the

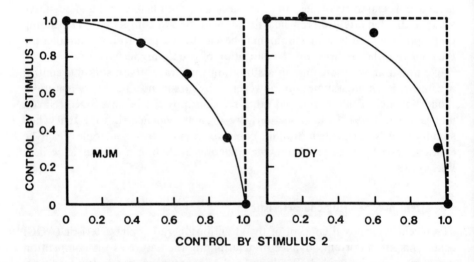

Figure 8.1   AOC analyses of data from Sperling and Melchner's experiment. Inner array detections (Stimulus 1) are plotted as a function of outer array detections (Stimulus 2). Adapted from Figure 1, Sperling and Melchner (1978), *Science*, **202**, 315–318. Copyright 1978 by the American Association for the Advancement of Science. Reprinted by permission

relation of values within the AOC space to the point at which the two lines intersect (upper right-hand corner), the 'point of independence' (Sperling and Melchner, 1978). This point designates the outcome when the two stimuli do not compete, in other words, the limiting case in which both tasks can be performed simultaneously as well as they can be performed singly. Values in other parts of the AOC space are indicative of the cost of divided attention—the extent to which performances decline relative to conditions of undivided attention.

The AOC function itself is represented by a line fitted to the values plotted within the AOC space. There are various ways that this might be done (Sperling and Melchner fitted straight lines), but when attention is divided between two similar tasks, a curve described by the following equation seems well suited:

$$S_1{}^a + S_2{}^a = 1 \qquad\qquad [8.2]$$

where S_1 and S_2 are normalized measures of stimulus control. The functions shown in Figure 8.1 are of this form and were fitted by an iterative procedure that adjusted the value of a until a maximum proportion of the variance had been accounted for.

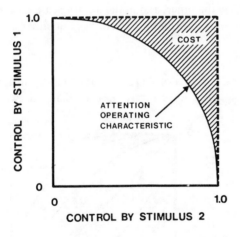

Figure 8.2 Somberg and Salthouse's method for quantifying the cost of divided attention. In the AOC plot, control by Stimulus 1 is plotted as a function of control by Stimulus 2, and the shaded area designates the attentional cost. In the example, cost = 0.32. Adapted from Figure 2, Somberg and Salthouse (1982), *Journal of Experimental Psychology: Human Perception and Performances*, **8**, 651–663. Copyright 1982 by the American Psychological Association. Reprinted by permission

Somberg and Salthouse (1982) proposed a method of quantifying the cost of divided attention using the difference between the total area of the AOC space and the area bounded by the AOC function. This expression of cost may be seen in Figure 8.2 as the cross-hatched area that falls above the function in the right-hand corner. With AOC functions of the form of equation 8.2, it may be shown that the area corresponding to divided attention cost is equal to $1/(1+a)$. Equation 8.2 has the advantage that it may be fit to data using only one free parameter. Moreover, the value of a leads directly to an index of the interference between concurrent tasks.

The value of the divided attention cost index depends on the extent of competition between the stimuli. Figure 8.3 gives a summary of values associated with various positions of the AOC function. When the cost index, $1/(1+a)$, is close to 0.0 both tasks can be performed simultaneously as well as either one alone. With increases in the cost from 0.0 to 0.5, the AOC assumes a convex form (similar to the results of the Sperling and Melchner study) whose curvature decreases as the intermediate value of 0.5 is approached and a linear tradeoff is reached. Indices exceeding 0.5 are associated with a series of concave functions. As the cost index approaches 1.0, control by one stimulus increasingly precludes control by the other, and in the limiting case, interference between the tasks is so profound as to prohibit performance of either one.

Age and the AOC

Although analyses in terms of AOC functions have considerable potential for the study of aging, they have rarely been used in this way. The value of the

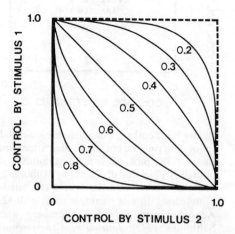

Figure 8.3 Fitted curves and cost indices associated with various forms of the AOC. The cost index can range from 0.00 (no interference) to 1.00 (complete interference)

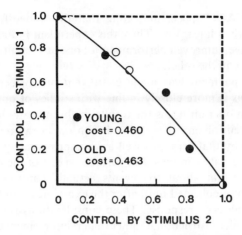

Figure 8.4   AOC analyses of data from Somberg and Salthouse's experiment. Outer array reports (Stimulus 1) are plotted as a function of inner array reports (Stimulus 2) for groups of young and old subjects. Adapted from Figure 1, Somberg and Salthouse (1982), *Journal of Experimental Psychology: Human Perception and Performance*, **8**, 651–663. Copyright 1982 by the American Psychological Association. Reprinted by permission

approach may be seen in an experiment by Somberg and Salthouse (1982) which extended Sperling and Melchner's procedures to include comparisons of older and younger adults (57–76 yrs versus 18–23 yrs). As before, different divisions of attention were accomplished through instructions. Depending on the condition, subjects were told to devote their attention in various ways to the two arrays (exclusively to one or the other, equally between the two, or 70 per cent to one array and 30 per cent to the other), and to report whether or not a target had appeared in each array. A new procedure was that subjects also were told that they would be paid for correct responses according to the way attention was to be divided. For example, when 70 per cent was to be directed toward the inner array and 30 per cent to the outer array, correct inner and outer array reports were worth 0.7 cents and 0.3 cents, respectively.

Figure 8.4 is a slight modification of the AOC analysis reported by Somberg and Salthouse (we normalized their group averages and fitted the functions using the procedures described above). The AOC functions for their older subjects are virtually identical to those for a young adult comparison group; according to our analyses, the cost indices were 0.463 and 0.460, respectively. Also apparent is that the values tend to be positioned along the negative diagonal of the AOC space, indicating that the tradeoff, although slightly convex, was nearly a linear one. Thus, this experiment found that regardless of the individual's age, improved performance of one task resulted in a nearly equal loss of proficiency in the other.

The fact that payment was made contingent on correct responses in this experiment brings it more closely in line with studies of operant conditioning variables. Cast in operant terms the results might indicate that increases in the relative rate of reinforcement associated with one array resulted in increased stimulus control by that array, as well as in approximately equal decreases in control by the alternate stimulus. But various aspects of the procedures make it difficult to be certain about the events actually controlling behavior. The reinforcers were not collected until after the experiment, and feedback was not provided following each response. These considerations suggest that behavior may have been under instructional rather than reinforcement control (Baron and Galizio, 1983). A different problem is that the data were averages of groups of subjects given brief exposure to the procedures rather than the outcome of a steady-state analysis of individual performances.

Nevertheless, the Somberg and Salthouse study provides important information about age and attention, and the research illustrates the utility of an AOC analysis in this regard. As they pointed out in their paper, other research on divided attention has not controlled for variables that might indirectly interfere with the performances of older adults, such as sensory problems, inappropriate motivation, deficits in undivided attention, and the like. The AOC analysis is designed to control for these factors by evaluating the cost of divided attention relative to performances under undivided conditions. And when the AOC analysis was applied to data from older and younger adults, older adults were found to be as capable of distributing their attention between two stimulus sources as were younger ones, a finding that contradicts the conventional wisdom about age and attention.

The AOC applied to operant discriminations

The value of further analyses using the AOC approach is apparent. Additionally, it is important to examine age–attention relationships with a range of experimental paradigms so that the generality of effects can be established. These considerations led us to undertake research on divided attention using procedures similar to those followed in the study of human operant conditioning. These included explicit reinforcement for responding, reduced reliance on instructions as the technique for controlling divided attention, and a single-subject rather than a group-statistical research design.

The research (Hale and Baron, 1984) employed a conventional operant paradigm, matching-to-sample discriminations. In this type of discrimination, brief exposure to a sample stimulus is followed by a pair of choice stimuli, and

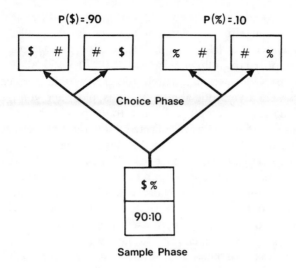

Figure 8.5 Diagram of matching-to-sample procedure used in the Hale and Baron (1984) experiment. The compound sample stimulus included information about the probabilities that the two elements would appear as the positive stimulus within the subsequent discrimination

only responses to the choice stimulus that match the sample are reinforced. As shown in Figure 8.5, division of attention was studied by using samples that were comprised of two-element compound stimuli (nonalphanumeric typewriter keyboard symbols, e.g. '%' and '$', positioned side by side). One of the sample elements was the positive member of the subsequent pair of discriminative stimuli; the negative member of the pair always was a symbol that was absent from the sample (e.g. #). Thus, accurate responses to the pair of choice stimuli required inspection of both elements of the compound sample. The stimuli used in each discrimination were drawn from a pool of eight items so that a given stimulus could be either positive or negative, depending on the trial.

Rather than employing pre-experimental instructions, division of attention was controlled on each trial by presenting information about the likelihoods that either of the elements would reappear. As illustrated in Figure 8.5, a compound stimulus ('$' and '%') might be preceded by the display, '90:10', which indicated that the left element of the sample ('$') would stand a 9 in 10 chance of reappearing as one of the choice stimuli, and the right element ('%') a 1 in 10 chance. Shown in the diagram are the four possible displays during the subsequent (delayed) choice phase of the discrimination. Delivery of the reinforcer (a signal of monetary payment) followed responses to the correct stimulus. Responses to the negative stimulus ('#') went unreinforced.

Within this procedure, the probability information was varied from trial to trial. The values at either extreme, '100:0' and '0:100', called for exclusive attention to either the left or right element of the sample. Intermediate conditions comprised the following values: 90:10, 70:30, 50:50, 30:70, and 10:90.

As is customary in operant research, the critical data were collected when performances were asymptotic and the subjects, older and younger men (65–75 yrs versus 19–25 yrs), were well acclimated to the procedures. An essential part of the analysis was that data were collected in the form of the speed with which the man selected one or the other of the choice stimuli. The tasks, although demanding, were designed to produce low error rates; these were no more than 3–4 per cent for men of either age. From the standpoint of age comparisons, this helped guarantee equivalent mastery of the information provided by the sample. Under conditions of high accuracy, response speed can serve as a highly sensitive behavioral index, one which has been used successfully to study such complex performances as memory and choice (Posner, 1978).

A general finding with regard to response speeds was that the older men were slower across the range of experimental conditions (this outcome is consistent with the well-known phenomenon of response slowing in older adults; see Cerella, Poon, and Williams, 1980). The speed data were subjected to AOC analyses, the results of which are shown for two young and two old subjects in Figure 8.6. It may be seen that in all four cases, the division of attention was accomplished only at some cost. Also apparent is that the tradeoffs were convex rather than linear. Such convex AOC functions indicate that the extent of the cost was moderate (cost indices ranged from 0.21 to 0.33). Finally, the analyses summarized in Figure 8.6 provide no basis for concluding that our procedures detected age differences in either the form of the AOC functions or the associated cost indices (we have not seen differences in these regards in work with other subjects). In other words, the older men were as capable of dividing attention as their younger counterparts.

The two studies discussed above, one conducted within a cognitive framework (Somberg and Salthouse, 1982) and the other within a behavioral one (Hale and Baron, 1984), demonstrate the utility of AOC analyses for the study of age differences. There was agreement about the absence of age differences in the cost of divided attention for individuals of different ages. A difference, however, concerns the nature of the tradeoff. Somberg and Salthouse's data, based on the accuracy of the choice response, suggested that the tradeoff is a linear one. But our work with a response speed measure indicated the tradeoff to be quite nonlinear (convex). It is not clear why the response measure should influence the shape of the AOC, and the fact that Sperling and Melchner's (1978) accuracy data also showed a nonlinear tradeoff implies the role of other factors. One possibility is simply that the task was more difficult for the subjects, both old and young, in Somberg and Salthouse's experiment.

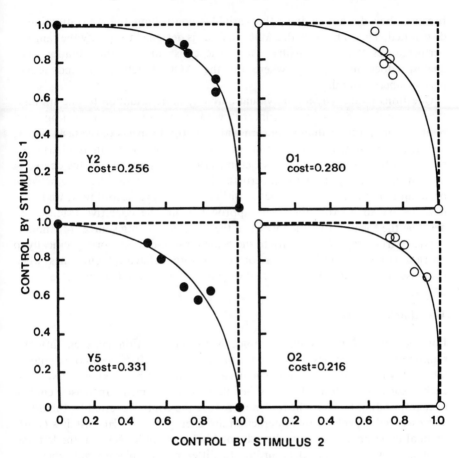

Figure 8.6 AOC analyses of data from two young and two old subjects exposed to a matching-to-sample procedure in which the samples were compound stimuli, one of which constituted the positive choice. Response speeds to the element contained in the left half of the sample (Stimulus 1) are plotted as a function of response speeds to the right half (Stimulus 2). Data are from Hale and Baron (1984)

Competition and concurrent schedules of reinforcement

We have discussed the concept of divided attention cost and the value of the AOC analysis as a mathematical description of attentional tradeoffs. The form assumed by the AOC characterizes the interaction between the particular tasks under study. Given this description, one then can investigate the variables that control the form of the tradeoff by analyzing the structure of the tasks and the nature of their incompatibility. But such analyses are necessarily incomplete because they do not address the variables controlling the way attention is distributed. This is because the AOC analysis is designed to specify the range of performances that are possible within the constraints of the situation. The analysis does not specify where on the AOC function the individual's performances will fall.

Questions about why an individual may pay more attention to one stimulus than another represent a concern with processes of motivation and reinforcement, rather than a concern with structural aspects of the tasks. Thus, identification of the variables that control the way attention is distributed requires a functional analysis. As Catania (1973) has pointed out, the degree of interest in functional rather than structural issues is a major difference between behavioral and cognitive approaches within psychology. Accordingly, we found it necessary to borrow the AOC approach from the cognitive tradition to describe the form of the tradeoff when there are competing sources of stimulus control (structure). We now turn to the behavioral tradition, more specifically to operant studies of choice behavior, to explore behavioral outcomes when responses to concurrent stimuli are differentially reinforced (function).

The Matching Law

For the operant psychologist, choice is the competition between different reinforcement schedules for the control of behavior. In a commonly studied laboratory procedure, a hungry pigeon can obtain food by pecking on two keys, each associated with a different schedule of reinforcement. Increased control over responding by one schedule must reduce the control exerted by the other. The essential aspects of this interaction are exemplified by Herrnstein's (1961) seminal experiment. In a two-key chamber, the pigeon's pecks on the left and right keys were reinforced according to different variable-interval schedules. Herrnstein discovered that a simple equation, now known as the Matching Law, described responding to pairs of schedules differing in their average rates of reinforcement. For each pair of schedules, the relative rate of pecking one of the keys (pecks on that key divided by total pecks) matched the relative rate of reinforcement (the number of reinforcers produced by pecks on that key divided by total reinforcers). This relation may be expressed mathematically as:

$$R_1/(R_1 + R_2) = r_1/(r_1 + r_2) \qquad\qquad [8.3]$$

where R_1 is the number of responses on one key, r_1 the rate of reinforcement for pecks on that key, and R_2 and r_2 are responses and reinforcers associated with the second key. For example, if responses on the left key produced three-quarters of all obtained reinforcers, then this relative reinforcement proportion is matched by relative responding on the two keys such that three-quarters of the total responses are made on the left key.

It may be obvious that an account of choice in terms of proportions necessarily implies a linear tradeoff. With two possible responses, any reduction in the relative rate of one response must be accompanied by an equal increase in the other. Even if the analysis considers performances in terms of the absolute number of responses, the procedures are biased toward linear relationships. In so far as the hungry bird spends most of its time pecking for food, responses on one key will reduce the time available for the other response. An important consequence of these methods is that they have led operant researchers away from analyses of the forms that tradeoffs can assume within choice situations. Instead, the overriding question in operant choice research has been: How does the distribution of responses between the two alternatives change as a function of the distribution of reinforcements?

The Matching Law was proposed as an answer to this question by Herrnstein more than 20 years ago, and considerable research with pigeons since then has demonstrated that the law provides an accurate description of choice between probabilistic schedules. Although most of this research has been conducted within the animal laboratory, it is most significant for the present discussion that the Matching Law also describes human choice (see de Villiers, 1977, and Pierce and Epling, 1983, for reviews).

Extension of the law to the human level is illustrated by results reported by Bradshaw, Szabadi, and Bevan (1976). In this experiment, the young adult subjects pressed a button (main key) to earn money according to variable-interval schedules (the maximum payoffs ranged from 5 to 211 reinforcers/hour, i.e. variable-interval 720 second to variable-interval 17 second schedules). Choice was introduced into the procedure by providing the subject with a second (changeover) button that allowed switching back and forth between the two schedules currently in effect. Although this choice procedure differs in some respects from the one described above (in that the choice response, i.e. responses on the changeover key, is separate from the reinforced response, i.e. responses on the main key) the essential relationships are the same.

Results for individual subjects may be seen in Figure 8.7. The graphs, based on stable performances under each schedule combination, express relative response rates as a function of relative reinforcement rates. If relative responding matches relative reinforcement, the data points should fall along the positive diagonal. Clearly this was the case in Bradshaw *et al.*'s experiment, showing that the Matching Law provided a good description of the data.

Matching and attention

The previous experiment was a straightforward extension of operant procedures commonly used with pigeons. Of special interest are the results of certain other tests of the applicability of the Matching Law to human choice. Although the term 'attention' has not been used in discussing these studies, they can be

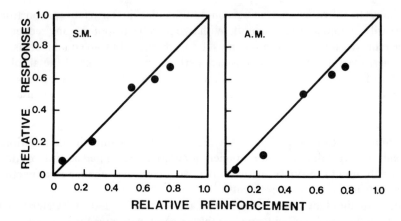

Figure 8.7 Matching analyses of data from Bradshaw *et al.*'s experiment. Relative response rates are plotted as a function of relative rates of obtained reinforcements for two subjects. Adapted from Figure 3, Bradshaw *et al.*, (1976), *Journal of the Experimental Analysis of Behavior*, **26**, 135–141. Copyright 1976 by the Society for the Experimental Analysis of Behavior. Reprinted by permission

conceptualized as investigations of divided attention as well as investigations of choice.

Consider in this regard a study reported by Baum (1975) in which concurrent operant schedules were incorporated into game-like procedures. The college-student subject was told that he was the captain of a spaceship under siege and that he could defend himself by 'detecting and destroying two types of enemy missiles: red missiles and green missiles'. By depressing either of two keys, sensors for one or the other type of missile were activated, thus allowing detection of the missile if it was present. Through operation of a second key, the missile could be destroyed. Within this procedure, detection and destruction of missiles constituted the reinforcer, and the rate at which the missiles were presented, the reinforcement schedule.

Figure 8.8 shows results for two subjects; note that data are presented as allocation of time (rather than responses) to the alternatives. The figure shows that the relative amount of time that the sensor for red missiles was activated closely matched the relative number of red missiles that were detected (again, a straight line with a slope of 1.00 provides a good fit to the points). In other words, the subjects divided their viewing time in accord with the probability that reinforcement would be obtained.

There is further evidence from operant experiments that division of viewing time matches the probability of the event being viewed. For example, Schroeder and Holland (1969) measured the eye movements of subjects, who were monitoring two pairs of meters. The relative number of fixations on each pair

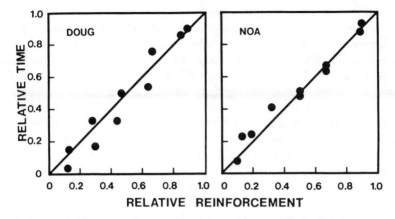

Figure 8.8   Matching analyses of data from Baum's experiment. Relative time is plotted as a function of relative rates of obtained reinforcements for two subjects. Adapted from Figure 1, Baum (1975), *Journal of the Experimental Analysis of Behavior*, **23**, 45–53. Copyright 1975 by the Society for the Experimental Analysis of Behavior. Reprinted by permission

matched the relative number of needle deflections detected by the subject. Conger and Killeen (1974) conducted an innovative test of the Matching Law within a social context. Their subjects participated in a group discussion in which the other members of the group (collaborators of the experimenter) systematically varied the extent to which they agreed with the subject's statements. Results indicated that the amount of time the subject spent looking at a particular individual matched the relative number of statements of agreement.

Because the above studies were motivated by efforts to test the Matching Law with humans, their status as experiments on divided attention has largely gone unrecognized. But the formal similarities are apparent. In each case, the procedures required that subjects divide their attention between stimuli that competed for the control of behavior. Thus, subjects directed their attention (although this is not the language used by the authors of the reports) to possible green missiles or red missiles, to the left pair of meters or the right pair of meters, or to one or another member of the discussion group. In each case, the results indicated that increased control by one stimulus was associated with decreased control by the other. Moreover, the results further indicated that the relative amount of attention paid to each stimulus was determined by the relative rate of reinforcement associated with that stimulus.

There are, of course, a number of differences between these operant experiments and the conventional investigations of divided attention described in previous sections. One difference is the detailed study of the behavior of a small number of subjects rather than brief observations of a larger number of subjects. Another is the response chosen for study. The operant studies relied on the time spend observing the stimuli, whereas the dependent measure in divided attention studies has been the accuracy of reports about the stimuli (Somberg and Salthouse, 1982, Exp. I; Sperling and Melchner, 1978), or less frequently, the speed of responding (Somberg and Salthouse, 1982, Exp. II; see also Hale and Baron, 1984). But the similarities appear to outweigh the differences, and the experiments raise some intriguing questions: Is the division of attention in all of these studies functionally equivalent? Is the competition between stimuli for control of behavior governed by the rates of reinforcement associated with the different stimuli? Do relative measures of control by different stimuli match the relative reinforcement rates associated with these stimuli, or are other relationships involved?

Answers to these questions are not simple because of the different conceptual frameworks in which the research was conducted. Nevertheless, there may be some promise in the strategy we have already adopted in the present effort—that of determining whether the data from experiments conducted in the different traditions will, if dealt with properly, present similar pictures. We presented the outcome of this strategy in a previous section where we took data from operant procedures (Hale and Baron, 1984) and subjected them to a type of analysis associated with cognitive experiments. The resulting AOC functions resembled those of a cognitive study of divided attention (Sperling and Melchner, 1978). In the following section, we describe outcomes when we reverse this strategy. We take the results of a cognitive study described above (Somberg and Salthouse, 1982) and reanalyze them using techniques associated with operant psychology. At issue is whether the data conform to the Matching Law.

Attention and matching

The main obstacle to the translation of results from cognitive experiments into operant terms is that the contingencies for responding usually are not made explicit. But a notable exception is the previously described Somberg and Salthouse (1982) experiment. It will be recalled that the payment for correct reports corresponded to the division indicated in the instructions (e.g. subjects told to divide their attention on a 70:30 basis received either 0.7 cents or 0.3 cents, respectively, for correct reports). This feature of the procedure provides a starting point for determining the effects of relative reinforcement on the competition between the stimuli for control.

Execution of the analysis is by no means straightforward. One problem pertains to the nature of the response. Somberg and Salthouse's procedure was arranged so that both stimuli (the inner and outer arrays) were well within the subject's central visual field, making simultaneous viewing possible. Consequently, the division of attention cannot be regarded as a simple tradeoff

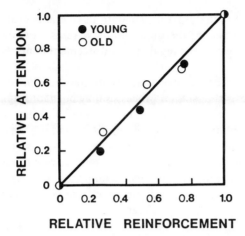

Figure 8.9 Matching analysis of data from
Somberg and Salthouse's (1982) experiment.
Relative attention is plotted as a function of
obtained relative reinforcements

between two viewing responses that were directly measured (as was the case in the operant procedures; see Baum, 1975), and we were forced to infer the relative control of responding from the data on response accuracy.

A further difficulty is that response accuracy was the dependent measure. Assessment of relative stimulus control must in some way take into account the extent to which responses were correct by chance, that is, correct guesses not a result of stimulus control. We dealt with this problem by assuming that the proportion correct for each array, C, equalled the proportion actually detected, S, plus the proportion correct by chance. The probability of a correct guess was 0.5; therefore, $C = S + 0.5 (1 - S)$ which rearranged yields $S = 2 (C - 0.5)$. It follows that the relative control by one stimulus (in the present case defined as the relative attention to the inner array) is given by:

$$S_1/(S_1 + S_2) = (C_1 - 0.5)/[(C_1 - 0.5) + (C_2 - 0.5)] \qquad [8.4]$$

Despite the above complications, the reanalysis of the Somberg and Salthouse data yielded remarkably clear results. The outcome may be seen in Figure 8.9, which expresses 'relative attention' (more precisely, relative stimulus control) as a function of relative reinforcement. The figure shows that the division of attention closely matched the relative rate of obtained reinforcements. Also apparent is that age differences were virtually absent. In this connection, it will be recalled that the AOC analysis reported by Somberg and Salthouse led to the conclusion that the older adults were as capable of dividing their attention as the younger ones. Our reanalysis of their data in operant terms sheds additional light on this phenomenon; the older adults were as capable of dividing their attention in accord with the prevailing reinforcement contingencies as were the younger ones.

The similarity of the Somberg and Salthouse results to those of operant experiments suggests that similar processes may be involved in cognitive studies of divided attention and operant studies of matching. Furthermore, the relative rate of reinforcement appears to be an important and precise determinant of the allocation of stimulus control across a range of response measures, including relative accuracy, relative viewing time, and relative rate of responding.

In the above discussion, we mentioned a number of differences and similarities between attention experiments and operant choice experiments. At this point, it is important to emphasize the difference that, in our estimation, has had the largest bearing on the models that have emerged from each approach. As we explained earlier, the practice in most operant experiments is to select the competing responses in such a way as to make them completely incompatible. The pigeon, for example, can peck only one key at a time, and human subjects may be admonished not to press both buttons simultaneously (in Baum's study, simultaneous responses were not reinforced). An associated feature of the matching analysis is that outcomes are characteristically represented as relative responding, expressed as proportions of ratios. As we explained earlier, the necessary result of these procedures is that tradeoffs are forced in the direction of linear relationships, i.e. relationships in which changes in one response are accompanied by equal but opposite changes in the other.

Now consider the usual procedure in experiments on divided attention. Here the experiment typically is arranged so that attention to the competing stimuli can occur simultaneously. Both stimuli are present within the visual field (or auditory field, e.g. dichotic listening) at the same time. Because the individual is exposed to both stimuli simultaneously, the nature of the tradeoffs in control is free to vary. Although tradeoffs may be linear under these circumstances (e.g. Somberg and Salthouse, 1982), they may assume nonlinear forms as well (e.g. Hale and Baron, 1984; Sperling and Melchner, 1978).

These considerations point to a limitation of operant research on choice that has been overlooked in discussions of research in this area. The methods used by operant psychologists have focused on linear tradeoffs to the exclusion of all other forms, because the linear form tends to emerge when competing responses are incompatible. Performances under such conditions are not unimportant, but the definition of choice is considerably broader, and a comprehensive analysis eventually will require consideration of compatible as well as incompatible responses. An analysis of tradeoffs between partially compatible operants modeled after the AOC and using an index of the cost of response incompatibility (mathematically equivalent to the divided attention cost index developed above) could prove quite useful in such an endeavor.

Summary and conclusions

The goal of this chapter was to examine some complex instances of stimulus control (divided attention) in human behavior. In the sections below, we outline the main conclusions of the effort: First, with regard to mathematical analyses of divided attention, as expressed by AOC and matching functions; second, with regard to the proposition that divided attention abilities decline with advancing age; and finally, with regard to the role of structure–function relations in the analysis of human conditioning.

The relation of the AOC to the Matching Law

The AOC and matching functions constitute mathematical descriptions of different aspects of divided attention, as this process has been investigated within cognitive and behavioral psychology. A common feature is that both approaches are directed toward the analysis of competition between psychological processes. Competition, however, is viewed from quite different vantage points. In the case of the AOC analysis, the focus is on the constraints surrounding the competition. The primary goal is to determine the cost of the competition. By comparison, the matching analysis is directed toward the outcomes of the competition. The goal is to specify the course of action expressed in the individual's behavior, given the constraints of the situation.

Descriptions exclusively in terms of one or the other approach necessarily are incomplete. Consider the limitations of the AOC analysis in this regard. To say that a subject's performance is described by a particular AOC function is to characterize the tradeoff when attention is divided in different ways. But the analysis leaves an essential question unanswered: Why was a specific data point (a specific combination of control by the two stimuli) obtained in a particular situation? Perhaps one might say, most simply, that the outcome reflected the way in which the subject *chose* to divide his attention. The trouble with this answer, from a behavioral standpoint at least, is that it raises, but leaves unanswered, the further question: Why did the subject choose this particular division of attention and not some other? It is with regard to questions of the latter sort that operant conceptions of choice and the associated Matching Law can be of use. Furthermore, it can be shown in mathematical terms that each of the two analyses represents an incomplete expression of the other.

Consideration of the exact mathematical relationship between the AOC and the Matching Law can be simplified by taking the intermediate step of expressing the law in terms of ratios rather than the proportions used previously (equation 8.3). The two expressions are, of course, mathematically equivalent. For example, if two-thirds of the total reinforcers are obtained for responding to one of two alternatives, the Matching Law predicts that two-thirds of total responding be allocated to that alternative, or, equivalently, that the reinforcement ratio of 2:1 be matched by a 2:1 ratio of responding. In general terms:

$$R_1/R_2 = r_1/r_2 \qquad\qquad [8.5]$$

where R_1/R_2 is the ratio of the alternative responses and r_1/r_2 is the ratio of the reinforcers for the responses.

For the present application of the Matching Law to the phenomenon of divided attention, the law also may be expressed as:

$$S_1/S_2 = r_1/r_2 \qquad\qquad [8.6a]$$

where S_1/S_2 refers to the ratio of the control by the two stimuli. Finally, to allow representation of the Matching Law's predictions in AOC space (where performances under the control of one stimulus are plotted as a function of control by the second stimulus), the terms of equation 8.6a may be rearranged so that:

$$S_1 = (r_1/r_2) S_2 \qquad\qquad [8.6b]$$

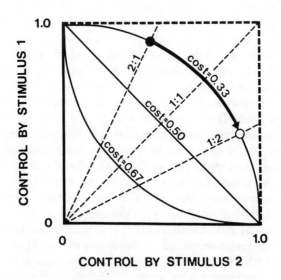

Figure 8.10   The relationship between the AOC and matching. AOC function (solid lines) are those associated with three levels of cost: 0.33, 0.50, and 0.67. Matching functions (thin dashed lines) are those associated with three ratios of reinforcement ($S_1:S_2$): 2:1, 1:1, and 1:2. Darkened arrow when cost = 0.33 indicates change when the reinforcement ratio is changed from 2:1 to 1:2

Equation 8.6b describes a straight line in AOC space that runs through the origin and which has a slope that is equal to the current reinforcement ratio (r_1/r_2). The relationship of the matching line to the AOC is illustrated in Figure 8.10. Three possible AOC functions are shown, one in which the cost index equals 0.67 (the concave function), one in which cost equals 0.50 (the linear function), and one in which cost equals 0.33 (the convex function). Also shown are the matching functions associated with three reinforcement ratios: 1:2, 1:1, and 2:1.

Consider data from a subject for whom there is a moderate cost of divided attention—a subject who trades off control by the first stimulus for control by the second stimulus according to a cost index of 0.33. According to the AOC analysis, this subject's performances can fall at any point along the convex AOC function, depending on how the individual 'chose' to divide attention between the two stimuli. But assume also that the reinforcement ratio was 2:1 for responses controlled by the two stimuli; that is, two reinforcers were received for attending to the first stimulus for every reinforcer received for the second. According to the Matching Law, this means that performances may fall anywhere along the line corresponding to that ratio of reinforcements (the line labeled 2:1). Thus, the subject's performance must satisfy two conditions: it must fall along a particular AOC function determined by the cost of divided attention and fall along a matching line determined by the reinforcement ratio. In our example, these two conditions are satisfied only at the point at which the 2:1 matching line interests the AOC function associated with a cost of 0.33 (the solid circle in the figure).

While the preceding discussion has emphasized the incompleteness of the AOC as a description of divided attention, it is apparent that the same arguments can be directed against the Matching Law. For a subject confronted with a particular pair of tasks, the AOC function specifies a line that limits the range of possible performances. The Matching Law specifies, for a given reinforcement ratio, a line (the matching line in AOC space) that likewise limits the range of possible performances. But only the AOC function and the matching line taken together specify a single point that predicts what an organism will do in a given situation in response to a particular pair of reinforcement rates.

A last consideration pertains to behavioral transitions. In the previous example, the reinforcement contingencies were arranged so that more attention was paid to the first stimulus than to the second (ratio = 2:1). Now consider a change in the procedure: The contingencies are reversed so that the subject gains one reinforcer for attending to the first stimulus for every two reinforcers received for the second (ratio = 1:2). According to the Matching Law, performances should adjust so that increasing attention is paid to the second stimulus relative to the first. But as the division of attention is altered by the new contingencies, it must do so in the manner prescribed by the AOC, that is, performances must move along the function until the division of attention matches the distribution of reinforcement. In the present case, this will be at the point at which the line labeled 1:2 in Figure 8.10 intersects the AOC function associated with a cost of 0.33 (the open circle at the point of the arrow). Thus, it may be seen that the AOC and the Matching Law, taken together, not only provide a theoretical basis for describing asymptotic (steady-state) performances, but also the transitions between steady states as responding adjusts to changes in the reinforcement contingencies.

As suggested earlier, analyses in terms of the AOC and the Matching Law represent concerns with structure and function, respectively. Catania (1973, 1984) discussed the important roles played by these concerns within psychology, tracing the distinction back to the writings of Titchener at the turn of the century. Catania made two important points that are well illustrated by the present effort. The first is that despite the antagonism that has existed between advocates of structural and functional analyses, the analyses themselves are complementary rather than mutually exclusive. Our analysis of divided attention shows that a comprehensive account must include the structural processes described by the AOC as well as the functional processes described by the Matching Law. The second point is that structural questions have been more the concern of cognitive than behavioral psychologists whereas the reverse is true with regard to functional issues. But this correlation appears to be more a matter of tradition than a necessary one, and the analysis presented here may encourage others to break with this tradition. As a behavioral psychologist, Catania advocated increased attention to structural questions, but his consideration of the issues was more programmatic than empirical. The present effort may be seen as an implementation of the inquiry that he proposed.

Age and divided attention

This brings us to the question of response competition as it pertains to the behavior of older adults. The phenomenon of divided attention has played a prominent role in the psychology of aging, in that deficits in divided attention are seen as a major contributor to deficiencies in a range of other performances (learning, memory, problem solving, etc.). But despite the widely held belief that older adults are deficient in their ability to divide attention, such a conclusion is not supported by the results reported by Somberg and Salthouse (1982) or the new data we presented here (Hale and Baron, 1984).

A critical difference from previous research was that performances were studied in terms of the AOC and the associated concept of divided attention cost. Equally important was that the procedures kept separate differences due to divided attention from differences that were not. We accomplished this by normalizing the data so that a subject's performance in the divided attention conditions was compared with performance in the undivided (100 per cent) condition. Somberg and Salthouse took the further step of adjusting the stimulus durations in a way that matched old and young subjects' performances under the undivided condition. The absence of age differences when these controls were included suggests that the age-related effects of previous experiments may have nothing to do with division of attention. Instead, the procedures may have picked up differences from other sources. Candidates here include differences in ability to perform under undivided conditions as well as differences in motivation, experience with the tasks, and, more generally, differences in the ways older and younger individuals react in laboratory situations.

Although previous reports about age-related deficits in divided attention may have been mistaken, one aspect of our analysis suggests an area of research that may reveal age differences. It is noteworthy that research on divided attention has been concerned primarily with how individuals respond to a given set of task conditions. Equally important is the question of how rapidly the division of attention can be altered in response to changing conditions. Thus, older individuals may have AOCs similar to younger ones, and ultimately they may adapt to changed reinforcement contingencies. Nevertheless, older adults may be slower in their ability to make adjustments in the way attention is divided when such changes occur. We know of no studies directly related to this question, however, and so its answer will have to await the results of future research.

Age and human conditioning

A final comment is in order about the relation of age to the study of human conditioning. As Catania (1973) pointed out, Titchener's effort to divide psychology into its fundamental components led him to describe not only a psychology of structure and a psychology of function, but a third psychology as well, that of 'psychogenesis'—a concern with 'the workings of the child's mind and the way in which it passes over into the adult mind'. Thus, the study of both structure and function must be placed within the context of the ways in which developmental variables influence behavioral outcomes. Considerable progress has been made since Titchener's time in the description of structural and functional aspects of the behavior of the developing child. By comparison, inquiry into structural and functional changes during the remainder of the life span remains a relatively untapped research area.

Behavioral changes in the adult often are seen as the continuation of a developmental process originating in childhood. In the case of the child, however, changes are characterized by a progression toward enhanced behavioral capabilities, and the acknowledged task of theories of child development is to account for increases in behavioral competence with age. The picture is different when one turns to the development of the older adult. Here the characteristic changes are those associated with declining capabilities—

slowing of reaction time, failure of memory, impairment of problem solving ability. The important questions, therefore, pertain to the processes leading to reduced behavioral competence. What are the variables controlling these losses? What are the implications of such losses for the personal and social adjustment of the older adult? Can remedial procedures be discovered that will restore lost functioning, or, at the least, retard the rate of loss?

It remains to be seen whether common analytic techniques can be employed to study increasing and decreasing competence, but the origins of both are to be sought in the interplay between structural and functional determinants of behavior. In the study of child development, important roles have been assigned to both maturation and learning. In the psychology of aging, by comparison, the preeminence of structural determinants is rarely challenged. Thus, the conventional wisdom has been that changes originating in biological aging overshadow the control that can be exerted by the enviroment. One might suppose that this notion has emerged from extensive study of the effectiveness of modifying the behavior of the elderly through environmental manipulation. To the contrary, and despite the status of conditioning as a highly effective technique of behavior modification, remarkably little is known about conditioning processes in the elderly.

The power of conditioning variables provides a basis for questioning the pessimistic view that changes in the elderly are exclusively a biological matter. From a conditioning standpoint, the environments to which older adults are exposed (or to which they expose themselves) are not especially conducive to the acquisition and maintenance of competent behaviors. Such environments may lack contingencies for rapid responding, for efficient memory, and, for that matter, for appropriate division of attention. Only future research can tell whether deficient behaviors of elderly individuals can be significantly remediated through conditioning-based interventions. A necessary preliminary to such efforts is the systematic laboratory study of basic conditioning processes in older adults.

While it is clearly the case that the proper understanding of aging must consider the interplay between structure and function, the reverse is also true. That is, in order to arrive at a complete account of structure and function, both must be placed within the context of developmental variables. Furthermore, from an analytic standpoint our knowledge of conditioning will be greatly enhanced by studying individuals whose structural and functional capabilities differ. And again, an ontogenetic approach seems particularly appropriate. To understand the interaction of structural and functional determinants of behavior, systematic examination of other age groups is needed.

The view taken here concerning the importance of a developmental approach is quite consistent with recent trends in the study of conditioning, in particular, the revival of interest in the comparative psychology of learning. There is increasing recognition that conditioning theories must come to grips with the structural constraints that phylogenetic differences place on the conditioning process. Similarly, the study of human conditioning must consider the possible constraints due to developmental differences. In this regard, it is important to note that the young adults who serve as subjects in the typical psychology experiment represent only one, somewhat arbitrarily selected, point along the developmental continuum. Systematic structural and functional analyses of the behavior of other age groups obviously are needed for a complete account. The present effort suggests an integrated approach which focuses on the interplay between structure and function. This approach should further understanding of the ways behavioral potentials and their realization change throughout the life span.

References

Baron, A., and Galizio, M. (1983). Instructional control of human operant behavior, *The Psychological Record*, **33**, 495–520.

Baron, A., and Menich, S. R. (1985). Age-related effects of temporal contingencies in response speed and memory, *Journal of Gerontology*, **40**, 60–70.

Baron, A., Menich, S. R., and Perone, M. (1983). Reaction times of older and younger men and temporal contingencies of reinforcement, *Journal of the Experimental Analysis of Behavior*, **40**, 275–287.

Baron, A., and Perone, M. (1982). The place of the human subject in the operant laboratory, *The Behavioral Analyst*, **5**, 143–158.

Baum, W. M. (1975). Time allocation in human vigilance, *Journal of the Experimental Analysis of Behavior*, **23**, 45–53.

Bradshaw, C. M., Szabadi, E., and Bevan P. (1976). Behavior of humans in variable-interval schedules of reinforcement, *Journal of the Experimental Analysis of Behavior*, **26**, 135–141.

Burke, D. M., and Light, L. L. (1981). Memory and aging: The role of retrieval processes, *Psychological Bulletin*, **90**, 513–546.

Catania, A. C. (1973). The psychologies of structure, function, and development, *American Psychologist*, **28**, 434–443.

Catania, A. C. (1984). *Learning* (2nd edn), Englewood Cliffs, NJ: Prentice-Hall.

Cerella, J., Poon, L. W., and Williams, D. M. (1980). Age and the complexity hypothesis. In L. W. Poon (ed), *Aging in the 1980s*, Washington, DC: American Psychological Association, pp. 332–340.

Conger, P., and Killeen, P. (1974). Use of concurrent operants in small group research, *Pacific Sociological Review*, **17**, 399–416.

Craik, F. I. M. (1977). Age differences in human memory. In J. E. Birren and W. K. Schaie (eds), *Handbook of the Psychology of Aging*, New York: Van Nostrand Reinhold, pp. 384–420.

de Villiers, P. (1977). Choice in concurrent schedules and a quantitative formulation of the law of effect. In W. K. Honig and J. E. R. Staddon (eds), *Handbook of Operant Behavior*, Englewood Cliffs, NJ: Prentice-Hall, pp. 233–287.

Eysenck, M. W. (1984). *A Handbook of Cognitive Psychology*, London: Lawrence Erlbaum Associates.

Hale, S., and Baron, A. (1984, May). Matching to compound samples: An operant paradigm to study divided attention in young and old adults. Paper presented at the meetings of the Association for Behavior Analysis, Nashville, TN.

Herrnstein, R.J. (1961). Relative and absolute strength of response as a function of frequency of reinforcement, *Journal of the Experimental Analysis of Behavior*, **4**, 267–272.

Jenkins, H.M., and Harrison, R.H. (1960). Effects of discrimination training on auditory generalization, *Journal of Experimental Psychology*, **59**, 246–253.

Kahneman, D. (1973). *Attention and Effort*, Englewood Cliffs, NJ: Prentice-Hall.

Kausler, D.H. (1982). *Experimental Psychology and Human Aging*, New York: Wiley.

Mackintosh, N.J. (1977). Stimulus control: Attentional factors. In W.K. Honig and J.E.R. Staddon (eds), *Handbook of Operant Behavior*, Englewood Cliffs, NJ: Prentice-Hall, pp.481–513.

Myerson, J., and Hale, S. (1984). Practical implications of the matching law, *Journal of Applied Behavior Analysis*, **17**, 367–380.

Navon, D., and Gopher, D. (1979). On the economy of the human-processing system, *Psychological Review*, **86**, 214–255.

Norman, D.A., and Bobrow, D.G. (1975). On data-limited and resource-limited processes, *Cognitive Psychology*, **7**, 44–64.

Pierce, W.D., and Epling, W.F. (1983). Choice, matching, and human behavior: A review of the literature, *The Behavior Analyst*, **6**, 57–76.

Posner, M.I. (1978). *Chronometric Explorations of Mind*, Hillsdale, NJ: Erlbaum.

Reynolds, G.S. (1961). Attention in the pigeon, *Journal of the Experimental Analysis of Behavior*, **4**, 203–208.

Rodewald, H.K. (1979). *Stimulus Control of Behavior*, Baltimore, MD.: University Park Press.

Schneider, W., and Schiffrin, R.M. (1977). Controlled and automatic human information processing: I. Detection, search, and attention, *Psychological Review*, **84**, 1–66.

Schroeder, S.R., and Holland, J.G. (1969). Reinforcement of eye movement with concurrent schedules, *Journal of the Experimental Analysis of Behavior*, **12**, 897–903.

Somberg, B.L., and Salthouse, T.A. (1982). Divided attention abilities in young and old adults, *Journal of Experimental Psychology: Human Perception and Performance*, **8**, 651–663.

Sperling, G., and Melchner, M.J. (1978). The attention operating characteristic: Examples from visual search, *Science*, **202**, 315–318.

Terrace, H.S. (1966). Stimulus control. In W.K. Honig (ed), *Operant Behavior: Areas of Research and Application*, Englewood Cliffs, NJ: Prentice-Hall, pp.271–344.

Thomas, D.R. (1970). Stimulus selection, attention, and related matters. In J.H. Reynierse (ed), *Current Issues in Animal Learning*, Lincoln, NE: University of Nebraska Press, pp.311–356.

Human Operant Conditioning and Behavior Modification
Edited by G. Davey and C. Cullen
© 1988 John Wiley & Sons Ltd

Chapter 9

Method and Theory in the Study of Human Competition

WILLIAM BUSKIST AND DAVID MORGAN
Auburn University

Perhaps as much as his propensity to produce championship football teams and the Super Bowl trophy which bears his name the late Green Bay Packer coach, Vince Lombardi, will be remembered for the one liner he offered the public regarding his coaching philosophy: 'Winning isn't everything, it is the only thing'. Such a statement aptly captures most of our attitudes about competition, athletic or otherwise. That is, we compete to win, to be the best, or merely to be awarded some prize that may not be had under other conditions. Indeed, the *raison d'être* for most athletes, professional or amateur, is to win. Roy Hobbes, the middle aged rookie of the New York Knights in Bernard Malamud's (1952) novel and later movie, *The Natural*, summed up what he hoped to accomplish by playing baseball: 'When I walk down the street, people will look and say "there goes Roy Hobbes, the best there ever was in the game"'.

Besides the personal satisfaction derived from besting rivals, there are often financial and prestigious rewards to be gained by being a successful competitor. Witness the astronomical salaries among today's professional athletes or the glory and financial gain to be had by winning a gold medal in the Olympics. Carl Lewis, for example, was estimated to have earned nearly 1 million dollars in advertising endorsements and related activities by winning four gold medals in the 1984 Los Angeles Olympic Games.

*We thank J. Castro, W. Chaplin, S. Green, and R. Morgan for reading and commenting on earlier versions of this work

Competition transcends sport though, and is present in most of our workaday lives. We compete for jobs, merit raises, and mates. Children are said to engage in sibling rivalry and compete for the attention of their parents and significant others. Students compete for grades and entrance to graduate schools. Academicians compete for peer respect and journal space. We even engage in competitive events in our leisure time; we golf or bowl against friends, play in recreational and intramural sports, participate in chili cookoffs and pie-baking contests. And as if this were not enough, most of us spend large, even excessive, amounts of time in front of the television watching sporting events, game shows, fishing and hunting tutorials, etc. In short, a good deal of our behavior, if not the bulk of it, is spent competing.

Given the ubiquity of competitive events in our society, it would seem that the study of competition is justified on *a priori* grounds and that there should exist an abundant database from which to draw and test theoretical and applied statements regarding competition. However, the extant literature, at least in psychology, is scant. For the most part, psychologists have focused on co-operation and have only studied competition *vis-à-vis* cooperation in order to identify the variables which govern an individual's choice to compete or cooperate. There are at least three reasons for the dearth of research on competition *per se*. First, social scientists have focused upon improving social relations between and within groups. After all, if science can determine the factors which produce a preference for cooperation over competition, such procedures might be implemented in classrooms, factories, businesses, etc., and as a prevailing belief goes, the more cooperative society we have, the greater the productivity and happiness we might all enjoy. Moreover, competition often produces negative emotional and behavioral by-products. Tempers are said to 'flare' when the ethics of good sportsmanship or the rules of competition are broken and name calling and fistfights ensue (e.g. hockey games often involve a brawl or two). In politics, competition for votes often results in spying (e.g. Watergate) and mudslinging (e.g. Carter–Reagan campaign). In business, misleading advertisements, and contrived product shortages are methods by which companies compete for consumer patronage. International military conflict and civil war are direct results of participants' competition for natural and political resources. Even spectators at sporting events, such as those at the Italian-English soccer game in Brussels in which 38 persons were killed and 437 injured, become involved in competition-related displays of aggression. Social psychological research supports these casual observations. For example, the classic research of Sherif *et al.* (1961) with small groups of children showed that while competition produces intra-group unity, it also produces inter-group prejudice, jealousy, and hostility. In contrast, cooperation produces intra- and inter-group unity, friendship, and happiness. Steigleder *et al.* (1978) highlighted the aversive properties of competition by showing that many subjects, particularly those led to believe that they are incompetent relative to another person, will terminate competition when given the opportunity.

Second, there has been a longstanding sentiment among social psychological researchers that competition increases quantity but not quality of performance. In fact, Allport (1924) noted that competition is likely to produce a deterioration in performance. For example, in one of the earliest studies of competion, Triplett (1897) showed that only half of his 40 subjects showed an increase in quality of performance (speed in winding line on a fishing reel). The other half either showed no improvement in speed or showed a marked decrease in performance. More recently, Johnson *et al.* (1981), in their meta-analysis of the interpersonal benefits to be derived from individual, cooperative, and competitive educational contingencies, concluded that cooperation is the most effective means by which to promote educational productivity and progress. Scott and Cherrington (1974), in their study of undergraduate scoring of test booklets, showed competitive contingencies produced higher output but less interpersonal attraction than cooperation contingencies.

Third, there are strong socio-religious reasons for promoting cooperative means of social behavior over competitive ones. Competition usually results in an inequitable distribution of rewards while cooperation usually involves an equitable or near-equitable distribution. Christ and the Biblical prophets taught that envy, strife and contention result from inequitable distributions of certain resources. For example, after Paul had learned that the church at Corinth had become divided and that certain factions were vying for the townspeople's loyalty and tithes, he wrote his first epistle to the Corinthians, advising them to join together in the common cause of the church: 'Now I beseech you, brethren... that ye all speak the same thing, and that there be no divisions among you; but that ye be perfectly joined together in the same mind and judgment. For it hath been declared unto me of you... that there are contentions among you' (1 Corinthians 1:10–11). Similarly, Paul urged the Phillipians to become of 'one mind': 'Let nothing be done through strife or vainglory but in lowliness of mind let each esteem other better than themselves' (Phillipians 2:3). Biblical teachings such as these are used by modern preachers, ministers and evangelists to promote cooperation, sharing, giving and other forms of noncompetitive social behavior among their followers.

Thus the deterrents to the study of competition have spanned several levels of society and provide an example of where science is guided by social trends. While cooperation has been promoted both in society at large and within scientific circles, it does not necessarily follow that competition *per se* cannot be a topic of scholarly inquiry. The fact is that competition is ever present in nearly every aspect of our culture. Granted the pervasiveness of competition and the lack of scientific inquiry into the variables governing competitive behavior, the purpose of this chapter is four-fold: (1) to review and assess well-known scientific definitions of competition in an attempt to identify the critical components of competition which might support theory development and research; (2) to integrate the methods and findings from the three major lines of research that have studied competition: nonhuman animal models, social psychological research involving matrix games, and human research involving reinforcement theory; (3) to propose an alternative method for the study of competition; and (4) to examine several empirical issues that future research might feasibly study.

Definitions of competition

Historically, there has been little agreement among researchers as to exactly what competition is or what its primary characteristics are. Allport (1924) spoke of competition in terms of both social facilitation and rivalry. Social facilitation is the increase in performance due to any stimulation from other persons while rivalry is the 'drive to excel others' (p. 280). Thus an increase in performance may be induced by either the desire to win or by the stimulation provided by another person, as with the distance runner trying to 'keep up' with, but not necessarily overtaking, another runner during a race. Margaret Mead (1937), in her socio-anthropological studies of primitive peoples, defined competition as the 'act of seeking or endeavoring to gain what another is seeking to gain at the same time' (p. 7). Further, competition is 'behavior oriented toward a goal in which the other competitors are secondary; rivalry is behavior oriented toward another human being, whose worsting is the primary goal' (p. 17). Outlining his theory of cooperation and competition, Deutsch (1949, 1962) noted that contrient interdependence is the defining characteristic of competition. 'Contrient interdependence is the condition in which individuals are so linked that there is a negative correlation between their goal attainments' (1962, p. 276).

Each of these definitions poses problems for the rigorous study of competition. While making an important distinction between social facilitation and rivalry, Allport's definition has all the problems ascribed to drive reduction theory. It is also difficult to isolate and manipulate experimentally an individual's desire to win. Mead's definition is problematic because competitive behavior might possibly be shaped and maintained by stimuli and events other than or in addition to 'worsting' an opponent. Deutsch's definition lacks precision as it is possible for a negative correlation to exist between competitors over a given number of trials, and for the score to be tied at the contest's end. It is also imaginable that certain forms of cooperation, such as altruism, might result in a negative correlation between goal attainments.

Potentially more feasible definitions of competition, at least in terms of specificity, have been offered by several experimental psychologists. For Skinner (1953) a competitive situation is one in which 'the behavior of one [person] can be reinforced only at the cost of the reinforcement to the other' (p. 311). Church (1968) focused on the social aspects of competition: 'A competitive situation is one in which the reinforcement to a subject depends upon his performance relative to that of the other subjects' (p. 152). Hake, Olvera, and Bell (1975) took the definition a step further and specified the response necessary: 'Competition is said to occur when two or more individuals make taking responses for the same reinforcer' (p. 343). In this way, competition produces maximal responding over the competitive episode or period. The advantages of definitions such as these is that the emphasis is placed on situational factors outside the organism rather than those which are merely descriptive. The response and its relation to that of another individual is also clearly specified, as is the relation between responding and reinforcement.

It is clear that most researchers have not viewed competition as a simple behavior or set of responses. Rather, competition is viewed as a complex relation between the behavior of one person and that of another with respect to a common stimulus or event that cannot be shared or divided among the persons involved. Each of the definitions offered above appears to focus on specific elements of the competitive situation and, when combined, point to the critical components of the competitive situation: (1) usually two or more organisms are involved; (2) behavior is directed toward obtaining or taking reinforcement (note, however, that the behavior of competitors need not occur simultaneously with respect to reinforcement, as in golf or bowling); (3) reinforcement is made contingent on some aspect of behavior, i.e. speed, accuracy, topography, frequency, etc., and some criterion must exist to determine which subject's response, relative to that of the other, will be reinforced; (4) reinforcement in any specified segment of the competitive event or episode is mutually exclusive; (5) trials or time criteria usually exist for termination of the competitive event.

Definitional constraints

This approach to defining competition has at least three qualifications. First, while it is possible that nearly any aspect of behavior may be made the basis for competition, it does not necessarily follow that all persons involved are under control of the competitive context. Take for example the buying of shoes at a shoe sale. I buy the last pair of shoes in my size which means that the next person coming in to buy that shoe in that size will not be able to do so. One could say that 'I beat him to the sale'. In this case, my behavior, relative to that of another shopper, results in my obtaining the shoes at the expense of someone else not being able to. Functionally, this could be considered a case of competition although (1) neither of us may have been aware that we each behaved toward the shoes relative to one another or (2) our behavior was not under the control of each other (see Keller and Schoenfeld, 1950, pp. 257–258), since we might have been responding to an advertisement regarding the sale or because we happened to be in the shoe store and noticed the shoes on sale. What is important in this case is not the *social* relation *per se* that exists between individuals but the *functional relation* (see, e.g. Hyten and Burns, 1986).

Second, competition need not involve another individual. For example, Parrott (1983) has discussed social behavior in terms of 'the functional relation obtaining between the responding of one person and the stimulating of another person or object' (p. 533). An instance of this type of competition might be self-competition or 'auto-competition' as Allport (1924) called it. This is the case in which an individual comes to respond to some standard such as time or the number of correct responses without direct respect to the presence of another individual. Such competition may have its roots in actual interpersonal competition. Thus a runner might compete 'against the clock' over a 10 kilometer course she will be running in a future race. This practice usually has the effect of narrowing the distance between the runner's time and times of others. It is the functional relation that exists between other runners' times and her time that imbues this situation with competitive stimulation. Other examples might include the bowler who goes to the alley by himself and bowls three or four games as practice or the golfer who goes out to the course by herself to tune up for a tournament. Such self-competition would not be considered social if the roots of such behavior could not be traced to actual interpersonal competition, such as in the card game of solitaire.

Third, some situations may have the appearance of being competitive when in fact they are not. Take, for instance, the case of the runner out on a leisurely run. He turns a corner and notices another runner about 100 meters ahead. The first runner also notices a street sign about 200 meters in front of the other runner and attempts to 'beat' the second runner to it. This 'race' is rather one-sided and is an instance of social facilitation rather than competition since the first runner's performance (speed) increased due to the mere presence of the second runner and because these runners are not making responses for the same reinforcer.

Definitions of related social phenomena

Other social behavior, particularly cooperation and sharing, are studied as alternatives to competition. Cooperation, as defined by Hake and associates (e.g. Hake, Vukelich, and Olvera, 1975; Hake and Olvera, 1978) is any social situation in which reinforcers for one person are at least partially dependent upon the behavior of at least one other person. Competition could be defined similarly since the reinforcers for one's own behavior are usually dependent upon some characteristic of another's behavior. In cooperation, however, the total number of responses increases as does equity of reinforcement, while in competition responding usually increases but reinforcer equity decreases. Sharing, the other major alternative to competition, involves equitable distributions of reinforcement but involves taking responses rather than giving responses. That is, cooperation usually involves both subjects giving reinforcers to one another, usually on alternate trials, while sharing involves each subject alternating turns taking reinforcers. While Hake (e.g. Hake and Olvera, 1978) has discussed cooperation and sharing in terms of equity effects, competition may also involve an equal distribution of reinforcers when both competitors are of equal ability (e.g. a tied race) or when cooperation or sharing develop as a secondary response pattern in competition (e.g. price fixing).

Some dimensions of competition

Our component approach to defining competition suggests several useful distinctions in discussing various types of competition. Three of the more obvious and useful forms are presented in this section.

Interactive and noninteractive

Interactive competitive events such as tennis, soccer, rugby, and squash require both offensive behavior, which is directed toward obtaining reinforcement, and defensive behavior, which is either directed toward preventing reinforcement of the opponent's behavior or which interferes with the opponent's responses directed toward reinforcement. Examples of interactive competition would be the execution of a tackle in football or one player attempting to return the serve of the other player in tennis. Since participants in interactive competition must respond to the behavior of other persons, these types of games usually require subjects to play simultaneously for some agreed upon time or trial period. (A notable exception to this may be the form of chess in which players make moves in each other's absence.)

Noninteractive contests do not involve participants intervening with one another with respect to the response chosen as the basis for competitive reinforcement or with stimuli (e.g. a baseball or football) contacted by an opponent; all that is necessary is that the participants' scores be compared at the end of some agreed upon time or trial period. In bowling, for instance, the opponents do have sensory contact with one another but they do not respond in such a manner that one's behavior prevents the other from successfully executing a response. Moreover, in noninteractive contests, one's behavior is neither necessary nor sufficient for the occurrence of the second competitor's behavior. This does not mean, however, that interaction may not take place on another level. For example, the mere execution of a response, say an exceptional tee-off in golf or a perfectly executed triple somersault with a half twist in diving, may affect an opponent's behavior (i.e. so called 'psychological pressure').

An important point regarding the differences between interactive and noninteractive competition is that in the latter there are few, if any, instances of negative emotional responses directed toward opponents. It is uncommon to hear of the bowler who yells obscenities at his opponent or of the golfer who hurls her clubs and balls at fellow golfers, although it is common to hear an occasional obscenity directed at the ball after a poor drive or to see a golfer slam an iron into the sod after a duffed shot. In interactive competitive contests, however, such outbursts are common among both players and spectators (e.g. hockey, soccer, football).

Individual and team competition

An obvious difference in competitive events is that some, like tennis and track, are considered to be individual sports while others, like soccer and basketball, are considered to be team sports. Individual and team competition may be either interactive (e.g. tennis, baseball, respectively) or noninteractive (e.g. golf, bobsleding, respectively). In individual competitive events an individual is competing against only one other individual and so responding, functionally, to stimulation from that person's behavior and objects physically contacted by that person (i.e. balls, pucks, etc). Team competition is more complex and difficult to study since team members must respond not only to stimuli related to opposing players but also to stimulation produced by teammates. That is, individual members of a team cooperate with one another in the execution of complex responses. Borrowing from Marwell and Schmitt's (1975) discussion of cooperation, teamwork may involve the following: Goal-directed behavior (obtaining reinforcement), rewards for each participant (recognition for a job well done), distributed responses (each player on a team makes the same or different response), and coordination (one player passes the ball to another). It is also possible that the variables controlling teamwork differ depending on whether the behavior of teammates is essentially similar (e.g. rowing) or different (e.g. basketball). Moreover, the variables governing competition in individual competitive events may be different from those controlling team competition.

Minimal and maximal competition

Competition may also be discussed in terms of equity of reinforcement among competitors. Allport (1924) noted that competition is greatest when the skill of the competitors is equally matched. That is, the performance of two or more competitors reflects the quality of competition in terms of the score or distribution of reinforcement at the end of the competitive episode. If one competitor is much more successful at obtaining reinforcement than an opponent she might alter her behavior to allow the other person to catch up (but not necessarily to the point of tying or surpassing her score). In contrast, the person receiving infrequent or no reinforcement may quit responding (i.e. extinction). An example of the former would be a football coach putting in his second or third string players to avoid 'running up the score' while an example of the latter would be the runner who stops and walks because he is so far behind the other runners. However, other factors such as verbal stimulation from coaches and others, as well as self-imposed standards, may prevent the loser from 'giving up'. Such is the case when a runner in a race has no chance to catch up to the lead runner, but instead 'runs against the clock' in an attempt to better a previous time or showing. In other cases, it may be the leader whose behavior comes under the control of the clock as in the case of the marathon runner who has outdistanced his fellow runners by 2000 meters, but continues to run hard to 'go for the record'.

Discussion of the types of competition underscores the diversity and complexity of competitive phenomena as well as pointing up the abundance of important research questions which need to be addressed. For example, clarification of the variables controlling behavior in individual versus team competition or in different types of team competition would not only advance our theoretical understanding of competition but also contribute significantly to applied concerns such as the development and refining of training and coaching strategies. Also important is the study of factors that contribute to individual differences in competitive performance such as in 'quitting' and 'persevering'. In the next section, we review competition research to date with respect to both the demonstration of competition in the laboratory and elucidation of some of its controlling variables in various settings.

Prevailing research strategies

Nonhuman animal models

As is true of so many other scientific pursuits, the analysis of human competitive behavior finds part of its history in the animal laboratory. Among the earliest of these investigations was Lepley's (1937) study of individual, noninteractive competitive straight alley running in rats. Animals were initially trained to run the length of the straight alley for food reinforcement, then were pair-matched according to running speeds. During competitive trials, animals ran simultaneously but only the first animal to reach its goal box received food. Pairs separated rapidly into consistent 'winners' and 'losers', but no response facilitation was apparent in either group; in fact, while 'winners' competitive running speed did not differ from individual running speed, 'losers' showed a marked decrease in running speed. Straight alley running in rats was also studied by Winslow (1940, 1944a) who similarly matched pairs according to individual running speed. Results were consistent with those of Lepley (1937) in demonstrating no increase in competitive over individual running speed. Winslow (1944b) also showed that time to escape from a puzzle box for food reinforcement did not differ significantly for cats tested in competitive pairs versus animals tested individually.

In contrast to these studies, Bayroff (1940) demonstrated response facilitation as an effect of individual, noninteractive competition in rats who swam the length of an experimental tank under water. Animals were initially matched according to individual swimming times. Reinforcement consisted of escape to air at the goal end of the swimming tank. During competitive trials, the first pair member to reach the goal was allowed immediate access to air while the 'loser' was kept under water an additional 20 seconds. Swimming speed under competitive conditions increased relative to individual trials and, as in Lepley's (1937) experiment, pair members separated early into 'winners' and 'losers'.

Highlighting the notion that competitive contingencies differentially reinforce particular response properties, Church (1961) demonstrated response facilitation in a lever-pressing procedure. In two experiments, food reinforcement was delivered to whichever of two rats emitted the most or the least number of responses in a 15-second period. Yoked noncompetitive animals received the same number and temporal distribution of reinforcement as their experimental counterparts. Reinforcement made contingent on slower or faster responding, respectively, produced higher probabilities of both relative to the performance of control animals. Kanak and Davenport (1967), using a similar yoking procedure with rats, obtained identical results.

Church (1962), in a study of minimal and maximal competition, later identified initial relative skill of competitors as an important component of the magnitude of response facilitation produced by competition. Relative skill was defined as the ratio of a subject's responses over both its own and its opponent's responses. Food reinforcement was delivered to whichever of two rats pressed a lever first when food was available according to a variable-interval (VI) 30-second schedule. The larger the performance differences during initial competitive inter-reinforcement intervals (IRIs), the more response facilitation obtained during competition. Finally, using a straight alley running procedure rather than the lever press response, Carnthan and Church (1964) differentially reinforced the slower of two rats and found that rats in this condition ran slower than did rats in a control group. The researchers argued, however, that differential reinforcement, and not the presence of the competitor, was sufficient to produce slower running. All experimental animals, whether they had visual contact or no contact with their competitor, showed reduced running speeds during competition.

Fukasawa, Lima, and Masur (1975) have shown that individual, noninteractive competitive performance entailing one response does not necessarily carry over to a different competitive behavior. Rats, selectively bred as offspring of winner-runway and loser-runway parents, were first trained and then competed in a standard straight alley runway, and then trained and competed in a food-hole apparatus. The food-hole apparatus contained milk and was designed such that only one animal at a given time could access it. Predictably, offspring of winner-runway animals dominated competitive runway performance. This ability did not generalize to the food-hole response, however, as no significant difference was found between animals on this task.

While behavior in several nonhuman species has been studied using a variety of competitive tasks, including straight alley running (Carnathan and Church, 1964), swimming (Bayroff, 1940), lever pressing (Church, 1961, 1962), and the food-hole response (Fukasawa, Lima, and Masur, 1975), competitive facilitation of behavior has, at the same time, proved experimentally intractable, as suggested by the negative findings of Lepley (1937) and Winslow (1940, 1944a, 1944b). This failure to produce response facilitation unequivocally has been attributed, by Church (1968), to an absence of differential reinforcement. Large differences in subjects' initial behavior result in the selection of consistent 'winners' and 'losers'. This occurrence leads to a positive feedback function. The slower responding organism is less likely to receive reinforcement (unless slower responding has been specifically selected for reinforcement), which only leads to a further reduction in responding. The end result of this feedback function is response extinction for the 'losing' animal and little, if any, response facilitation on the part of the 'winning' animal for whom increased responding is unnecessary to obtain competitive reinforcement. There are, of course, other methodological differences characterizing research in this area which likely contribute to the disparate results. It might be argued, for example, that animals in Bayroff's (1940) swimming experiment were exposed to a particularly aversive contingency; hence, the rapidly obtained response facilitation. It is clear from the research on animal competition that the manner in which competitive reinforcement controls behavior depends both on the nature of the task as well as the competitors' initial performance on the task (i.e. minimal versus maximal competition).

Social psychology: The gaming literature

To date the most extensive and systematic analyses of competition have derived from the use of matrix games by social psychologists. Among the more popular of these games are the Prisoner's Dilemma (Luce and Raiffa, 1957) and the trucking game (Deutsch and Krauss, 1960). Such games, typically referred to as mixed-motive games, present subjects with a conflict whose resolution results in either individual or collective gains. While the specific game conflicts faced by subjects may vary, the general dilemma represents a common theme; subjects face a forced choice to cooperate with or compete against one another in order to maximize the payoffs made possible by the game's matrix structure. The game's formal matrix is composed of a number of contingency cells, each designating the specific consequence of each subject's response. In the case of the Prisoner's Dilemma, subjects play the role of imprisoned convicts who must decide whether to confess to a crime or implicate the other convict in the crime. The degree of sentence handed down depends upon the combination of subjects' responses; all possible response combinations are represented in the game's cell matrix. The trucking game entails rival trucking firms, each requiring access to a one lane road over which only one can travel at a given time. At each end of this road are toll gates which can be operated by players either to provide (cooperate) or prohibit (compete) one another from entering the road. Payoffs, usually in the form of points or money, are delivered at the end of each trial in accordance with the subjects' responses. The purpose of the present section is to discuss briefly the more commonly manipulated variables in matrix gaming and their effects upon subjects' game behavior. Comprehensive reviews and critical assessments of this voluminous literature are available elsewhere (see, e.g. Vinacke, 1969; Wrightsman, O'Connor, and Baker, 1972).

The independent variables examined in matrix game research typically fall into one of three general categories: (1) task variables; (2) situational variables; and (3) personality variables. Task variables include structural conditions of the experiment which remain unaltered across sessions independent of subjects' behavior. The game's payoff matrix, for instance, is a structural property of the task which, while perhaps strongly affecting game playing responses, is not reciprocally altered by them. Much game research has investigated the effects of varying matrix payoffs on subjects' response preferences. With few exceptions, however, varying relative payoff magnitudes has little influence upon response preference (Dolbear and Lave, 1966; Jones *et al.*, 1968).

Situational variables include all other aspects of the experimental task, other than the structural properties of the game itself, that are manipulated by the experimenter. Since a subject's behavior seems intuitively to be at least partly a function of the coactor's behavior, a logical variable of interest would be players' responses. For this variable to be experimentally manipulated, of course, requires the use of confederates or experimental settings in which subjects believe themselves to be interacting with another person when, in fact, they are interacting with the experimenter. Conflicting findings have emerged from this type of research. Neither Bixenstine, Potash, and Wilson (1963) nor McClintock *et al.* (1963) were able to demonstrate any stable pattern or change in subjects' performance as a result of randomly ordered experimental conditions. In contrast, Solomon (1960) demonstrated that when subjects played against a matching strategy (responses of experimenter matched those of the subject), more cooperation obtained than when the imposed strategy was either solely cooperative or competitive. In addition, Bixenstine and Wilson (1963) found that subjects responded in a like fashion to a strategy which was either 95 per cent cooperative or competitive and varied systematically over trials. Even conditions of this sort, however, failed to produce more than 50 per cent cooperative play in subjects. Similarly, Komorita (1965) revealed little cooperative reciprocity when confederates' responses matched those of subjects on previous trials. However, as the number of trials increases, so does the likelihood that players will cooperate (Morehous, 1966). Thus, examination of game playing strategies suggests that subjects' behavior may be only weakly related to partners' responding. Also, Swinth (1967) has observed that subjects in matrix games are often confused as to exactly what differentiates coopera- tive from competitive responding. Games that allow for expression and clarification of interest and purpose, usually through verbal and/or written communication as well as through visual contact, markedly reduce this ambiguity; they also, not surprisingly, occasion more cooperative behavior (see, e.g. Deutsch and Krauss, 1962; Bixenstine, Levitt, and Wilson, 1966; Swensson, 1967; Wichman, 1970). In addition, while fixed experimental contingencies seldom affect behavior, contingencies which change over the games' course do (Deutsch *et al.*, 1967).

The types of instruction given to subjects have also been demonstrated to affect response choice. Level of cooperative behavior, for instance, is strongly related to the degree to which investigators emphasize cooperation in instructing subjects (Deutsch, 1960; Raven and Eachus, 1963; Evans, 1964). Several researchers have also shown response preference to be a function of the relationship between players. In general, subjects are more likely to cooperate with friends than with nonacquaintances or disliked individuals (Oskamp and Perlman, 1965; Swingle and Gillis, 1968), although some exceptions have been reported (e.g. Oskamp and Perlman, 1966). Married couples also are more likely to cooperate than strangers (Schoeninger and Wood, 1969). Marlowe, Gergen, and Doob (1966) demonstrated that subjects who were led to believe they would see their opponents after the game were found to engage in cooperative play more often than players who were not so instructed.

A significant portion of the gaming literature focuses upon the relationship between various personality attributes, traits, dispositions, etc., and cooperative and/or competitive responses. This research is primarily correlational in that game playing behavior is measured as a function of personal characteristics rather than of aspects of the experimental task itself. While this type of research may represent a creative interface between experimental social psychology and traditional personality theory, it will not be reviewed here. It has, instead, been our intention to communicate the general findings of an equally large body of research in which some measure of control over independent variables was exercised. The reader interested in the relationship between personality characteristics and behavior in mixed-motive games is referred to Vinacke (1969) who has adequately canvassed this literature. It should also be noted that the gaming literature suffers no theoretical impoverishment; in particular, we note the equity theories of Homans (1961) and Adams (1965) as well as Kelley and Thibaut's (1978) significant work on interpersonal relations.

Operant analyses of competitive behavior

The application of behavior analytic techniques to the study of human competition originated with the exploratory research of Ogden Lindsley (1966; see also Cohen, 1962). Pairs of human subjects were seated in adjacent experimental cubicles, each containing a panel with a response plunger. According to the reinforcement schedule in effect, plunger pulling dispensed pennies into a small opening in the response panel. A sliding partition allowed subjects to view one another but no physical contact was possible. The primary dependent measures were the temporal and sequential relations between subjects' responses. While reinforcement was usually contingent upon cooperative team responses, defined as responses by pair members occurring within 0.5 second of one another, competitive reinforcement was also studied. During competition, if the second subject's response occurred within 0.5 second of the first subject's response, only the second subject received reinforcement. If the first subject's response, however, caught the second subject 'off guard' and the second subject did not respond within 0.5 second, only the first subject received reinforcement. During all conditions, leadership was uncontrolled (i.e. whichever subject emitted the first response after the last reinforcement was designated leader). In general, competitive responding could be produced only with difficulty as subject pairs usually resolved the conflict cooperatively by alternating leadership.

Lindsley's (1966) work was followed by a systematic program of research conducted by Schmitt (1976) and Schmitt and Marwell (1971), part of which examined the conditions under which subject pairs chose to cooperate or compete interactively or work individually. In the first study, pair members could respond to take $1.00 of their coactor's earnings during specified periods of a cooperative procedure (Schmitt and Marwell, 1971). Introduction of taking responses disrupted cooperation, as subjects chose to work under relatively safer individual conditions. When taking was allowed during both cooperative and individual conditions, subjects either cooperated or terminated the experiment. A later study revealed that when given the opportunity to cooperate, compete or work alone, competitive responding occurred only when reinforcement magnitude for competition exceeded that for cooperation (see also Matthews, 1979). Schmitt (1976) obtained similar results with triads although triad members were more likely to quit the experiment than were dyad members since overall earnings were less (i.e. split three ways instead of two).

In a more recent program of research, Schmitt (in press) has investigated performance differences under alternative interpersonal contingencies rather than the factors affecting subjects' preferences for cooperative, competitive or individual responding. Results of initial experiments demonstrated that both cooperative and competitive contingencies produce greater cost-effectiveness (e.g. responses per unit of reinforcement) than do individual contingencies, and that cooperative contingencies occasion highest overall response rates. This latter finding, however, is tempered by the disclosure that subjects spent comparatively less session time competing than cooperating. Indeed, when local competitive response rate was calculated (i.e response rate during only those portions of a session in which the competitive contingency was in effect), rate differences between cooperative and competitive responding were minimal.

Stewart, Zelman, and Mithaug (1971) investigated the effects of three different competitive contingencies on subjects' cooperative responding. Subjects were junior high school dropouts who could show up at the experiment at their own discretion. Subjects were divided into three-member teams without respect to previous task experience. The task was to accumulate points/money on a counter by holding down three buttons simultaneously. According to how team members divided their labor, several types of button pressing were possible, with the method of two subjects holding and one pressing rapidly as the most effective in producing points. Teamwork was studied under three different conditions: (1) an experimenter-imposed standard which had to be surpassed before receiving reinforcement (an additional 30 seconds of game time in which subjects could earn more points/money); (2) inter-team competition in which one team had to surpass another team's response total to receive reinforcement; and (3) inter-team competition in which one team had to emit either a greater or lesser number of responses than another before receiving reinforcement. Responding was highest in the second and third groups where subjects had to surpass a standard set by another triad.

Weinstein and Holzbach (1972) showed competitive contingencies to be superior to cooperative ones in producing response output. In each of their experimental phases, monetary reinforcement was contingent upon total group response output. In the competitive phase there was an individual contingency in which reinforcement magnitude was dependent upon performance level of each individual relative to that of teammates. Thus the more responses emitted by a subject the greater the amount of reinforcement to be shared among group members and the greater the chance that each individual's share of the total would be larger. In the cooperative condition reinforcement was divided equally among group members regardless of individual effort. Competitive conditions produced more responding than cooperative conditions.

Hake and his associates (Hake, Olvera, and Bell, 1975; Olvera and Hake, 1976) employed a matching-to-sample procedure to investigate task choice in dyads and found that when reinforcement was equal across cooperative and competitive conditions, subjects chose to cooperate rather than compete. Subjects distributed matching-to-sample problems to themselves by fulfilling a schedule requirement on one lever, and distributed problems to their coactor by fulfilling the requirement on a second lever. Responses which distributed problems to oneself, designated 'taking' responses, were considered competitive while responses which distributed problems to a coactor, designated 'giving' responses, were identified as cooperative. Requirements on each lever varied from FR10 to FR120 (Hake *et al.*, 1975). Subjects preferred competition only at low ratio values. Moreover, subjects frequently resolved high response requirements by sharing, i.e. alternating taking responses. Sharing represents an advantageous means of ensuring an equitable distribution of reinforcement while simultaneously maintaining minimum individual effort. In a follow-up study, subjects were exposed either to immediately low or high ratio requirements or adjusting high or low requirements (Olvera and Hake, 1976). Consistent with earlier findings, subjects chose to share problems when ratio requirements were high. In addition, the adjusting ratio groups developed sharing as a response much earlier than did the simple ratio group. Thus, responding on competitive ratio schedules may acquire aversive properties because competition requires responding on every trial whereas cooperation and sharing do not.

A similar line of operant research, bearing considerable implications for an understanding of competition, has addressed phenomena more commonly identified as social comparison processes (Festinger, 1954). In general, these investigations have highlighted the importance played by information concerning one's own performance relative to that of a coactor in social situations (Hake, Vukelich, and Kaplan, 1973; Seta, 1982; Vukelich and Hake, 1974). Seta (1982) has studied the effects of providing feedback pertaining to a coactor's performance on a subject's subsequent behavior. Pair members sat opposite one another in front of separate response consoles and were allowed both visual and auditory contact. When subjects fulfilled response requirements on a button pressing task, a tone sounded which was audible to both subjects. No response interaction took place; subjects were engaged in parallel, identical tasks (noninteractive competition). However, subjects responded according to different schedule parameters, producing differences in tone density. Feedback indicating a coactor's slightly superior performance resulted in response facilitation. Facilitation was not occasioned, however, by clearly superior or inferior coactor performance as indicated by feedback rate.

Hake and his colleagues (Hake, Vukelich, and Kaplan, 1973; Vukelich and Hake, 1974) conducted a similar series of studies on social comparison using the matching-to-sample procedure discussed earlier. However, in contrast to Seta's (1982) work, comparison responses or audits were treated as the dependent rather than independent variable. Information pertaining to coactor performance was contingent upon fulfilling a schedule requirement on a designated 'audit' button. The initial study revealed auditing of coactor performance to be a robust social phenomenon. In addition, when access to one's own score was made contingent upon self-audits, such responses occurred more frequently under social than under nonsocial (individual) conditions. A second study demonstrated auditing to be a function of the correspondence of subjects' scores over the course of experimental sessions. Matching-to-sample problems were distributed to subjects according to a preprogrammed schedule. Under some conditions, problems were equitably distributed while under other conditions problems were disproportionately distributed. Both self- and coactor-audits were more frequent under conditions of high score correspondence. Auditing seldom occurred, however, when large discrepancies in subjects' scores developed. Maintenance of auditing thus appears to depend upon the extent to which its consequence provides a discriminative function. During sessions of equitable reinforcer distribution, auditing provided important information about the relevant social reinforcer, namely being ahead of one's coactor. With large score discrepancies, auditing provided only redundant information, for the likelihood of a change in one's relative status from one trial to the next was minimal. Thus, research on the audit response tends to support one of the more central hypotheses of social comparison theory (Festinger, 1954): Subjects are more likely to compare themselves to individuals of similar abilities as determined by specific performance measures.

In summary, the study of social relations has not been the sole responsibility of social psychologists and animal researchers, but has more recently attracted the attention of operant psychologists as well. Operant research into social processes has eschewed the more traditional practice of evaluating correlations between response strategies and personality variables, and has, instead, focused on the functional relations obtaining between subjects' responses and task variables. Research in this area has both supplemented the social psychological literature on factors affecting the choice to cooperate or compete, and provided a method for the study of social comparison processes.

An alternative procedure: Use of reinforcement schedules to study competition

While all three approaches to the study of competition just reviewed have contributed to the database for our present understanding of social behavior, each has its shortcomings. Nonhuman animal models of social behavior are probably better models of nonhuman animal social behavior than human social behavior since no matter what pains are taken to assure similarity across conditions, the rat environment cannot ever be made isomorphic to ours. Thus despite evidence for interspecies generality, there is an equally plausible argument for interspecies differences (Buskist, Morgan, and Barry, 1983; Lowe, 1979; Lowe, Beasty, and Bentall, 1983). Hake has also pointed out that 'If an animal is simply not observed to engage in cooperation, trust ... in its natural habitat and only with extreme difficulty in an experiment arranged to produce these behaviors, then that animal is not the species to use' (Hake, 1982, p.25). Since much human competition, such as athletics and business, takes place far from the rodent operant chamber, it is difficult to imagine how nonhuman animal models would give us the complete story with respect to human competition. Thus future competition research might augment nonhuman animal research with detailed laboratory studies of human competition, starting with simple cases (e.g. individual, noninteractive competition) and gradually working up to complex ones (e.g. interactive team competition), as warranted by the database.

Both traditional social psychological research on games and experiments involving application of reinforcement theory to human competition have used humans as subjects but have studied only the choice to cooperate or compete. Thus, we now know something about the variables that govern one's choice to cooperate or compete but little about the variables which govern competition *per se.* Social psychological research has also tended to focus on variables that are beyond the experimenter's control such as personality traits or subjects' expectations, so that at best, much of this line of research is correlational and does not lend itself well to understanding the factors necessary and sufficient for competition.

An alternative approach might consist of combining the best features of each of these approaches into a single procedure that would allow for a thorough-going analysis of competition. Consider the advantage of developing a 'game' in which persons compete for reinforcers, such as points or money, by being the first to satisfy the requirements of a given reinforcement schedule. Such a procedure would have the appeal of a game and the experimental control found in nonhuman animal and reinforcement theory research. In addition, it might incorporate any or all of the components of the definition of competition discussed at the outset of this chapter: (1) any number of subjects might be involved so that either individual or team competition might be feasibly studied; (2) interactive or noninteractive competitive contingencies might be studied by simple rearrangement of reinforcement contingencies; (3) the experimenter controls reinforcement which might be made contingent upon any aspect of responding such as speed, accuracy, latency, etc.; (4) reinforcement may be made mutually exclusive on either a trials or sessions basis. In addition to the types of competition which subjects might be required to engage in, a large number of other variables might be effectively isolated and studied, for example reinforcement delivery systems (schedules), reinforcement magnitude, task requirements, instructional or coaching strategies, team size, role of visual and auditory stimulation produced by competitors and/or teammates, the effects of score discrepancies between competitors, social comparison, etc.

Some exemplars

Competition and instructions to compete

Over the past five years, we have used performance on FI, FR and DRL schedules of reinforcement as a baseline for the study of human competition. Each of these schedules has been shown to produce characteristic patterns of responding in our subjects. Moreover, competitive versions of these schedules differentially select for response characteristics somewhat distinguishable from those maintained under independent conditions. Competitive FR contingencies, for example, favor absolute response rate; the emphasis is upon total output. Fixed-interval schedules, on the other hand, differentially reinforce pauses after reinforcement followed by response bursts near the end of the inter-reinforcement interval (IRI). The DRL schedule, though also interval based, selects for rather precise temporal discriminations which, under competitive contingencies, become even more highly refined. The use of various reinforcement schedules is in keeping with Church's (1962) significant observation that competitive reinforcement exerts influence over various topographical properties of behavior. Most instances of skilled competition do indeed bear this notion out; winning or losing is typically made contingent upon a complex aggregate of qualitative and quantitative performance criteria.

An initial series of three experiments examined the role of orienting instructions in competitive fixed-interval (FI) performance (Buskist *et al.*, 1984). Orienting instructions are general verbal descriptions of the apparatus and experimental task whose functions include both setting the occasion for the response of interest and enhancing response acquisition. In the first experiment, pairs of subjects were trained, independently of one another, on a FI 30-second schedule of reinforcement. Responding consisted of pressing a standard primate lever and points accumulated on a game console in parcels of 25 according to the FI schedule. Subjects were next instructed that they would be competing against the other person for counter points and then immediately exposed to the competitive FI 30 schedule. During this condition, reinforcement was delivered to the first pair member to satisfy the schedule requirements. The other subject was notified of his opponent's success via the illumination of a red stimulus light on his game console. Responding under competitive conditions increased well above that obtained under independent training. Competitive responding for each subject was also characterized by a long post-reinforcement pause (PRP) followed by an abrupt and rapid response burst which continued until reinforcer delivery. This 'break and run' pattern of responding it atypical of human performance on FI schedules. More common among human subjects is either a continuously high or low response rate with the latter being marked by the occurrence of only a few responses just prior to the end of the IRI (for a review of human FI performance, see Lowe, 1979). A return to the independent condition produced a drop in response rates comparable to those obtained during initial training, and a return to a second competitive condition replicated the results of the first competitive condition. In a second experiment, subjects were exposed to a regular FI 30 schedule and then read competition instructions identical to those described above. During this 'pseudocompetitive' phase, however, no competitive contingency was in effect. Instead, subjects received reinforcement according to individual completion of the regular FI schedule. Three of four subjects increased response rates during the initial 'pseudocompetitive' session, only to decrease with continued exposure to the noncompetitive contingency. In a third experiment, subjects were not given instructions concerning the competitive phase of the experiment, but were, nevertheless, exposed to the competitive contingency after first being trained on the noncompetitive FI schedule. These subjects gradually increased responding during exposure to the competitive contingency. The aggregate results of these experiments lead to the conclusion that while orienting instructions may act as an effective discriminative stimulus for rapid acquisition of responding in competitive contexts, they are, nevertheless, unnecessary for its development.

Parametric analyses of FI and DRL competition

Generality of the competitive facilitatory effect was the subject of a further series of experiments in which subject pairs were exposed to three values of a FI schedule: 30 seconds, 60 seconds, and 90 seconds (Buskist and Morgan, 1987). Subjects were first exposed to several independent sessions followed by competitive sessions at each schedule parameter. Results replicated those of the earlier experiment across each parameter value. Also, PRPs during competitve sessions were an increasing function of schedule value. In a subsequent experiment, subject pairs were trained on a noncompetitive FI 30-second schedule and exposed to a competitive version of the same schedule. They were then trained on either independent differential reinforcement-of-low-rate (DRL) or fixed-ratio (FR) schedules after which they were re-exposed to the original competitive FI schedule. Thus, subjects' performance during the initial exposure to the competitive FI schedule served as a baseline against which the effects of training on independent DRL or FR schedules were assessed on subsequent re-exposure to the competitive FI schedule. Subjects exposed to intervening DRL training showed a reduction in response rate upon re-exposure to competitive FI contingencies; conversely, subjects exposed to intervening FR training showed increased rates relative to rates during initial exposure to FI competition. However, the break and run pattern of competitive FI responding persisted.

In a similar study, responding was brought under the exclusive control of a competitive DRL contingency (Morgan and Buskist, 1985). Subjects were initially exposed to sessions of independently programmed DRL 5-second and 12-second schedule values. Subjects were next read competitive instructions and then exposed to a competitive DRL contingency in which the first pair member to respond when reinforcement became available received counter points and the other subject received the red 'loss' light. If either subject responded before the programmed interval had elapsed, that subject's console was reset. The other subject's console did not reset; instead, points became available for that subject according to the original interval. Upon delivery of reinforcement to either subject, both pair members' consoles were automatically reset. Since absolute response rate would not seem to be affected by this competitive contingency, duration of post-stimulus pause (PSP) was used as the dependent measure (PSP was that time elapsing between illumination of the red 'loss' light or the green 'reinforcement' light and the subject's next response). For all subjects, PSPs under competitive conditions were reduced relative to PSPs obtained under independent conditions. The effect of the competitive contingency was to enhance sensitivity to the reinforcement schedule. Pauses which only slightly exceeded the programmed schedule value were better suited to capitalize on the DRL schedule's temporal requirement than were the longer pauses characteristic of independent performance. These findings also support Church's (1961) notion that differential reinforcement can be delivered contingent upon arbitrary response dimensions in competitive contexts.

Reduced reinforcement availability and competitive FI performance

Two features of the experimental context change when a subject is exposed to FI competition after FI training: First, for most subjects, reinforcement probability decreases since now the available reinforcement is divided two ways; and, second, once the programmed interval has elapsed, reinforcement availability decreases since either subject may take the reinforcement upon its immediate availability. Indeed, Church (1968) speculated that competitive performance on interval schedules was likely due to the development of a limited hold-like contingency. The relative contributions of these factors to competitive facilitation were examined in an additional experiment. Subjects never experienced FI 30 competition nor were they given instructions pertaining to competition. Instead, subjects performed under conditions in which competitive FI contingencies were stimulated. For subjects in the reinforcement probability condition, several different probabilities of reinforcement were preprogrammed for each subject. During IRIs for which reinforcement was programmed for a particular subject, lever presses resulted in accumulation of counter points. If reinforcement was not programmed, the subject's red light illuminated upon termination of the 30-second interval irrespective of the subject's behavior. For subjects in the limited hold condition, reinforcement was available upon termination of the 30-second interval, but only for 1 second. Failure to respond during this limited hold interval resulted in illumination of the red light and commencement of the next IRI. In both conditions subjects were informed of each other's scores after each session. Subjects exposed to the limited hold condition showed response rate increases and break and run response patterns similar to those commonly obtained under actual competitive FI contingencies. No such change in rate or pattern of response was observed in subjects for whom reinforcement probability underwent a reduction from baseline conditions. Thus competitive FI performance appears to be controlled by the decreased availability of reinforcement upon termination of the programmed schedule parameter.

Competition and auditing

Although operant investigations have provided some support for Festinger's (1954) hypotheses concerning social comparison processes, it is curious that this support has derived from research in which reinforcement was not delivered competitively. Instead, subjects either worked on parallel tasks (e.g. Seta, 1982), or in cooperative contexts (e.g. Hake *et al.*, 1973). This is particularly interesting considering Vukelich and Hake's (1974) assertion that auditing may be maintained because of its function in clarifying the presence or absence 'of the major social reinforcer of being ahead' (p. 70).

We have conducted preliminary investigations of auditing during competition. Pairs of subjects were first trained independently on either a FI 30-second or a FR 50 reinforcement schedule. When responding stabilized, an audit lever was introduced and pair members could monitor, at any time, their coactor's performance on the independent task by fulfilling a FR 5 requirement on that lever. Once responding had stabilized on both task and audit levers, subjects were exposed to competitive conditions in which reinforcement was delivered to whichever pair member first completed the schedule requirement on the task lever. Response facilitation was observed on the task lever similar to that obtained in previous studies. The focal dependent measure, however, was response rate on the audit lever. Little if any change in rate of auditing was observed in subjects who responded on the task lever according to a FR 50 schedule of reinforcement. For most FI 30 subjects, however, auditing underwent a considerable reduction upon condition change. Differences between FI and FR subjects were possibly due to the fact that FR subjects characteristically developed large score differences early in their independent training due to large individual differences in response rate. These differences were usually maintained or even widened during competition. Auditing, therefore, served no more of a discriminative function during competition than it did during training (i.e. it was redundant). For FI subjects, however, scores tended to be very similar during training, as all subjects eventually maximized reinforcement during these sessions. Only during competition did large differences between subjects' scores develop. Corresponding to these large score discrepancies was a reduction in audit responses thus extending the generality of Vukelich and Hake's (1974) findings.

A further study was conducted to confirm the relation between auditing and score discrepancy during competition. In contrast to the first study, however, some measure of control over score correspondence was exercised. Pairs of subjects were initially trained on independent FI 30 or FR 50 schedules with the audit lever (FR5) also present. When FR pairs were shifted to competition, one subject's schedule parameter was adjusted from session to session in order to produce very high or very low score correspondences. For FI subjects, reinforcement was made available disproportionately to subjects on an IRI by IRI basis, also producing either high score correspondence (50 per cent/50 per cent) or low correspondence (90 per cent/10 per cent). Auditing was maintained by high score correspondence and, unexpectedly, by low correspondence, at least for subjects who were behind during competition. Auditing occurred rarely for subjects who were far ahead of their opponent.

These preliminary analyses demonstrate that reinforcement schedules can be easily contrived which establish criteria for reinforcement delivery in competitive contexts. Instructions orienting subjects to the experimental task facilitate rapid contact with the competitive contingency, though they are clearly not necessary for competition to develop. In addition, subjects' competitive performance on these schedules can serve as baselines against which the effects of other variables such as training history and social comparison are readily studied. Competitive performance under different reinforcement schedules is likely affected by the unique properties of each schedule; FI competitive performance, for example, may be due to transformation of this schedule into a fixed-interval with a limited hold. These are, of course, merely a few of the myriad variables which might be ostensibly implicated in the control of human competition. Indeed, as Schmitt (1984, 1986) has recently suggested, the number of independent and dependent variables which might be incorporated within the experimental analysis of human competition is enormous. A look at our research reveals several possible avenues of future research. For example, it is likely that the situation in which the competitive contingencies are embedded affects subjects' performances. Thus, factors such as a subject's knowledge of the opponent's score during (or after) competitive episodes may contribute to that subject's subsequent response output and timing. Stimuli associated with reinforcement and nonreinforcement are also likely candidates for controlling variables. Finally, by experimentally pitting small 'teams' of subjects against one another on various competitive schedules of reinforcement, the development and enhancement of cooperation (i.e. 'teamwork') within a competitive situation might be feasibly studied.

Summary

The writing of this chapter has been guided by three central objectives: (1) to examine the manner in which social scientists have conceptually and operationally discussed competition; (2) to review the empirical literature from three methodologically distinct disciplines that share a common interest in competitive behavior; and (3) to provide an experimental methodology for the study of human competitive performance which can be used to examine a wider variety of competitive phenomena than heretofore investigated.

Perusal of the social scientific literature revealed numerous definitions of competition. Further, these definitions have emphasized very different features of the competitive context including the motivation to excel others (Allport, 1924), behavior oriented toward mutually exclusive goals (Mead, 1937), negative correlation between competitors' goal attainments (Deutsch, 1962), and the delivery of reinforcement based upon the relative performance of competitors (Church, 1968). While each of these conceptualizations serves to highlight the many subtleties of competitive phenomena, those which make explicit the response to be reinforced and the method of reinforcement delivery were recognized as most efficacious for research purposes (Skinner, 1953; Church, 1968; Hake, Olvera, and Bell, 1975). It was also observed that while the conceptual status of competition remains equivocal, commonalities from the research literature signify the following as likely defining characteristics: (1) the involvement of two or more organisms; (2) behavior directed toward reinforcement; (3) reinforcement delivered contingent upon preselected features of response topography and made contingent on the relative performances of competitors; (4) reinforcement of only one competitor at a particular time; and (5) existence of time or trials criteria for termination of competition.

The psychological study of competitive behavior has been dominated by no single research tradition. It has, instead, composed a portion of the knowledge base of at least three diverse disciplines: Nonhuman animal research; social psychological matrix game research; and research from a reinforcement perspective. With respect to facilitation of competitive performance, research from the animal laboratory has produced inconsistent findings. While some researchers have demonstrated changes in responding due to competitive contingencies (e.g. Bayroff, 1940; Church, 1961, 1962), failure to do so has been at least as common (Lepley, 1937; Winslow, 1940, 1944a, 1944b). These discrepancies in experimental findings are likely due to various methodological idiosyncracies, though Church (1968) has identified differential reinforcement as one of the more crucial variables determining response facilitation under competitive conditions. It may also be the case that certain studies employed more aversive contingencies than did others, thus producing more rapid response adaptation (e.g. Bayroff, 1940).

A prodigious contribution to the literature on human competition emerged from the use of matrix games by social psychologists during the 1950s and 1960s. The primary objective of most of these studies was to identify specific task, situational, and personality characteristics correlated with cooperative and/or competitive choice behavior. Included among the findings of such investigations is that the choice to cooperate or compete is related to game duration (Morehous, 1966), type and level of communication between game participants (Deutsch and Krauss, 1962; Bixenstiwe, Levitt, and Wilson, 1966; Swensson, 1967; Wichman, 1970), instructions given subjects regarding the game (Deutsch, 1960; Evans, 1964), and the relationship between players (Oskamp and Perlman, 1965; Swingle and Gillis, 1968; Schoeninger and Wood, 1969).

Although more recent than either its animal or social psychological counterparts, the analysis of human competition through reinforcement procedures boasts both a powerful methodology and an aggregate of preliminary findings, many of which corroborate results found in the more traditional literature. In particular, a good deal of this research has demonstrated that preference for competitive over cooperative means of social responding is affected by such variables as relative magnitude of reinforcement (Schmitt and Marwell, 1977; Schmitt, 1976; Matthews, 1979) and response requirements (Hake *et al.*, 1975; Olvera and Hake, 1976). Studies of inter-personal comparison processes have identified the importance of such behavior even within contexts which are only implicitly competitive (e.g. Seta, 1982). Social comparison behavior, in the form of auditing, has been demonstrated to be functionally related to degree of score correspondence obtaining between coactors (Hake *et al.*, 1973; Vukelich and Hake, 1974).

We have described both a method for the study of human competition through the use of reinforcement schedules as well as some introductory experiments on the role of orienting instructions in competitive FI performance (Buskist *et al.*, 1984). Also reported are results from parametric analyses of FI, history effects of FR and DRL training, competitive performance, and the role of a limited-hold-like contingency in engendering the increased response rate and 'break and run' response pattern characteristic of human competitive behavior on FI schedules. We have also demonstrated that sensitivity to DRL parameters can be enhanced through competitive reinforcement and that auditing, during competitive situations, is maintained by high score correspondence and, at least for the less fortunate competitor, by low corres-pondences as well.

Finally, we have outlined a modest program of research which systematically addresses part of a large residuum of questions left by previous studies. We are, moreover, enthusiastic in suggesting that operant methodologies, in particular schedules of reinforcement, are well suited to examine what will no doubt prove to be a vast and intricate array of human competitive phenomena, including self-competition, variations of interactive versus noninteractive competition and individual versus team competition, instructional and demonstrational coaching, and a host of others.

In closing, we would like to proffer a note on the operant psychologist's timely emergence as somewhat of a middle-man in the study of human social behavior. The recent application of the techniques of the experimental anlaysis of behavior to the study of interpersonal relations is an encouraging augmentation of what we consider to be a rich theoretical groundwork (e.g. Skinner, 1953). The role of the operant psychologist in the prosecution of a science of behavior is exemplified in Alexander and Simpson's (1971) assertion that '...the theoretical contribution of small-group research has consisted in showing how the kinds of microscopic variables usually ignored by sociologists can explain the kinds of social situations usually ignored by psychologists' (pp. 69–70).

References

Adams, J.S. (1965). Inequity in social exchange. In L. Berkowitz (ed), *Advances in Experimental Social Psychology*, New York: Academic Press, pp. 267–299.

Alexander, C.N., Jr., and Simpson, R.L. (1971). Balance theory and distributive justice. In H. Turk and R.L. Simpson (eds), *Institutions and Social Exchange*, New York: Bobbs-Merrill, pp. 69–80.

Allport, F. H. (1924). *Social Psychology*, Boston, Mass.: Houghton Mifflin.

Bayroff, A. G. (1940). The experimental social behavior of animals: II. The effect of early isolation of white rats on their competition in swimming, *Journal of Comparative Psychology*, **9**, 293–306.

Bixenstine, V. E., Levitt, C. A., and Wilson, K. V. (1966). Collaboration among six persons in a Prisoner's Dilemma game, *J. Con. Res.*, **10**, 488–496.

Bixenstine, V. E., Potash, H. M., and Wilson, K. V. (1963). Effects of level of cooperative choice by the other player on choices in a Prisoner's Dilemma game, Part I, *Journal of Abnormal and Social Psychology*, **66**, 308–313.

Bixenstine, V. E., and Wilson, K. V. (1963). Effects of level of cooperative choice by the other plater on choices in a Prisoner's Dilemma game, Part II, *Journal of Abnormal and Social Psychology*, 139–147.

Buskist, W. K., and Morgan, D. (1987). Competitive fixed interval performance in humans, *Journal of the Experimental Analysis of Behavior*, **47**, 145–158.

Buskist, W. F., Morgan, D., and Barry A. (1983). Interspecies generality and human behavior: An addendum to Baron and Perone, *Behavior Analyst*, **6**, 107–108.

Buskist, W. F., Barry, A., Morgan, D., and Rossi, M. (1984). Competitive fixed interval performance in humans: Role of 'orienting' instructions, *Psychological Record*, **34**, 241–257.

Carnathan, J., and Church, R. M. (1964). The effect of competitive allocation of reinforcements to rats in the straight alley', *Journal of General Psychology*, **71**, 137–144.

Church, R. M. (1961). Effects of a competitve situation on the speed of response, *Journal of Comparative and Physiological Psychology* **2**, 162–166.

Church, R. M. (1962). Effect of relative skill on the amount of competitive facilitation, *Psychological Reports*, **11**, 603–614.

Church, R. M. (1968). Applications of behavior theory to social psychology: Imitation and competition. In E. C. Simmel, R. A. Hoppe, and G. A. Milton (eds), *Social Facilitation and Imitative Behavior*, Boston, Mass.: Allyn & Bacon, pp. 135–167.

Cohen, D. J. (1962). Justin and his peers: An experimental analysis of a child's social world, *Child Development*, **33**, 697–717.

Deutsch, M. (1949). A theory of co-operation and competition, *Human Relations*, **2**, 129–151.

Deutsch, M. (1960). Trust, trustworthiness, and the F scale, *Journal of Abnormal and Social Psychology*, **61**, 138–140.

Deutsch, M. (1962). Cooperation and trust: Some theoretical notes. In M. R. Jones (ed), *Nebraska Symposium on Motivation*, Lincoln, NE.: University of Nebraska Press, pp. 275–319.

Deutsch, M., and Krauss, R. M. (1960). The effect of threat upon interpersonal bargaining, *Journal of Abnormal and Social Psychology*, **61**, 181–189.

Deutsch, M., and Krauss, R. M. (1962). Studies of interpersonal bargaining, *J. Con. Res.*, **4**, 52–76.

Deutsch, M., Epstein, V., Canavan, D., and Gumpert, P. (1967). Strategies of inducing cooperation: An experimental study, *J. Con. Res.*, **11**, 345–360.

Dolbear, R. T., and Lave, L. B. (1966). Risk orientation as a predictor in the Prisoner's Dilemma, *J. Con. Res.*, **10**, 506–515.

Evans, G. (1964). Effect of unilateral promise and value of rewards upon cooperation and trust, *Journal of Abnormal and Social Psychology*, **69**, 587–590.

Festinger, L. (1954). A theory of social comparison processes, *Human Relations*, **7**, 117–140.

Fukasawa, T., Lima, M.P., and Masur, J. (1975). The behavior of genetically selected loser and winner-runway rats in different competitive situations, *Behavioral Biology*, **15**, 333-342.

Hake, D.F. (1982). The basic-applied continuum and the possible evolution of human operant social and verbal research, *Behavior Analysis*, **5**, 21-28.

Hake, D.F., and Olvera, D. (1978). Cooperation, competition and related social phenomena. In A.C. Catania and T. Brigham (eds), *Handbook of Applied Behavior Analysis*, New York: Irvington Publishers, pp. 208-245.

Hake, D.F., Olvera, D., and Bell, J.C. (1975). Switching from competition to sharing or cooperation at large response requirements: Competition requires more responding, *Journal of the Experimental Analysis of Behavior*, **24**, 343-354.

Hake, D.F., Vukelich, R., and Kaplan, S.J. (1973). Audit responses: Responses maintained by access to existing self or coactor scores during non-social, parallel work, and cooperative procedures, *Journal of the Experimental Analysis of Behavior.*, **19**, 409-423.

Hake, D.F., Vukelich, R., and Olvera, D. (1975). The measurement of sharing and cooperation as equity effects and some relationships between them, *Journal of the Experimental Analysis of Behavior*, **23**, 63-79.

Homans, G.C. (1961). *Social Behavior: Its Elementary Forms*, New York: Harcourt, Brace & World.

Hyten, C., and Burns, R. (1986). Social relations and social behavior. In L.J. Parrott and H. Reese (eds), *Behavior Science: Philosophical, Methodological, and Empirical Advances*. Hillsdale, NJ: Erlbaum.

Johnson, D.W., Maruyama, G., Johnson, R., Nelson, D., and Skon, L. (1981). Effects of cooperative, competitive and individualistic goal structure on achievement: A meta-analysis, *Psychological Bulletin*, **89**, 47-62.

Jones, B., Steele, M., Gahagan, J., and Tedeschi, J. (1968). Matrix values and cooperative behavior in the Prisoner's Dilemma game, *Journal of Personality and Social Psychology*, **8**, 148-153.

Kanak, N.J., and Davenport, G. (1967). Between-subject competition: A rat race, *Psychological Science*, **7**, 87-88.

Keller, F.S., and Schoenfeld, W.N. (1950). *Principles of Psychology: A Systematic Text in the Science of Behavior*, New York: Appleton-Century-Crofts.

Kelley, H.H., and Thibaut, J.W. (1978). *Interpersonal Relations: A Theory of Interdependence*, New York: Wiley.

Komorita, S.S. (1965). Cooperative choice in a Prisoner's Dilemma game, *Journal of Personality and Social Psychology*, **2**, 741-745.

Lepley, W.M. (1937). Competitive behavior in the albino rat, *Journal of Experimental Psychology*, **21**, 194-204.

Lindsley, O.R. (1966). Experimental analysis of cooperation and competition. In T. Verhave (ed), *The Experimental Analysis of Behavior*, New York: Appleton-Century Crofts, pp. 470-501.

Lowe, C.F. (1979). Determinants of human operant behavior. In M.D. Zeiler and P. Harzem (eds), *Advances in the Analysis of Behavior: Vol. 1. Reinforcement and the Organization of Behavior*, Chichester, England: Wiley, pp. 159-192.

Lowe, C.F., Beasty, A., and Bentall, R.P. (1983). The role of verbal behavior in human learning: Infant performance on fixed-interval schedules, *Journal of the Experimental Analysis of Behavior*, **39**, 157-164.

Luce, R.D., and Raiffa, H. (1957). *Games and Decisions*, New York: Wiley.

Malamud, B. (1952). *The Natural*, New York: Farrar, Strauss & Giroux.

194   *Human operant conditioning and behavior modification*

Marlowe, D., Gergen, K. J., and Doob, A. N. (1966). Opponent's personality, expectation of social interaction, and interpersonal bargaining, *Journal of Personality and Social Psychology*, 3, 206–213.

Marwell, G., and Schmitt, D. R. (1975). *Cooperation: An Experimental Analysis*, New York: Academic Press.

Matthews, B. A. (1979). Effects of fixed and alternated payoff inequity on dyadic competition, *Psychological Record*, 29, 329–339.

McClintock, C. G., Harrison, A. A., Strand, S., and Gallo, P. (1963). Internationalism-isolationism, strategy of the other player, and two-person game behavior, *Journal of Abnormal and Social Psychology*, 67, 631–636.

Mead, M. (1937). *Co-operation and Competition among Primitive Peoples*, New York: McGraw-Hill.

Morehous, G. (1966). One-play, two-play, five-play, ten-play runs of Prisoner's Dilemma, *J. Con. Res.*, 10, 354–362.

Morgan, D., and Buskist, W. (1985). Competitive DRL performance in humans: Differential reinforcement of short poststimulus pausing, *Bulletin of the Psychological Society*, 23, 462–464.

Olvera, D. R., and Hake, D. F. (1976). Producing a change from competition to sharing: Effects of large and adjusting response requirements, *Journal of the Experimental Analysis of Behavior* 26, 321–333.

Oskamp, S., and Perlman, D. (1965). Factors affecting cooperation in a Prisoner's Dilemma game, *J. Con. Res.*, 9, 359–374.

Oskamp, S., and Perlman, D. (1966). Effects of friendship and disliking on cooperation in a mixed-motive game, *J. Con. Res.*, 10, 221–226.

Parrott, L. J. (1983). Defining social behavior: An exercise in scientific system building, *Psychological Record*, 33, 533–551.

Raven, B. H., and Eachus, H. T. (1963). Cooperation and competition in means-interdependent triads, *Journal of Abnormal and Social Psychology*, 67, 307–316.

Schmitt, D. R. (1976). Some conditions affecting the choice to cooperate or compete, *Journal of the Experimental Analysis of Behavior*, 25, 165–168.

Schmitt, D. R. (1984). Interpersonal relations: Cooperation and competition, *Journal of the Experimental Analysis of Behavior*, 42, 377–383.

Schmitt, D. R. (1986). Competition: Some behavioral issues, *Behavior Analysis*, 9, 27–34.

Schmitt, D. R. (in press). Interpersonal contingencies: Performance differences and cost-effectiveness, *Journal of the Experimental Analysis of Behavior*.

Schmitt, D. R., and Marwell, G. (1971). Taking and the disruption of cooperation, *Journal of the Experimental Analysis of Behavior*, 15, 405–412.

Schoeninger, D., and Wood, W. (1969). Comparison of married and ad hoc mixed-sex dyads negotiating the division of a reward, *Journal of the Experimental Society of Psychology*, 5, 483–499.

Scott, W. E., and Cherrington, D. J. (1974). Effects of competitive, cooperative and individualistic reinforcement contingencies, *Journal of Personality and Social Psychology*, 30, 748–758.

Seta, J. J. (1982). The impact of comparison processes on coactors' task performance, *Journal of Personality and Social Psychology*, 42, 281–291.

Sherif, M., Harvey, O. J., White, J. B., Hood, W. E., and Sherif, C. W. (1961). *Intergroup Conflict and Cooperation: The Robber's Cave Experiment*, Norman, OK: University of Oklahoma Press.

Skinner, B. F. (1953). *Science and Human Behavior*, New York: The Free Press.

Solomon, L. (1960). The influence of some types of power relationships and game strategies upon the development of interpersonal trust, *Journal of Abnormal and Social Psychology*, 61, 223–230.

Steigleder, M. K., Weiss, R. F., Cramer, R. E., and Feinberg, R. A. (1978). Motivating and reinforcing functions of competitive behavior, *Journal of Personality and Social Psychology*, **36**, 1291–1301.

Stewart, J. E., Zelman, W. N., and Mithaug, D. E. (1971). The effects of different competitive contingencies on cooperative behavior, *Journal of Experimental Child Psychology*, **11**, 461–479.

Swensson, R. G. (1967). Cooperation in the Prisoner's Dilemma game. I: The effects of asymmetric payoff information and explicit communication, *Behavioral Science*, **12**, 314–322.

Swingle, P. G., and Gillis, J. S. (1968). Effects of the emotional relationships between protagonists in the Prisoner's Dilemma, *Journal of Personality and Social Psychology*, **8**, 160–165.

Swinth, R. L. (1967). The establishment of the trust relationship, *J. Con. Res.*, **11**, 335–344.

Triplett, N. (1897). The dynamagenic factors in pacemaking and competition, *American Journal of Psychology*, **9**, 507–533.

Vinacke, W. E. (1969). Variables in experimental games: Toward a field theory, *Psychological Bulletin*, **71**, 293–318.

Vukelich, R., and Hake, D. F. (1974). Effects of the difference between self and coactor scores upon the audit responses that allow access to these scores, *Journal of the Experimental Analysis of Behavior*, **22**, 61–71.

Weinstein, A. G., and Holzbach, R. L. (1972). Effects of financial inducements on performance under two task structures, *Proceedings of the 80th Annual Convention of the American Psychological Association*, **7**, 217–218.

Wichman, H. (1970). Effects of isolation and communication on cooperation in a two-person game, *Journal of Personality and Social Psychology*, **16**, 114–120.

Winslow, C. N. (1940). A study of experimentally induced competitive behavior in the white rat, *Comparative Psychological Monographs*, **15** (6).

Winslow, C. N. (1944a). The social behavior of cats: I. Competitive and aggressive behavior in an experimental runway situation, *Journal of Comparative and Physiological Psychology*, **37**, 297–313.

Winslow, C. N. (1944b). The social behavior of cats: II. Competitive, aggressive, and food-sharing behavior when both competitors have access to the goal, *Journal of Comparative and Physiological Psychology*, **37**, 315–326.

Wrightsman, L. S., O'Connor, J., and Baker, N. J. (eds), (1972). *Cooperation and Competition: Readings on Mixed-Motive Games*, Belmont, CA: Brooks/Cole.

Chapter 10

Some Neglected Problems in the Analysis of Human Operant Behavior

J. H. WEARDEN
Department of Psychology, University of Manchester

A dog cannot be a hypocrite, but neither can he be sincere.

Wittgenstein, quoted by Benford and Eklund (1978)

In spite of the more than 50 years that the study of operant conditioning has been in existence, it is only relatively recently that the operant behavior of normal adults has been systematically investigated in laboratory conditions. Prior to this, discussions often simply assumed that principles of operant conditioning were applicable to human behavior, usually on the basis of little or no experimental evidence (e.g. Skinner, 1953). Laboratory studies, reviewed by Lowe (1979), have suggested that operant techniques developed in the animal laboratory do not transfer well to the behavior of normal humans, at least those old enough to speak (Bentall, Lowe, and Beasty, 1985; Lowe, Beasty, and Bentall, 1983). For example, the behavior of human adults under reinforcement schedules often appears conspicuously less orderly than that of animals, and seems different in some other respects such as response patterning and sensitivity to schedule parameter.

Most researchers now appear aware that animal and human operant behavior in laboratory settings is more likely to be different than it is to be similar. Nevertheless, in spite of this awareness, factors which seem likely candidates for determinants of these interspecies differences still receive little genuine analysis. It is often apparently merely assumed, for example, that 'reinforcement' operations are an appropriate explanatory term for both human and animal behavior, even though the reinforcers themselves may obviously differ in the two cases. Furthermore, other variables that seem to apply uniquely to human behavior, such as instructional effects or relations between verbal statements and nonverbal performance, generally appear to be regarded as unimportant or peripheral issues (an exception is Bentall *et al.*, 1985, and other work from the same laboratory), particularly when orderly performance can be obtained from humans without detailed consideration of these factors. Even experiments which study these issues explicitly (e.g. the instructional manipulations of Buskist, Bennett, and Miller, 1981) often rest content with demonstrations of clear behavioral effects, without further experimental or theoretical analysis (such as considering how instructions should be conceived and how they operate).

The present chapter is concerned with three areas which seem to me to have been neglected, or at least not given the type or depth of analysis that they deserve. The first is the nature of 'reinforcement' and motivation in adult human learning. Do the response-contingent events which manipulate human behaviors function as classical reinforcers? If not, what do they do? The second area of interest is instructional effects. What does it mean to say that behavior is instructed? Does instructed behavior differ from that arrived at by some different means? Are there fundamentally different types of instructions, for example instructions to do something as opposed to instructions about something? How do instructions operate to change behavior? The final area concerns relations between verbal behavior and nonverbal performance on operant tasks.

Reinforcement and motivation in human operant learning

It is obvious that when a normal adult voluntarily participates for a brief time in an experiment in which his or her performance is rewarded by small amounts of money, he or she faces a game-like social situation, governed by a set of complex, if largely implicit, rules. As such, experiments with human adults may have aspects which have no equivalent in studies in which animals are used, and research on the social psychological aspects of the experimental situation (Adair, 1973; Rosenthal and Rosnow, 1969) seems obviously relevant. Much recent work in the laboratory analysis of adult operant behavior has, however, proceeded by assuming that terms derived from animal studies, such as reinforcement, may be directly applied to work with humans, without substantial qualification or analysis. For various reasons, as will be argued below, such an attitude, particularly to the use of the term 'reinforcement' in adult human learning, seems questionable.

In the overwhelming majority of studies of operant behavior with animals, a state of food or water deprivation is instituted and the consequences of behavior are reinforcers which tend to redress the induced deprivation. A common exception is that in which behavior can be maintained by stimuli which have been reliably associated with reinforcer delivery (Fantino, 1977; Killeen, 1982), although these depend for their efficacy on the continued associated delivery of the primary reinforcer. In the above cases, hedonic accounts of animal performance, in which animals respond to produce reinforcement (Mackintosh, 1974), to optimize the rate of return from the experimental conditions (Baum, 1981), or to maintain certain levels of body weight or water intake (Collier, Hirsch, and Kanarek, 1977) seem natural. It is not, however, clear that the operant behavior of normal adult humans in laboratory experiments can be understood in such terms. On the contrary, there is evidence to suggest that the events which manipulate human behavior are of a different type from those that control animal behavior, and operate in a way fundamentally different from the way the reinforcers operate in the animal laboratory.

Almost all studies of reinforcement schedule performance with human adults deliver response-contingent points (usually in terms of incrementation of a counter) which are later exchangeable for small amounts of money (e.g. Bradshaw, Szabadi, and Bevan, 1976). In some cases, however, it is difficult to believe that the nominal value of the 'reinforcer' accurately assesses its utility to the subject, as very high response rates can be apparently maintained by low rates of return. For example, in the 'no punishment' condition of Bradshaw, Szabadi, and Bevan (1979), subjects responded at between 100 and 200 button presses per minute under variable-interval 720 seconds, which delivers at most 5p per hour. Not only did subjects respond apparently enthusiastically for this Dickensian remuneration, but they also appeared to attach almost no value to any other activity during experimental sessions. DeVilliers and Herrnstein (1976) argue that the reponse rates emitted by a subject under a range of variable-interval schedules can be used to estimate the 'value', in reinforcers per hour, that the subject attaches to any activity other than responding. Following this analysis, the 'value' of nonresponding (or 'leisure') in the Bradshaw *et al.* condition mentioned above was, for different subjects, between 1.9p and 8.6p per hour.

These figures seem incredible if the nominal value of the reinforcer accurately represents its utility to the subject. It seems far more plausible to suppose that, for some reason, the subjects value the point incrementation far more than its exchange value would suggest. Why this might be so is discussed further below.

Another example suggesting that it might be unwise to take 'reinforcers' in experiments with normal adults at their face value comes from Miller's laboratory at Brigham Young University. Miller's group of researchers have frequently employed dispensations of small amounts of food as reinforcers (e.g. Buskist and Miller, 1981; Buskist, Miller, and Bennett, 1980). However, Miller (personal communication) reports that subjects frequently fail to consume, or even taste, these snacks preferring instead to throw them out of the window of the experimental room. Furthermore, Miller discovered that orderly performance was most readily obtained from his subjects when their scores, in the form of graphs showing the number of 'reinforcers' obtained each day by each subject, were posted. Without this competitive spur, results were more variable and disorderly. What was the subjects' motivation and reinforcement in these experiments? It certainly does not seem to have been food, even though delivery of food reinforcers apparently resulted in many cases of orderly behavioral control by the experimental contingencies.

These results may make more sense if 'reinforcers' in operant studies with normal adults are conceived in informational, rather than hedonic or response-strengthening, terms. That is, to assume that 'reinforcers' provide subjects with information that their performance was correct or appropriate. Following from this, the nominal monetary value of reinforcer delivery may be less important than informational properties of the event, such as the way that its rate changes with variations in behavior, the relations that it has to particular behaviors (for example, immediacy, temporal asynchrony, and so on), and the way the subject uses the information provided by reinforcer delivery to vary performance.

Many conventional reinforcement schedules are informationally very poor, in the sense that wide variations in performance may produce little obvious change in consequences. Variable-interval schedules are a clear example, since delivered reinforcement rate may vary little with gross variations in response rate. The delivery of the reinforcer thus provides the subject with little performance-relevant information, and it is perhaps unsurprising that in some laboratories (e.g. Lowe and Horne, 1985), including my own, adult performance under variable-interval (VI) schedules is extremely variable between subjects, and even variable between different sessions of training with the same subject. Participants in these studies in my own laboratory also routinely complained that they are unable to work out 'what to do' on a VI schedule. In contrast, some temporal differentiation schedules, which impose time constraints on responses (e.g. that they should be spaced apart by more than a certain time), might be thought to be informationally richer, since performance changes may be reflected in large and obvious changes in consequences and, in addition, certain types of behavior are obviously 'better' than others in terms of return from the schedule. Consistent with this, under conditions in which each inter-response time (irt) greater than some value produces a point reinforcer (e.g. Lowe, Harzem, and Bagshaw, 1978), adult human performance can approach theoretically perfect levels. However, when the irt contingency is obscured by having reinforcers arranged by a VI schedule (Wearden and Quinn, 1982), so that performance variations have less clear effects on reinforcer delivery, performance adjusts more crudely to the contingency, if it adjusts at all.

If adults are working, in laboratory settings, wholly or partly for informational feedback that enables them to solve the problem that the experimenter's contingencies pose them, then providing informational feedback richer than that normally available on conventional schedules may manipulate behavior rapidly and precisely. Consistent with this, Wearden and Shimp (1985) exposed subjects to an irt contingency in which irts within a target band (e.g. between 1 and 3 seconds) were occasionally (according to a random-interval

10-seconds schedule) followed by a feedback event. This was the word 'GOOD' displayed on a computer screen if the irt that produced it was within the target band, and the word 'POOR' if it was not. Such a contingency shaped the temporal distribution of irts from about half the subject population used in a single half-hour experimental session. This compares favorably with rates of learning in more conventional temporal differentiation conditions with human adults (e.g. Lowe, Harzem, and Bagshaw, 1978), even though no monetary reinforcement was used in this study.

Even Wearden and Shimp's procedure is, however, informationally rather primitive. If subjects are given even more precise feedback about performance appropriateness, behavior change can be even more rapid and accurate. Figure 10.1 shows some examples of this, obtained in an unpublished experiment in my laboratory.

The task employed was a discrete-trial temporal differentiation task in which a contingency was imposed on the time taken to complete a fixed ratio of ten button presses (for a similar experiment with animals see DeCasper and Zeiler, 1974). A trial was initiated by a brief tone, which was presented for a second time when the trial was completed by emission of the tenth button press. The time that the trial took (measured from the delivery of the tone initiating the trial) was noted and compared with a target time (e.g. 5 or 10 seconds). If the completion time was within 10 per cent of the target time, the words 'VERY GOOD' were displayed on a computer screen, and a points counter incremented by 3, if within 10 and 20 per cent, the word 'GOOD' was presented, and so on with evaluation becoming progressively more negative as deviation from the target time increased, until with deviations of more than 50 per cent the words 'VERY POOR' occurred. Points delivered in this study had no monetary value, although subjects were instructed to obtain as many as they could.

The data shown in Figure 10.1 are the completion times produced by two subjects during the first three experimental sessions. One subject (T) achieved accurate performance on the temporal differentiation of 5- and 10-second completion times with remarkable rapidity, showing almost perfect adjustment of behavior to the imposed contingency within five or ten trials, and little subsequent change. With inter-trial intervals, this represents about 1–3 minutes' exposure to the contingency before behavioral 'steady state' is apparently reached. At the 15-second target time condition, a little longer is needed by T, and the second subject (C) shows more irregular behavior changes in the 10- and 15-second conditions, but still is emitting completion times close to the target value in the last few trials of the single session.

It is important to contrast these results with those obtained under more conventional reinforcement schedules with time constraints. For example, under fixed-interval schedules (Lowe, 1979) subjects may take several sessions to stabilize performance, and performance rigidity, in the form of lack of response changes when schedule parameters or types are varied, is common. In contrast,

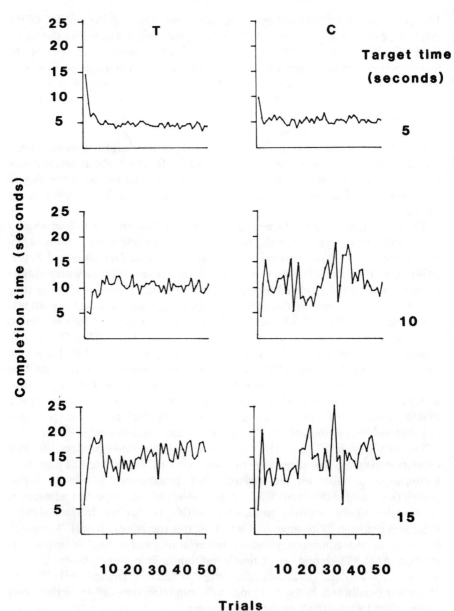

Figure 10.1   Time to complete ten button presses during the 50 trials of consecutive experimental sessions for two subjects. Target time was varied across 5 (upper), 10 (middle), and 15 seconds (lower panel)

the informationally rich procedures like those used for Figure 10.1 apparently produce behavior which changes flexibly when schedule values are varied, as they were between the consecutive sessions shown in Figure 10.1.

The orderliness of data produced when 'reinforcement' in laboratory experiments with adults was conceived in informational terms led to the general idea that reinforcement in such cases should always be conceived informationally, and that motivation of subjects under such conditions was also informationally based. The tendency of experimental subjects to perceive experimental procedures as tests, or problems to which there is a correct or exact solution, has been documented by social psychologists under the name of 'evaluation apprehension' (Rosenberg, 1969). Informal observations in my own laboratory strongly support the view that subjects are highly motivated to know about the appropriateness of their behavior. Indeed, in multiple-session experiments, post-session conversations between experimenter and subject were dominated by this topic, and great care had to be taken to avoid communicating to the subject what the experimenter regarded as 'good' performance. Without such hints, subjects' performance under, for example, VI schedules appeared to be under the control of idiosyncratic response strategies based on the subject's conception of the task. Since a VI schedule is informationally poor, and the experimenter uncommunicative, such strategies were often complex, bizarre, and inappropriate to the task. In my own laboratory, when experimental procedures similar to those used with animals were employed with normal adults, the more carefully controlled the experiment was in terms of presenting subjects only with automatically delivered events, and taking care to avoid cuing subjects about appropriate performance, the more disorderly human performance became.

Conceiving of operant experiments with normal adults in informational terms also helps resolve some of the odd results in other experiments, discussed above. If the delivery of a 'reinforcer' serves an informational function, then it may not matter if it is consumed (Miller), or what its value is in monetary terms (Bradshaw *et al.*). Posting scores of different subjects may likewise operate by encouraging subjects to treat the procedure as a game or puzzle and suggesting that there might be optimal solutions to the problems posed.

The idea that normal adults will work in operant experiments for informational feedback is not new. The implications of equating information and reinforcement are discussed further below, but confusion about informational factors in experiments with adult humans has given rise to a recent controversy. It is well known (e.g. Fantino, 1977) that animals will not emit observing responses if the consequence of such responses is 'negative' information, that is, information that reinforcement is not available for another response. Perone and Baron (1980), however, showed that observing responses in normal adults could be maintained by such negative information, a result consistent with an informational account of operant experiments since negative information may be just as useful for problem-solving purposes as positive information, even though it may be less pleasant to receive. Fantino and Case (1983) contested this finding, by arranging an experimental situation in which subjects did not respond to produce informative stimuli when these were 'negative', in this case associated with extinction. However, subjects in Fantino and Case's experiment had previously been accurately instructed that their behavior could not influence the delivery of point reinforcers (which were exchangeable for money) in any way. When Case, Fantino, and Waxted (1985) arranged conditions so that the negative information could be used to improve performance efficiency (which it obviously could not in the Fantino and Case study, since point delivery was response-independent), adults responded to produce it, but they did not do so if the negative information delivered could not change task efficiency.

Obviously, informational conceptions of adult operant behavior do not predict that subjects will respond to produce all informational stimuli, however irrelevant the information might be to the task in hand. For example, in a temporal discrimination experiment, a response manipulandum that produced illumination of a digital clock (Lowe, Harzem, and Hughes, 1978) might provide task-relevant information and be used, whereas one that produced some irrelevant event would not.

In spite of the suggestion that many putative 'reinforcers' in operant experiments with adults provide information, it is unclear whether informational feedback and reinforcement can be considered to be simply equivalent, as informational feedback events may not alter the probability of emission of the behavior they follow in a direct manner. That is, as well as having no clear hedonic value, they may not have the functional role ascribed to classical reinforcers by the Law of Effect. In addition, they may not shape behavior gradually, but instead produce abrupt changes in rate and pattern of responses. Some examples of very rapid behavior change in experiments with normal adults were illustrated in Figure 10.1, and others are provided in another section below, but such effects can even occur with conventional 'reinforcers' such as points exchangeable for money. Figure 10.2 shows an unpublished example from Wearden and Quinn (1982).

The subject shown had experienced training sessions under contingencies which were intended to differentially reinforce irts longer than various values. Such contingencies resulted in low rates of responding. Conditions were then changed such that irts less than certain values were now reinforced, although the subject was not informed that any change had occurred. The data in Figure 10.2 come from the first and fifth session after the change. After persisting for about four minutes with the rate of responding appropriate to the previous condition, the subject's performance shifted abruptly (at point A in Figure 10.2) to responding at a much higher rate. This higher rate persisted without any systematic change for the remaining several hours of the experiment (e.g. results

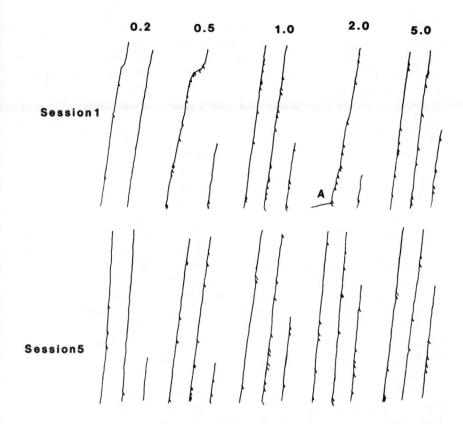

Figure 10.2   Cumulative records of button pressing by S13 from Wearden and Quinn (1982), during the first and fifth session in which irts less than various values (shown above the columns) were reinforced according to a VI 30-second schedule. On the first session the Irt < 2.0 second condition was presented first

from session 5). It is difficult in Figure 10.2 to observe any gradual response shaping by the reinforcement contingency. It seems more reasonable to suppose that a change in response strategy occurred (perhaps occasioned by the failure of the previous low rate responding to produce any reinforcers), and that this strategy was confirmed by subsequent point delivery. The relations between expressed response strategies, knowledge, and performance are discussed in more detail in a later section, but the question of interest here is whether such abrupt changes in behavior, as shown in Figure 10.2, are consistent with a reinforcement process.

One way to make them so is to revise principles of reinforcement to encompass very rapid behavior changes, particularly in the case of human adults. However, this solution may create more problems than it solves. For one thing, if the abrupt changes in behavior shown in Figures 10.1 and 10.2 are examples of reinforcement, it is difficult to explain why such powerful reinforcers do not always produce such rapid behavior change. For example, in an experimental setting identical to that in which the data for Figure 10.2 were collected, another subject worked for fifteen hours for such point reinforcers without exhibiting reliable temporal differentiation of responding (Wearden and Quinn, 1982). In addition, it is not always obvious what preceding behavior has been strengthened when human behavior changes quickly. The steady rapid responding emerging at point A in Figure 10.2, for example, had never previously occurred during the experiment, and only a single short irt was needed to deliver the 'reinforcer' that the schedule had already set up.

It seems equally risky to translate the procedures used to generate the data of Figure 10.1 into reinforcement terms. Although it might be reinforcing (in the casual sense of pleasurable) to obtain information that one's behavior is accurate or appropriate, the informational feedback which generates performance may not exert any direct shaping or strengthening effect on behavior. It may, for example, influence response strategies, as suggested by results presented in a section below. Are events which alter behavior in this way 'reinforcers'? Both a positive and a negative answer to this question pose difficulties. A positive one does so because the concept of reinforcement is then expanded to cover situations very different from those, such as animal studies, for which it was originally devised. Is 'reinforcement' in adult humans different from the same process in animals? If so, in what ways is the process the same? It seems unlikely that continuity between the results of the animal and human laboratory can be maintained if the concept of reinforcement is extended too much, since conventional response-strengthening notions seem adequate to explain animal performance even in sophisticated modern accounts of complex schedule effects (e.g. Vaughn, 1985). However, deciding that informational feedback events are not reinforcers erodes continuity between animal and human studies in a more direct way, and also raises complex questions about the determinants of human performance. For example, does animal-like reinforcement operate in normal adults as well as informational feedback? Is human behavior controllable by types of events which have no equivalent in animal studies?

The concept of reinforcement as a response-strengthening process has done, and continues to do, useful service in the explanation of results from the animal laboratory. Changing it to encompass very rapid changes in behavior accomplished by contingent events with no obvious hedonic value, by means of processes which do not seem to involve response shaping, flirts with the assertion that any event which produces orderly behavioral change when arranged in an operant contingency is a reinforcer. This development would, of course, give reinforcement explanations an *ad hoc* character, make such explanations virtually irrefutable, and render a powerful concept vacuous.

The argument that human behavior is sometimes disorderly under laboratory conditions because of the feebleness of reinforcers used, compared with those used in the animal laboratory, and the unstated implication that human and animal performance would be the same if more powerful reinforcers were used with humans deserves some brief comment, as there are several obvious objections to it. Firstly, it is not clear what would have to be done to equate reinforcer magnitude across, say, pigeons and people, given that it cannot be equated for rats and pigeons. Furthermore, it is not clear how one would ever know that the equation had been achieved. Secondly, in some studies, as argued above, orderly behavior and high response rates are observed from humans even when reinforcers of very low exchange value are delivered. Thirdly, as shown in Figure 10.1, human behavior can apparently by very rapidly manipulated by informationally rich feedback events in the absence of any monetary reinforcement at all. These arguments all suggest that the hedonic value of reinforcers used in laboratory experiments with human adults is of little consequence. Following from this, it seems unlikely that differences in performance between animals and humans are due to reinforcer magnitude effects. However, the argument that they are is irrefutable if the operations of equating reinforcer magnitude cannot be specified (as they cannot), and thus it is difficult to take this position seriously as a scientific argument.

It is obvious that much remains to be discovered about the effects of performance-contingent events in experiments with normal adults. Once more empirical work on the nature of 'reinforcers' in human adult learning has been done, however, problems may principally involve definition. For example, what properties do 'reinforcers' in experiments with normal adults have, and what are the consequences of defining such events as reinforcers? It may be that traditional notions of reinforcement need to be abandoned when studying what normal adults do in laboratory settings. Taking this position, however, may not be a step away from a rigorous experimental analysis of human performance, but a step toward one.

Instructions and human operant performance

When normal adults in laboratory settings are instructed to behave in a certain way, their behavior frequently shows obvious conformity to the instructions given. For example, Buskist, Bennett, and Miller (1981) exposed subjects to a FI 27-second schedule, with different groups differing as to the instructions they were given about what to do (e.g. to respond a certain number of times during each interval, and/or to take a certain time to complete the session). These instructions produced clear performance differences between the groups, even though the experimental schedule was the same for all of them.

Some authors have suggested that behavior which is instructed and that which is generated by some other means differs in critical ways. In particular, in several studies Catania and his associates (Matthews *et al.*, 1977; Shimoff, Catania, and Matthews, 1981) have distinguished between instructed button pressing which occurs when subjects are instructed directly to press a button, and 'shaped' button pressing, which arises when no such instructions are given and a response-shaping procedure is employed. These workers claim that 'shaped' button pressing is more sensitive to experimental contingencies (for example by exhibiting consistent rate differences when interval or ratio schedules are imposed, or showing performance changes when schedule values are altered) than is responding which is instructed. This claim deserves some examination since if true it may be the basis of the well-known performance differences between adult human and animal behavior under reinforcement schedules (Lowe, 1979). It could be argued, for example, that 'shaped' responding in humans is under contingency control in some animal-like way, whereas that which is instructed is not. If human performance is generally intructed then differences between animals and humans might usually occur, even though in certain circumstances adult human and animal performance would be similar and controlled in similar ways.

It seems, however, that the claim of Catania's group that instructed performance is insensitive to schedule contingencies is not supported clearly by data from other laboratories. For example, the numerous studies from Bradhaw's laboratory in which most subjects exhibit clear sensitivity to the rate of reinforcement received on single (Bradshaw, Szabadi, and Bevan, 1976) and concurrent VI schedules (Bradshaw, Szabadi, and Bevan, 1979), as well as sensitivity to the imposition of punishment contingencies (Bradshaw, Szabadi, and Bevan, 1978), all employ what seem to be instructed conditions. Subjects are clearly told to button press in these experiments, although they are not told to press at particular rates. Differences in behavioral sensitivity to FI schedule contingencies, likewise, may depend on procedural factors such as addition of various sorts of clock (Lowe, Harzem, and Hughes, 1978), but adults do apparently exhibit sensitivity to schedule requirements even when told to button press, as under various sorts of irt schedules (e.g. Wearden and Quinn, 1982; Wearden and Shimp, 1985).

Even in the experiments in Catania's laboratory, differences in performance between instructed and shaped groups are not always strikingly large. For example, in experiment 1 of Shimoff, Catania, and Matthews (1981), an irt contingency, scheduled according to a random-interval schedule, was arranged to maintain low rates of responding. This irt contingency was subsequently removed. Of the shaped subjects, eight out of eleven showed a response rate increase when this was done, although only three subjects showed rate increases of more than 100 per cent. Of the ten instructed subjects, one showed no rate change, four out of nine showed rate increases and two of these increased rates by 100 per cent or more.

Other difficulties also arise when considering a distinction between 'shaped' and instructed human performance. For example, if subjects are responding on a schedule which is intended to reinforce irts differentially, and they are instructed to button presss, is the behavior instructed or 'shaped'? The problem arises because although the subjects are instructed to press the button, they may not be instructed to emit particular irt values, and it is upon these irt values rather than button pressing *per se* that contingencies are imposed. More generally, adult humans are always instructed to do something in operant experiments, if only turn up at the appropriate time for the session, make themselves comfortable in the experimental room, and so on. Does this make all behavior 'instructed', or does behavior count as 'instructed' only when certain types of instructions are given, for example, those that, in some way, critically relate to some aspect of the experimental contingency, or tell subjects what to do? If so, who decides when behavior counts as instructed, and on what basis? In the Shimoff *et al.* (1981) experiment, for example, subjects who were instructed were not only instructed to press the response manipulandum, but instructed to 'press slowly; pressing too rapidly will not work' (p. 209). This is clearly a performance-related instruction, suggesting some particular behavior. An instruction to press the button without any specific rate requirement may, obviously, have produced different results.

Considering the single example of instructing subjects to press buttons which act as response manipulanda, is 'shaping' of such a response a possible procedure when adults are used? Buttons and similar manipulanda, particularly those which are prominently displayed in otherwise rather uninteresting experimental environments, have the 'demand characteristic' (Orne, 1962, 1969) of being there to be pressed. The manipulanda for the 'uninstructed' subjects of Shimoff *et al.* (1981) were a red button and a black telegraph key. Subjects in this condition were instructed to press the red button but allegedly 'shaped' to press the telegraph key. It is obvious that when a shaping contingency is applied to button pressing, the response itself may not in any way be shaped (as presumably all normal adults know how to press buttons), the procedure may, rather, convince the subject to press at some particular moment rather than to wait until instructed to press. It is not obvious that this process is similar to the 'shaping' of responses in animals, by which previously non-occurring behaviors can be inserted into their repertoire. It may, therefore, be safer to say that all button-pressing behavior in normal adults in laboratory experiments is instructed either directly or by means of demand characteristics of the experimental situation.

It seems *a priori* that instructions of significantly different types can be discerned. As well as being instructed to respond in particular ways, subjects may be instructed that something is true, for example that different schedule conditions will deliver different rates of reinforcement. Do these kind of instructions differ in some critical way from instructions to do something? In my own laboratory, for example, informing subjects that different VI schedules differed in the rates of reinforcement obtainable from them appeared to have little effect on performance, compared with conditions in which subjects did not receive this instruction. This obviously contrasts with the effectiveness of instructions about what to do, as in Buskist *et al.*, 1981. However, in some cases providing information about contingencies does seem to produce clear behavioral effects. For example, Galizio (1979) exposed adults to avoidance schedules in which they could postpone loss of points (for 10, 30, or 60 seconds) by turning a handle. The different postponement values did not produce clearly different rates of responding until they were associated with the labels '10', '30', etc., in which case different response rates reliably occurred in the different conditions.

This finding suggests that instructions to perform in a certain way and instructions about contingencies may not always differ in effectiveness, but similarity between them may only occur when the instruction about the contingency obviously gives rise to some self-instruction about performance. To give an exaggerated example, an instruction that pressing a response manipulandum would result in an excruciating electric shock may well produce similar behavior to a direct instruction not to press the manipulandum, even though in the first case the instruction does not specify what subjects should do in a direct manner.

Another problem arising when considering instructional effects on adult behavior is how instructions operate. Do they, for example, change behavior in some direct way (possibly analogous to the way in which contingencies are supposed to change behavior), or do they operate indirectly, by means of altering response strategies or cognitions, which then produce behavioral changes? Little interest has been shown in the question of how instructions operate, although some evidence to be given in the next section suggests that instructional differences are correlated with shifts in response strategies, specifically by constraining the response strategies used by the subject during early learning to those of particular types. This issue is obviously worthy of more detailed investigation. It was argued above that we do not know how (or if) 'reinforcement' works in experiments with adults: It is certainly true that even less is known about the details of instructional effects.

Lowe (1979) has argued convincingly that many results in the literature on adult operant behavior might be understood with reference to the concept of 'self-instruction', that is, an instruction that the subject generates (on the basis of past history as well as current experimental events), and which serves in some way to control behavior. An 'uninstructed' subject, in Shimoff *et al.*'s (1981) terms, can therefore be self-instructed. The relation between such cognitions and behavior is discussed more fully in the next section, but for present purposes it is sufficient to note that the concept of self-instruction is compatible with the arguments given above, both about the possibly informational nature of 'reinforcement' and about instructional effects. A more radical possibility than merely that self-instructional effects occur is that the formation of such instructions acts as a 'final common path' of behavior control in a variety of, if not all, circumstances when human adults learn in laboratory experiments.

One particularly difficult problem arises with instructional effects. Suppose that a normal adult is instructed in a very direct way to emit particular behavior in an experimental situation, for example, the subject is told what to do, in the fullest possible manner, so that his or her behavior under a series of presented VI schedules varies in accordance with Herrnstein's equation (Herrnstein, 1970). The subject then performs in accordance with the instructions, as experiments suggest he or she would (e.g. Buskist *et al.*, 1981). Does the resulting behavior, in this case conformity to Herrnstein's equation, then represent a 'law' to which human performance conforms? At first sight the answer is obviously no, since the subject presumably could have been instructed to behave in a totally different way under the schedule conditions. It seems, initially, that the subject is obeying some other sort of behavioral law, for example that of conformity to experimental instructions. However, further consideration suggests that the problem raised above may not be solved so easily. The instructed behavior, for example, may be identical to that of another subject who has not been so instructed. It may exhibit characteristics of orderliness, and sensitivity to the schedule parameter. On what basis, then, is what our hypothetical instructed subject does different from what some other subject did, apart from the means of arriving at the result? Furthermore, how could the behavior of our instructed subject and another person who behaved in a very similar way be distinguished by an experimenter who did not know how the behavior was generated, and for some reason was not allowed to question the subjects? If the behaviors could not be distinguished, then in what ways are they different, and why does Herrnstein's equation act as a 'law' when behavior conforms to it for one reason, but not when behavior conforms to it for another?

It is possible, of course, that a change of conditions would readily distinguish the instructed subject from another person (e.g. Shimoff *et al.*, 1981). For example, if a VI schedule that had never previously been presented was administered, the two subjects may behave very differently in this condition. However, it is also possible that they would not, given the variability of human performance that occurs in operant experiments with adults. Furthermore, if the underlying logic of Herrnstein's equation had been explained to the subject as part of the instructional procedure, he or she might subsequently adjust response rates to a novel VI schedule to maintain conformity to the equation, unless instructed otherwise.

Part of the acuteness of the problems outlined above probably derives from arbitrarily defining button pressing as the only interesting behavior that could be emitted, for example by forbidding the use of verbal probes with our instructed and uninstructed subjects. It is this restriction, of course, that makes two examples of conformity to Herrnstein's equation the same. If the restriction was lifted, and the button pressing regarded as just part of a totality of behavior which could occur, including verbalizations, then the behavior of our two hypothetical subjects is no longer seen to be the same, as they could narrate their past histories, which differ. Arbitrary restrictions on what counts as behavior can easily generate pseudoproblems. For example, it may be difficult to explain why the 'behavior' generated by two very different reinforcement schedules is 'the same' if the only thing measured is whether or not a response occurred at some time (e.g. in the tenth minute) during an experimental session. More realistic observations of behavior would reveal a host of differences (e.g. in rate and patterning of responding), of course. However, although in this example the definition of 'behavior' is absurd, it may be equally absurd to restrict the 'behavior' of adult humans in operant learning experiments to button pressing. Doing so gives rise to part of the problem described above (about the ways in which the behaviors of an instructed and uninstructed subject differ), but may seem a reasonable procedure to experimenters familiar with animal subjects, or to those for whom only responses such as button presses for some reason count as objective.

However, the problem of when human behavior is lawful (or 'natural') still remains and appears difficult to argue away. If subjects can be instructed to conform to Hernstein's equation or its opposite, as they almost certainly can, then which of these two contradictory actions reflects what humans would 'naturally' do? A similar problem arises if conformity to some behavioral principle is wholly or partly due to inadvertent communication of the experimenter's expectancies or wishes (Rosenthal, 1969), or demand characteristics of the experimental setting (Orne, 1969). A possible escape route is to suggest that neither Herrnstein's equation nor its opposite is a law of behavior. What subjects do depends on circumstances, for example, what they are instructed to do, or what they instruct themselves to do. Setting up one situation leads to one behavior, another situation a different one. Perhaps human adults do not have any 'natural' behavior in conditions as artificial as operant experiments in laboratories. The difficulty with this view, of course, is that it may make prediction and control of human behavior in such cases extremely difficult. This, however, may actually be the case.

Verbal behavior and human operant performance

Throughout the history of research on the operant behavior of normal humans, consistencies have been found between what subjects do, and what they say. For example, Lippman and Meyer (1967) found that different individuals performed differently under FI schedules of points, with some responding at high rates consistently throughout the interval, and others pausing for almost the entire interval before emitting a few responses at the end (see also Lowe, 1979). Such differences in performance under FI schedules were found to be correlated with different verbal descriptions of the schedule contingencies. High rate responders usually described the FI schedule in ratio terms (i.e. as involving the emission of a number of responses), whereas the low rate subjects often described the schedule in terms of time. Other workers such as Harzem, Lowe, and Bagshaw (1978) have found similar effects. Most recently, Wearden and Shimp (1985) found clear differences in verbal descriptions of task requirements between subjects who adapted behaviorally to their temporal differentiation contingency, and those who did not. The former subjects were found, by means of a post-experimental questionnaire, to describe contingency requirements invariably in terms of timing or spacing of responses in time, whereas nonadapting subjects only rarely employed time or response-spacing descriptions, exhibiting instead a wide variety of complex suggestions about the contingency.

One procedural difficulty of such studies is that correlations between what subjects do and what they say are assessed only by means of post-experimental questionnaires. It is not clear how behavior and statements about behavior or strategies developed as learning proceeded. Presumably, the subject is biased toward verbal reports describing final performance, if only on the grounds of memory limitations.

Catania, Matthews, and Shimoff (1982), however, obtained verbal reports from subjects every three minutes during a learning task. As well as responding under a multiple schedule (the components of which were random-ratio and random-interval schedules), subjects had to 'guess' the appropriate strategy (e.g. pressing rapidly during the ratio and less rapidly during the interval schedule). Points exchangeable for money were given for guesses, as well as for responding on the schedules. Different subjects received different types of procedures applied to the guesses. In one case, guesses were 'shaped' by having progressively more points awarded for closer and closer approximations to expressions of certain response strategies. In another, subjects were directly instructed what to guess. Catania *et al.* reported that when subjects were successfully 'shaped' as to what to guess, nonverbal responding was closely correlated with guesses, whereas this was not the case when guessing was unsuccessfully shaped, or when subjects were instructed what to guess.

As a study of relations between verbal and nonverbal behavior in human adults, Catania *et al.*'s study, although in many respects innovative, leaves much to be desired. For one thing, assessment of verbal behavior every three minutes may be too infrequent to capture changes in verbalizations accompanying rapid changes in human performance, such as shown in Figures 10.1 and 10.2 above. Secondly, the procedure of awarding points for guesses makes the overall operant task extremely complicated since it involves a multiple schedule with ratio and interval components, followed by a discriminably different condition in which points are available for another response, guessing, with conditional relations between behavior in the various experimental phases. Thirdly, the procedure of 'shaping' guesses raises the same problems as earlier work on 'shaping' responses in adult humans, namely of what is being shaped, and what shaping means in this context. Finally, instructing subjects what to emit as guesses may produce inconsistent effects not because of some fundamental difference between the effects instructed and shaped verbal behavior have on nonverbal performance but merely because this procedure violates demand characteristics of experiments. The subjects seem to be posed a problem (what to write on a guess sheet) while almost simultaneously being given the answer. Such a procedure may have little face-validity as an experimental manipulation, and consequently produce inconsistent behavioral effects, for example by arousing suspiciousness of the experimenter's intent (McGuire, 1969).

In general, however, Catania *et al.* (1982) confirmed the finding of other studies that statements generated under operant schedules and performance on the schedules are frequently related. Statements about what contingencies involve (e.g. that different conditions deliver different rates of reinforcement, or involve schedules of different types) may, of course, be more poorly correlated with performance than statements about what the subject should do. A subject may, for example, be able to describe several aspects of a schedule without being able to describe a behavior appropriate for it. The condition in which a subject expressed an allegedly ideal behavioral strategy but did not use it is surely rarer. All these considerations lead to the unsurprising prediction that statements about what the subject should do will be more highly correlated with what he or she does do than are statements about aspects of the schedule, a prediction confirmed by Matthews, Shimoff, and Catania (1985).

In spite of the above problems, work from Catania's laboratory shows that relations between what subjects say and what they do occur during learning, rather than merely in the form of post-experimental generalizations.

Lowe and his associates (Bentall *et al.*, 1985; Lowe *et al.*, 1983) also manipulated verbal behavior during operant learning using the ingenious expedient of testing children of different ages, and consequently different levels of verbal development. Firstly, Lowe *et al.* (1983) showed that pre-verbal infants responded differently from adults on FI schedules (showing a range of behaviors noted previously only in animals). Secondly, when children from four different age ranges were tested under FI schedules, older groups behaved like adults, pre-verbal infants behaved as mentioned above, whereas children in the two-and-a-half to four-year age range (in whom verbal behavior was developed to some extent but less so than in older children) performed in an intermediate way, showing aspects of behavior similar to that of both the younger and older children (Bentall *et al.*, 1985).

These studies obviously show a strong developmental correlation between verbal behavior and nonverbal performance, and suggest that the responding shown by adult subjects under FI schedules may be due, at least in part, to their being able to describe events which occur.

Although many studies have found strong correlations between verbal and nonverbal behavior on reinforcement schedules, opinion seems divided about the importance of verbal behavior under such conditions (Bentall *et al.*, 1985). A persistent problem is the charge that verbal behavior is in some way ephiphenomenal, that is, merely a correlate of nonverbal performance rather than a controlling variable. An analogy might be with the commentary on a sporting event and action on the field. The commentary and the play are obviously highly correlated, but the commentary merely reflects action and performs no causal or controlling role in it.

The charge of epiphenomenalism is not addressed by studies which show positive correlations between statements in post-experimental questionnaires and previous nonverbal behavior. It can even withstand the results of studies such as Lowe *et al.* (1983) and Bentall *et al.* (1985) showing developmental correlations between verbal and nonverbal behavior. For example, it could be argued that children of different ages learned in different ways for some reason which was reflected both in the verbal and nonverbal behavior.

Can the charge of epiphenomenalism be refuted experimentally? One method which seems promising is to investigate the time-course of verbal and nonverbal behavior during learning. On the one hand, nonverbal behavior may change before verbal behavior does, in which case the argument that verbal behavior plays no causal role in determining nonverbal performance is strengthened. On the other hand, verbal behavior changes may occur first, a result which, at first sight, tends to imply that verbal behavior may have a controlling role. Results from post-experimental questionnaires cannot resolve this issues since verbal behavior is assessed retrospectively. Even assessing verbal behavior every three minutes (as in Catania *et al.*, 1982) may miss changes occurring over shorter time periods (e.g. Figures 10.1 and 10.2 above).

A procedure which is perhaps useful in investigating the time-course of verbal and nonverbal behavior is to use very frequent verbal probes during learning (as suggested by Wearden and Shimp, 1985). This technique was developed in my own laboratory (in collaboration with Julia Ward) in an investigation of nonverbal and verbal behavior during acquisition of temporal differentiation of response latency. The basic procedure was a discrete-trial task in which a constraint was placed on the time taken to emit a single response, timed from the delivery of a signal which started a trial. An evaluative feedback contingency, similar to that used to generate the data in Figure 10.1, above, was imposed on each trial of a 50-trial experimental session. Between each trial, the subjects filled in a response sheet describing what they thought they had to do perform properly on the task, although no points were available for verbal behavior. Different groups of subjects received either neutral instructions, or those indicating that the time the trial took was important. Target latencies for different subgroups were 2, 4, and 8 seconds.

Figure 10.3 shows data from four typical subjects, two of whom (SR and JD) showed good temporal differentiation of response latency and two others who did not. The upper part of each panel shows the response latencies produced when the target latencies were 4 (SR and VC) and 8 seconds (JD and KD). The lower part of each panel shows the class into which the expressed response strategy fell. A wide range of verbal formulations of appropriate behavior were produced by subjects, and these were classified by the experimenters into 12 categories. Category 1 was variations on 'don't know' or 'no idea', numbers from 2–8 reflected a variety of response strategies not involving explicit reference to timing (for example pressing with some particular force). Categories 9, 10, and 11 reflected more and more precise time-based strategies, moving from the expression of the strategy of waiting for some unspecified time, to category 11, an explicit 'wait x-seconds and then respond' strategy. Category 12 was used as a 'miscellaneous' classification.

The subjects achieving good temporal differentiation (SR and JD) not only produced similar nonverbal performance, involving a rapid adjustment of response latency to target time, but also very similar verbal behavior. In particular, accurate temporal differentiation was associated with timing strategies (9, 10, and 11), and final performance accompanied in both cases by strategy 11, a correct expression of the contingency requirement. In both subjects only a few strategies were tried, and timing-based formulations of the appropriate behavior dominated the session after the first few trials.

In contrast, VC and KD used a wide variety of frequently changing strategies. Categories not involving timing tended to predominate, although VC's performance improvement toward the end of the session seemed associated with the development of a vague timing strategy (category 9). In general, both nonverbal and verbal behavior from subjects showing poor temporal differentiation of responding was less orderly than that from SR and JD.

These results, along with others such as Catania *et al.* (1982), show that verbal and nonverbal behavior may covary during experimental sessions. Furthermore, the present results (as well as Wearden and Shimp, 1985) suggest that good performance on temporal differentiation tasks is associated with verbal statements that the contingency involves time, and consequent time-related performance strategies. Such verbal formulations and the feedback events arranged by the schedule seem to operate in concert, as for example when KD's performance was not improved by receiving a 'VERY GOOD' evaluation in the absence of a time-related strategy.

Inspection of the time-course of verbal and nonverbal behavior for SR and JD suggests that time-related strategies emerge slightly before good temporal differentiation of response latency is evident (see also Catania *et al.*, 1982). Further evidence supporting this conclusion is shown in Figure 10.4.

Here, mean response latencies in the five trials preceding and the five trials following adoption of a timing strategy are shown, with the data coming from all subjects in the experiment who developed clear timing strategies. It is evident that most subjects show more accurate temporal differentiation of latency after the timing strategy has been adopted than before. It seems unlikely in the light of these results that timing strategies are mere commentaries on nonverbal behavior changes that occur independently.

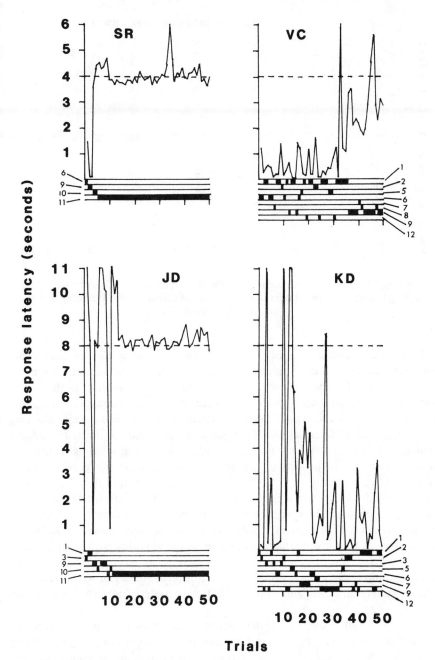

Figure 10.3   Response latencies and expressed response strategies from four subjects. Target latency was 4 (upper) or 8 seconds (lower panels)

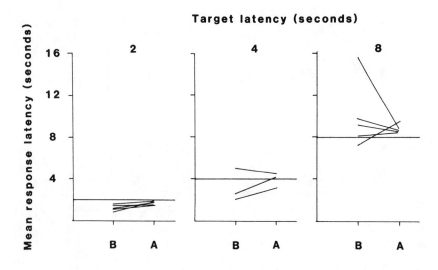

Figure 10.4   Mean respone latencies in the five trials before (B) and after (A) adopting timing strategies. Target time values varied across 2 (left), 4 (centre), and 8 seconds (right panel)

Subjects SR and JD in Figure 10.3 show more examples of very rapid behavior change in human adult learning, as both achieve accurate temporal differentiation of response latency in five to ten trials. The path to this stable nonverbal behavior was, however, marked by abrupt changes in response latency. In general, this type of behavior was characteristic of subjects achieving good temporal differentiation. Such subjects also showed initially variable strategies, followed most commonly by adoption and gradual refinement of timing strategies. In particular, almost all subjects achieving good temporal differentiation reported strategies 9, 10, and 11 in that temporal sequence. Once timing was adopted, the strategy was refined, a result reminiscent of the gradual 'shaping' of behavior by reinforcement contingencies in animals. Although the present results are insufficiently elaborate to substantiate the assertion fully it seems possible that if operant contingencies shape anything with normal adults they shape what they say about what they have to do (see also Catania *et al.*, 1982). Paradoxically, this suggests that it is nonverbal behavior which may be in a sense 'epiphenomenal', and a mere reflection of underlying verbal or cognitive changes.

Another result from the verbal probe study was that pre-experimental instructions that time was an important dimension in the contingency apparently influenced the response strategies reported. In particular, time-cued subjects tended to use more time-related strategies and fewer of other sorts. For example, time-cued subjects reported 255 trials on which strategies 9, 10, and 11 were used, versus 106 for the other subjects. Although this result is not surprising, it does illustrate a possible mechanism of action of instructions, a restriction or constraint on the population of response strategies (or 'self-instructions', Lowe and Higson, 1981) employed in learning sessions.

At first sight the results above are inconsistent with the belief that verbal behavior is epiphenomenal and plays no controlling role in nonverbal behavior. Verbal reports are not only apparently associated with nonverbal behavior during learning, but appear to change before nonverbal behavior does. The epiphenomenalist argument can still be salvaged, however, by positing a third entity of which both verbal and nonverbal behaviors are manifestations, with the temporally prior emergence of verbal reports accounted for by supposing that the 'threshold' for their production is lower than for nonverbal changes. Such a development would make the epiphenomenalist argument very difficult, perhaps impossible, to refute by examination of the time-course of verbal and nonverbal behavior changes, and possibly almost impossible to refute by any conceivable experimental evidence. It may, in addition, have the disadvantage of inventing and additional hypothetical internal variable to account for verbal and nonverbal behavior changes. It seems more parsimonious to assume that some underlying cognitive change, of which verbal reports are a direct if possibly slightly inaccurate expression, occurs and is then translated, once again perhaps inaccurately, into nonverbal behavior. Cognitive changes can obviously act as antecedent controlling variables of nonverbal actions, as in the case discussed in the previous section where the subject is directly instructed what to do, and subsequently does it (see also Skinner, 1969, p. 147). Although such an 'experiment' raises some difficulties mentioned previously, there is little doubt that it would produce clear behavior change.

It may be that the general acceptance of verbal or cognitive factors as controlling variables of operant performance will depend more on theoretical developments articulating more clearly how the various types of events are related, rather than experimental results. At the present time, most theoretical analysis (e.g. Skinner, 1969) seems to regard verbal and cognitive factors, as well as other sorts of private events, as having discriminative stimulus properties, and thus setting the occasion for nonverbal performance. A similar interpretation of instructional control has also been attempted (see Galizio, 1979). Although this analysis may draw interesting parallels between events controlling the behavior of animals and normal humans, and serves to maintain continuity of explanatory concepts across species boundaries, the characterization of private events as 'stimuli' is not without its difficulties. For one thing, the 'stimuli' appear to be generated by the subject, rather than arranged by the experimenter, and in addition there may be no history of reinforcement of behavior in the presence of these 'stimuli'.

Emphasis on verbal or cognitive factors as presented above is obviously not intended to suggest that operant contingencies play no role in determining behavior. What the subject decides it is appropriate to do clearly depends critically on information received from the scheduled experimental events, as in Figure 10.3 above. The operant contingencies may not, however, operate directly without the involvement of some sort of cognitive mediation, usually in the form of development of rules, self-instructions, or response strategies. This implies that all the behavior observed from normal adults in operant conditioning experiments in the laboratory may be 'rule-governed', rather than 'contingency-governed'. The fact that changing contingencies produces behavior change does not, of course, challenge this argument.

Finally, what relations can be discerned between the response strategies and self-generated rules discussed above and the concept of 'awareness'? Awareness, like knowledge, must have a content, unless it is proposed that human subjects in operant experiments are unaware in the sense of being unconscious. Since subjects are always aware of something, if only that they are in a psychological experiment, questions about 'conditioning without awareness' are reducible to questions about what subjects are aware of in operant experiments. It seems from the above results that awareness of dimensions of the contingencies (for example that time is involved), leading to some self-instruction about performance is a necessary concomitant of successful performance on temporal differentiation tasks (see also Wearden and Shimp, 1985). Subjects who can report features of the experimental situation without developing appropriate response strategies may perform more poorly (Matthews *et al.*, 1985), but cannot be said to be 'unaware'. In general, there has been little interest in questions about what subjects can and cannot report during and after operant experiments, although techniques involving verbal probes provide some promising experimental methods.

As illustrated above, almost all investigations of relations between verbal and nonverbal behavior on operant tasks illustrate 'conditioning with awareness', that is, strong correlations between performance and verbal reports. The possibility remains, however, that a subject's behavior may adjust to contingencies without the subject being able to verbalize contingency requirements, as has been claimed by Hefferline, Keenan, and Harford (1959). Whether this type of effect is restricted to occasions when the response employed is some very small movement, as in Hefferline *et al.*'s study, remains to be seen, but even if some types of responses such as autonomic changes (Brener, 1977) can show conditioning without concomitant verbal reports, this does not mean that such effects are common (or even possible) when behaviors such as button pressing are used.

A more subtle difficulty which does arise in conventional operant studies might be called 'coincidental awareness'. This is when the subject's behavior adapts appropriately to the experimenter's contingency, but is accompanied by a verbalization of a response strategy which is 'incorrect' from the experimenter's point of view. For example, in the experiment from which the data for Figures

10.3 and 10.4 were taken, a few subjects showed reasonably good temporal differentiation of response latency in the 2-second target time condition by means of strategies not explicitly involving time. These included holding down the response button (which they were expressly instructed not to do), or sequences of actions terminating in a button press. Subjects were able to describe their strategies accurately, and their execution resulted in reliably positive evaluation by the feedback contingencies. It seems unreasonable to class these subjects as 'unaware', although they were 'unaware' of the 'real' basis of the contingency imposed. A related problem is that subjects may make erroneous statements about their own performance, or experimental events (Nisbett and Wilson, 1977). However, just because some response systems may show conditioned changes without concomitant verbal descriptions, and subjects may, occasionally, produce obscure or inappropriate verbalizations, there are no sound reasons for the currently prevalent disinclination to collect and investigate verbal reports. It seems likely that the more studies conducted on relations between nonverbal and verbal behavior on operant tasks, the more light will be shed on the relations between these factors. Human subjects are uniquely able to respond to verbal probes: It may be dangerously shortsighted to assume that the experimental analysis of adult operant behavior can proceed without consideration of what such probes can reveal.

Concluding comments

The main issues raised in the material above may be summarized by several series of questions.

1. Do the 'reinforcers' used in laboratory experiments with normal adults have hedonic and/or informational properties? What are the consequences of defining informational feedback events as 'reinforcers'? How do such contingent events influence the behavior of normal adults?
2. What does it mean to say that behavior is instructed? Can certain types of behavior in normal adults ever be 'shaped'? Do different types of instructions have different behavioral effects? How do instructions operate? What is the status of behavior which is generated solely by instructions relative to that which occurs by other means?
3. What relations can be discerned between what people say and what they do during operant learning? Can verbal behavior be shown to be a controlling variable of nonverbal performance? What does it mean to say that subjects are 'aware' in operant experiments?

The above questions concern the principal issues discussed in this chapter. Another field of inquiry, if possible even more neglected than those described previously, is the social psychology of the operant experiment. This particularly involves the possibility that much of what happens in experiments with normal adults is not generated by the operation of the arranged experimental contingencies but by 'artifacts' (Rosenthal and Rosnow, 1969) such as inadvertent communication of experimenter expectancies, some other type of unintentional cuing of subjects, or demand characteristics of experimental procedures.

Many of the issues discussed in this chapter may seem unfamiliar, peripheral, or irrelevant to experimenters whose main experience has been work in the animal laboratory. These individuals may be inclined to apply to humans only those procedures closely analogous to ones used with animals, and may prefer to explain human behavior only in terms which are applicable to the behavior of lower animals. The present chapter, obviously, takes the view that the behavior of normal adults has unique characteristics, and needs treatment different from that applicable to animal performance if it is to be understood. This view is advocated not on the basis of a belief that humans possess any metaphysical or mystical properties, but arises from the possibility that the great cognitive complexity of humans, particularly their elaborate verbal behavior, may make the principles of their learning different from those of animals. To discover what these principles are, and to provide rigorous accounts of human learning, experimental analysis may need to disencumber itself of much baggage picked up over many years in the animal laboratory.

References

Adair, J.G. (1973). *The Human Subject*, Boston: Little, Brown and Company.

Baum, W.M. (1981). Optimization and the matching law as accounts of instrumental behavior, *Journal of the Experimental Analysis of Behavior*, **36**, 387–403.

Benford, G., and Eklund, G. (1978). *If the Stars are Gods*, London: Gollancz.

Bentall, R.P., Lowe, C.F., and Beasty, A. (1985). The role of verbal behavior in human learning: II. Developmental differences, *Journal of the Experimental Analysis of Behavior*, **43**, 165–181.

Bradshaw, C.M., Szabadi, E., and Bevan, P. (1976). Behavior of humans in variable-interval schedules of reinforcement, *Journal of the Experimental Analysis of Behavior*, **26**, 135–141.

Bradshaw, C.M., Szabadi, E., and Bevan, P. (1978). Effect of variable-interval punishment on the behavior of humans in variable-interval schedules of monetary reinforcement, *Journal of the Experimental Analysis of Behavior*, **29**, 161–166.

Bradshaw, C.M. Szabadi, E., and Bevan, P. (1979). The effect of punishment on free-operant choice behavior in humans, *Journal of the Experimental Analysis of Behavior*, **31**, 71–81.

Brener, J. (1977). Sensory and peripheral determinants of voluntary visceral control. In G.E. Schwartz and J. Beatty (eds), *Biofeedback, Theory and Research*, London: Academic Press, pp. 29–66.

Buskist, W.F., Bennett, R.H., and Miller, H.L. Jr. (1981). Effect of instructional constraints on human fixed-interval performance, *Journal of the Experimental Analaysis of Behavior*, **35**, 217–225.

Buskist, W. F., and Miller, H. L. Jr. (1981). Concurrent operant performance in humans: Matching when food is the reinforcer, *Psychological Record*, **31**, 95–100.

Buskist, W. F., Miller, H. R. Jr., and Bennett, R. H. (1980). Fixed-interval performance in humans: Sensitivity to temporal parameters when food is the reinforcer, *Psychological Record*, **30**, 111–121.

Case, D. A., Fantino, E., and Waxted, J. (1985). Human observing: Maintained by negative stimuli correlated with improvement in response efficiency, *Journal of the Experimental Analysis of Behavior*, **43**, 289–300.

Catania, A. C., Matthews, B. A., and Shimoff, E. (1982). Instructed versus shaped human verbal behavior: Interactions with non-verbal responding, *Journal of the Experimental Analysis of Behavior*, **38**, 233–248.

Collier, G., Hirsch, E., and Kanarek, R. (1977). The operant revisited. In W. K. Honig and J. E. R. Staddon (eds), *Handbook of Operant Behavior*, Englewood Cliffs, NJ: Prentice-Hall, pp. 28–52.

DeCasper, A. J., and Zeiler, M. D. (1974). Time limits for completing fixed ratios, III: Stimulus variables, *Journal of the Experimental Analysis of Behavior*, **22**, 285–300.

DeVilliers, P. A., and Herrnstein, R. J. (1976). Toward a law of response strength, *Psychological Bulletin*, **83**, 1131–1153.

Fantino, E. (1977). Conditioned reinforcement: Choice and information. In W. K. Honig and J. E. R. Staddon (eds), *Handbook of Operant Behavior*, Englewood Cliffs, NJ: Prentice-Hall, pp. 313–339.

Fantino, E., and Case, D. A. (1983). Human observing: Maintained by stimuli correlated with reinforcement but not extinction, *Journal of the Experimental Analysis of Behavior*, **40**, 193–210.

Galizio, M. (1979). Contingency-shaped and rule-governed behavior: Instructional control of human loss avoidance, *Journal of the Experimental Analysis of Behavior*, **31**, 53–70.

Harzem, P., Lowe, C. F., and Bagshaw, M. (1978). Verbal control in human operant behavior, *Psychological Record*, **28**, 405–423.

Hefferline, R. F., Keenan, B., and Harford, R. A. (1959). Escape and avoidance conditioning in human subjects without their observation of the response, *Science*, **130**, 1338–1339.

Herrnstein, R. J. (1970). On the law of effect, *Journal of the Experimental Analysis of Behavior*, **13**, 243–266.

Killeen, P. (1982) Incentive theory II: Models for choice, *Journal of the Experimental Analysis of Behavior*, **38**, 217–232.

Lippman, L. G., and Meyer, M. E. (1967). Fixed-interval performance as related to subjects' verbalizations of the reinforcement contingency, *Psychonomic Science*, **8**, 135–136.

Lowe, C. F. (1979). Determinants of human operant behavior. In M. D. Zeiler and P. Harzeml (eds), *Reinforcement and the Organization of Behaviour*, Chichester: Wiley, pp. 159–192.

Lowe, C. F., Beasty, A., and Bentall, R. P. (1983). The role of verbal behavior in human learning: Infant performance on fixed-interval schedules, *Journal of the Experimental Analysis of Behavior*, **39**, 157–164.

Lowe, C. F., Harzem, P., and Bagshaw, M. (1978). Species differences in the temporal control of behavior, II: Human performance, *Journal of the Experimental Analysis of Behavior*, **29**, 351–361.

Lowe, C. F., Harzem, P., and Hughes, S. (1978). Determinants of human operant behavior: Some differences from animals, *Quarterly Journal of Experimental Psychology*, **30**, 373–386.

Lowe, C. F. and Higson, P. J. (1981). Self-instructional training and cognitive behavior modification: A behavioral analysis. In G. Davey (ed), *Applications of Conditioning Theory*, London: Methuen, pp. 162–188.

Lowe, C. F., and Horne, P. J. (1985). On the generality of behavioral principles: Human choice and the matching law. In C. F. Lowe, M. Richelle, D. Blackman, and C. M. Bradshaw (eds), *Behaviour Analysis and Contemporary Psychology*, pp. 97–115. London: Erlbaum.

Mackintosh, N. J. (1974). *The Psychology of Animal Learning*, London: Academic Press.

Matthews, B. A., Catania, A. C., and Shimoff, E. (1985). Effects of uninstructed verbal behavior on nonverbal responding: Contingency descriptions versus performance descriptions, *Journal of the Experimental Analysis of Behavior*, **43**, 155–164.

Matthews, B. A., Shimoff, E., Catania, A. C., and Sagvolden, T. (1977). Uninstructed human responding: Sensitivity to ratio and interval contingencies, *Journal of the Experimental Analysis of Behavior*, **27**, 453–467.

McGuire, W. J. (1969). Suspiciousness of the experimenter's intent. In R. Rosenthal and R. L. Rosnow (eds), *Artifact in Behavioral Research*, New York: Academic Press, pp. 13–57.

Nisbett, R. E., and Wilson, T. D. (1977). Telling more than we can know: Verbal reports on mental processes, *Psychological Review*, **84**, 231–259.

Orne, M. T. (1962). On the social psychology of the psychological experiment: With particular reference to demand characteristics and their implications, *American Psychologist*, **17**, 776–783.

Orne, M. T. (1969). Demand characteristics and the concept of quasi-controls. In R. Rosenthal and R. L. Rosnow (eds), *Artifact in Behavioral Research*, New York: Academic Press, pp. 143–179.

Perone, M., and Baron, A. (1980). Reinforcement of human observing behavior by a stimulus correlated with extinction or increased effort, *Journal of the Experimental Analysis of Behavior*, **34**, 239–261.

Rosenberg, M. J. (1969). The conditions and consequences of evaluation apprehension. In R. Rosenthal and R. L. Rosnow (eds), *Artifact in Behavioral Research*, New York: Academic Press, pp. 280–349.

Rosenthal, R. (1969). Interpersonal expectations: Effects of the experimenter's hypothesis. In R. Rosenthal and R. L. Rosnow (eds), *Artifact in Behavioral Research*, New York: Academic Press, pp. 181–277.

Rosenthal, R., and Rosnow, R. L. (1969). *Artifact in Behavioral Research*, New York: Academic Press.

Shimoff, E., Catania, A. C., and Matthews, B. A. (1981). Uninstructed human performance: Sensitivity of low-rate performance to schedule contingencies, *Journal of the Experimental Analysis of Behavior*, **36**, 207–220.

Skinner, B. F. (1953). *Science and Human Behavior*, New York: MacMillan.

Skinner, B. F. (1969). *Contingencies of Reinforcement: A Theoretical Analysis*, New York: Appleton-Century-Crofts.

Vaughn, W. Jr. (1985). Choice: A local analysis, *Journal of the Experimental Analysis of Behavior*, **43**, 383–405.

Wearden, J. H., and Quinn, M. (1982). Human performance under inter-response time contingencies, *Behavior Analysis Letters*, **2**, 309–319.

Wearden, J. H., and Shimp, C. P. (1985). Local temporal patterning of operant behavior in humans, *Journal of the Experimental Analysis of Behavior*, **44**, 315–324.

Human Operant Conditioning and Behavior Modification
Edited by G. Davey and C. Cullen
© 1988 John Wiley & Sons Ltd

Chapter 11

Quantitative Analysis of Human Operant Behavior*

C. M. BRADSHAW AND E. SZABADI
Department of Psychiatry, University of Manchester

The discovery of simple quantitative relationships between the parameters of reinforcement and the rate or probability of operant responding must rank as a major landmark in the history of the experimental analysis of behavior. Even the most casual observer of the behavior analysis literature cannot fail to detect the great impact which Herrnstein's discovery of the 'matching' relation (Herrnstein, 1961) and the subsequent formulation of the 'quantitative Law of Effect' (Herrnstein, 1970) made both on empirical research and on theoretical thinking about operant behavior. One is reminded of similar empirical and theoretical advances in other biological sciences which ensued from the discovery of simple quantitative laws: For example Clark's (1933) analysis of the pharmacological dose–response relation, or Weber's (1834) analysis of psychophysical judgments.

It is a fundamental assumption of biological science that there are certain basic principles of the structure and function of organisms that transcend species differences. For example, the same laws of enzyme-catalyzed reactions and drug–receptor interaction apply to protozoa and to man, even though the particular enzyme or receptor molecules may differ between species. Does the quantitative Law of Effect enjoy the same universality? Most of the studies reviewed in the chapter are in some measure concerned with this question, in that they constitute attempts to verify with human subjects quantitative predictions derived from the Law of Effect which have previously been verified only with animals.

*Preparation of this chapter was supported by the Sir Jules Thorn Charitable Trust.

In the first section of the chapter we will outline the quantitative Law of Effect and its corollaries. The next two sections will address the question of whether these quantitative relationships apply to the operant behavior of humans, as well as to that of animals. And finally we will discuss the possible implications of these relationships for the analysis of human behavior in social and clinical settings.

Theoretical background

Single schedules

The rate of responding in single variable-interval schedules of positive reinforcement is an increasing, negatively accelerated function of reinforcement frequency. This relationship was first revealed by a systematic study by Catania and Reynolds (1968), who recorded the steady-state response rates of pigeons in a series of variable-interval schedules specifying a wide range of reinforcement frequencies. Herrnstein (1970) proposed that the relationship could be described by a simple hyperbolic equation:

$$R = R_{max} . r \,/\, (K_H + r) \qquad\qquad [11.1]$$

where R is response rate and r is reinforcement frequency; R_{max} and K_H are constants expressing the theoretical maximum response rate and the reinforcement frequency corresponding to the half-maximal response rate, respectively (see Figure 11.1). The empirical validity of Herrnstein's equation has been supported by numerous studies using pigeons and rats as subjects (for reviews, see de Villiers and Herrnstein, 1976; Bradshaw *et al.*, 1983).

Inspection of equation 11.1 shows that any variable which affects the rate of responding in variable-interval schedules must alter the value of one or other, or both, of the two constants R_{max} and K_H. There are in fact eight, and only eight, theoretically possible patterns of effect on the two constants; three patterns of pure response suppression, three patterns of pure response facilitation, and two patterns of mixed effect (see Figure 11.2). These eight patterns form the basis of an empirical classification of variables which affect operant performance in interval schedules (Bradshaw, Szabadi, and Bevan, 1976, 1977, 1978a).

In addition to affording an empirical classificatory scheme, the patterns of effect on R_{max} and K_H may also provide insights into the behavioral mechanisms underlying observed changes in operant performance. Since R_{max} is measured in units of response rate, and expresses the maximum rate which can be maintained by an infinitely high reinforcement frequency, a change in the value of this parameter may be interpreted as a change in the maximum response capability of the organism. K_H, on the other hand, is measured in units of reinforcement frequency, and expresses the frequency of a given reinforcer which is required to

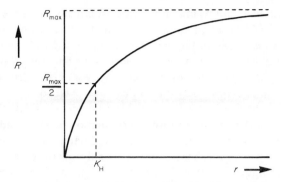

Figure 11.1 Hyperbolic curve defined by Herrnstein's equation (equation 11.1). *Ordinate*: response rate (R); *abscissa*: reinforcement frequency (r). R_{max} is the asymptote of the curve (i.e. the theoretical maximum response rate: $R \rightarrow R_{max}$ as $r \rightarrow \infty$), and K_H is the reinforcement frequency needed to maintain the half-maximal response rate ($r = K_H$ when $R = R_{max}/2$)

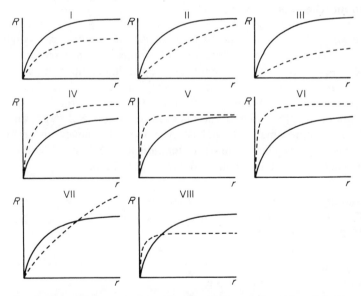

Figure 11.2 Patterns of effect of hypothetical variables influencing R_{max} and K_H. Each graph shows the hyperbolic curve relating response rate (R) to reinforcement frequency (r), under control conditions (continuous line) and in the presence of the hypothetical variable (broken line). *Top row*, patterns of pure suppression of response rate: I, R_{max} reduced; II, K_H elevated; III, R_{max} reduced and K_H elevated. *Middle row*, patterns of pure facilitation of response rate: IV, R_{max} elevated; V, K_H reduced; VI, R_{max} elevated and K_H reduced. *Bottom row*, patterns of mixed effect: VII, R_{max} and K_H both elevated; VIII, R_{max} and K_H both reduced

maintain responding at half its maximum rate; thus a change in the value of this parameter may be interpreted as a change in the organism's sensitivity to reinforcement. An example of the application of this kind of interpretation of the effects of variables on operant performance is the analysis of the behavioral effects of d-amphetamine. This drug exerts a Type VIII effect on variable-interval performance (Bradshaw, Ruddle, and Szabadi, 1981b; Morley, Bradshaw, and Szabadi, 1985), which has been taken to indicate that the drug reduces the organism's capacity to respond (reduction of R_{max}) and at the same time sensitizes the organism to the reinforcer (reduction of K_H) (Morley *et al.*, 1985). A similar approach has been adopted in analyzing the effects of a number of variables, including some psychiatric conditions, on human operant behavior (see below). This type of analysis has considerable appeal; however, it should be handled with a certain amount of caution, because there is as yet no unanimous agreement about the precise interpretation of the two constants (see Herrnstein, 1970, 1974; Catania, 1973; Staddon, 1977; McDowell and Kessel, 1979; McDowell, 1980; Killeen, 1979, 1982).

Concurrent schedules

When a pigeon or a rat is exposed to a concurrent schedule consisting of two variable-interval components, the rate of responding in each component is directly related to the reinforcement frequency in that component, and inversely related to the reinforcement frequency in the other component (Catania, 1963). The relative rate of responding in each component (i.e. the rate of responding in that component, expressed as a fraction of the overall rate of responding in both components) approximately 'matches' the relative frequency of reinforcement (Herrnstein, 1961). These empirical relationships can be described by the following equations (Herrnstein, 1970) (see Figure 11.3):

$$R_A = R_{max} \cdot r_A / (K_H + r_A + r_B) \qquad [11.2]$$
$$R_B = R_{max} \cdot r_B / (K_H + r_A + r_B) \qquad [11.3]$$
$$R_A / (R_A + R_B) = r_A / (r_A + r_B) \qquad [11.4]$$

where the subscripts A and B designate the two component schedules. An alternative form of equation 11.4 is

$$R_A / R_B = r_A / r_B \qquad [11.5]$$

Equations 11.4 and 11.5 (the 'Matching Law') can be derived from equations 11.2 and 11.3 if the values of R_{max} and K_H are assumed to be invariant between the two components, a prerequisite which may be realized in some concurrent schedule situations, but which may be violated in others (see below).

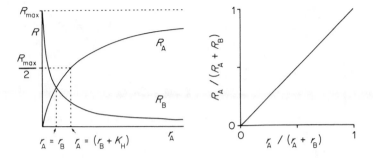

Figure 11.3 Herrnstein's model of concurrent performances. *Left-hand graph*: hyperbolic curves showing absolute rates of responding in components A and B (R_A and R_B) as a function of the reinforcement frequency in component A (r_A); the reinforcement frequency in component B is held constant (cf. equations 11.2 and 11.3). *Right-hand graph*: linear relationship between relative response rate and relative reinforcement frequency specified by the Matching Law (cf. equation 11.4)

In practice, performance in concurrent schedules often shows systematic departures from equations 11.4 and 11.5. These departures can be accommodated by a modification of equation 11.5 (Staddon, 1968; Baum, 1974):

$$R_A / R_B = k (r_A / r_B)^a \qquad [11.6]$$

Equation 11.6 (the 'Generalized Matching Law': Baum, 1974) is illustrated in Figure 11.4. Values of k deviating from unity indicate a 'bias' in favor of one or other of the component schedules. A value of a less than unity signifies 'undermatching', a weaker preference for the component with the higher reinforcement frequency than that predicted by equation 11.5; a value of a greater than unity signifies 'overmatching', a stronger preference for the component with the higher reinforcement frequency than that predicted by equation 11.5. The Generalized Matching Law may also be used to describe the distribution of available time (T) between the components:

$$T_A / T_B = k (r_A / r_B)^a \qquad [11.7]$$

Conformity to equations 11.6 and 11.7 is usually assessed by fitting a linear function to double-logarithmically transformed data (cf. Figure 11.4); the slope of the linear function expresses the value of a (the 'sensitivity' parameter; Baum, 1974). Empirical values of a have generally been found to be less than 1.0 (i.e. undermatching) (see Myers and Myers, 1977; Baum, 1979; Wearden and Burgess, 1982). The origin of undermatching is a topic of current debate. It has

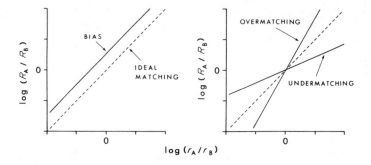

Figure 11.4   The Generalized Matching Law (equation 11.6). The ratio
of the response rates in the two components (R_A/R_B) is plotted against
the ratio of the reinforcement frequencies (r_A/r_B) in double-logarithmic
coordinates. In each graph, the broken line shows the ideal matching
relation. *Left-hand graph*: continuous line shows performance biased in
favour of component A ($k > 1$). *Right-hand graph*: continuous lines
show overmatching ($a > 1$) and undermatching ($a < 1$)

been proposed that it results from 'subjective transformation' of reinforcer
values (Allen, 1981; Prelec, 1984), from inadequate discrimination between the
component schedules (Wearden, 1983), or that it may constitute a cumulation of
procedural artifacts (Baum, 1979). Other authors (e.g. Davison, 1981) have
favored the view that undermatching, rather than ideal matching, should be
regarded as the 'true' description of concurrent performance (see below for
further discussion).

An important, and aesthetically pleasing, aspect of Herrnstein's model is that
it provides a coherent set of equations which embraces both single and
concurrent schedules of reinforcement. Comparison of equations 11.1 and 11.3
shows how response rates in single variable-interval schedules are predicted to be
affected by the introduction of a concurrent source of reinforcement. The two
equations specify the same asymptotic response rate, R_{max}; however, a higher
reinforcement frequency is needed to maintain the half-maximal response rate in
the concurrent schedule than in the single schedule:

From equation 11.1, $R = R_{max}/2$ when $r = K_H$
From equation 11.2, $R_A = R_{max}/2$ when $r_A = K_H + r_B$

Thus a concurrent source of reinforcement is expected to act as a Type II
suppressor of operant behavior (cf. Figure 11.2). This prediction, which has been
confirmed in the case of animals (Bradshaw, 1977), has been the subject of
several investigations with humans (see below).

Human performance in single schedules

Conformity of performance in single schedules to Herrnstein's equation

Most published studies investigating the conformity of human variable-interval performance to equation 11.1 have used a button-pressing or lever-pulling task and monetary reinforcement. Typically, subjects are trained under four or five variable-interval schedules specifying a wide range of reinforcement frequencies. Reinforcement consists of the addition of points to a score displayed on a counter, the points being exchanged for money at the end of the experiment. A common procedure is to present all the schedules in every session, using a four or five-component multiple schedule (e.g. Bradshaw *et al.*, 1976). This bestows several advantages. Firstly, since training under all frequencies of reinforcement proceeds simultaneously, contaminating effects of baseline drift are avoided. Secondly, breaking the session up into segments of five to ten minutes helps to mitigate the boredom which subjects experience during long uninterrupted sessions. Thirdly, and perhaps most importantly, the reduction in the number of sessions needed to complete an experiment allows much more detailed studies to be carried out than would be feasible using successive training under a series of single schedules (e.g. Bradshaw, Szabadi, and Bevan, 1979; McDowell and Wood, 1984). The use of five-ply multiple schedules carries some risk of behavioral interaction between the components; however, this risk can be minimized by the use of long component durations and long time-out periods between successive components, and by varying the order of presentation of the schedules (see Bradshaw, Szabadi, and Bevan, 1976; McLean, 1983). The relative complexity of this procedure might suggest that it would be unsuitable for use with young children or mentally handicapped subjects. However, it is noteworthy that five-component multiple schedules have been used successfully in studies of Herrnstein's equation with animals (Heyman, 1983).

Using the above procedures, stable performance which is sensitive to variation in reinforcement frequency has been observed in numerous experiments. The degree of conformity to equation 11.1 which has been found in humans is comparable to that observed in pigeons and rats (see Figure 11.5 for example). When equation 11.1 was fitted to the data obtained from 42 individual animals (de Villiers and Herrnstein, 1976; de Villiers, 1977), the fitted functions accounted for more than 80 per cent of the data variance in 39 cases, and for more than 90 per cent in 32 cases. (A recent reanalysis of the data presented by de Villiers and Herrnstein (1976) and de Villiers (1977) suggests that these figures may have somewhat overestimated the conformity of individual subject data to equation 11.1 (Warren-Boulton *et al.*, 1985).) Comparable data obtained from human subjects are shown in Table 11.1, which lists all the published reports known to us, in which human variable-interval performance was analyzed in terms of equation 11.1. In many of the studies the subjects contributed several

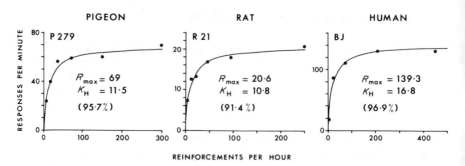

Figure 11.5   Conformity to Herrnstein's equation in different species. Each graph shows the relationship between steady-state response rate and reinforcement frequency in single variable-interval schedules. Curves are best-fit hyperbolic functions (equation 11.1); the values of R_{max}, K_H, and percentage of variance accounted for are shown in each case. *Left-hand graph*: data from one pigeon (Catania and Reynolds, 1968; data replotted by Herrnstein, 1970). *Middle graph*: data from one rat (Bradshaw, Szabadi, and Bevan, 1978b). *Right-hand graph*: data from one human (Bradshaw, Szabadi, and Bevan, 1976). Reproduced by permission of the Society for the Experimental Analysis of Behavior, Inc

sets of data (in some cases as many as ten: McDowell and Wood, 1985); however, the table only includes one set of data from each subject. It can be seen that equation 11.1 accounted for more than 80 per cent of the data variance in 27 out of the 31 cases, and for more than 90 per cent in 22 cases. The conclusion from these studies seems clear: Equation 11.1 provides at least as good a description of the behavior of human subjects in variable-interval schedules as it does in the case of animals.

Variables affecting R_{max} and K_H

The good conformity of human variable-interval performance to equation 11.1, together with the possibility afforded by human subjects of conducting rather complex studies within a relatively small number of sessions, suggest that studies with humans may be well suited to addressing certain issues of theoretical importance for the quantitative analysis of behavior which have proved difficult to study using animals. One such issue is the question of whether the value of R_{max} remains constant across variations in reinforcer magnitude and response-force requirement. According to Herrnstein's interpretation of R_{max} ('k' in Herrnstein's notation), this constant should be influenced by changes in response-force requirement, but should be impervious to changes in the parameters of reinforcement (Herrnstein, 1970, 1974, 1979). Alternative interpretations (McDowell and Kessel, 1979; McDowell, 1980) predict that the

Table 11.1 *Fit of equation 11.1 to data obtained from individual human subjects*

Study	Number of schedules	Subject	Sex	R_{max} (resp/ min)	K_H (rft/hr)	% variance accounted for by equation 11.1
Bradshaw, Szabadi, and	5	BH	M	392	9.8	98
Bevan (1976)	5	BF	M	399	6.8	96
	5	SM	F	271	5.8	97
	5	AM	F	287	7.6	99
Bradshaw, Szabadi, and	5	BJ	F	139	16.8	97
Bevan (1977)	5	JL	F	103	1.3	99
	5	VG	F	219	13.8	99
Bradshaw, Szabadi and	5	CW	F	300	1.4	92
Bevan (1978a)	5	JC	F	82	14.2	96
	5	HB	F	87	2.7	89
	5	KD	M	295	67.7	99
Bradshaw and Szabadi (1978)[a]	5	JA	F	185	2.9	99
Bradshaw, Szabadi and	5	BB	F	251	1.9	88
Bevan (1979)	5	LK	F	275	3.6	88
	5	MS	F	291	8.6	98
McDowell (1981a)	5	—	?	213	3.2	96
Ruddle, Bradshaw and	5	PK	M	289	2.0	93
Szabadi (1981)	5	SF	M	247	248.1	98
	5	JG	F	290	2.0	59
Szabadi, Bradshaw, and Ruddle (1981)[a]	5	AK	M	287	127.7	94
McDowell and Wood	5	H09	F	37	7.7	92
(1984)[b]	5	H13	F	57	92.0	95
	5	H15	F	61	0.6	67
	5	H17	F	41	14.2	98
	5	H18	F	63	32.5	99
	4	H19	F	64	6.0	81
	4	H20	F	46	1.1	62
	4	H23	M	179	7.3	96

(continued overleaf)

Table 11.1 *continued*

Study	Number of schedules	Subject	Sex	R_{max} (resp/ min)	K_H (rft/hr)	% variance accounted for by equation 11.1
McDowell and Wood	5	H06	F	59	10.5	78
(1985)[c]	5	H09	F	67	0.6	81
	5	H11	M	73	104.6	94

Note In many of the studies several functions were obtained from each subject under different experimental conditions. Only one representative function is shown for each subject in this table.

[a] Manic-depressive patients: data obtained during periods of remission.

[b] Data from the 1-cent-per-reinforcer condition. Values of K_H computed from raw data presented in original paper.

[c] Data from the high-force-requirement, 0.5-cent-per-reinforcer condition. H13 omitted because her data also feature in McDowell and Wood (1984). Values of K_H computed from raw data presented in original paper.

value of R_{max} should be inversely related to reinforcer value. De Villiers, reviewing the available data in 1977, concluded that the evidence was equivocal. Subsequent experiments with rats confirmed the prediction that R_{max} is sensitive to response-force requirement (Bradshaw, Szabadi, and Ruddle 1983), and indicated that R_{max} may be sensitive to some parameters of reinforcement (e.g. concentration of a liquid reinforcer: Bradshaw *et al.*, 1978b) but not to others (e.g. volume of a liquid reinforcer: Bradshaw, Ruddle, and Szabadi, 1981a; deprivation level: Bradshaw *et al.*, 1983).

Recent experiments with humans have confirmed the sensitivity of R_{max} to response-force requirement (Bradshaw *et al.*, 1981c; McDowell and Wood, 1984, 1985). Bradshaw *et al.* (1981c), using a concurrent schedule paradigm, also found that response-force requirement did not influence the value of K_H, indicating that an increase in force requirement acts as a Type I suppressor of operant responding (Figure 11.6). A detailed analysis of the sensitivity of R_{max} to reinforcer magnitude has recently been undertaken by McDowell and Wood (1984, 1985). In one study (McDowell and Wood, 1984), hyperbolic curves relating response rate to reinforcement frequency were obtained for a wide range of reinforcer magnitudes (0.25–35 cents per reinforcer; three to five functions obtain from each of eight subjects). The value of R_{max} was a monotonically increasing function of reinforcer magnitude, the function being approximately hyperbolic, as indicated by the good fit of a straight line to the data plotted in

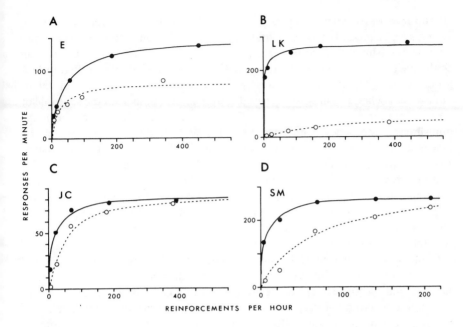

Figure 11.6 Human performance in single variable-interval schedules. The graphs show examples of the effects of different variables on the hyperbolic function relating response rate to reinforcement frequency (cf. Figure 11.2); each graph obtained from one subject. Closed symbols, continuous lines: control performance; open symbols, broken lines: performance in the presence of the variable in question. A: Type I suppression of response rate produced by an increase in response-force requirement (Bradshaw, Ruddle, and Szabadi, 1981c). B: Type III suppression produced by a variable-ratio punishment schedule (Bradshaw, Szabadi, and Bevan, 1977). C: Type II suppression produced by a variable-interval punishment schedule (Bradshaw, Szabadi, and Bevan, 1978a). D: Type II suppression produced by a concurrent source of reinforcement (Bradshaw, Szabadi, and Bevan, 1976). Reproduced by permission of the Society for the Experimental Analysis of Behavior, Inc

double-reciprocal coordinates (cf. Lineweaver and Burk, 1934; Cohen 1973). A second study (McDowell and Wood, 1985) confirmed this relationship, and in addition revealed an interaction between the effects of response force and reinforcer magnitude; increasing the response-force requirement enhanced the sensitivity of R_{max} to changes in the monetary value of the reinforcer.

The effect of punishment, in the form of monetary penalties for responding, was the subject of a series of experiments by the present authors. An interesting finding in these experiments was that punishment exerted different patterns of effect on R_{max} and K_H depending on the particular punishment schedule used. When punishment was delivered according to a variable-ratio schedule, a Type

III suppression of responding was observed (Bradshaw, Szabadi, and Bevan, 1977, 1979; Szabadi, Bradshaw, and Ruddle, 1981). In contrast, when a variable-interval punishment schedule was used, the pattern of response suppression conformed to Type II (Bradshaw, Szabadi, and Bevan, 1978a) (see Figure 11.6 for examples). The basis for the different patterns of effect exerted by different punishment schedules may lie in their differing interactions with the schedule of positive reinforcement. In the case of variable-interval punishment, both the punishment frequency and the reinforcement frequency are essentially independent of response rate over a wide range of response rates (see Baum, 1973). Thus the punishment schedule simply acts to reduce the effective reinforcement frequency, thereby elevating the value of K_H. In contrast, variable-ratio punishment has a dual effect; as well as reducing the effective reinforcement frequency, it also penalizes responding in direct proportion to response rate, a contingency which might well be expected to reduce the value of R_{max} (cf. Herrnstein, 1974).

Conformity of operant performance to equation 11.1 has been demonstrated in the case of free-operant avoidance responding. de Villiers (1974), using rats as subjects and electric shock as the aversive stimulus, showed that the rate of responding in variable-interval avoidance schedules was a hyperbolic function of the frequency of shocks successfully avoided. Ruddle *et al.* (1982), using humans as subjects and monetary loss as the aversive stimulus, also found a hyperbolic relationship between response rate and avoidance frequency. Free-operant avoidance schedules have been employed in some studies of choice behavior in humans (see below).

The studies reviewed in this section indicate that equation 11.1 provides an accurate description of human variable-interval performance. An important goal of future research in this area will be to identify the types of variable that influence the values of R_{max} and K_H. This may help to resolve some of the controversies which currently surround the interpretation of the hyperbolic equation (Herrnstein, 1970, 1974; Catania, 1973; Staddon, 1977; McDowell and Kessel, 1979; McDowell, 1980; Killeen, 1979, 1982).

Human performance in concurrent schedules

Conformity of performance in concurrent schedules to the Matching Law

This section will consider a question which has preoccupied most workers in this field to date: Does the choice behavior of human subjects conform to the Matching Law?

The first published study to address this question was the now famous experiment by Schroeder and Holland (1969). These authors used a vigilance task in which subjects were required to detect deflections of a needle in an array of dials. Two variable-time schedules programmed the deflections ('reinforcers') on the left- and right-hand dials, and eye-movement responses were recorded by a corneal reflection technique. In the absence of a changeover delay the pooled data from six subjects showed little sensitivity to relative reinforcement frequency (i.e. undermatching). However, the imposition of a 1 second changeover delay resulted in good conformity to equation 11.4 in all but one subject, and this subject's performance conformed to the matching equation when the changeover delay was increased to 2.5 seconds (see Figure 11.7). The finding that conformity to the matching relationship depended on the presence of a changeover delay is in accord with the observation of Catania and Cutts (1963) that a changeover delay served to prevent the development of 'concurrent superstitions', and thus ensured the functional independence of the component schedules.

A vigilance task was also used by Baum (1975). The subjects were required to detect signals which could be presented in either of two components. The changeover procedure (Findley, 1958) was used, and a changeover delay and response cost for changing over were imposed in order to reduce the frequency of changeovers. The task was presented as a game in which the subject tried to detect missiles which were attacking his spaceship. The dependent variable was time distribution. In all three subjects studied, performance conformed closely to equation 11.7. In two subjects the value of a was close to 1.0; in the third, an initial tendency towards undermatching could be eliminated by increasing the response cost for changing over.

Conger and Killeen (1974) studied verbal behavior in a small group setting. Two experimenters, who were 'planted' in the group, delivered verbal reinforcement (approving comments) for spontaneous remarks, according to independent variable-interval schedules. The subjects' remarks were addressed more frequently to the experimenter from whom more reinforcers were received, the pooled data from five subjects conforming closely to equation 11.4 (see Figure 11.7).

More recent studies have mostly employed button-pressing or lever-pulling tasks and monetary reinforcement. Bradshaw, Szabadi, and Bevan (1976, 1979a) and Bradshaw *et al.* (1979b), using the changeover procedure, presented five different concurrent schedule pairs in each session. The reinforcement frequency in one component was held constant, and the reinforcement frequency in the other component was varied over a wide range. This allowed conformity of the absolute response rates to equations 11.2 and 11.3, as well as conformity of the response rate and time ratios to equations 11.6 and 11.7, to be assessed. Good conformity to the relevant equations was obtained in all the subjects studied, the slopes of the matching functions being close to 1.0.

Buskist and Miller (1981) also observed good conformity to equations 11.6 and 11.7 using the changeover procedure; their experiment is of especial interest because it is the only published study with humans in which food (peanuts, etc.) was used as the reinforcer.

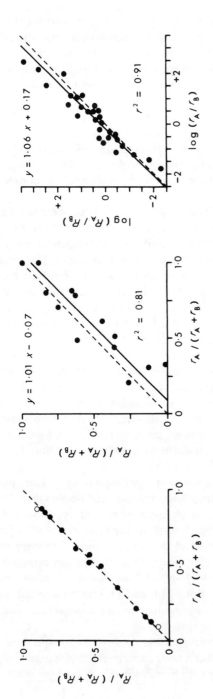

Figure 11.7　Concurrent performance by humans. *Left-hand graph*: pooled data from six subjects in a concurrent vigilance task; the response was eye-movement, and the reinforcer was deflection of a dial. Relative rate of responding in one component is plotted against relative frequency of reinforcement. Broken line indicates ideal matching (equation 11.4). A 1-second changeover delay was imposed, except in the case of one subject (open circles) for whom a 2.5-second delay was necessary (Schroeder and Holland, 1969). *Middle graph*: pooled data from five subjects in a small group discussion; the response was verbal utterance, and the reinforcer was approving comment from a 'planted' participant. Relative rate of responding is plotted against relative reinforcement frequency. Broken line indicates ideal matching (equation 11.4); continuous line is best-fit linear function (Conger and Killeen, 1974). *Right-hand graph*: pooled data from six subjects in a concurrent lever-pulling task with monetary reinforcement. Response rate ratio is plotted against reinforcement frequency ratio in double-logarithmic coordinates. Broken line indicates ideal matching (equation 11.6); continuous line is best-fit linear function (data from Ruddle *et al.*, 1979). Reproduced by permission of the Society of the Experimental Analysis of Behavior, Inc. and the Pacific Sociological Review, and Sage Publications, Inc

DeWaard (1980) carried out a series of experiments employing the changeover procedure. A high degree of conformity to equations 11.6 and 11.7 was observed. Individual values of *a* ranged from 0.5 to 1.89, with a general tendency toward slight undermatching (median slope approximately 0.8). DeWaard's experiments provide much valuable information about the effects of various superimposed contingencies upon concurrent performances, and will be discussed in greater detail below.

Cliffe and Parry (1980) carried out a detailed study of a sexually deviant subject using sexually stimulating pictures as the reinforcers. Equations 11.6 and 11.7 provided good descriptions of the data, the slopes of the matching functions ranging from 0.72 to 0.96. The clinical implications of Cliffe and Parry's study are discussed below.

The two-operandum procedure (Herrnstein, 1961) was used by Ruddle *et al.* (1979) and Bradshaw *et al.* (1981c). The subjects responded on two levers which were separated by a barrier which prevented both levers from being operated at once. In other respects, the procedure was similar to that used by Bradshaw, Szabadi, and Bevan (1976, 1979) and Bradshaw *et al.* (1979). Good conformity to equations 11.2, 11.3, and 11.6 was observed in these studies. Slopes of the matching functions obtained from individual subjects ranged from 0.25 to 1.30, the pooled data yielding a value of *a* very close to 1.0 (see Figure 11.7).

The two-operandum procedure was also used by Schroeder (1975) in a study of mentally subnormal subjects. The pooled data showed near-perfect matching (equation 11.4). In Schroeder's experiment a 5-second changeover delay was found to be essential in order to preserve sensitivity to relative reinforcement frequency. Interestingly, conformity to the matching relation was due almost entirely to responses emitted outside the changeover delay, responses emitted within the delay being largely insensitive to relative reinforcement frequency. Similar findings have been reported in the case of hens (Scown, Foster, and Temple, 1981).

In contrast to the studies reviewed so far, several authors have reported gross undermatching. Schmitt (1974) studied two subjects using the changeover procedure with a 1.5 second changeover delay. Neither subject's performance showed any appreciable sensitivity to relative reinforcement frequency. However, these results are difficult to interpret, since only two different reinforcement frequency ratios were used (1:2 and 1:5).

Wurster and Griffiths (1979), also used the changeover procedure and a button-pressing task. Three concurrent schedule pairs were presented, the reinforcement frequency in one component being held constant, and that in the other component varied. Response rates in the variable component tended to increase and those in the fixed component to decrease, as a function of increasing reinforcement frequency in the variable component (cf. equations 11.2 and 11.3). Undermatching was found in each of the three subjects studied (values of *a*, recalculated from original data, 0.51 to 0.79).

Marked undermatching was also observed by Oscar-Berman *et al.* (1980), Navarick and Chellson (1983), and McLean (1983). In Oscar-Berman *et al.*'s study, six normal subjects and six patients suffering from Korsakoff's psychosis were compared. The degree of undermatching was greater in the patient group; this may have reflected an inability of the patients to retain the essentials of the task from one session to the next, resulting in a failure to establish stable control of performance by the schedule contingencies.

Lowe and Horne (1985) conducted a series of experiments using the changeover procedure. Five different reinforcement frequencies, associated with different geometrical shapes, were used in one component, the reinforcement frequency in the other component being held constant. In the first experiment, four out of five subjects showed complete insensitivity to relative reinforcement frequency (slope values less than 0.1). In the second experiment, the imposition of a 3-second changeover delay resulted in somewhat greater sensitivity (slope values of 0.15–0.62). In the third experiment, the stimuli associated with the various schedules were arranged from left to right in the order of descending reinforcement frequency; slopes greater than 0.5 were obtained in three out of five subjects (range 0.56–0.98), the remaining two subjects showing little sensitivity.

The studies described in this section may be considered in the context of two related questions: Firstly, 'Does human concurrent-schedule performance conform to the Matching Law?' and secondly, 'Is the performance of humans fundamentally different from that of animals?' Table 11.2 lists all the relevant individual subject data known to the present authors, which are amenable to analysis in terms of equations 11.6 and 11.7. The criteria for inclusion of a study in this table were: (1) at least three reinforcement frequency ratios were used; (2) conventional concurrent variable-interval schedules of positive reinforcement and arbitrary motor responses (e.g. button pressing) were used; and (3) individual subject data were available. Pooled data (Schroeder and Holland, 1969; Conger and Killeen, 1974), and data obtained from psychiatric patients (Schroeder, 1975; Cliffe and Parry, 1980; Oscar-Berman *et al.*, 1980) were excluded. The table lists the values of *a* and the proportion of the data variance accounted for by the Generalized Matching Law (r^2), for each data set. It is clear from table 11.2 that the values of *a* and r^2 vary considerably between subjects and between experiments. The frequency distributions of the values of *a* are shown in Figure 11.8. For the purposes of comparison, the corresponding data from rats and pigeons, obtained from the exhaustive reviews of Baum (1979) and Wearden and Burgess (1982), are also shown. As those reviewers have pointed out, there are inherent problems in drawing conclusions from data of this kind. Nevertheless, certain trends can be identified in the data shown in Figure 11.8. Firstly, there is a tendency, in both animals and humans, for response rate ratios to exhibit undermatching. Secondly, the degree of undermatching is somewhat greater in humans (mean value of $a \pm SD = 0.68 \pm 0.41$) than in animals ($a = 0.82$

Table 11.2 *Fit of equation 11.6 to data obtained from individual human subjects*

Study	COD (seconds)	Number of rft frequency ratios	Subject	Response rate ratio		Time ratio	
				Slope	r^2	Slope	r^2
Baum (1975)	2	7	Doug	—	—	1.16	0.91
			John	—	—	0.67	0.96
			Noa	—	—	0.98	0.93
Bradshaw, Szabadi, and Bevan (1976)[a]	—	5	SM	0.98	0.99	—	—
			AM	1.11	0.98	—	—
Bradshaw, Szabadi and Bevan (1979)	—	5	BB	1.20	0.99	1.04	0.98
			LK	1.36	0.98	1.10	0.97
			MS	1.38	0.96	1.11	0.95
Bradshaw *et al.* (1979)	—	5	AD	1.15	1.00	1.17	1.00
			MW	0.90	0.98	0.96	0.96
			SW	1.13	0.99	1.10	0.95
Ruddle *et al.* (1979)	—	5	JJ	1.01	1.00	—	—
			MD	0.68	0.99	—	—
			PD	1.30	0.99	—	—
			LD	0.54	0.83	—	—
			MH	1.26	1.00	—	—
			GB	1.14	0.95	—	—
Wurster and Griffiths (1979)[b]	3	3	S1	0.67	0.97	—	—
			S2	0.51	0.90	—	—
			S3	0.79	0.99	—	—
Buskist and Miller (1981)	3	3	LO	0.87	0.95	0.92	0.83
			NS	1.00	0.97	1.08	0.99
			CL	0.93	0.98	0.98	0.98
DeWaard (1980) Experiment 1	2	3	625	0.52	0.92	0.51	0.97
			172	0.95	0.99	0.93	0.99
			384	0.63	0.81	0.63	0.94
			399	0.96	0.99	0.96	0.99
DeWaard (1980) Experiment 2	2	5	048	0.76	0.99	0.89	0.97
			484	0.77	0.99	0.91	0.99
			291	0.94	0.99	0.91	0.99
			127	1.89	0.93	1.86	0.93
Oscar-Berman *et al.* (1980)	5	3	N1	0.36	—	—	—
			N2	0.67	—	—	—
			N3	0.27	—	—	—
			N4	0.45	—	—	—
			N5	−0.04	—	—	—
			N6	0.40	—	—	—
Bradshaw, Ruddle, and Szabadi (1981c)[c]	—	5	B	1.30	0.88	—	—
			C	0.68	0.94	—	—
			D	0.25	0.98	—	—

(*continued overleaf*)

Table 11.2 *continued*

Study	COD (seconds)	Number of rft frequency ratios	Subject	Response rate ratio		Time ratio	
				Slope	r^2	Slope	r^2
Navarick and Chellson (1983)	1.5	3	PA	0.38	0.78	0.42	0.85
Experiment 1			RP	0.53	0.81	0.34	0.54
			HT	0.24	0.09	0.11	0.03
			LC	0.25	0.19	0.15	0.26
Navarick and Chellson (1983)	1.5	3	FY	0.60	0.60	0.55	0.61
Experiment 2			RC	0.57	0.75	0.45	0.78
McLean (1983)	—	5	Lynne	0.63	—	—	—
			Sally	0.51	—	—	—
Lowe and Horne (1985)	—	5	CT	0.53	0.88	—	—
Experiment 1			KW	0.07	0.62	—	—
			JT	0.04	0.23	—	—
			TM	0.03	0.66	—	—
			JB	−0.06	0.32	—	—
Lowe and Horne (1985)	3	5	1	0.62	0.92	—	—
Experiment 2			2	0.59	0.94	—	—
			3	0.45	0.78	—	—
			4	0.37	0.77	—	—
			5	0.15	0.25	—	—
Lowe and Horne (1985)	3	5	NL	0.98	0.96	—	—
Experiment 3			SP	0.79	0.99	—	—
			SC	0.56	0.98	—	—
			CL	0.14	0.22	—	—
			PB	0.07	0.40	—	—

Note: In many of the studies several functions were obtained from each subject under different experiment conditions. Only one representative function is shown for each subject in this table.

[a]These data were originally presented as relative response rates; the response rate ratios were calculated from the raw data.
[b]Data points calculated by averaging five days' performance (presented in original paper).
[c]The data from subjects A, E and F feature under Ruddle *et al.* (1979).

± 0.17). Thirdly, the variability of the slope values is greater in the case of humans, as indicated by the larger standard deviation. Fourthly, time distribution ratios approximate ideal matching more closely than do response rate ratios; this is true both of humans ($a = 0.84 \pm 0.37$) and of animals ($a = 0.87 \pm 0.20$).

A tendency toward undermatching in the case of response rate ratios has been widely recognized in the literature on concurrent performances in animals

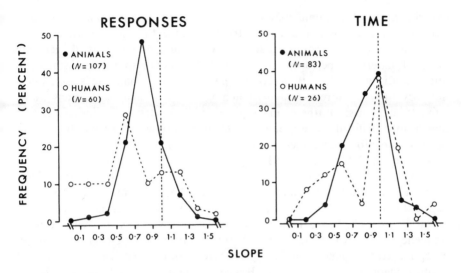

Figure 11.8   Percent frequency distribution of the slopes of the generalized matching functions obtained for individual human (open circles, broken lines) and animal (closed circles continuous line) subjects. Data from human subjects were derived from the studies summarized in Table 11.2; data from animal subjects derived from Baum (1979) and Wearden and Burgess (1982). *Left-hand graph*: data obtained for response rate ratios (equation 11.6). *Right-hand graph*: data obtained for time distribution ratios (equation 11.7)

(Myers and Myers, 1977; Baum, 1979; Davison, 1981; Wearden and Burgess, 1982). It seems that humans are no exception to this general rule. A tendency for time distribution ratios to approximate ideal matching more closely than response rate ratios has also been noted in the literature on animal choice behavior (e.g. Baum, 1979). The interpretation of this observation is difficult, as noted by Wearden and Burgess (1982), because the data relating to time distribution and response rate ratios derive, in part, from different sets of experiments. This caveat also applies to the data obtained with humans (cf. table 11.2, Figure 11.8); nevertheless the similar pattern seen with humans and animals is striking.

The quantitative disparity between the results obtained with humans and animals, namely the more marked undermatching of response rate ratios and greater variability shown by humans, requires explanation. Lowe and Horne (1985) regard the extreme undermatching shown by some human subjects as evidence for a qualitative difference between the choice behavior of humans and animals, and attribute this difference to the propensity for verbal behavior in humans. It is difficult to reconcile this interpretation with the results of experiments in which humans show the same pattern of performance as animals (see table 11.2). Lowe and Horne try to resolve this inconsistency in the following way. They propose that even when humans and animals generate identical patterns of performance, the similarity may be spurious, arising from idiosyncratic 'verbal hypotheses' on the part of some humans. This assertion is not easy to test. Moreover, undermatching is not peculiar to humans; some animals (e.g. cows: Matthews and Temple, 1979) are staunch undermatchers. It may be more fruitful, therefore, to look for methodological factors which might be responsible for undermatching in humans (Baron and Perone, 1982).

Navarick and Chellson (1983) suggested that the range of reinforcement frequency ratios used may influence the slope of the matching function. They point out that most of the studies in which marked undermatching was found (e.g. Schmitt, 1974; Wurster and Griffiths, 1979; Oscar-Berman et al., 1980; Navarick and Chellson, 1983) employed a narrow range of reinforcement frequency ratios. However, Lowe and Horne's (1985) experiments constitute an exception to this generalization, since these authors used the same range of reinforcement frequency ratios as Bradshaw, Szabadi, and Bevan (1979) and Bradshaw et al. (1979b) and Ruddle et al. (1979) who found good conformity to matching.

McLean (1983) has drawn attention to the common practice, in studies with humans, of presenting a number of concurrent schedule pairs within each session, a procedure which might be expected to generate interactions between the component schedules and hence give rise to undermatching. He examined performances in concurrent schedules presented either individually or in a multiple schedule paradigm. The results indicated that performance in concurrent schedules was essentially unaffected by other schedules presented successively within the same session. Lowe and Horne (1985), however, obtained evidence that concurrent schedule performance may be affected by the spatial position of the stimuli used to signal the various schedules. Steeper slopes were obtained when the stimuli were arranged in the order of descending reinforcement frequency than when no such 'ordinal cues' were provided. It is possible that 'ordinal cues' facilitate discrimination between the reinforcement frequencies offered by the various schedules. This interpretation is consistent with the widely accepted view that one of the main causes of undermatching is a failure to discriminate between the component schedules (Baum, 1974, 1979; Wearden, 1980, 1983).

An important methodological factor in concurrent schedule performance is the changeover delay. Although it has generally been found in studies with animals that a changeover delay is a prerequisite for observing matching (see de Villiers, 1977), its precise role is uncertain. Two important effects of the changeover delay appear to be the prevention of behavioral chains involving responses in both components (Herrnstein, 1961; Catania and Cutts, 1963) and the reduction of the frequency of changeovers (Baum, 1974). The minimum effective delay differs between species (possibly reflecting differences in response topography), rats requiring longer delays than pigeons (see de Villiers, 1977). The effect of changeover delays on human concurrent performances is uncertain. Some authorts report that sensitivity to relative reinforcement frequency was enhanced by the imposition of a changeover delay (Schroeder and Holland, 1969; Schroeder, 1975; Ruddle *et al.*, 1982; Lowe and Horne, 1985). However, others have observed good conformity to matching in the absence of a changeover delay (Bradshaw, Szabadi and Bevan 1976, 1979; Bradshaw *et al.*, 1979). These apparently conflicting results are difficult to interpret because details of changeover behavior have seldom been reported in studies with humans (but see Baum, 1975; Bradshaw *et al.*, 1979).

It will be apparent from this discussion that the available data do not allow a complete explanation for the gross undermatching reported in some studies with humans, and it is to be hoped that future research will address this issue. Another feature of human concurrent performances which deserves comment is the between-subject variability, which, as noted above (cf. Figure 11.8), is considerably greater than that found in animals. This may be largely due to methodological factors. In particular, the level of experimental control which can be achieved with humans is poor by comparison with the rigors of an animal laboratory. It would be remarkable indeed if this were not reflected in greater variation in human than in animal operant behavior (see Baron and Perone, 1982).

Variables affecting human concurrent performances

As described above, comparison of equations 11.1 and 11.3 indicates that the introduction of a concurrent source of reinforcement should exert a Type II suppression of the absolute rate of responding in variable-interval schedules. This prediction has been confirmed in two studies with humans using the changeover procedure (Bradshaw, Szabadi, and Bevan, 1976, 1979); an example is shown in Figure 11.6. Although the finding of a Type II suppression of responding is in qualitative agreement with the prediction based on equations 11.1 and 11.3, the findings obtained with some subjects showed a quantitative departure from the prediction. According to the equations, the increase in reinforcement frequency needed to maintain the half-maximal response rate should be exactly equal to the rate of reinforcer delivery in the alternative schedule of reinforcement. Although this could be said to have occurred in some subjects (within the limits of error of the curvefitting parameters) the change in the value of the parameter seen in other subjects was clearly less than predicted (Bradshaw, Szabadi, and Bevan 1979). Although the reason for this discrepancy is unclear, it is of interest that similar discrepancies have been found in experiments with animals (Bradshaw, 1977). The discrepancy is no doubt related to the common finding in studies of concurrent performances, both in animals (e.g. McSweeney, Melville, and Whipple, 1983) and in humans (e.g. Bradshaw *et al.*, 1981c), that the reinforcement frequency needed to obtain the half-maximal response rate in each component is sometimes less than the frequency of reinforcer delivery in the other component. Some authors have regarded this observation as indicating a negative value of K_H (McSweeney *et al.*, 1983). However, this may not be the most appropriate interpretation. Negative values of K_H have no clear behavioral meaning in any current theory of operant behavior, and they are in any case clearly incompatible with the increasing negatively accelerated function relating response rate to reinforcement frequency in single schedules. In our view it may be more appropriate to view these quantitative departures from the theoretical predictions as reflecting a smaller than expected interaction between the component schedules; the reinforcers delivered in one component may occasionally exert a smaller suppressant effect on responding in the other component than is predicted by equations 11.2 and 11.3.

The nature of the interaction between the component schedules is of considerable theoretical interest. Equations 11.2 and 11.3 imply that the reinforcers delivered in one component are responsible for suppressing behavior in the other component; the suppression is not brought about simply by competition between the two responses for available time. This principle is known as 'response independence', since the suppressant effect of an alternative source of reinforcement is deemed to be independent of any responding which it may generate (see Catania, 1966). Evidence favoring response independence has been obtained in several studies with pigeons, which have shown that the rate of responding in Component A is inversely related to the reinforcement frequency in Component B even if the rate of responding in Component B is reduced to very low levels by signaling the availability of reinforcement (Catania, 1963; Rachlin and Baum, 1969, 1972). The question of response independence has also been examined in the case of humans. Bradshaw *et al.* (1979) exposed three subjects to a series of concurrent schedules using the changeover procedure. The reinforcement frequency in Component A was varied over a wide range, while the reinforcement frequency in Component B was held constant. Absolute response rates conformed closely to equations 11.2 and 11.3, and the response-rate and time-distribution ratios approximated closely to ideal matching. When the availability of reinforcers in Component A was signaled by a light, the rate of responding in Component A was greatly reduced and there was a concomitant increase in the rate of responding in Component B. These changes in the absolute response rates were reflected in a large shift in bias in favor of Component B, sensitivity to relative reinforcement frequency remaining unaltered. At first sight these results appear to be at variance with previous findings with animals (e.g. Catania, 1963), and also seem to be irreconcilable with the principle of response independence. However, Bradshaw *et al.* pointed out that not all studies with animals have found response rates in Component B to be unaffected by signaling reinforcer availability in Component A (e.g.

Marcucella and Margolius, 1978). Moreover, the signal procedure may not constitute a fair test of response independence. Signaling reinforcer availability effectively changes Component A from a simple variable-interval schedule to a multiple schedule in which the absence of the signal is associated with an extinction schedule. Thus, except for the brief periods when the signal is present, the subject is exposed to a concurrent variable-interval extinction schedule. In these circumstances equation 11.3 predicts an elevation of the response rate in Component B due to the reduction of r_A to zero.

DeWaard (1980) carried out a series of experiments in order to determine the circumstances which favor response independence. Using conventional concurrent variable-interval schedules and the changeover procedure, DeWaard obtained very similar results to Bradshaw *et al.* (1979). However, the superimposition of a continuous punishment contingency ('response cost') on to both component schedules greatly reduced the effect of the signal on response rate in the alternative component. In two further experiments, DeWaard demonstrated that the effect of the response-cost was probably brought about by a general reduction of response rates in both components. A superimposed temporal differentiation (inter-response time > 2 seconds) contingency, which markedly suppressed response rates without reducing the subjects' earnings, was just as effective as response cost in attenuating the effect of the signal upon responding in the alternative component. In contrast, a superimposed variable-interval punishment contingency, which had a less profound suppressant effect on response rates, was ineffective in attenuating the effect of the signal. DeWaard concluded that the failure of the signal procedure to reveal response independence in some experiments may be attributable to adventitious reinforcement resulting from high response rates; when response rates are suppressed by response cost or temporal differentiation contingencies, the chances of a signal closely following (and thereby reinforcing) a response in the alternative component is reduced thus allowing uncontaminated response independence to become apparent.

We have discussed response independence in some detail because of its salience for the theoretical analysis of behavior, and because of the complexity of the procedures used to investigate it. It is to be hoped that further research, using both animals and humans, will be addressed to this important topic.

The effects of punishment, in the form of monetary penalties for responding, have been the subject of several experiments. DeWaard (1980) superimposed a continuous punishment contingency (i.e. punishment of every response) on to both components of a concurrent variable-interval schedule. In the absence of the punishment contingency the performance of all four subjects was well described by the Generalized Matching Law (equation 11.6). The addition of the punishment contingency reduced the absolute rates of responding by approximately 90 per cent; however, there was no consistent change in the slopes or intercepts of the matching function (see Figure 11.9).

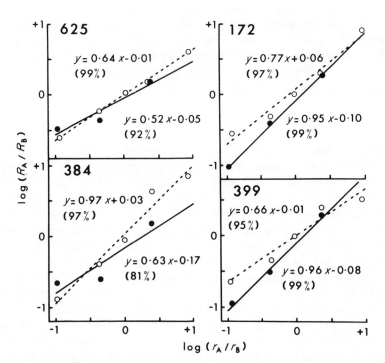

Figure 11.9 Performance of humans in concurrent schedules of monetary reinforcement. Response rate ratio is plotted against reinforcement frequency ratio in double-logarithmic coordinates. Closed symbols, continuous lines: performance in the absence of punishment. Open symbols, broken lines: performance in the presence of a continuous punishment schedule (response cost) imposed in both components. Punishment suppressed absolute response rates by about 90 percent, but had no consistent effect on generalized matching functions (DeWaard, 1980).
Reproduced by permission of the University of Milwaukee-Wisconsin

Two studies have employed 'asymmetric' punishment contingencies, one using a variable-interval and the other a variable-ratio punishment schedule. DeWaard (1980) superimposed a variable-interval punishment contingency on to one component of a concurrent schedule. This procedure produced a bias in favor of the other component in all four subjects tested; sensitivity to relative reinforcement was not markedly affected (median slope 0.8). Bradshaw, Szabadi, and Bevan (1979) also superimposed a punishment schedule on to one component of a concurrent schedule; however, in this case a variable-ratio rather than variable-interval punishment contingency was used. In the absence of the punishment contingency the absolute response rates conformed closely to equations 11.2 and 11.3, and the response-rate and time-distribution ratios showed good approximation to matching. In the presence of the punishment contingency response rates in the 'punished' components were suppressed and response rates in the other component were concomitantly elevated. This was reflected in a reduction of the reinforcement frequency needed to maintain the half-maximal response rate. A marked bias developed in favor of the 'unpunished' component, and in all three subjects this was accompanied by gross undermatching.

The different patterns of effect of variable-interval and variable-ratio punishment upon concurrent performances are of considerable interest, especially in view of the different patterns of effect of these two punishment procedures on single-schedule performance. It should be noted, however, that the variable-ratio punishment procedure used by Bradshaw *et al.* produced a much more profound suppression of responding than the variable-interval punishment procedure used by DeWaard. It remains to be determined whether the change in absolute response rate, the type of punishment contingency, or both, are responsible for the different effects produced on the slope of the matching function.

The effect of a change in response-force requirement on concurrent schedule performance was studied by Bradshaw *et al.* (1981c), using the two-operandum procedure. In the first phase of the experiment, when the force requirements were equal for the two components, all the subjects showed a slight bias toward the right-hand lever, possibly reflecting the hand-preference of the subjects. When the force required to operate the right-hand lever was increased from 7.9 to 135N all the six subjects showed a shift in bias in favor of the left-hand lever; the sensitivity parameter was not consistently affected. Interestingly, the marked suppression of the absolute response rate on the right-hand lever was not accompanied by any significant change in the rate of responding on the left-hand lever.

The effect of a superimposed temporal differentiation contingency was studied by DeWaard (1980). An inter-response time greater than 2 seconds contingency was superimposed on to the variable-interval schedules operating in both components of a concurrent schedule. This produced low response rates (less than 25 responses per minute) in all four subjects tested. However, good conformity to matching was preserved both in the case of response-rate ratios (median slope = 0.77) and time-distribution ratios (median slope = 1.05). It is of interest that very similar results have been obtained with animals (Staddon, 1968; Moffitt and Shimp, 1971).

Ruddle, Bradshaw, and Szabadi (1981) and Ruddle *et al.* (1982) examined performance maintained under concurrent schedules in which one component was a positive reinforcement schedule and the other was an avoidance schedule. The response-rate and time-distribution ratios conformed to analogs of the Generalized Matching Law (equations 11.6 and 11.7), in which reinforcement frequency in the avoidance component was expressed as the frequency of aversive events (monetary penalties) successfully avoided. There was no consistent bias in favor of either component, suggesting a 'functional symmetry' between positive and negative reinforcement (cf. de Villiers, 1977, 1981). Performance in these schedules was found to be sensitive to the presence or absence of a changeover delay; good approximation to ideal matching was found in the presence of a 5-second changeover delay, but undermatching ensued when the duration of the changeover delay was reduced (Ruddle *et al.*, 1982) or if no delay was imposed (Ruddle *et al.*, 1981).

The studies reviewed in this section demonstrate the utility of concurrent schedule paradigms for studying the effects of a wide range of variables on choice behavior in humans. The effects of some of these variables raise questions of general importance for the quantitative analysis of behavior. One such question is whether choice in concurrent schedules is 'response independent', as implied by Herrnstein's model. Another question, which in our view deserves further attention, is whether the effects of variables on single-schedule performance allow predictions to be made about their effect on concurrent performances (for discussion, see Bradshaw *et al.*, 1981a). Herrnstein's model implies that such predictions are possible and thus the testing of such predictions could provide a rigorous approach to examining the model itself.

Clinical and social applications

Single schedules

There have been few attempts to apply Herrnstein's equation to clinical situations. However, the equation would seem to have potential application both in the analysis of pathological behavior and for the design of behavior therapy strategies.

Bradshaw and Szabadi (1978) and Szabadi *et al.* (1981) studied the behavior of two manic-depressive patients in single variable-interval schedules. The patients were first trained under five schedules during a period of euthymia, and then continued to undergo testing sessions several times a week for many months. In one patient (Bradshaw and Szabadi, 1978) the period of observation encompassed two depressive and one manic episode, as well as interspersed periods of remission. Depression was accompanied by a reduction of operant response rates, which took the form of a lowering of the value of R_{max} and an elevation of the value of K_H (i.e. Type III suppression: see above). This pattern of suppression was confirmed in a second patient (Szabadi *et al.*, 1981). The observation that operant responding is suppressed during depressive illness is consistent with the notion that depression involves a general reduction of reinforcer effectiveness (Costello, 1972; Akiskal and McKinney, 1975). Moreover, the pattern of change of the two constants may provide some insight into the mechanisms underlying this reduced effectiveness of reinforcers. Szabadi *et al.* noted that Type III suppression of responding also occurs when behavior is punished at a constant probability per unit response (variable-ratio punishment: see above), and indeed confirmed in one patient that the effects of variable-ratio punishment during a period of normal mood mimicked the pattern of suppression seen in a subsequent depressive episode. These findings raise the possibility that the reduced effectiveness of reinforcers in depression involves an enhancement of the aversive consequences of responding. However, this suggestion must remain tentative at present, since it is likely that other variables, whose effects on human variable-interval performance have not yet been examined, may also produce the same pattern of suppression (Szabadi *et al.*, 1981). The observation that mania was accompanied by a Type VI facilitation of responding (Bradshaw and Szabadi, 1978) clearly needs to be replicated in further studies; the observation is potentially of great interest because it suggests that mania and depression may have opposing effects on reinforcemnt processes.

The reduced value of R_{max} seen during depressive episodes has implications for behavioral treatment strategies aimed at increasing the level of appropriate behavior in depressed patients by enriching their environments with reinforcers (e.g. Lewinsohn, Weinstein, and Alper, 1970). Since a reduction of the value of R_{max} implies that the behavioral suppression cannot be surmounted by increasing the frequency of reinforcement, behavioral interventions of this kind may be of limited value, at least in the case of patients suffering from endogenous depression.

The implications of Herrnstein's equation for behavior therapy have been reviewed by McDowell (1981b, 1982). This author reported a case study of self-injurious behavior in an eleven-year-old boy. Direct observation revealed that this behavior was maintained by attention from the child's parents, in the form of verbal reprimands. The rate of self-injurious behavior was related to the rate of verbal reprimands according to a hyperbolic function, equation 11.1 accounting for more than 99 per cent of the data variance. McDowell argues that the recognition that many clinically relevant behaviors may be governed by Herrnstein's equation has important implications for designing intervention strategies. One such strategy is the use of alternative sources of reinforcement. It has been known for many years that reinforcing appropriate behavior can result in a decline in the frequency of maladaptive behavior (e.g. Ayllon and Roberts, 1974). This effect is often attributed to competition between mutually incompatible behaviors for available time. This interpretation is criticized by McDowell, who argues that alternative reinforcers need not be contingent upon appropriate behavior in order to effect a suppression of the 'target' behavior. Enriching the environment with 'free' reinforcers should be equally effective since all reinforcers contribute to the value of K_H, irrespective of the behaviors which they maintain. It should be noted, however, that this argument relies on the principle of 'response independence', whose applicability to human behavior is still in question (see above).

A potential problem with the use of alternative reinforcement relates to the type of suppression (Type II) which it exerts on the target behavior. As discussed above, Type II suppression implies that the suppressant effect of alternative reinforcers is most effective when the target behavior occurs at a relatively low frequency, and that the suppression can be surmounted by an increase in the frequency of reinforcement for the target behavior. In the case of preponderant maladaptive behaviors, which may be occurring at rates close to R_{max}, a variable exerting a Type II suppression might be less useful than one exerting a Type III suppression. One such variable is punishment delivered at a constant probability per unit response. Although the use of punishment in therapeutic behavior modification is offensive to most clinicians, there may be some occasions (e.g. when maladaptive behavior occurs at a very high frequency) when it is likely to provide the most effective suppression of target behavior.

Concurrent schedules

We have already alluded to the few published studies of concurrent performances in psychiatric patients (Schroeder, 1975; Cliffe and Parry, 1980; Oscar-Berman *et al.*, 1980). Cliffe and Parry's study deserves special mention because it used a concurrent schedule paradigm to address a clinically relevant problem, the quantitative assessment of the sexual preferences of a convicted pedophile offender. The two-operandum procedure was used, with brief presentations of sexually provocative photographic slides serving as the reinforcers. Three groups of slides were used, which depicted women, men, and children respectively; in three phases of the experiment the subject was faced with choice between men versus women, men versus children, and women versus children. Choice behavior conformed to the Generalized Matching Law (equations 11.6 and 11.7), the slopes of the linear functions ranging between 0.72 and 0.96. The bias parameters indicated that slides depicting women were preferred to those depicting men or children. Cliffe and Parry comment that despite his history of sexual offences against children, the subject was known to have a strong sexual orientation toward adult women, and his failure to establish close relations with women may have been a contributing factor to his deviant behavior. His performance in the concurrent schedule paradigm was, therefore, probably a valid reflection of his sexual preference. However, the authors also point out that procedural problems (e.g. poorer technical quality of the child pornographic material) may have contaminated the results.

The applicability of concurrent schedule theory has been reviewed by Myerson and Hale (1984). These authors argue that many clinical or classroom situations in which 'problem' behaviors arise may be viewed as choice situations, and that the Matching Law may provide a sound basis for planning treatment strategies, especially strategies which entail reinforcing alternative behaviors. Some aspects of this type of strategy were discussed in the preceding section;

here we shall restrict ourselves to Myerson and Hale's analysis of the relative merits of ratio and interval schedules of reinforcement in clinical interventions. Myerson and Hale point out that problem behavior may be maintained under either an interval or a ratio schedule; the task for the behavior therapist is to select the optimal schedule for reinforcing appropriate behavior. They argue that, given that there is an upper limit to the frequency of reinforcement which the therapist can reasonably dispense, interval schedules are generally superior to ratio schedules. Myerson and Hale's argument is based on an analysis of the Matching Law's implications for concurrent ratio/ratio and ratio/interval schedules.

When an organism is faced with a choice between two ratio schedules, adherence to the Matching Law entails exclusive choice in favor of the richer alternative (i.e. the schedule specifying the lower ratio of responses to reinforcers) (Herrnstein, 1970; Herrnstein and Loveland, 1975). Thus, a target behavior maintained under a ratio schedule may be totally eliminated by provision of a richer ratio schedule for appropriate behavior. This, however, is an all-or-none effect; an alternative schedule which is only marginally leaner than the schedule maintaining the target behavior will have no effect whatever on the frequency of the target behavior. In contrast, when an organism is faced with a choice between a ratio and an interval schedule, the Matching Law implies a graded preference depending on the reinforcement frequency offered by the interval schedule (Herrnstein and Loveland, 1975; Herrnstein and Heyman, 1979). Thus even when the therapist is not in a position to offer a higher reinforcement frequency for appropriate behavior than is already available for the target behavior, he may still be able to effect a reduction in the rate of the target behavior.

Similar considerations apply in the case of target behaviors maintained under interval schedules. Intervention using a ratio schedule of reinforcement for appropriate behavior will only start to become effective when the ratio schedule yields a higher reinforcement frequency than the interval schedule. In contrast, intervention using an interval schedule will exert a graded suppression of the target behavior according to the dictates of the Matching Law (i.e. Type II suppression).

Myerson and Hale's recommendations for the use of concurrent sources of reinforcement in clinical and classroom situations are soundly based both on matching theory (Herrnstein, 1970) and on empirical findings with animals (Herrnstein and Loveland, 1975; Herrnstein and Heyman, 1979; Herrnstein and Vaughan, 1980). However, as yet they remain untested in applied settings.

A potentially fruitful area of application of the Matching Law is the analysis of social behavior. Encouraged by Conger and Killeen's (1974) experimental finding that verbal behavior in a small group discussion conformed to equation 11.4, Hamblin (1977, 1979) undertook a reanalysis of published data on social interactions. In general, the Matching Law provided an excellent account of the data. For example, Bales, Stodtbeck and Mills (1951) reported the matrix of social interactions between the members of a six-man group; reanalyzing their data in terms of equation 11.4, Hamblin (1977) found a linear relationship between the relative frequency of verbal behavior by individuals, and the relative frequency of behavior directed toward the individuals, which accounted for more than 99 per cent of the data variance.

Conclusions

The experimental analysis of behavior has traditionally relied heavily on animal subjects, particularly the pigeon and the rat, and has tended to eschew the human subject. There are sound reasons for this policy. The early successes of the experimental analysis of behavior are to a great extent attributable to the previously unattainable level of experimental control which operant techniques afforded (Skinner, 1956). Ethical and practical considerations preclude such rigorous control over the history and environment of human subjects.

The exclusion of the human subject from the operant behavior laboratory did not pose a serious problem to applied behavior analysis 30 years ago because the principles of behavior revealed in the animal laboratory had clear relevance for human behavior (e.g. Skinner, 1953). However, the increasing technical sophistication and the current trend toward quantification in the analysis of operant behavior have prompted some workers to question whether findings obtained with animals still have relevance for human behavior. In addition, the increasing popularity of cognitive explanations of human behavior has led some psychologists even to doubt whether the basic principles of reinforcement apply to humans (e.g. Brewer, 1974). It is difficult to take such doubts seriously, since they would seem to imply the untenable proposition that human behavior is not influenced by its consequences. Nevertheless, it must be acknowledged that as the theoretical analysis of operant behavior becomes increasingly complex, so it may become increasingly difficult to demonstrate the validity of newly discovered principles of operant behavior in humans whose history and environment are less easy to control than those of laboratory animals. An important goal of future research on human operant behavior may be to devise techniques for achieving a more satisfactory level of control over the 'extraneous' variables which can mask the operation of fundamental behavioral processes in humans (cf. Baron and Perone, 1982).

It would be unfortunate, however, if research on human operant behavior were to be restricted to attempts to confirm or refute the applicability to humans of established principles of operant behavior. As discussed above, human subjects may offer some advantages over animals which have yet to be exploited. A case in point is the analysis of concurrent performances, where simultaneous training under a range of schedules may allow more detailed parametric studies to be undertaken with humans than would be feasible with animals. Perhaps the time to ripe for abandoning the controversy over whether humans 'match' (clearly they do under some circumstances but not under others); a more profitable approach may be to exploit the experimental conditions which reveal matching in humans in order to examine questions of more general relevance to the quantitative analysis of behavior.

Finally, the application of the quantitative Law of Effect to social and clinical problems has already yielded some new insights and behavioral treatment strategies. Only future work can reveal the full scope of this promising approach.

References

Akiskal, H. S., and McKinney, W. T. (1975). Overview of recent research in depression, *Archives of General Psychiatry*, **32**, 285–305.

Allen, C. M. (1981). On the exponent in the 'generalized' matching equation, *Journal of the Experimental Analysis of Behavior*, **35**, 125–127.

Ayllon, T., and Roberts, M.D. (1974). Eliminating discipline problems by strengthening academic performance, *Journal of Applied Behavior Analysis.*, **7**, 71–76.

Bales, R. F., Stodtbeck, F. L., and Mills, T. M. (1951). Channels of communication in small groups, *American Sociological Review*, **16**, 461–468.

Baron, A., and Perone, M. (1982). The place of the human subject in the operant laboratory, *Behavior Analyst*, **5**, 143–158.

Baum, W. M. (1973). The correlation-based law of effect, *Journal of the Experimental Analysis of Behavior* **20**, 137–153.

Baum, W. M. (1974). On two types of deviation from the matching law: Bias and undermatching, *Journal of the Experimental Analysis of Behavior*, **22**, 231–242.

Baum, W. M. (1975). Time allocation and human vigilance, *Journal of the Experimental Analysis of Behavior*, **23**, 45–53.

Baum, W. M. (1979). Matching, undermatching, and overmatching in studies of choice, *Journal of the Experimental Analysis of Behavior*, **32**, 269–281.

Bradshaw, C. M. (1977). Suppression of response rates in variable-interval schedules by a concurrent schedule of reinforcement, *British Journal of Psychology*, **68**, 473–480.

Bradshaw, C. M., Ruddle, H. V., and Szabadi, E. (1981a). Relationship between response rate and reinforcement frequency in variable-interval schedules: II. Effect of the volume of sucrose reinforcement, *Journal of the Experimental Analysis of Behavior*, **35**, 263–269.

Bradshaw, C. M., Ruddle, H. V., and Szabadi, E. (1981b). Relationship between response rate and reinforcement frequency in variable-interval schedules: III. The effect of d-amphetamine, *Journal of the Experimental Analysis of Behavior*, **35**, 29–39.

Bradshaw, C. M., Ruddle, H. V., and Szabadi, E. (1981c). Studies of concurrent performances in humans. In C. M. Bradshaw, E. Szabadi, and C. F. Lowe (eds), *Quantification of Steady-State Operant Behaviour*, Amsterdam: Elsevier/North-Holland Biomedical Press, pp. 79–90.

Bradshaw, C. M., and Szabadi, E. (1978). Changes in operant behavior in a manic-depressive patient, *Behavior Therapy*, **9**, 950–954.

Bradshaw, C. M., Szabadi, E., and Bevan, P. (1976). Behavior of humans in variable-interval schedules of reinforcement, *Journal of the Experimental Analysis of Behavior*, **26**, 135–141.

Bradshaw, C. M., Szabadi, E., and Bevan, P. (1977). Effect of punishment on human variable-interval performance, *Journal of the Experimental Analysis of Behavior*, **27**, 275–279.

Bradshaw, C. M., Szabadi, E., and Bevan, P. (1978a). Effect of variable-interval punishment on the behavior of humans in variable-interval schedules of monetary reinforcement, *Journal of the Experimental Analysis of Behavior*, **29**, 161–166.

Bradshaw, C. M., Szabadi, E., and Bevan, P. (1978b). Relationship between response rate and reinforcement frequency in variable-interval schedules. The effect of the concentration of sucrose reinforcement, *Journal of the Experimental Analysis of Behavior*, **29**, 447–452.

Bradshaw, C. M., Szabadi, E., and Bevan, P. (1979). The effect of punishment on free-operant choice behavior in humans, *Journal of the Experimental Analysis of Behavior*, **31**, 71–81.

Bradshaw, C. M., Szabadi, E., and Ruddle, H. V. (1983). Herrnstein's equation: Effect of response-force requirement on performance in variable-interval schedules, *Behaviour Analysis Letters*, **3**, 93–100.

Bradshaw, C. M., Szabadi, E., Bevan, P., and Ruddle, H. V. (1979). The effect of signaled reinforcement availability on concurrent performances in humans, *Journal of the Experimental Analysis of Behavior*, **32**, 65–74.

Bradshaw, C. M., Szabadi, E., Ruddle, H. V., and Pears, E. (1983). Herrnstein's equation: Effect of deprivation level on performance in variable-interval schedules, *Behaviour Analysis Letters*, **3**, 267–273.

Brewer, W. F. (1974). There is no convincing evidence for operant or classical conditioning in adult humans. In W. B. Weimer and D. S. Palermo (eds), *Cognition and Symbolic Processes*, Hillsdale, NJ: Erlbaum, pp. 1–42.

Buskist, W. F., and Miller, H. L. (1981). Concurrent operant performance in humans: Matching when food is the reinforcer, *Psychological Record*, **31**, 95–100.

Catania, A. C. (1963). Concurrent performances: Reinforcement interaction and response independence, *Journal of the Experimental Analysis of Behavior*, **6**, 253–263.

Catania, A. C. (1966). Concurrent operants. In W. K. Honig (ed), *Operant Behavior: Areas of Research and Application*, New York: Appleton-Century-Crofts, pp. 213–270.

Catania, A. C. (1973). Self-inhibiting effects of reinforcement, *Journal of the Experimental Analysis of Behavior*, **19**, 517–526.

Catania, A. C., and Cutts, D. (1963). Experimental control of superstitious responding in humans, *Journal of the Experimental Analysis of Behavior*, **6**, 203–208.

Catania, A. C., and Reynolds, G. S. (1968). A quantitative analysis of the responding maintained by interval schedules of reinforcement, *Journal of the Experimental Analysis of Behavior*, **11**, 327–383.

Clark, A. J. (1933). *The Mode of Action of Drugs on Cells*, London: Edward Arnold.

Cliffe, M. J., and Parry, S. J. (1980). Matching to reinforcer value: Human concurrent variable-interval performance, *Quarterly Journal of Experimental Psychology*, **32**, 557–570.

Cohen, I. L. (1973). A note on Herrnstein's equation, *Journal of the Experimental Analysis of Behavior*, **19**, 527–528.

Conger, R., and Killeen, P. (1974). Use of concurrent operants in small group research, *Pacific Sociological Review*, **17**, 399–416.

Costello, C. G. (1972). Depression: Loss of reinforcers or loss of reinforcer effectiveness, *Behavior Therapy*, **3**, 240–247.

Davison, M. C. (1981). Choice between concurrent variable-interval and fixed-ratio schedules: A failure of the generalized matching law. In C. M. Bradshaw, E. Szabadi, and C. F. Lowe (eds), *Quantification of Steady-State Operant Behaviour*, Amsterdam: Elsevier/North-Holland Biomedical Press, pp. 91–100.

De Villiers, P. A. (1974). The law of effect and avoidance: a quantitative relationship between response rate and shock-frequency reduction, *Journal of the Experimental Analysis of Behavior*, **21**, 223-235.

De Villiers, P. A. (1977). Choice in concurrent schedules and a quantitative formulation of the law of effect. In W. K. Honig and J. E. R. Staddon (eds), Englewood Cliffs NJ: Prentice-Hall, pp. 233-287.

De Villiers, P. A. (1981). Quantitative studies of punishment: The negative law of effect revisited. In C. M. Bradshaw, E. Szabadi, and C. F. Lowe (eds), *Quantification of Steady-State Operant Behaviour*, Amsterdam: Elsevier/North-Holland Biomedical Press, pp. 139-151.

De Villiers, P. A., and Herrnstein, R. J. (1976). Toward a law of response strength, *Psychological Bulletin*, **83**, 1131-1153.

DeWaard, R. J. (1980). *Matching and failure of response independence by human subjects on concurrent VI VI schedules of reinforcement*, doctoral dissertation, University of Milwaukee, Wisconsin.

Findley, J. D. (1958). Preference and switching under concurrent scheduling, *Journal of the Experimental Analysis of Behavior*, **1**, 123-144.

Hamblin, R. L. (1977). Behavior and reinforcement: A generalization of the matching law. In R. L. Hamblin and J. H. Kunkel (eds), *Behavioral Theory in Sociology: Essays in Honor of George C. Homans*, New Brunswick NJ: Transaction Books, pp. 469-509.

Hamblin, R. L. (1979). Behavioral choice and social reinforcement: Step function versus matching, *Social Forces*, **57**, 1141-1156.

Herrnstein, R. J. (1961). Relative and absolute strength of response as a function of frequency of reinforcement, *Journal of the Experimental Analysis of Behavior*, **4**, 267-272.

Herrnstein, R. J. (1970). On the law of effect, *Journal of the Experimental Analysis of Behavior* **13**, 243-266.

Herrnstein, R. J. (1974). Formal properties of the matching law, *Journal of the Experimental Analysis of Behavior*, **21**, 159-164.

Herrnstein, R. J. (1979). Derivatives of matching, *Psychological Review*, **86**, 486-495.

Herrnstein, R. J., and Heyman, G. M. (1979). Is matching compatible with reinforcement maximization on concurrent variable-interval, variable-interval, variable ratio? *Journal of the Experimental Analysis of Behavior*, **31**, 209-223.

Herrnstein, R. J., and Loveland, D. H. (1975). Maximizing and matching on concurrent ratio schedules, *Journal of the Experimental Analysis of Behavior*, **24**, 107-116.

Herrnstein, R. J., and Vaughan, W. (1980). Melioration and behavioral allocation. In J. E. R. Staddon (ed), *Limits to Action* New York: Academic Press, pp. 143-176.

Heyman, G. M. (1983). A parametric evaluation of the hedonic and motoric effects of drugs: Pimozide and amphetamine, *Journal of the Experimental Analysis of Behavior*, **40**, 113-122.

Killeen, P. R. (1979). Arousal: Its genesis, modulation and extinction. In M. D. Zeiler and P. Harzem (eds), *Reinforcement and the Organization of Behaviour*, New York: Wiley.

Killeen, P. R. (1982). Incentive theory: II. Models for choice, *Journal of the Experimental Analysis of Behavior*, **38**, 217-232.

Lewinsohn, P., Weinstein, M., and Alper, T. (1970). A behavioral approach to the group treatment of depressed persons: A methodological contribution, *Journal of Clinical Psychology*, **26**, 525-532.

Lineweaver, H., and Burk, D. (1934). The determination of enzyme dissociation constants, *Journal of the American Chemical Society*, **56**, 657-666.

Lowe, C. F., and Horne, P. J. (1985). On the generality of behavioural principles: Human choice and the matching law. In C. F. Lowe, M. Richelle, D. F. Blackman, and C. M.

Bradshaw (eds), *Behaviour Analysis and Contemporary Psychology*, London: Erlbaum, pp. 97-115.

McDowell, J.J. (1980). An analytic comparison of Herrnstein's equations and a multivariate rate equation, *Journal of the Experimental Analysis of Behavior*, **33**, 397-408.

McDowell, J.J. (1981a). Wilkinson's method of estimating the parameters of Herrnstein's hyperbola, *Journal of the Experimental Analysis of Behavior*, **35**, 413-414.

McDowell, J.J. (1981b). On the validity and utility of Herrnstein's hyperbola in applied behavior analysis. In C.M. Bradshaw, E. Szabadi, and C.F. Lowe (eds), *Quantification of Steady-State Operant Behaviour*, Amsterdam: Elsevier/North-Holland Biomedical Press, pp. 311-324.

McDowell, J.J. (1982). The importance of Herrnstein's mathematical statement of the law of effect for behavior therapy, *American Psychologist*, **37**, 771-779.

McDowell, J.J., and Kessel, R.A. (1979). A multivariate rate equation for variable-interval performance, *Journal of the Experimental Analysis of Behavior*, **31**, 267-283.

McDowell, J.J., and Wood, H.M. (1984). Confirmation of linear system theory prediction: Changes in Herrnstein's k as a function of changes in reinforcer magnitude, *Journal of the Experimental Analysis of Behavior*, **41**, 183-192.

McDowell, J.J., and Wood, H.M. (1985). Confirmation of linear system theory prediction: Rate of change of Herrnstein's k as a function of response-force requirement, *Journal of the Experimental Analysis of Behavior*, **43**, 61-73.

McLean, A.P. (1983). Independence of successive human concurrent performances, *Behaviour Analysis Letters*, **3**, 275-284.

McSweeney, F.K., Melville, C.L., and Whipple, J.E. (1983). Herrnstein's equation for the rates of responding during concurrent schedules, *Animal Learning Behavior*, **11**, 275-289.

Marcucella, H., and Margolius, G. (1978). Time allocation in concurrent schedules: The effect of signalled reinforcement, *Journal of the Experimental Analysis of Behavior*, **29**, 419-430.

Matthews, L.R., and Temple, W. (1979). Concurrent schedule assessment of food preference in cows, *Journal of the Experimental Analysis of Behavior*, **32**, 245-254.

Moffitt, M., and Shimp, C.P. (1971). Two-key paced variable-interval schedules of reinforcement, *Journal of the Experimental Analysis of Behavior*, **16**, 39-49.

Morley, M.J., Bradshaw, C.M., and Szabadi, E. (1985). The effect of *d*-amphetamine on operant behaviour maintained under variable-interval schedules of reinforcement, *Psychopharmacology*, **87**, 207-211.

Myers, D.L., and Myers, L.E. (1977). Undermatching: A reappraisal of performance on concurrent variable-interval schedules of reinforcement, *Journal of the Experimental Analysis of Behavior*, **25**, 203-214.

Myerson, J., and Hale, S. (1984). Practical implications of the matching law, *Journal of Applied Behavior Analysis*, **17**, 367-380.

Navarick, D.J., and Chellson, J. (1983). Matching versus undermatching in the choice behavior of humans, *Behaviour Analysis Letters*, **3**, 325-335.

Oscar-Berman, M., Heyman, G.M., Bonner, R.T., and Ryder, J. (1980). Human neuropsychology: Some differences between Korsakoff and normal operant performance, *Psychological Research*, **41**, 235-247.

Prelec, D. (1984). The assumptions underlying the generalized matching law, *Journal of the Experimental Analysis of Behavior*, **41**, 101-107.

Rachlin, H., and Baum, W.M. (1969). Response rate as a function of amount of reinforcement for a signalled concurrent response, *Journal of the Experimental Analysis of Behavior*, **12**, 11-16.

Rachlin, H., and Baum, W. M. (1972). Effects of alternative reinforcement: Does the source matter?*Journal of the Experimental Analysis of Behavior*, **18**, 231–241.

Ruddle, H. V., Bradshaw, C. M., and Szabadi, E. (1981). Performance of humans in variable-interval avoidance schedules programmed singly, and concurrently with variable interval schedules of positive reinforcement, *Quarterly Journal of Experimental Psychology*, **33**, 213–226.

Ruddle, H. V., Bradshaw, C. M., Szabadi, E., and Bevan, P. (1979). Behaviour of humans in concurrent schedules programmed on spatially separated operanda, *Quarterly Journal of Experimental Psychology*, **31**, 509–517.

Ruddle, H. V., Bradshaw, C. M., Szabadi, E., and Foster, M. (1982). Performance of humans in concurrent avoidance/positive-reinforcement schedules, *Journal of the Experimental Analysis of Behavior*, **38**, 51–61.

Schmitt, D. R. (1974). Effects of reinforcement rate and reinforcer magnitude on choice behavior of humans, *Journal of the Experimental Analysis of Behavior*, **21**, 409–419.

Schroeder, S. R. (1975). Perseveration in concurrent performances by the developmentally retarded, *Psychological Record*, **25**, 51–64.

Schroeder, S. R., and Holland, J. G. (1969). Reinforcement of eye movement with concurrent schedules, *Journal of the Experimental Analysis of Behavior*, **12**, 897–903.

Scown, J. M., Foster, T. M., and Temple, W. (1981). Some effects of changeover-delay on the concurrent-variable-interval schedule performance of hens. In C. M. Bradshaw, E. Szabadi, and C. F. Lowe (eds), *Quantification of Steady-State Operant Behaviour*, Amsterdam: Elsevier/North-Holland Biomedical Press, pp. 353–356.

Skinner, B. F. (1953). *Science and Human Behavior*, New York: Macmillan.

Skinner, B. F. (1956). A case history in scientific method, *American Psychologist*, **11**, 221–233.

Staddon, J. E. R. (1968). Spaced responding and choice: A preliminary analysis, *Journal of the Experimental Analysis of Behavior*, **11**, 669–682.

Staddon, J. E. R. (1977). On Herrnstein's equation and related forms, *Journal of the Experimental Analysis of Behavior*, **28**, 436–444.

Szabadi, E., Bradshaw, C. M., and Ruddle, H. V. (1981). Reinforcement processes in affective illness: Towards a quantitative analysis. In C. M. Bradshaw, E. Szabadi, and C. F. Lowe (eds), *Quantification of Steady-State Operant Behaviour*, Amsterdam: Elsevier/North-Holland Biomedica Press, pp. 299–310.

Warren-Boulton, F. R., Silberberg, A., Gray, M., and Ollom, R. (1985). Reanalysis of the equation for simple action, *Journal of the Experimental Analysis of Behavior*, **43**, 265–277.

Wearden, J. H. (1980). Undermatching on concurrent variable-interval schedules and the power law, *Journal of the Experimental Analysis of Behavior*, **33**, 149–152.

Wearden, J. H. (1983). Undermatching and overmatching as deviations from the matching law, *Journal of the Experimental Analysis of Behavior*, **40**, 333–340.

Wearden, J. H., and Burgess, I. S. (1982). Matching since Baum (1979), *Journal of the Experimental Analysis of Behavior*, **38**, 339–348.

Weber, E. H. (1834). *De pulsu, resorptione, auditu et tactu*, Leipzig: Koehler.

Wurster, R. M., and Griffiths, R. R. (1979). Human concurrent performances: Variation of reinforcer magnitude and rate of reinforcement, *Psychological Record*, **29**, 341–354.

Author Index

Subject Index